Lecture Notes in Computer Science

Edited by G. Goos and J. Hartmanis

38

P. Branquart · J.-P. Cardinael · J. Lew
J.-P. Delescaille · M. Vanbegin

An Optimized Translation Process and Its Application to ALGOL 68

Springer-Verlag
Berlin · Heidelberg · New York 1976

Authors
Paul Branquart
Jean-Pierre Cardinael*
Johan Lewi**
Jean-Paul Delescaille
Michael Vanbegin

MBLE Research Laboratory
Avenue Em. van Becelaere 2
1170 Brussels/Belgium

* Present address: Caisse Générale d'Epargne et de Retraite, Brussels, Belgium

** Present address: Katholieke Universiteit Leuven, Applied Mathematics and Programming Division, Leuven, Belgium

Library of Congress Cataloging in Publication Data
Main entry under title:

An Optimized translation process and its application to ALGOL 68.

(Lecture notes in computer science ; 38)
Bibliography: p.
Includes index.
1. ALGOL (Computer program language)
2. Compiling (Electronic computers) I. Branquart, Paul, 1937- II. Series.
QA76.73.A24067 001.6'424 75-45092

AMS Subject Classifications (1970): 68-02, 68A05, 90-04
CR Subject Classifications (1974): 4.1, 4.12

ISBN 3-540-07545-3 Springer-Verlag Berlin · Heidelberg · New York
ISBN 0-387-07545-3 Springer-Verlag New York · Heidelberg · Berlin

Printed in Germany
Offsetdruck: Julius Beltz, Hemsbach/Bergstr.

FOREWORD

In the late sixties, the definition of ALGOL 68 [1] , for a long time called ALGOL X, reached some stability. It is at that period (1967) our team started the project of writing a compiler for that language. We had two goals in mind :

(1) to make significant research in the field of compiler methodology,

(2) to point out the special difficulties encountered in the design of the compiler and thus possibly influence the definition of the language.

This book is concerned with the first goal only ; ALGOL 68 should be considered a support to explain and develop compiling principles and techniques.

The whole book is directly based on the actual compiler we have written for the Electrologica-X8 computer ; this compiler has been operational since early 1973. Since May 1975, it is available on the "BS-computer", the Philips prototype developed by MBLE and which is at the origin of the UNIDATA 7720. In fact, the X8 has been microprogrammed on the BS [22] ; it is worthwhile to mention that microprogramming did not introduce any significant loss in efficiency.

The book does not require a very deep knowledge of ALGOL 68 except in some special cases described here for the sake of completeness only. The reading of some general description of the language as provided by [17] is however assumed.

Acknowledgments

We should like to express our thanks to Mrs Micheline Mispelon for her excellent typing of the manuscript and to Mr Claude Semaille for his careful drawing of the figures.

SUMMARY

The book describes a translation process which generates efficient code while remaining machine independent. The process starts from the output stream of the syntactic analyzer.

(1) Code optimization is based on a mechanism controlling a number of static properties and allowing to make long range previsions. This permits to minimize the dynamic (run-time) actions, replacing them by static (compile-time) ones whenever possible. In particular, much attention is paid on the minimization of run-time copies of values, of run-time memory management and of dynamic checks.

(2) Machine independency is improved by translating the programs into intermediate code before producing machine code. In addition to being machine independent, intermediate code instructions are self-contained modules which can be translated into machine code independently, which improves modularity. Only trivial local optimizations are needed at the interface between intermediate code instructions when machine code is produced.

The description of the translation process is made in three parts :

-PART I defines the general principles on which the process is based. It is made as readable as possible for an uninitiated reader.

-PART II enters the details of translation into intermediate code : particular problems created by all ALGOL 68 language constructions and their interface are solved.

-PART III shows the principles of the translation of the intermediate code into machine code ; these principles are presented in a completely machine independent way.

CONTENTS

PART I : GENERAL PRINCIPLES

0. INTRODUCTION

A programming language is defined by means of a *semantics* and a *syntax*.

- the *semantics* defines the meaning of the programs of the language. It is based on a number of *primitive functions (actions)* having parameters, delivering a result and/or having some side-effects, and on a number of *composition rules* by which the result of a function may be used as the parameter of another function.
- the *syntax* provides means for program representations. It defines a structure of programs, reflecting both the primitive functions and the composition rules of the semantics.

A *compiler* translates programs written in a given *source language* into programs written in *an object language* and having the same meaning. Ultimately the object language is the machine code. Generally, the transformation is performed in two steps at least conceptually separated : the *syntactic analysis* and the *translation proper.*

0.1 BASIC CONCEPTS

The *syntactic analysis* is a program transformation by which the structure of the source program is made explicit. We can distinguish three parts in the syntactic analysis, namely :

- the *lexical analysis* by which atoms of information semantically significant in the source language are detected,
- the *context-free analysis* by which the primitive functions of the source language and their composition rules are made explicit, and
- the *declaration handling* by which the declared objects are connected to their declaration.

Conceptually, the output of the syntactic analysis has the form of a tree in which :

- the terminal nodes are the atoms delivered by the lexical analyzer. These atoms may represent values (value denotations, identifiers) or they may just be source language syntactic separators or key-words,
- nonterminal nodes represent functions (actions) the parameters of which are the values resulting from the subjacent nodes ; in turn, these functions may deliver a value as their result, and
- the initial node is obviously the syntactic unit "particular program".

The translation proper produces machine code. Elementary functions of, and values handled by *machine codes* are much more primitive than primitive functions of high level languages and their parameters. The translation process has to decompose the source functions and source values. Machine instructions are executed as independent modules : the interface between them is determined by the sequence in which they are elaborated and by the storage allocation scheme on which the program they constitute is based. More concretely, the result of each instruction is stored in a memory cell and it can be used by another instruction in which the access (address) of the same memory cell is specified.

Roughly speaking, machine code generation for a given program is based on the following informations :

- the program tree resulting from the syntactic analysis,
- the semantics of the source functions as defined by the source language, and
- the semantics of the machine instructions as defined by the hardware.

The main task of the compiler reduces to decompose source functions into equivalent sequences of machine instructions. Obviously, a storage allocation scheme must first be designed in order to be able to take the composition rules of the source language into account.

It is not required to produce machine code in one step ; our translation scheme first produces an intermediate form of programs called *intermediate code* (IC). Among other things, this permits to remain machine independent during a more significant part of the translation process and hence to increase the compiler portability. We propose an intermediate code consisting of the same primitive functions as the source language, but provided with explicit parameters making it possible, these functions to be considered separate self-contained modules. As it is the case for the machine code, these modules are elaborated sequentially except when explicit breaks of sequence appear. The composition rules of the source language are taken into account through the sequential elaboration of the modules and the strategy of storage allocation. In this respect, as opposed to the source language dealing with abstract instances of values, the intermediate code deals with stored values characterized by the static properties corresponding both to the abstract instances of values [1] (mode ...) and to the memory locations where the values are stored (access ...). It is those properties which are used as the parameters of the intermediate code (object) instructions (ICI) ; more precisely, the parameters of an ICI consist of one set of static (compile-time) properties for each parameter of the corresponding source function and one set for the result of this function.

Coming back to our translation scheme, we can say that intermediate code generation for a given program is based on the following information :

- the program tree resulting from the syntactic analysis,
- the semantics of the source functions, and
- the storage allocation scheme.

We see that the semantics of machine instructions has disappeared, only the storage allocation can be influenced by the hardware. In fact, we only make two hypotheses at the level of the intermediate code :

- the memory is an uninterrupted sequence of addressable units,
- there exists an indirect addressing mechanism.

Machine independent optimizations are performed at the level of the intermediate code generation. In particular
- run-time copies of values,
- run-time memory management, and
- dynamic checks

are minimized up to a great extent.

Moreover, precautions are taken in order to allow to retrieve machine dependent optimizations in a further step ; such optimizations take care of :
- register allocation and
- possible hardware literal and/or display addressing.

Now, machine code generation can be based on the following :
- the intermediate code form of the programs,
- the semantics of the source functions, and
- the semantics of the machine code.

Note that each intermediate code instruction can be translated independently into machine code which improves the compiler modularity. This translation mainly consists in decomposing source functions and data into machine instructions and words (bytes) respectively. Only local optimizations(peephole [16]) at the interface between ICI's will still be needed to get the final machine code program.

Gathering information to be able to translate a program efficiently and automatically requires a non trivial static (compile-time) information management. The method explained in this book has many similarities with the one described by Knuth [6] , although it has been developed independently. We explain it using Knuth's terminology.

Attributes are static properties attached to the tree nodes ; there are *synthetized* and *inherited* attributes.

In our system, the *synthetized attributes* of a node are the static properties (mode, access ...) of the value attached to the node, i.e. the value of a terminal construction (denotation, identifier) or the value resulting from a function (nonterminal node).

These synthetized attributes are deduced from each other in a bottom-up way. For a terminal node, they are obtained from the terminal construction itself (and from its declaration in case of a declared object). For nonterminal nodes, they are calculated by the process of *static elaboration.*

The *static elaboration* of a function is the process by which the static properties of the result of the function are derived from the static properties of its parameters (i.e. the synthetized attributes of the subjacent nodes) and according to the code generated for the translation of the function.

Again, in our system, *inherited attributes* of a node are attributes which are transmitted in the tree in a top-down way along a path leading from the initial node to the current node.

Translating a function is based on the synthetized attributes of the parameters of the function, and on the inherited attributes of the function itself. Moreover, the translation can also take into account all the functions associated to the nodes situated on the path between the node of the current function and the initial node ; this allows us to make previsions on what will happen to the result of that function, and in some cases to generate better code. As we shall see in the next section, a very simple and efficient automaton can be used to implement the above principles.

<u>Example</u> 0.1

Source program :

$$x := a \times b + 3$$

Syntactic tree : {the part of the tree used to translate '×' is bold faced}

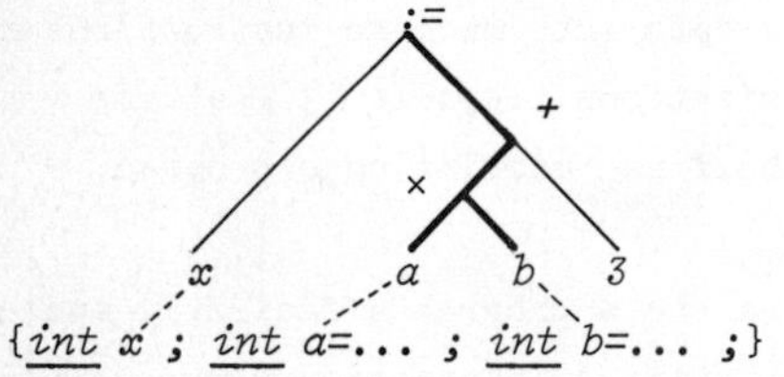

Intermediate code :

× (<u>proc</u> (<u>int</u>, <u>int</u>)<u>int</u>, *access a*, *access b*, *access w*)
+ (<u>proc</u> (<u>int</u>, <u>int</u>)<u>int</u>, *access w*, *access 3*, *access w1*)
:= (<u>int</u>, *access x*, *access w1*)

Machine code without local optimizations :

```
LDA access a
MPY access b
STA access w

LDA access w
ADA    = 3
STA access w1

LDA access w1
STA access x
```

Characteristics of the program at different stages of the compilation.

Source language	Result of the syntactic analysis	Intermediate code	Machine code
Semantics - Primitive functions - Primitive data	The syntactic structure is made explicit :	Same primitive functions and data as the source language, but	Primitive functions = instructions Primitive data = words, bytes ...
- Composition rules	-syntactic tree	-independent modules, the parameters of which are static properties of stored values	-independent modules, the parameters of which are machine addresses
	-links between declared objects and their declaration		
Syntax - Means for program representation - Defines a structure reflecting the semantics		-interface ensured through (1)storage allocation and (2)sequential elaboration -machine independency	-interface ensured through (1)storage allocation and (2)sequential elaboration
-Lexical analysis -Context-free analysis -Declaration handling →	-Static elaboration -Storage allocation →	-Decomposition of source functions and values -Local optimizations →	
SYNTACTIC ANALYSIS →	TRANSLATION PROPER →		

Machine code with local optimizations :

```
LDA access a
MPY access b
ADA    = 3
STA access x
```

0.2 *THE TRANSLATOR AUTOMATON*

In practice, the syntactic analyzer should deliver a form of tree well suited for the translator automaton ; we propose here a *linear prefixed form* of the tree(†). In this form, the terminals representing declared objects are connected to their declaration by means of a symbol table (*SYMBTAB*). In this table there is one entry for each declaration. For a declared object, both its declaration and applications are connected to the same *SYMBTAB* entry. This allows to make the static properties of the objects, defined at their declaration, available at each of their applications.

The translator automaton scans the linear prefixed form from left to right, accumulating top information on a so called top stack (*TOPST*) and bottom information on a so called bottom stack (*BOST*), while intermediate code is generated. Static properties of declared objects are obtained through *SYMBTAB*. More precisely, the automaton consists of :

(1) *An input tape* containing the source program ; this consists of prefix markers for the nonterminal nodes of the tree, and of basic constructions (i.e. denotations, identifiers ...) for the terminal nodes.

(2) *An output tape* where the intermediate code is generated.

(3) The so called *bottomstack* (*BOST*) where static information is stored in such a way that when an action is translated, the static properties, i.e. the synthetized attributes of its n parameters, can be found in the n top elements of *BOST*.

(4) The so called *topstack* (*TOPST*) containing at each moment the prefix markers and the inherited attributes of the not completely translated actions, in such a way, each time an action is translated, the complete future story of its result can be found on *TOPST*.

(5) The *symbol table* (*SYMBTAB*) where the static properties of each declared object deduced from its declaration are stored in order to be retrieved at each of its application, thus allowing to initialize the process of static elaboration.

(†) In ALGOL 68, coercions are a kind of implicit monadic operators ; in the sequel they will be supposed to have been made explicit by the syntactic analysis [15].

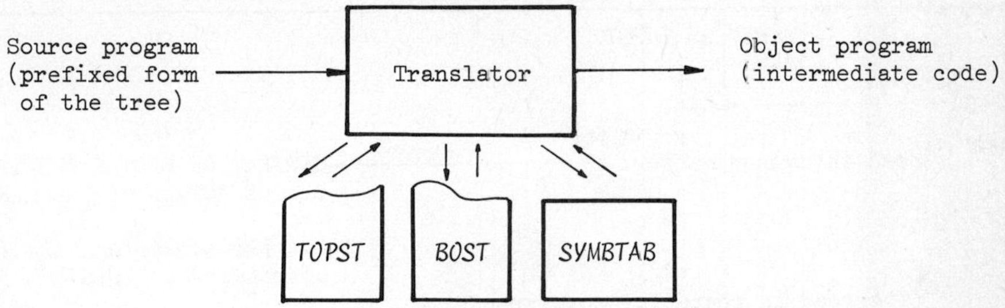

fig. 0.1

The translation of a given action can be separated in three parts :

(1) the *prefix translation* which is performed when the prefix marker of the action is scanned in the source program ; it may consist of the generation of prefix code.

(2) the *infix translation* which is performed in between the translation of two subjacent actions ; it may consist of code generation by which the value of a parameter will be copied at run-time, together with the corresponding updating of the static properties of the parameter at the top of *BOST*.

(3) the *postfix translation* which corresponds to the translation proper of the current action ; it consists of the generation of the corresponding object instructions, together with the replacement, at the top of *BOST*, of the static properties of the parameters of the current action by the static properties of its result (static elaboration).

This is described in a more precise way by the flowchart of fig. 0.2.

PART I is mainly devoted to the description of static properties. Beforehand, the principles of a storage allocation scheme are recalled (I.1).

Example 0.2

Source program :

$$x := a \times b + 3$$

Result of the syntactic analysis :

```
:= x + × a  b    3
            ↑    ↑
           (1)  (2)
```

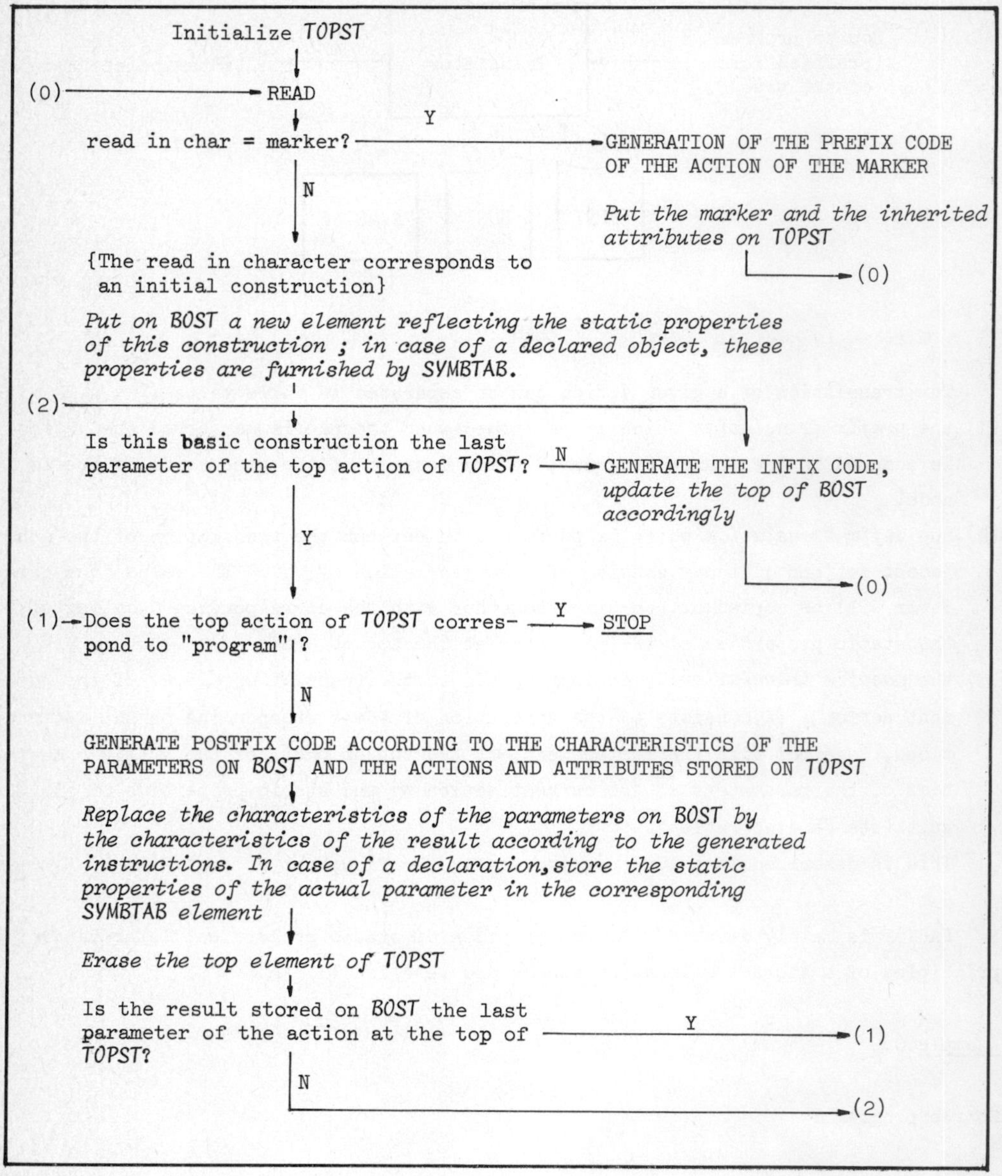
Initialize *TOPST*
(0)
READ
Y
read in char = marker?
GENERATION OF THE PREFIX CODE OF THE ACTION OF THE MARKER
Put the marker and the inherited attributes on TOPST
(0)
N
{The read in character corresponds to an initial construction}
Put on BOST a new element reflecting the static properties of this construction ; in case of a declared object, these properties are furnished by SYMBTAB.
(2)
Is this basic construction the last parameter of the top action of *TOPST*?
N
GENERATE THE INFIX CODE, *update the top of BOST accordingly*
(0)
Y
(1)
Does the top action of *TOPST* correspond to "program" ?
Y
STOP
N
GENERATE POSTFIX CODE ACCORDING TO THE CHARACTERISTICS OF THE PARAMETERS ON *BOST* AND THE ACTIONS AND ATTRIBUTES STORED ON *TOPST*
Replace the characteristics of the parameters on BOST by the characteristics of the result according to the generated instructions. In case of a declaration, store the static properties of the actual parameter in the corresponding SYMBTAB element
Erase the top element of TOPST
Is the result stored on *BOST* the last parameter of the action at the top of *TOPST*?
Y
(1)
N
(2)

fig. 0.2 : The translator automaton.

(1) Snapshot of the stacks when *b* is being translated :

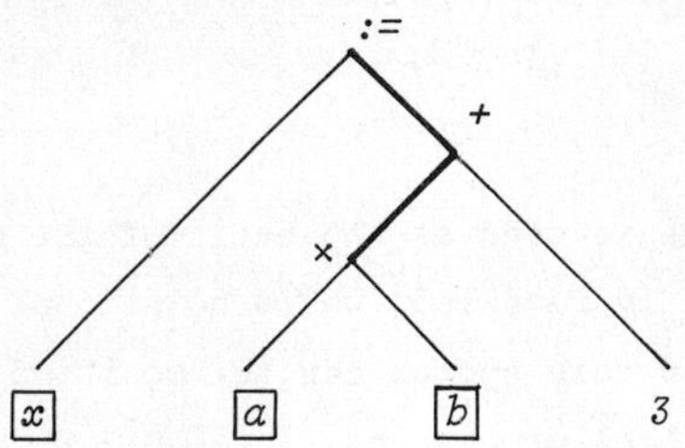

BOST □	TOPST
x	:=
a	+
b	×

(2) Snapshot of the stacks when *3* is being translated :

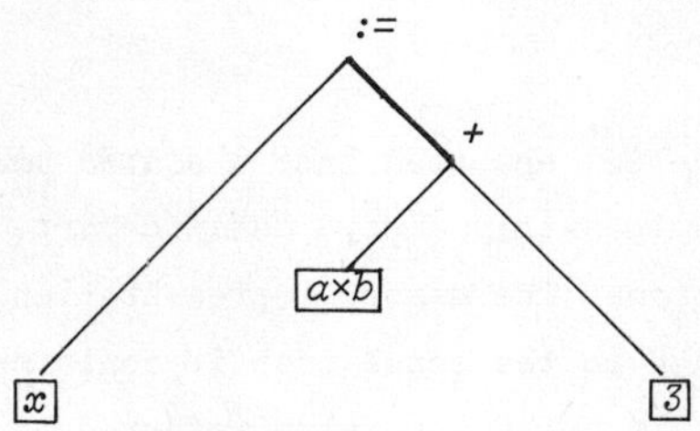

BOST □	TOPST
x	:=
$a \times b$	+
3	

1. RECALL OF STORAGE ALLOCATION PRINCIPLES

The storage allocation scheme of [12] is used as the basis of the run-time system described here ; this scheme is briefly recalled, while notational conventions are introduced. Moreover, it is shown how this system can be modified in order to be implementable on a computer with parallel processing. In II.0.3.3 a more formal description of the memory representation of values and of the memory organization can be found.

1.1 MEMORY REPRESENTATION OF VALUES

The memory representation of a value is separated into a *static part*, the size of which is known at compile-time and a (possibly empty) *dynamic part*, the size of which may result from run-time calculations. The memory representation of a name of mode ref [ ] μ is somewhat particular [14] in the sense that it contains space, not only for the name but also for the descriptor of the value referred to ; this makes it possible to avoid the use of the heap for storing the descriptors of slices and rowed coercends of mode *ref* [ ] μ.

For some values, the memory representation as described in [12] has to be completed(†). For example, names have to be provided with a scope indication, so are routines and formats . Moreover, routines and formats must be provided with additional information in order to ensure the link between the calls and the routines, as it is generally not known at the time a call is translated which routine is called.

1.2 CONCEPTUAL MEMORY ORGANIZATION

Conceptually, four storage devices can be considered in the run-time memory organization namely the identifier stack (*IDST%*(††)), the local generator stack (*LGST%*), the working stack (*WOST%*) and the heap (*HEAP%*). If a paging mechanism is available the conceptual memory organization can be implemented as such ; in [12] and [13] it has been shown how for a continuous memory a practical scheme can be deduced from the conceptual one.

1.3 PRACTICAL MEMORY ORGANIZATION

In practice, *IDST%*, *LGST%* and *WOST%* can be merged in one same run-time device, the range stack (*RANST%*) ; this merging does not significantly affect the stack

(†) Moreover, it has appeared that the master descriptor pointer foreseen for the garbage collection can be cancelled (III.6.4).

(††) As a convention, all notations for run-time devices end with %.

mechanism and leads to a memory organization with only two devices of varying size : the *RANST%* and the *HEAP%*. The dynamic control of these devices lies on two run-time pointers indicating the first free cell of each device namely *ranstpm%* and *heappm%* respectively.

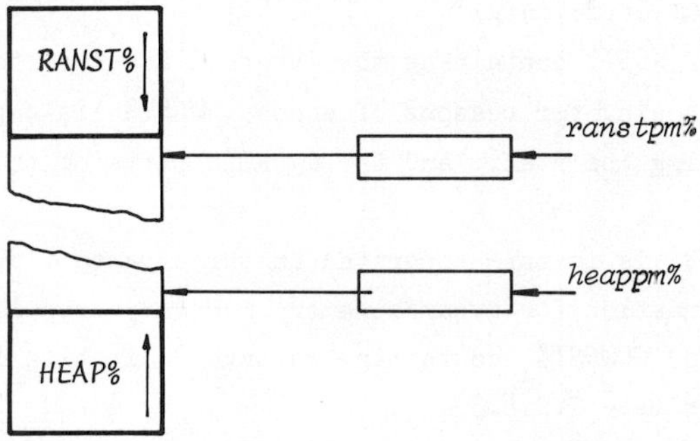

fig. 1.1

In the merging, *RANST%* is separated in several parts called range stack blocks (*BLOCK%*'s). A *BLOCK%* corresponds to a piece of program which has been entered but not definitively left ; in practice, which piece of program gives rise to a *BLOCK%* depends on implementation : in *"range oriented implementations"* mode declarations with dynamic bounds, dynamic replications of formats, and ranges with declarations and/or local generators give rise to *BLOCK%*'s; in *"procedure oriented implementations"*, mode declarations with dynamic bounds, dynamic replications of formats and routines give rise to *BLOCK%*'s. In the sequel, the term *block* will refer to a range giving rise to a *BLOCK%*. As shown in PART II, hardware considerations may guide the choice determining which ranges will be regarded as *blocks* (†).

Let $BLOCK\%_i$ (i≥0) be a particular *BLOCK%*, corresponding to a (program) *block* called $block_i$.

$BLOCK\%_i$ is separated in several parts :

(1) a heading $H\%_i$ containing linkage information between $BLOCK\%_i$, its calling block, and the block in which it is declared.

(2) a part $IDST\%_i$ of *IDST%* containing the values possessed by the identifiers declared in $block_i$ (at the exclusion of the inner *blocks*). For reasons of access, each $IDST\%_i$ is separated into $SIDST\%_i$ and $DIDST\%_i$ containing the static and the dynamic parts respectively of the values of $IDST\%_i$.

(3) a part $LGST\%_i$ of *LGST%* containing the locations reserved at the elaboration of

(†) In the sequel, unless the contrary is explicitely stated, when a *block* is mentioned, it always excludes inner *blocks*.

the local generators of the *block*$_i$. In the merging, *LGST%*$_i$ is combined with *DIDST%*$_i$.(We define here the notion of *variable (variable-identifier)* : a *variable* is an identifier possessing a local name created by the elaboration of a local generator which is the actual parameter of its declaration. In this case, the memory location of the name is reserved on *IDST%* instead of *LGST%*, which results in an increase of efficiency).

(4) a part *WOST%*$_i$ of *WOST%* containing the intermediate results of the expressions of the *block*$_i$. Again, for reasons of access, *WOST%*$_i$ is separated in *SWOST%*$_i$ and *DWOST%*$_i$ containing the static and the dynamic parts of the values of *WOST%*$_i$ respectively.
Moreover, *SWOST%*$_i$ is in turn separated in three parts : *SWOST%*$_i$ proper, *DMRWOST%*$_i$ containing information for dynamic memory recovery associated to *WOST%*$_i$ values (see I.2.4.2) and *GCWOST%*$_i$ containing garbage collection information associated to *WOST%*$_i$ values (see I.2.4.3).

In the merging, *H%*$_i$, *SIDST%*$_i$, *DMRWOST%*$_i$, *GCWOST%*$_i$, and *SWOST%*$_i$ will be grouped together, thus forming *SBLOCK%*$_i$; it is to be remarked that the size of each of these parts of *SBLOCK%*$_i$ is known at compile-time. The remaining part of *BLOCK%*$_i$ (*DIDST%*$_i$, *LGST%*$_i$ and *DWOST%*$_i$) will be called *DBLOCK%*$_i$ (<u>fig</u>. 1.2).

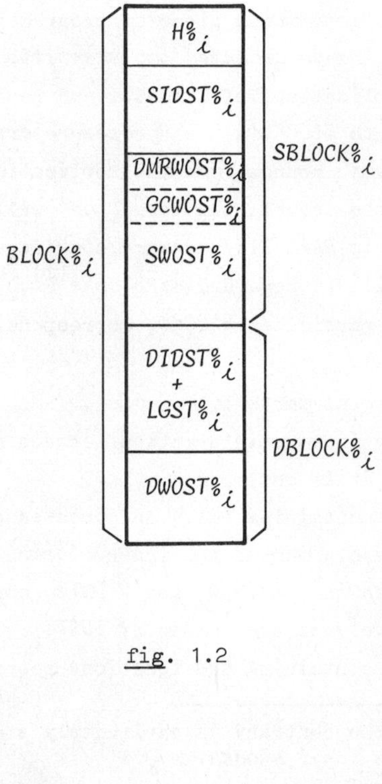

<u>fig</u>. 1.2

1.4 RANGE STACK ACCESSES

$IDST\%_i$ values and $WOST\%_i$ values together with the corresponding properties stored on $DMRWOST\%_i$ and $GCWOST\%_i$ must be statically accessible ; this means that it must be possible to provide the machine instructions which are the translation of the actions on the corresponding values with appropriate addresses (i.e. giving access to those values). More precisely, at each run-time moment, both the $IDST\%_j$ and $WOST\%_j$ values of all $blocks_j$ lexicographically surrounding the current $block_c$ have to be statically accessible. $BLOCK\%_j$'s are made accessible through the well known display mechanism [3] : the *DISPLAY%* is a run-time device containing at each run-time moment the addresses of the headings $H\%_j$ of all accessible $BLOCK\%_j$'s ; in fact, accessible $block_j$'s are those lexicographically surrounding the current $block_c$, they can be characterized by a depth number n sometimes noted bn_j and called the block number of $block_j$. Clearly the *DISPLAY%* must be updated each time a block is entered and left, this is performed thanks to two fields stored in $H\%_j$'s, namely

- the *static chain* ($stch\%_j$) containing the address of $BLOCK\%_k$, assuming that $block_j$ is declared in $block_k$.
- the *dynamic chain* ($dch\%_j$) containing the address of $BLOCK\%_\ell$, assuming that $block_j$ has been called from $block_\ell$. Remark that *dch%* links all *BLOCK%*'s of *RANST%* together in the reverse order of their creation.

<u>Example</u> 1.1

Source program structure :

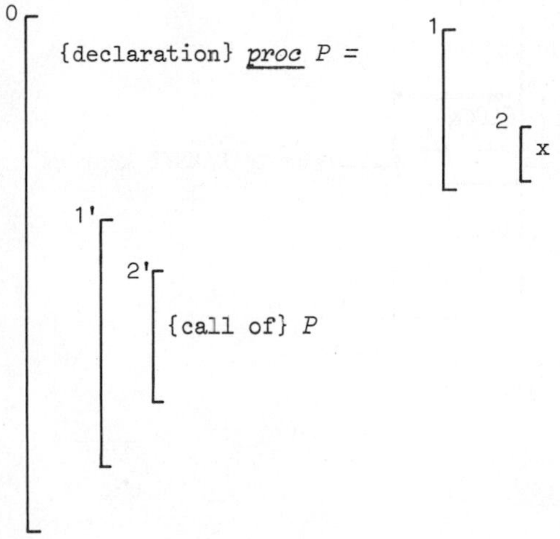

Figure 1.3 gives the contents of *DISPLAY%* and *RANST%* at x.

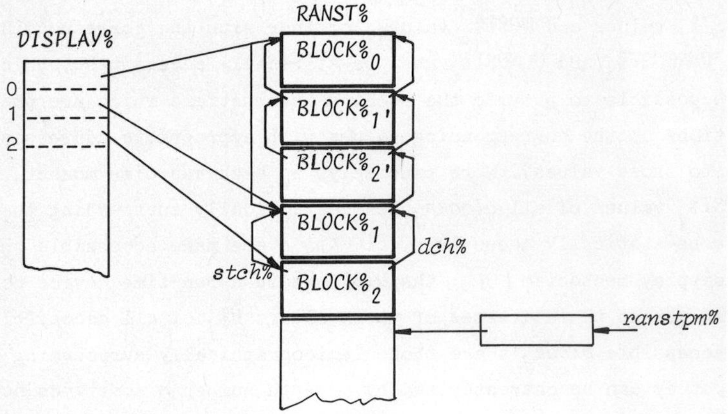

fig. 1.3

On the other hand, inside each SBLOCK%$_i$, the relative address p of each value or of each piece of information is known at compile-time. In short, thanks to the DISPLAY% mechanism, each information of SBLOCK%$_i$ is statically addressable through the doublet $n.p$; such a doublet will be called a static RANST% address.

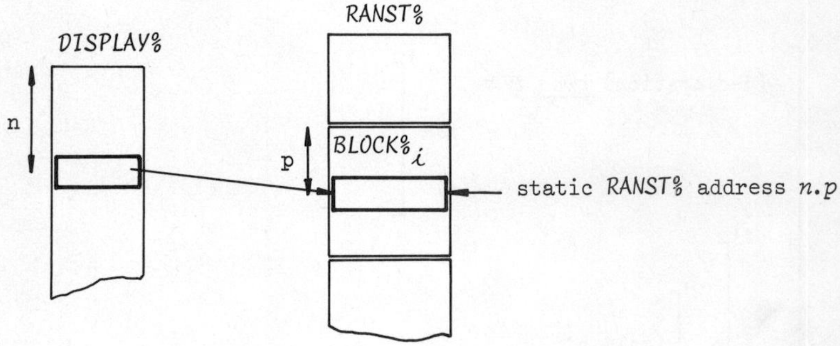

fig. 1.4

Some computers have a hardware device allowing to implement the DISPLAY% mechanism very easily. In this case the RANST% address $n.p$ itself may be used in the machine instruction, for example for loading the contents of the cell $n.p$ in the A-register, the instruction

LDA n.p

is generated.
Otherwise the display mechanism has to be simulated by means of index registers :
- if there is an index register B_n per *DISPLAY%* element, a very efficient object program can be generated, for example the above load instruction becomes

LDA p, B_n

- the availability of one single index register B forces however to simulate the *RANST%* addressing by means of two instructions instead of one at least when it cannot be decided at compile-time whether the old contents of B already is DISPLAYADD+n

```
LDB DISPLAYADD+n
LDA p, B
```

1.5 REMARK ON THE IMPLEMENTATION OF PARALLEL PROCESSING

When parallel processing is actually implemented, *RANST%* is no longer a simple stack, but a tree of stacks, i.e. a stack which is split up into several stacks at each node of the tree. Each terminal branch of the tree corresponds to a particular job being elaborated or halted. Clearly, each job has its own values accessible and must be provided with its own *DISPLAY%*. Again if we have a paging at our disposal, to each branch can be associated a set of pages, and hence, branches may grow and decrease independently.
When no paging is available we can merge the tree-stack with the *HEAP%* deleting the last-in-first-out principle as far as the memory recovery is concerned, and implementing what is called a linked stack. The implementation of such a stack simply consists in reserving space for *SBLOCK%*$_i$'s on *HEAP%* each time a *block* is entered in a given job and in updating the corresponding *DISPLAY%* accordingly, which makes the elements of *SBLOCK%*$_i$ accessible exactly as in the usual mechanism. Parts of *DBLOCK%*$_i$ are also reserved on *HEAP%* as they are created at run-time ; clearly, parts of different *DBLOCK%*'s can be mixed, the only constraint being that entities of *DBLOCK%* which have to be contiguous are reserved at one time. The memory recovery is performed by garbage collection only.
In order to implement semaphores we build a list of jobs, with for each job a pointer to its semaphore telling whether the job is halted or not ; when a job is not halted, it can be either in course of elaboration or waiting for a free unit : a flag stored with each job in the list is representative of this state. As soon as a unit has become free, a master program goes through the list, looking for a waiting job. The process stops when all units are free and the list of jobs is empty. Clearly,

when only one unit is available this unit has to perform one job at a time until it is either terminated or halted, whereafter, the unit starts executing the master program, looking for a new job if any.

<u>Example</u> 1.2

Tree of jobs :

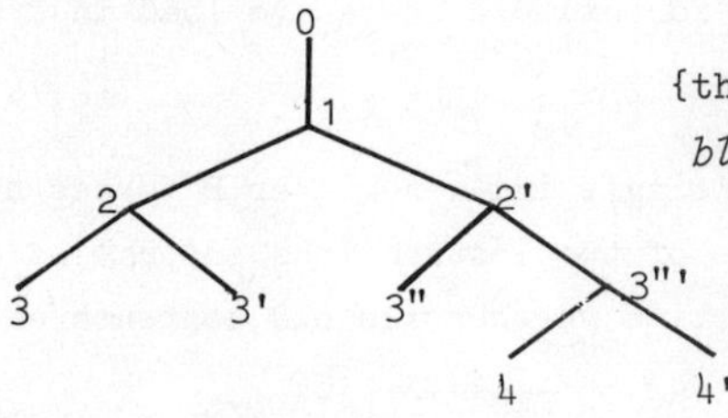

{the figures correspond to *block* depth numbers}

Contents of the *DISPLAY%*'s

0	1	2	3	
0	1	2	3'	
0	1	2'	3"	
0	1	2'	3"'	4
0	1	2'	3"'	4'

2. *STUDY OF THE STATIC PROPERTIES OF VALUES*

The *static properties* of a stored value are classified as follows :

- the *mode* of the value, from which the storage structure of the value can be deduced.
- the *access* to the location where the value is stored, from which the machine address of the location can be obtained.
- the *memory recovery* of the location of the value, telling how to recover the memory space of the location once the value is no longer needed, and allowing to minimize the dynamic memory management.
- the *dynamic check information* allowing to minimize the dynamic checks (scope and flexibility) and in case they cannot be avoided, to provide them with error diagnostic information.

These properties are now reviewed and described in a more precise way. Beforehand, a new static property called *origin* is introduced, it is essentially used for the static control of other properties.

An exhaustive study of the static elaboration of all ALGOL 68 actions showing the full power of the system is given in PART II. In the present section, only a few illustrations helping the understanding are given.

2.1 *THE ORIGIN*

The *origin* of a value is a static property keeping track of the story of the value, i.e. the way it has been obtained. At this stage, the aims of this property may be difficult to understand, they will become clearer when the properties controlled by the origin are discussed.

The origin of a value consists of six fields called *kindo*, *bno*, *derefo*, *geno*, *flexo* and *diago*.

- *kindo* (*kind of the origin*) keeps track of the fact that a value is issued from an identifier (*kindo* = <u>*iden*</u>), a variable (*kindo* = <u>*var*</u>), a generator (*kindo* = <u>*gen*</u>) or another construction (*kindo* = <u>*nil*</u>) ; it remains invariant through the static elaboration of a number of actions such as slices, selections and dereferencings.
  Kindo has to be considered together with *bno* (*block number of the origin*) which,
  - in case *kindo* is <u>*iden*</u> or <u>*var*</u>, indicates the depth number of the *block* where the identifier or the variable is declared.

- in case *kindo* is gen and corresponds to a local generator, indicates the depth number of the *block* where the generator appears.
- in case *kindo* is gen and corresponds to a heap generator, is equal to 0.

Among other things, *kindo* and *bno* are useful when a *block* is left : they allow to decide whether the resulting value has to be copied in the calling *block* ; they are also useful in order to be able to decide whether a value copied on *WOST%* has to be provided with garbage collection information (see I.2.4.3).

- *derefo* (*flag dereferencing of the origin*) indicates whether a dereferencing action has taken place starting from the construction in which *kindo* has been set up. The usefulness of this flag will appear in the static control of accesses in some actions where it allows to detect the absence of side-effects, and subsequently to avoid some copies of values (see I.2.3.3.c). It may also be useful in the static control of the memory recovery property, where it allows to minimize the garbage collection information attached to *WOST%* values (see I.2.4.3.b).
- *geno* (*flag local generator of the origin*) indicates whether a local generator is implied in the construction of the value. This is useful to control the memory recovery on *DWOST%* during the elaboration of row or structure display actions (see I.2.4.2, Remark 3).
- *flexo* (*flag flexible of the origin*) indicates whether the last name which has been dereferenced, starting from the construction where *kindo* has been set up, was flexible, not flexible or if this is not known at compile-time. This property is useful for minimizing the garbage collection information attached to *WOST%* values (see I.2.4.3.b), it is initialized by means of *flexbot* used in the checks of flexibility (see I.2.5.2).
- *diago* (*diagnostics of the origin*) furnishes error diagnostic information with which dynamic checks will be provided. For example *diago* may contain the line numbers of the source program construction giving rise to the value involved in the dynamic check.

2.2 *THE MODE*

The *mode* of a value is a static property on which the storage structure of the value is based. It is clear that the translation process of an action into machine code depends on the mode of the values involved in the action ; as already stated, the mode allows to decompose the primitive source actions and values into the elementary functions and values available in the hardware.

The mode handling implies the detection of the coercions and the identification of the operators(†). We assume from now on that coercions explicitely appear (in

(†) These two processes fall outside the scope of this study, they will be supposed to have been performed beforehand.

prefixed form) in the source program and that all operators are associated with their defining occurrence (through the symbol table as explained above [11]). Clearly, this makes the static elaboration of modes quite trivial.

2.3 THE ACCESS

2.3.1 GENERALITIES ON ACCESSES

The *access* of a stored value is a static property thanks to which the value can be reached at run-time. It is important to realize that the static control of accesses is the key of the system as far as the minimization of copies of values is concerned.

The machine independency of the access mechanism is submitted to the same rules as stated in I.0.1 for the storage allocation scheme, namely :

- the memory of the computer is considered an uninterrupted sequence of memory cells,
- an indirect addressing mechanism exists.

Provisions are made in order to be able to retrieve machine dependent optimizations :

- register allocation,
- possible hardware literal and/or display addressing.

An access is represented by means of a two-field record : a *class field* and a *specification field*. The *class field* gives information on how to interpret the *specification field* ; the *specification field* may have the form of one integer or a pair of integers. Follows an enumeration of the fundamental classes which are considered for a given value. This enumeration is given a priori, it will be justified thereafter, and in III.1 it will be shown how accesses can be transformed into machine addresses very systematically.

(1) (*constant* v) stands for "constant (literal) of value v" ; it means that v has to be considered as the given value itself. As stated above, this takes into account the possible existence in some hardwares of literal operand instructions. In such hardwares, the use of these instructions results in an increase of efficiency. Clearly, this applies to the denotations of simple values such as short(†) integers, short(†) bits, characters and Boolean values, or also to the identifiers which, according to their declaration, are made to possess such simple values.

(2) (*dirctab* a) stands for "direct constant-table address a". It means that the given value is stored in the constant-table CONSTAB at the address a. CONSTAB is a table which is filled at compile-time and available at run-time ; it consists essentially of values of denotations.

(†) i.e. fitting in the address part of a machine instruction.

(3) (*diriden* *n.p*) stands for "direct identifier stack address *n.p*". It means that the given value is stored on *IDST%* at the static *RANST%* address *n.p*. Such an access is used for values possessed by identifiers as long as the block in which they are declared has not been left. It is also used for values resulting from actions such as the selection from a value possessed by an identifier or the dereferencing of a name corresponding to a variable.

(4) (*variden* *n.p*) stands for "variable-identifier stack address *n.p*". The variable (name) is given the access (*variden* *n.p*) where *n.p* is the static *RANST%* address of the location of the name on *IDST%*. As already said under (3), the static elaboration of the dereferencing of a variable with the access (*variden* *n.p*) gives rise to the access (*diriden* *n.p*) thus implying no run-time action. Moreover, it is to be noted that the result of a selection applied to a variable of access (*variden* *n.p*) will be provided with the access (*variden* *n.p*+Δ*p*) where Δ*p* is the relative address of the field referred to by the resulting name, relative address in the static part of the structured value referred to by the initial variable ; such a selection does not imply any run-time action.

(5) (*indiden* *n.p*) stands for "indirect identifier stack address *n.p*". It means that the given value is stored in a memory location, the address of which can be found on *IDST%* at the static *RANST%* address *n.p*. This kind of access can be obtained through the static elaboration of a dereferencing applied to a value of access (*diriden* *n.p*). Again such a dereferencing does not imply any run-time action.

(6) (*dirwost* *n.p*) stands for "direct working stack address *n.p*". Its interpretation is similar to (*diriden* *n.p*) except that *n.p* is a static *RANST%* address in *WOST%*. Such an access is used for the result of an action, when this result does not preexist in memory and hence has to be constructed on *WOST%*.

(7) (*dirwost'* *n.p*) is similar to (*dirwost* *n.p*) but it is used when only the static part of a value having a non empty dynamic part is stored on *WOST%*. Such an access results in particular from the static elaboration of slices and rowings, for which only the descriptor does not preexist in memory.

(8) (*indwost* *n.p*) stands for "indirect working stack address *n.p*" ; its interpretation is similar to (*indiden* *n.p*). Such an access can be obtained e.g. through the static elaboration of the dereferencing of a name the access of which is (*dirwost* *n.p*).

(9) (*nihil* *0*) is used to characterize the absence of value ; this kind of access allows, for example, at the output from a *block* delivering a void result to keep track that no value has to be transmitted to the calling *block*. Such an access is set up by the static elaboration of a jump, a voiding or a call with a void result.

2.3.2 RESTRICTIONS ON ACCESSES

As it appears from the above section, each time an action is translated, advantage is taken from the fact that in many cases the resulting value can be characterized by a static access to an already existing stored value or part of it, thus avoiding run-time copies to a large extent.

Some restrictions have been introduced in the implementation of the access mechanism in order to keep the translation process within reasonable limits of complexity. Thus it may happen that values or part of them are copied while a new access class could avoid this. The following rules summarize the restrictions made on accesses :

a. Restrictions on the number of access classes

Rule a1 : only one level of indirect addressing is considered ; this implies e.g. that two consecutive dereferencings may result in some run-time action (copy of a machine address on *WOST%*). The exception is the case where a variable of access (*variden n.p*) is dereferenced twice ; the access of the result being (*indiden n.p*), no run-time action is implied (II.11.2).

Rule a2 : the above list of accesses requires that for all values involved in an action, at least their static part is stored in consecutive cells in memory. As a consequence, the static part of the value resulting, e.g. from a structure display, has always to be in consecutive cells (II.15) ; in other words, this means that a composed value is never represented by several static accesses to its elements.

b. Restrictions at the level of the access classes themselves

Rule b1 : no access of the type (*indwost n.p*) may correspond to a pointer (stored at the address *n.p*) pointing to *WOST%*. For *DWOST%*, this has particular implications in the handling of the action slice applying to a value of access (*dirwost n.p*) and delivering a value of mode NONROW (II.11.3, step 9, case B4). Theoretically it would be sufficient to copy the *DWOST%* address of the resulting element on *SWOST%* for example at the address *n'.p'*, and to characterize the result by the access (*indwost n'.p'*). With the above restriction, the whole static part of the resulting element has to be copied on *SWOST%* giving rise to the access (*dirwost n'.p'*) or (*dirwost' n'.p'*). For *SWOST%*, this restriction is of some consequence in the translation of choice actions (for example conditional or case actions, see II.14).

Rule b2 : the dynamic part of an intermediate result will never be stored on *SWOST%*. This rule has an implication in the translation of the action rowing applying to a value of access (*dirwost n.p*) and of mode NONROW. Theoretically, it would be sufficient to construct the descriptor of the result on *SWOST%*. In addition, the present rule implies to copy the static part of the original value on *DWOST%*.

Rule b3 : all offset pointers of *WOST%* values must point to the same direction (from the bottom to the top of the stack). This means that parts of *WOST%* values always appear in a well defined order which makes copies of values from *WOST%* to *WOST%* more efficient (when such copies are needed for the transmission of the result of a procedure for example).

Rule b4 : the dynamic part of a value has to be completely stored either on the *HEAP%* or in one same *BLOCK%* of *RANST%*. Moreover, when stored in a *BLOCK%*, supposing the static part of the value consists of several elements with a dynamic part (the whole of these dynamic parts forming the dynamic part of the value), these last ones must be stored in the same order as the corresponding descriptors in the static part of the value.

This rule is intended to make copies of values easier. Suppose for example the result of $BLOCK\%_i$ has an access class *diriden* which is originated from *variden*. Suppose also that the value referred to by the name of the variable has several elements of mode [] μ, the ones being flexible the others not. Strictly speaking the dynamic parts of the non flexible elements are stored on $DIDST\%_i$ and the flexible ones on the *HEAP%*. Suppose now the block is left and the value has to be copied on the $WOST\%_j$ of the calling block $BLOCK\%_j$; if all dynamic parts of the elements are not in the same device, the copy of the value must be made with much care (implying dynamic checks) in order to be sure that the copy of a dynamic part from *HEAP%* to $DWOST\%_j$ does not overwrite a dynamic part stored on $DIDST\%_i$ and which has not yet been copied in $BLOCK\%_j$. These difficulties are avoided by the present rule ; in particular, this implies that the whole dynamic part of the location of a local name is reserved on the *HEAP%* as soon as a subname of the name is flexible. (This is the case for location reserved for e.g.
loc struct ([*1:2*] *int i*, ..., [*1:2 flex*] *real r*)).

Example 2.1 (fig. 2.1)

Let S be a structured value with three fields F_1, F_2 and F_3 ; S_s (F_{s1},F_{s2},F_{s3}) is stored on $SIDST\%_i$, the dynamic parts F_{d1} of F_1 and F_{d3} of F_3 are stored on $DIDST\%_i$, and the one F_{d2} of F_2 is stored on the *HEAP%*. If S is the result of $BLOCK\%_i$, it has to be copied in the calling $BLOCK\%_j$. Clearly, the copy of F_{d2} risks to supersede F_{d3} before F_{d3} has been copied, if no precaution is taken (see also I.2.4.3, Remark 3-3).

Rule b5 : when a value is copied from *WOST%* to *WOST%* and when source and object values may overlap, the source value is always stored at a lower *WOST%* address than the object value such that the value can be copied cell by cell in natural order. (see II.14.1.2.B, Case C and III.5.4.3).

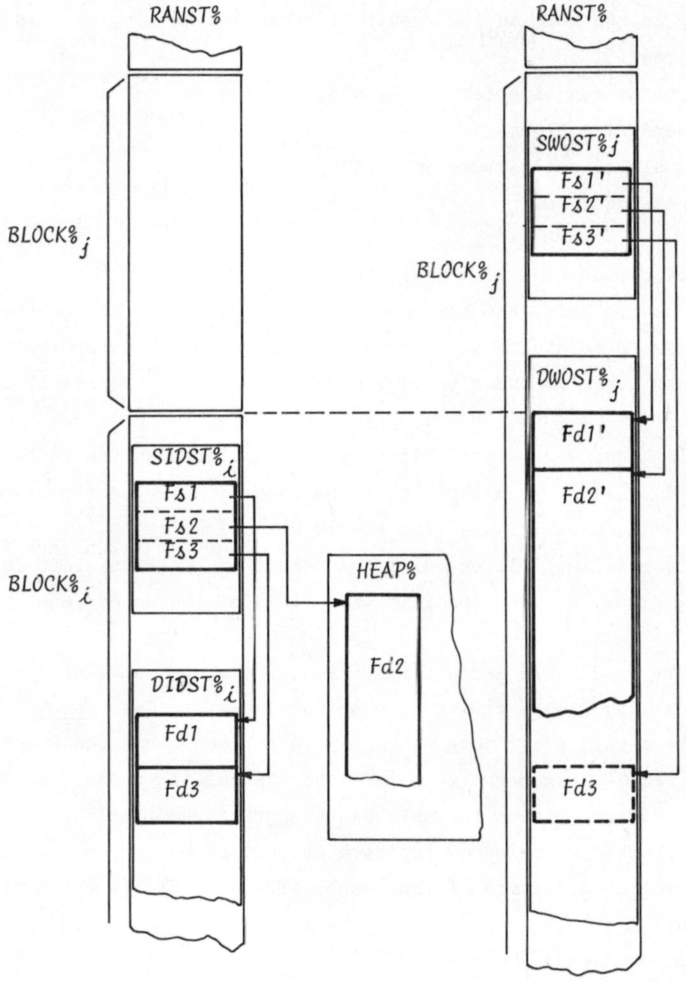

a. Before exit from *block*$_i$

b. After exit from *block*$_i$ during the copy *Fd2'* of *Fd2*

fig. 2.1

2.3.3 VALIDITY OF ACCESSES

The validity of an access to a stored value is based on the following principle: a stored value may be used as the result of an action as long as this stored value is not overwritten.

There are three run-time actions by which stored values can be lost :

- the end of a block,
- the call of the garbage collector,
- the assignation.

a. End of block action

When a $block_i$ is left, the corresponding $IDST\%_i$, $LGST\%_i$ and $WOST\%_i$ are lost ; it is the study of the origin of the value of the block which determines which run-time action has to be taken in order to keep a valid access to the result of this block (II.1).

If *kindo* is *iden*, *var* or *gen* and if *bno* is smaller than the depth number *bn* of the *block* which is left, assuming that scope rules(†) have been performed, the access remains valid. Clearly, when the access class is *dirwost*, *indwost* or *dirwost'*, a run-time action is implied, by which the result of the block left is transmitted to the calling block, and the specification field of the access must be modified accordingly.

If the above conditions are not fulfilled, the whole value has to be copied on *WOST%* of the calling *block*, giving rise to an access of class *dirwost*.

NB. What has been said above does not apply to a block corresponding to a procedure, for which the result is generally copied into the calling block, and this to ensure the static connection between the call and the procedure itself (II.5.1.3). On the other hand, in procedure oriented implementations, at non procedure block returns, the copies of the static parts of the results stored on *SWOST%* are avoided.

b. Call of the garbage collector

The garbage collection must be provided with run-time information about all accessible values. As explained in I.2.4.3 the updating of this run-time information is based on the access mechanism itself, which solves the problem of its validity.

c. Assignation

The effect of an assignation is the overwriting of a stored value, value which, according to the access management described so far, may be used as the parameter

---

(†) Scope rules (I.2.5.1) imply the *bn* of the block where a value is stored is always smaller or equal to the *bno* of this stored value. Hence, the above check takes the worst case into consideration.

of a future action. Such a situation may only appear for actions where side-effects are allowed, which brings itself in ALGOL 68 [1] to three cases where an order of elaboration is implied(†) :

- the primary of a call has to be elaborated before the actual parameters,
- the right part of a conformity relation has to be elaborated before its left part, if this left part is elaborated at all,
- a semicolon appearing between two formal parameters of a routine denotation implies an order in the elaboration of the corresponding actual parameters.

The problem may be solved by systematically copying the value of the primary of the call, of the right part of the conformity relation and of the actual parameters satisfying the above conditions. Obviously when the *derefo* of such values is zero, i.e. when no dereferencing has taken place since their origin, these values can never be overwritten by an assignation and no copy is needed.

2.3.4 LOCAL OPTIMIZATIONS

A computer possesses a specific number of registers each with its own properties; an optimal use of registers implies to take them into consideration during the static access management. It would e.g. be possible to have additional classes of accesses as *dirregister* and *indregister*, the meaning of which is obvious. The static management of such accesses supposes the updating of a list of register information reflecting their current occupation. Starting from this, we could for each action being translated choose the optimal strategy in the use of registers. The policy of the scheme described here requires machine independency, which can be obtained either in ignoring the existence of registers or in parametrizing the system. For lack of criteria for choosing a sound parametrization, the first solution has been adopted with, as direct consequence, a decrease in the efficiency of the generated object programs. This is only admissible as far as the price to pay is not to heavy; for this purpose a simple system of local optimizations is used.

The principle of this system consists essentially in suppressing pairs of consecutive store and load instructions of one same register and with the same address part [16]. Clearly, this is only valid if the value to be loaded and stored is used only once, which is the case for intermediate results stored on *WOST%*, i.e. when the instructions have a *WOST%* address part. In the examples below, the sequence STA w, LDA w is cancelled by local optimization (Example 2.2). When a similar sequence appears with a non-*WOST%* address STA y, LDA y, only the second instruction of the pair may be cancelled (Example 2.3).

Example 2.2

Source program :

$x := a + b \times c$

(†) In the revision [8] side-effects are no longer allowed.

Result of the syntactic analysis :

:= x + a × b c

Intermediate code :

$\times$*(<u>proc</u> (<u>int</u>, <u>int</u>)<u>int</u>, (<u>diriden</u> b), (<u>diriden</u> c), (<u>dirwost</u> w))*

+(<u>proc</u> (<u>int</u>, <u>int</u>)<u>int</u>, (<u>diriden</u> a), (<u>dirwost</u> w), (<u>dirwost</u> w_1*))*

:=(<u>int</u>, (<u>variden</u> x), (<u>dirwost</u> w_1*))*

Machine code without local optimization :

```
LDA b
MPY c
STA w

LDA w     {When the second operand of a commutative dyadic
ADA a      operator is stored on WOST% the order of the two
STA w1     operands is inverted in machine code}

LDA w1
STA x
```

Machine code after local optimizations :

```
LDA b
MPY c
ADA a
STA x
```

The only price to pay in the above example is the reservation of the memory cells w and w_1 (actually w and w_1 may be the same cell), which will in fact never be used at run-time.

<u>Example</u> 2.3

Source program :

x := y := a

Result of the syntactic analysis :

:= x <u>deref</u> := y a

Intermediate code :

:=(<u>int</u>, (<u>variden</u> y), (<u>diriden</u> a))

:=(<u>int</u>, (<u>variden</u> x), (<u>diriden</u> y))

Machine code without local optimizations :

```
LDA a
STA y

LDA y
STA x
```

Machine code after local optimizations :

```
LDA a
STA y
STA x
```

A more difficult case is the one of retrieving efficient machine code when choice actions (i.e. conditional, case or serial with completer actions) are involved. For these actions, special object instructions "*<u>loadreg</u> (mode, access)*" and "*storereg (mode, access)*" are generated in the intermediate code (Example 2.4) ; these instructions are ignored when translated into a machine code where no register exists for values of the *mode* specified in the instructions, otherwise they are replaced by load and store machine instructions respectively, for such registers. As shown by the example, the generation of these instructions allows one to obtain more efficient object code simply by applying the principles of local optimizations :

Example 2.4

Source program :

$x := (d \mid a_1 \mid a_2) + c$

Result of the syntactic analysis :

$:= x + (d \mid a_1 \mid a_2)\ c$

Intermediate code (without *storereg* and *loadreg* instructions) :

```
      jump no    ((diriden d), L)
      copy       (int,(diriden a1),(dirwost w))
      jump       (L')
L   : copy       (int,(diriden a2),(dirwost w))
L'  : +          (proc(int,int)int,(dirwost w),(diriden c),(dirwost w1))
      :=         (int,(variden x),(dirwost w1))
```

{in this intermediate code the instructions "*copy*" are intended to force the value of the first operand of the operator "+" in the same location *w* whatever the boolean value of *d* would be. In this way the single access *w* can be used when the action "+" is translated.}

Machine code :

```
       LDC d {C is supposed to be an addressable comparison register}
       IFJ L
       LDA a1
       STA w
       UNJ L'
  L  : LDA a2
       STA w
  L' : LDA w
       ADA c
       STA w1
       LDA w1
       STA x
```

Clearly, local optimizations applied to this machine code do not lead to optimal object code. It is the reason why, in case of choice actions, special instructions have to be generated in the intermediate code :

(1) At the end of each element of a choice, the following instruction is generated :

loadreg (mode, access)

where mode and access are the mode and access of the value of the element ; this instruction will be translated into the machine instruction "LDA access" if it appears that a value of the specified mode fits into the A register, otherwise the instruction will be disregarded.

(2) At the end of each choice action the following instruction will be generated:

storereg (mode, access)

giving rise to "STA access" in machine code if a value of the specified mode fits into the A register ; it is disregarded otherwise. Then the intermediate code becomes :

```
     jump no     ((diriden d), L)
     copy        (int, (diriden a1), (dirwost w))
     loadreg     (int,w)
     jump        (L')
L  : copy        (int, (diriden a2), (dirwost w))
     loadreg     (int,w)
L' : storereg    (int,w)
     + (proc(int,int)int, (dirwost w),(diriden c), (dirwost w1))
    := (int,(variden x), (dirwost w1))
```

and the machine code :

```
     LDC d
     IFJ L
     LDA a1
     STA w
     LDA w
     UNJ L'
L  : LDA a2
     STA w
     LDA w
L' : STA w
     LDA w
     ADA c
     STA w1
     LDA w1
     STA x
```

After local optimizations the program becomes optimal :

```
     LDC d
     IFJ L
     LDA a1
     UNJ L'
L  : LDA a2
L' : ADA c
     STA x
```

Other examples of local optimizations can be found in II.14.1.2 and III.3.

2.4 MEMORY RECOVERY

The problems of memory recovery treated in this section are related to the intermediate results on *WOST%*. These problems have three aspects each of which is controlled by a static property attached to the *WOST%* values (i.e. the values with access classes *dirwost*, *dirwost'* and *indwost*) :

- the static property "*static memory recovery*" *(smr)* controls the memory recovery on *SWOST%*,
- the static property "*dynamic memory recovery*" *(dmr)* controls the memory recovery on *DWOST%*,
- the static property "*garbage collection*" *(gc)* controls the storage of garbage collection information attached to *WOST%* values.

2.4.1 STATIC WORKING STACK MEMORY RECOVERY

A *WOST%* value is accessed through a static *RANST%* address *n.p* which is the static address of a location of *SWOST%* ; each part $SWOST\%_i$ of *SWOST%* is completely controlled at compile-time, and no dynamic pointer management is needed. It is shown below by means of a few examples how the static property *smr* allows the static control of *SWOST%* and at the same time permits to minimize the number of copies without endangering the last-in-first-out principle, but sometimes at the price of some delay in the recovery of "holes" on *SWOST%*.

Smr associated to a *SWOST%* value has the form of a *RANST%* address *n.p* which indicates up to where the memory can be statically recovered on *SWOST%* when the associated value is deleted ; as opposed to classical memory recovery methods, $n_s.p_s$ may be different from the static address *n.p* of the access of the value.

Example 2.5 (fig. 2.2)

Suppose a structured value *S* is stored on *SWOST%* with an *access (dirwost n.p)* and a *smr* $n_s.p_s$ identical to *n.p*. The translation of a selection of a field *F* from *S* consists simply in transforming the access into *(dirwost* $n.p{+}\Delta p$*)*, where Δp is the relative address of *F* in *S*. *SWOST%* memory is recovered as follows : the static address $n_f.p_f$ indicating the first free cell on *SWOST%* before the selection, is transformed into $n.p{+}\Delta p{+}stsz$, where *stsz* is the size of the static part of *F*. Clearly the hole of size Δp cannot be recovered at once if we want to avoid a shift of the value of the selected field, but it will be recovered at the same time as the space of the field itself, and this thanks to the static property *smr* which has remained unchanged. The process is recursive and the hole may grow, but it will not become bigger than $\Delta p{+}stsz$. Note that if the access itself of a value were used for recovering its *SWOST%* memory, the hole would only be recovered when the previous value is deleted ; in this case, holes risk to accumulate (e.g. when several values appear successively on *SWOST%* before the previous value is deleted), which is avoided by the present solution.

Example 2.6 (fig. 2.3)

Suppose m values $V_1,\ldots,V_m$ of *access* $n_1.p_1,\ldots,n_m.p_m$ and of *smr* $smr_1,\ldots,smr_m$, are respectively stored on $SWOST\%_i$ and are the *m* parameters of an action. Suppose moreover that the result of the action does not preexist in memory and hence has to be construted on *SWOST%*.

Generally speaking, it is impossible to construct the result of the action directly on *SWOST%* by overwriting the values of the parameters and this for two reasons :

(1) the whole of all parameters may be needed up to the end of the action,

(2) heap values accessible through parameters may remain accessible through the result. If such heap values are protected through garbage collection information associated with the parameters, the value of the parameter must remain available for the garbage collector up to the end of the action, where the result itself will be associated with a garbage collection information. (An alternative process consists in protecting the result as it is constructed, but this is more expensive in run-time actions).

A solution consists in constructing the result from $n_f.p_f$ and in shifting it to smr_1 at the end of the action in order to avoid the accumulation of unused memory on *SWOST%*, the price being an extra copy of the result.

The other solution consists in searching if there is a hole hi(smr_i to $n_i.p_i$) big enough to contain the static part of the result, in which case it is constructed in this hole with an *access* equal to (dirwost smr_i) and an *smr* equal to smr_1. It is to be remarked that the research of the hole is completely static. If the result does not fit in any hole it is constructed from $n_f.p_f$ but not shifted.

This last process avoids a copy of the resulting value, at the price of delaying the recovery of holes on *SWOST%* ; but it is not cumulative in the sense that the more one is lead to construct the results from $n_f.p_f$, the more the holes are growing, and the greater is the chance to find a hole big enough for the result of the next action.

Example 2.7 (fig. 2.4)

Suppose a value *V* has to be stored on *SWOST%* and that, according to the prevision mechanism described in I.3, we know that the next action to be applied to *V* will provide this value with an overhead (uniting or rowing for example) giving rise to *V'*. Instead of storing the value at the first free cell *n.p*, it is stored at *n.p+ohsz* where *ohsz* is the size of the overhead ; clearly, the *smr* of the value will be *n.p*. In this way, the dynamic effect of the next action will be to store the overhead without moving the value *V* on *SWOST%*.

Fig. 2.5 shows the situation where the selected field *F* of fig. 2.2 is provided with an overhead.

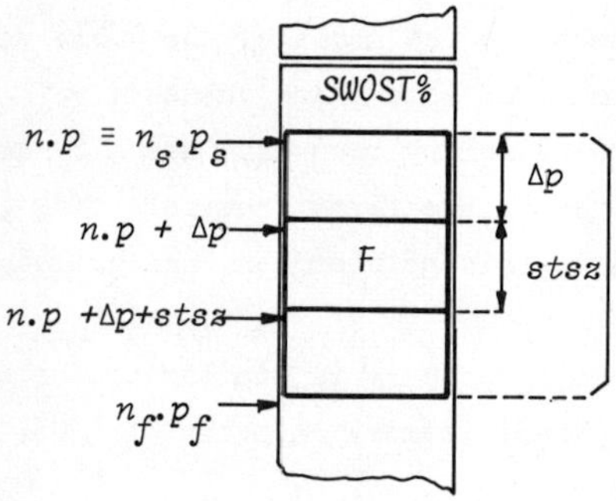

S : *access* : (*dirwost* *n.p*)
smr : *n.p*

F : *access* : (*dirwost* *n.p+Δp*)
smr : *n.p*

fig. 2.2

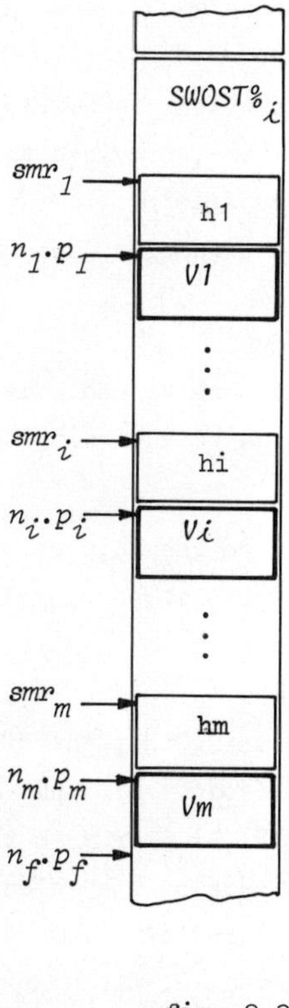

fig. 2.3

2.4.2 DYNAMIC WORKING STACK MEMORY RECOVERY

DWOST% parts of values are accessed at run-time through a dynamic interpretation of the descriptor offsets contained in their respective *SWOST%* parts ; the addresses of the offsets can be deduced from the accesses and the modes of the *WOST%* values either at compile-time or possibly at run-time (for some union values).

DWOST% memory recovery, as opposed to *SWOST%* memory recovery, has a dynamic effect, namely the updating of a run-time pointer to the first free cell of *DWOST%* (which is also the first free cell of *RANST%*) ; this pointer has been called *ranstpm%*.

Nevertheless, the strategy of dynamic memory recovery is similar to the strategy of static memory recovery : to separate the dynamic memory recovery of *DWOST%* values from their access, giving rise to the static property *dmr*.

The property *dmr* has three possible forms :

(<u>nil</u> o) shortened into <u>nil</u>

(<u>stat</u> $n_d.p_d$),

(<u>dyn</u> $n'_d.p'_d$).

1) <u>nil</u> is used for values without dynamic part on *DWOST%*, it allows to detect that no object instruction has to be generated for recovering *DWOST%* memory when such values are deleted.

2) (<u>stat</u> $n_d.p_d$) is used when the *DWOST%* pointer up to which the *DWOST%* memory can be recovered is at an address $n_d.p_d$ known at compile-time, provided the contents of the address do not risk to be lost before the value is deleted.

a) This is the case when the pointer is the first offset in the static part of a non-union value on *SWOST%*.

<u>Example</u> 2.8 (<u>fig</u>. 2.6)

Let *V* be a non-union *WOST%* value with a static part *Vs* and a dynamic part *Vd*, and let $n_d.p_d$ be the address of the first offset in *Vs* according to the mode of *V* ; *dmr* attached to *V* has the form (<u>stat</u> $n_d.p_d$).

b) It is also the case when the pointer is stored in the hole situated between the *access* and the *smr* of the value at $n_d.p_d$ known at compile-time.

<u>Example</u> 2.9 (<u>fig</u>. 2.7)

Suppose a structured value *S* of mode <u>struct</u> $([\,]\mu_1 s_1, \ldots, [\,]\mu_i s_i, \ldots, [\,]\mu_m s_m)$ is stored on *WOST%* with an access (<u>dirwost</u> n.p). Assuming that the offset of a descriptor is stored in its first cell, *dmr* of *S* is (<u>stat</u> n.p). This *dmr* remains invariant through the selection of a field *Fi* of *S*. Similarly to the static memory recovery, there is a hole above the dynamic part of the selected value and the *DWOST%* memory space *Fdi+1* ... *Fdm* can be recovered after the selection by adjusting *ranstpm%* ; obviously this recovery is dynamic, the compiler must generate the corresponding object instructions.

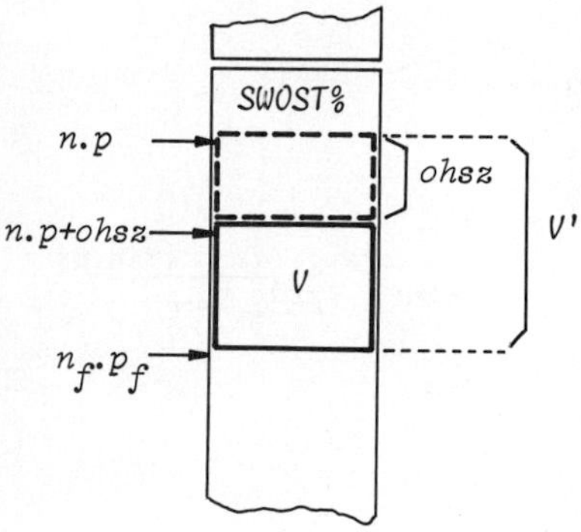

V : access : (<u>dirwost</u> n.p+ohsz)
smr : n.p

V' : access : (<u>dirwost</u> n.p)
smr : n.p

<u>fig</u>. 2.4

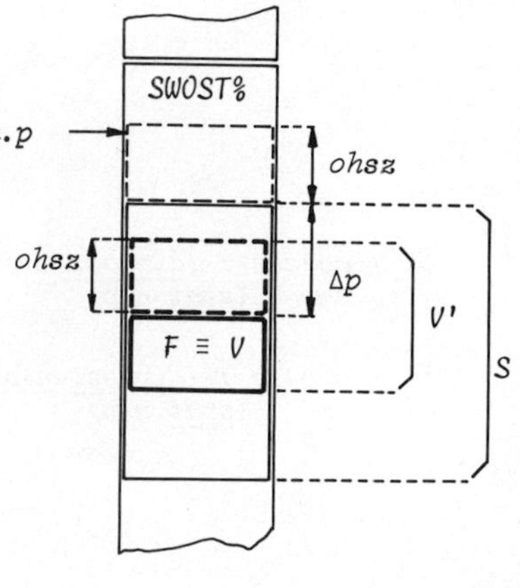

S : access : (<u>dirwost</u> n.p+ohsz)
smr : n.p

F : access : (<u>dirwost</u> n.p+ohsz+Δp)
smr : n.p

V' : access : (<u>dirwost</u> n.p+Δp)
smr : n.p

<u>fig</u>. 2.5

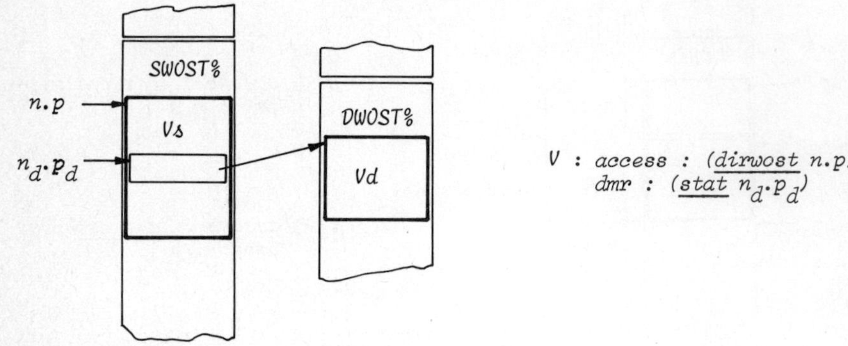
SWOST%
n.p
Vs
$n_d.p_d$
DWOST%
Vd
V : access : (dirwost n.p)
dmr : (stat $n_d.p_d$)

fig. 2.6

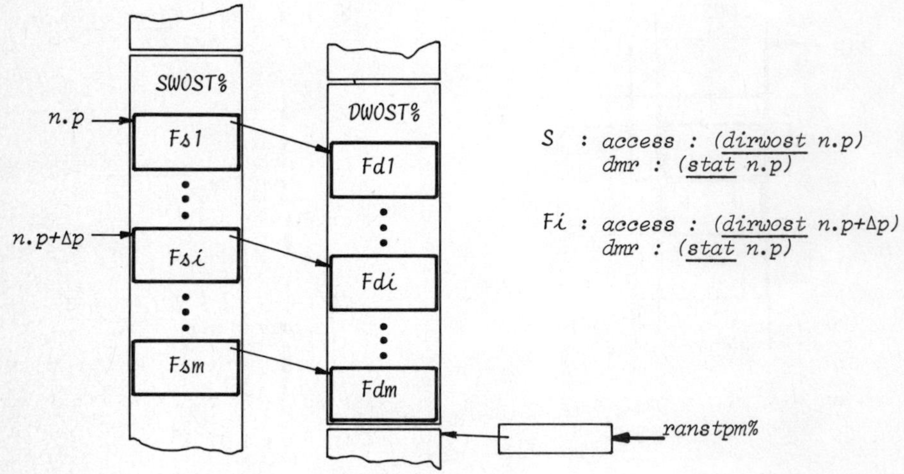
SWOST%
n.p
Fs1
n.p+Δp
Fsi
Fsm
DWOST%
Fd1
Fdi
Fdm
ranstpm%
S : access : (dirwost n.p)
dmr : (stat n.p)
Fi : access : (dirwost n.p+Δp)
dmr : (stat n.p)

fig. 2.7

3) *(<u>dyn</u> $n'_d.p'_d$)* is used when the *DWOST%* pointer up to which *DWOST%* space can be recovered is stored at an address known at compile-time but whose contents risk to be lost before the value is deleted. In this case, a special object instruction is generated by which this pointer is saved in a *SWOST%* memory cell $n'_d.p'_d$, where it can be retrieved when the value is deleted. There are several ways of choosing $n'_d.p'_d$, we explain one of them : a new part is distinguished in each *SWOST%*$_i$ in addition to *SWOST%*$_i$ proper : *DMRWOST%*$_i$, where the cells of address $n'_d.p'_d$ are reserved. As for *SWOST%*$_i$, the size of *DMRWOST%*$_i$ is known at compile-time and its management is completely static.

a) A first case in which the above situation appears is when some values of mode union have to be stored on *WOST%*.

<u>Example</u> 2.10 (<u>fig</u>. 2.8)

Suppose a value *U* of mode *<u>union</u>* (μ_1,[] μ_2), where μ_1 is a NONROW mode, has to be stored on *WOST%*. Before the value is stored, *ranstpm%* contains the address up to which *DWOST%* memory has to be recovered when the value is deleted ; clearly the copy of the value on *WOST%* causes the overwriting of *ranstpm%*. The proposed solution consists in generating an object instruction by which *ranstpm%* is stored at the *DMRWOST%* address $n'_d.p'_d$, just before the value is stored on *WOST%*. Statically, this gives rise to a *dmr* equal to *(<u>dyn</u> $n'_d.p'_d$)* for the value.

Clearly, the *DWOST%* memory recovery, when *U* is deleted, consists in dynamically restoring the initial value of *ranstpm%* by means of the contents of the cell $n'_d.p'_d$. Note that in this case there is another solution for recovering the *DWOST%* memory of *U*, which consists in a dynamic interpretation of the overhead, this solution seems to be less efficient.

b) The second case where *dmr* of class <u>dyn</u> has to be used occurs when an action on a value with *dmr* equal to *(<u>stat</u> $n_d.p_d$)* is translated, action which provides the value with an overhead which appears to overwrite the cell $n_d.p_d$.

<u>Example</u> 2.11 (<u>fig</u>. 2.9)

Let us come back to Example 2.9 with m=2 and suppose that the field *F2* of mode [] μ_2 is selected and that the result of the selection is rowed several times thereafter. If the overhead corresponding to the rowing supersedes the cell $n.p$, its contents must be saved beforehand on *DMRWOST%* at $n'_d.p'_d$.

Note that a similar situation may arise when the static part of the result of an action is constructed in a hole of a parameter as it is the case in the example 2.6.

<u>Remark</u> 1.

No example similar to example 2.6 about static memory recovery has been considered for the dynamic memory recovery. Such an example would be related to the translation of an action with several parameters stored on *WOST%* and with a result to be stored on *WOST%*, all corresponding values being supposed to have dynamic parts. A solution similar to the one described in I.2.4.1 can be imagined here, for storing

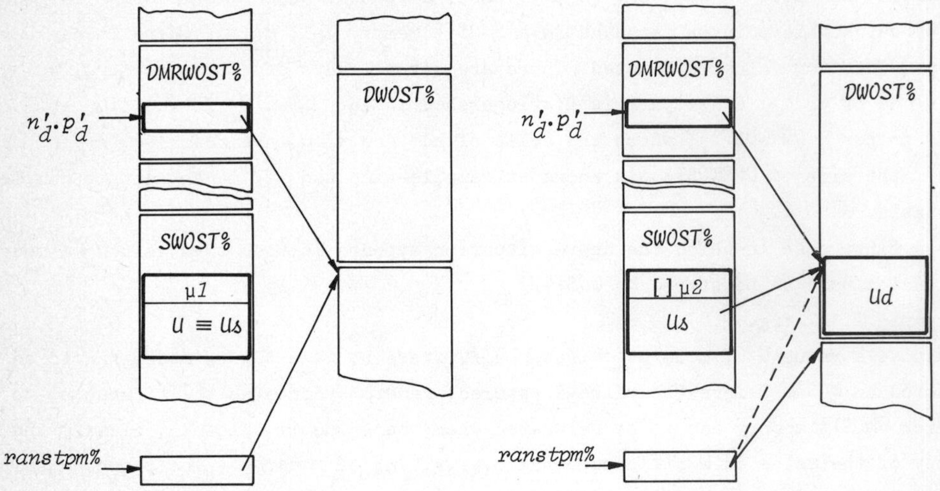

a. dynamic mode of *U* is μ_1 *b*. dynamic mode of *U* is $[\,]\mu_2$

<u>fig</u>. 2.8

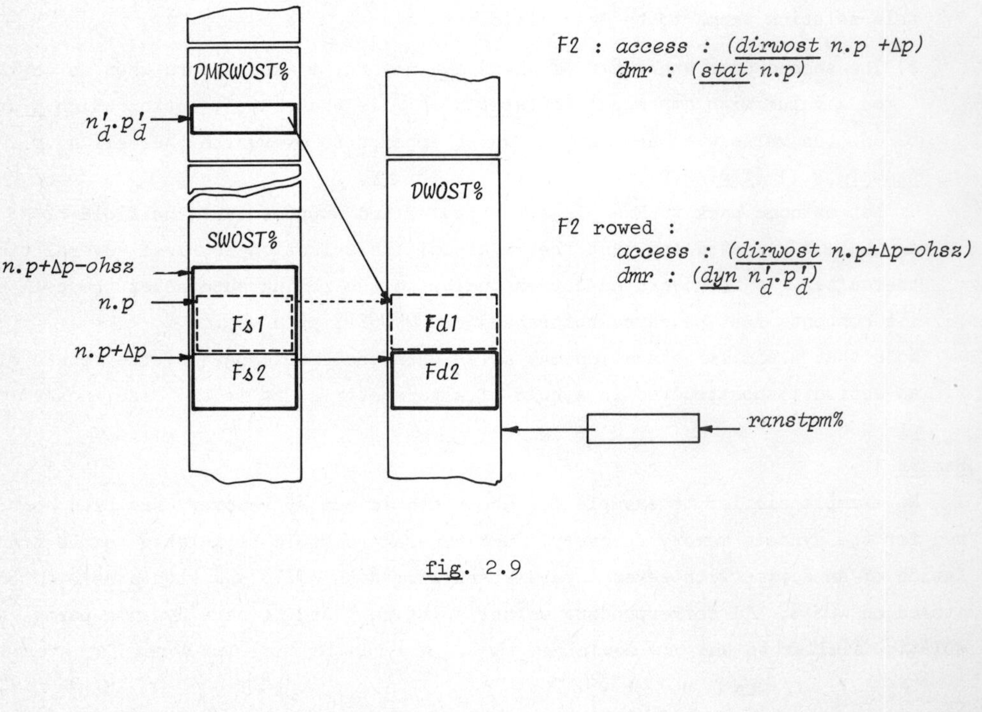

<u>fig</u>. 2.9

the dynamic part of the result of the action without overwriting the parameters. The solution also consists in searching between the *access* and the *dmr* of the dynamic part of a parameter, a hole big enough to store the dynamic part of the result. However the main difference is that the searching of the hole would take place at run-time. The question is, is it better to make this run-time search or to allow an extra copy of the dynamic part of the result?

On the other hand, no standard ALGOL 68 operator delivers a result with a dynamic part, and moreover, the system explained in this book avoids the copies of dynamic parts of values on *DWOST%* to a large extent for most of ALGOL 68 actions.

For these reasons, the mechanism explained in I.2.4.1 for static memory recovery, seems not worthwhile to be extended to the dynamic memory **recovery** in an ALGOL 68 compiler.

Remark 2.

According to the restrictions on accesses (see I.2.3.2), no ALGOL 68 action may cause the creation of an overhead to a *DWOST%* value ; however there is a situation where a similar problem occurs.

Suppose (fig. 2.10) that a value *V*(*Vs* and *Vd*) of mode *struct* ([] μs) is stored on *WOST%* and that this value has to be rowed ; *Vs* and *Vd* will form together the dynamic part of the result *V'* of the rowing, which will be of mode [] *struct* ([] μs). According to rule b2 (see I.2.3.2) by which the dynamic parts of the *WOST%* values may not be stored on *SWOST%*, *Vs* has to be copied on *DWOST%*. On the other hand, according to rule b3 by which the different parts of a *WOST%* value have to be stored in a well defined order, *Vs* has to be stored on the top of *Vd*. In order to avoid a shift of *Vd* freeing space for *Vs*, the prevision mechanism is used for generating an object instruction by which *ranstpm%* is increased with the size of *Vs* before *V* is stored on *WOST%*. Clearly, thereafter, there is space on top of *Vd* to store *Vs* (see also II.11.5).

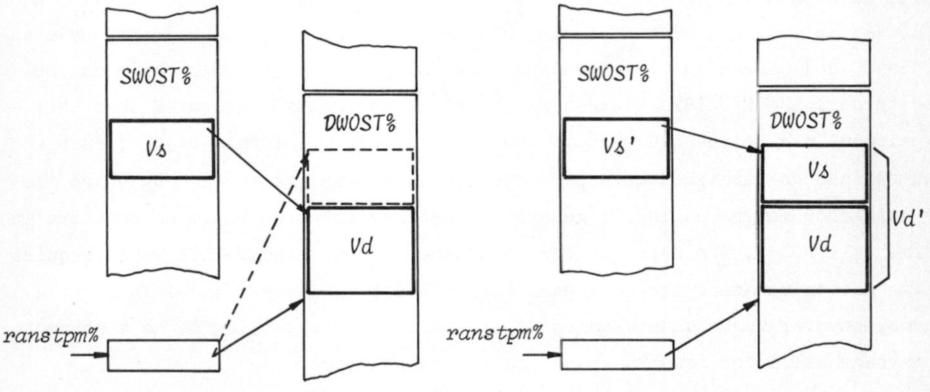

a. before rowing of *V*　　*b*. after rowing of *V*

fig. 2.10

Remark 3

It has been explained in [13] how the presence of local generators may hamper the last-in-first-out principle of *WOST%*, when *LGST%* and *WOST%* are merged in *RANST%*. The solution of [13] implies an order of elaboration ; more precisely, it implies that "syntactically accessible" generators of collateral clauses are elaborated before the other elements of the clause.

We propose here a solution implying no order of elaboration but by which we accept the freezing of some parts of $DWOST\%_i$ for the duration of $BLOCK\%_i$. The solution is based on *geno*(I.2.1). *Geno* is set to 1 when a local generator is elaborated, and is transmitted to the previous *BOST* elements corresponding to *WOST%* values of the same $BLOCK\%_i$. The effect of *geno* equal to 1 is to inhibit the *DWOST%* memory recovery of the corresponding value, which at the same time inhibits the recovery of merged *LGST%* locations (see also II.15.2, step 4.2).

2.4.3 HEAP MEMORY RECOVERY

HEAP% memory recovery is performed by the garbage collector ; this one proceeds in two steps, namely the marking and the compacting which are both based on the modes and the accesses of *IDST%* and *WOST%* values.

How garbage collection routines are generated starting from the mode and the access of a value is explained in [12] ; the remaining problem is to link all routines together in order that each time the garbage collector is activated the routines corresponding to the current state of *IDST%* and *WOST%* are called (*a*).

In addition, providing *WOST%* values with garbage collection information requires dynamic actions. It will be shown how these actions can be minimized (*b*).

a. Linkage of garbage collection information.

We know that *IDST%* and *WOST%* have been split in several parts $IDST\%_i$ and $WOST\%_i$ on *RANST%*, in such a way $IDST\%_i$ and $WOST\%_i$ are parts of one same block $BLOCK\%_i$. A block $BLOCK\%_i$ is provided with a heading $H\%_i$ and blocks are linked together by means of the field *dch%* stored in their heading. The entry point into this chain can be obtained through the *DISPLAY%* element of the *block* currently elaborated, and this display element can be reached through the depth number *bn* of this *block* ; such a depth number can be furnished as a parameter each time an instruction by which the garbage collector may be called, is generated. Another solution would be to store in a run-time cell *rtbn%*, the depth number *bn* of the current block. This would require a run-time action updating the cell each time a block is entered and left (<u>fig</u>. 2.11). This seems, however to be counterbalanced by the fact that passing *bn* as a parameter to the garbage collector is also space and time consuming.

Garbage collection information for each $IDST\%_i$ and $WOST\%_i$ will be stored in the corresponding $BLOCK\%_i$ (<u>fig</u>. 2.12) as follows :

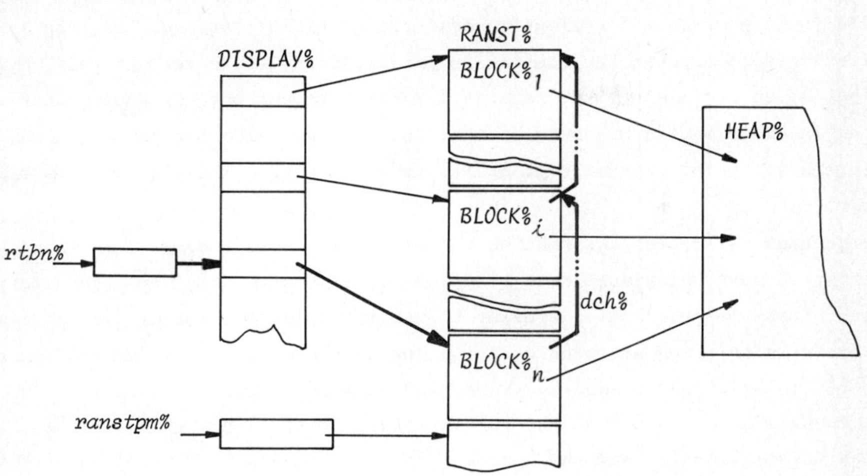

fig. 2.11

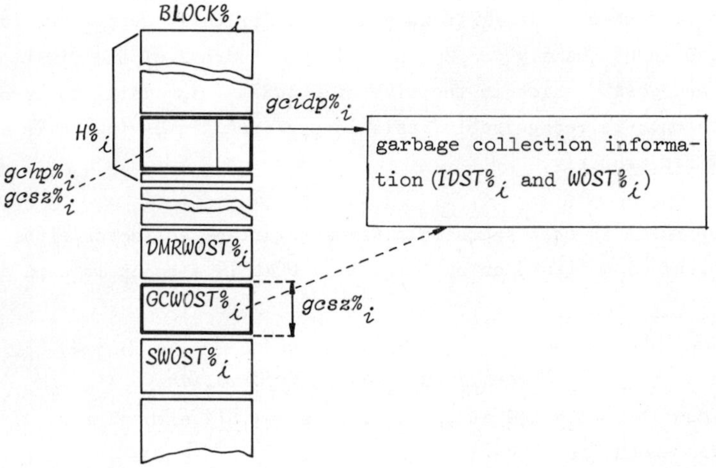

fig. 2.12

(1) The garbage collection information for $IDST\%_i$ mainly consists of a pointer $gcidp\%_i$ stored in $H\%_i$. This pointer gives access at run-time, either to a precompiled routine or to a compile-time constructed table ; when called, the garbage collector will execute the routine or interpret the table respectively. $Gcidp\%_i$ is set up at block entry and remains invariant throughout the whole block execution. In addition, in order to prevent the garbage collector to be misled, all pointers and union overheads of $SIDST\%_i$ must be initialized (to <u>*nil*</u>) at block entry.

(2) The garbage collection information for $WOST\%_i$ is continuously varying and, in principle, must be updated each time the contents of $WOST\%_i$ vary. For storing this information a solution similar to the one used for storing dynamic memory recovery information has been used : a new part has been distinguished in each $SWOST\%_i$ in addition to $SWOST\%_i$ proper and $DMRWOST\%_i$, namely $GCWOST\%_i$.(†)
The management of each $GCWOST\%_i$ is completely static, in particular its size is known at compile-time and the accesses to its elements have the form of *RANST%* addresses $n_g.p_g$; there will be one $GCWOST\%_i$ element for each $WOST\%_i$ value giving access to *HEAP%* values which risk to be lost when the garbage collector is called. The static property *gc* associated to each *WOST%* value will be the static address $n_g.p_g$ of the corresponding *GCWOST%* element when it exists, it will be given a special representation (<u>*nil*</u>) otherwise.
A *GCWOST%* element furnishes information about the mode and the access of the corresponding *WOST%* value ; moreover the garbage collector must be provided with information telling where *GCWOST%* starts and ends. For this purpose two informations are stored in $H\%_i$ namely $gchp\%_i$ which is the address of the first $GCWOST\%_i$ cell and $gcsz\%_i$ which is the size of $GCWOST\%_i$. In addition, irrelevant *GCWOST%* elements must be recognizable, this is performed in having their contents always initialized properly.

<u>Definition</u>. A value which is made accessible for the garbage collector either through an *IDST%* value of a *BLOCK%* or by means of a *GCWOST%* element is said to be *protected*.

b. Minimization of working stack garbage collection information

A *WOST%* value must be protected at run-time by a *GCWOST%* element :

- if it gives access to a *HEAP%* value and
- if this heap value is not already protected through an *IDST%* value, or if there exists such a protection but which can be destroyed by a side-effect.

These conditions are generally not completely known at compile-time ; a *GCWOST%*

(†) It is acknowledged that this solution is not optimal, although it works quite satisfactorily ; in appendix 1 the main lines of a better solution are sketched. However, for historical reasons, it is the first solution which is developped in the main text.

protection will be based on known information in order to allow full security. Clearly, the number of situations where at compile-time a *GCWOST%* protection has to be foreseen is larger than the number of run-time situations with the above conditions. The present study shows how the static properties *access*, *mode* and *origin* of a *WOST%* value allow to minimize the cases where this value has to be protected.
For the sake of clarity, it will be successively shown how these properties allow to determine at compile-time whether :
(1) the *WOST%* value risks to give access to a *HEAP%* value,
(2) a *HEAP%* value accessible through a *WOST%* value is protected through an *IDST%* value (assuming no side-effects have occurred),
(3) side-effects invalidating the above presumed protection risk to be present.

In practice the distinction has not to be made in such an explicit way. In particular, when translating an action on a given value, the presence or absence of *GCWOST%* protection for this value and its access class sometimes give additional information about the fact that the value resulting from the action has to be protected on *GCWOST%* or not (see Example 2.17, fig. 2.24).

(1) A *WOST%* value *V*(*Vs* and *Vd*) may give access to a *HEAP%* value *Vh* in the following conditions :
   a) the access class of the value is *dirwost* and, according to its *mode*, the value contains a name *N* (fig. 2.13). Clearly, a value with an access class *dirwost* and of plain mode (*int*, *bool*, ...) will never have to be protected.
   b) the access class of the value is *dirwost*', and according to its *mode*, the value contains a name *N* (fig. 2.14 and 2.15).
   c) the access class of the value is *dirwost*' and, according to its origin, its dynamic part risks to be on the *HEAP%* :

   Example 2.12 (fig. 2.16)
   Suppose a value *V* (*Vs* and *Vd*) with an access class *dirwost*' has the following *origin* properties
   - *kindo* = *var*
   - *derefo* = *1*
   - *flexo* = *1*

   This means that the last dereferenced name was referring to a value with flexible bounds, and hence that the dynamic part of this value is stored on the *HEAP%*. As a consequence *Vd* is on the *HEAP%*. Such a situation happens e.g. when a variable of mode *ref* [...] μ is first dereferenced giving rise to a multiple value *M*(*Ms* and *Md*) with flexible bounds and then sliced giving rise to *V*.
   However, (fig. 2.17), if the value *V* were originated from an identifier which is only sliced (*kindo* = *iden* and *derefo* = *0*) the access class of *V* would be *dirwost*' but *Vd* would not be on the *HEAP%*.

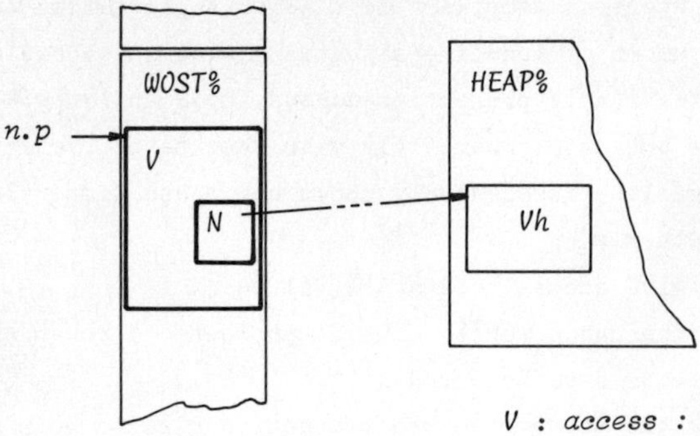

V : access : (<u>dirwost</u> n.p)

<u>fig</u>. 2.13

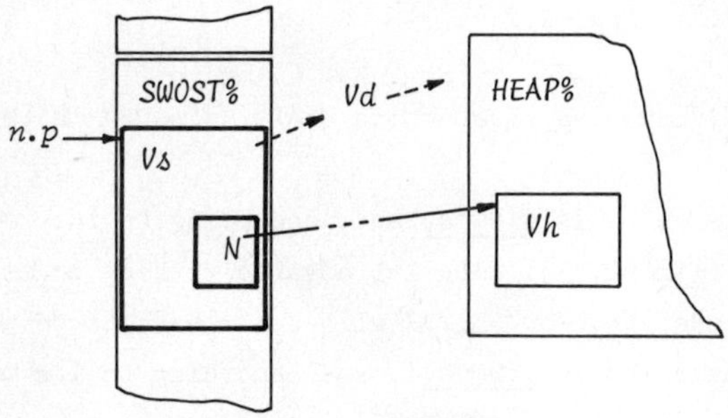

Vs : access : (<u>dirwost'</u> n.p)

<u>fig</u>. 2.14

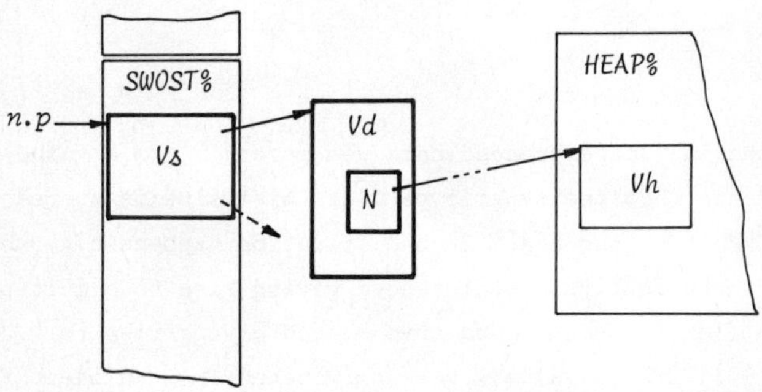

Vs : access : (<u>dirwost'</u> n.p)

<u>fig</u>. 2.15

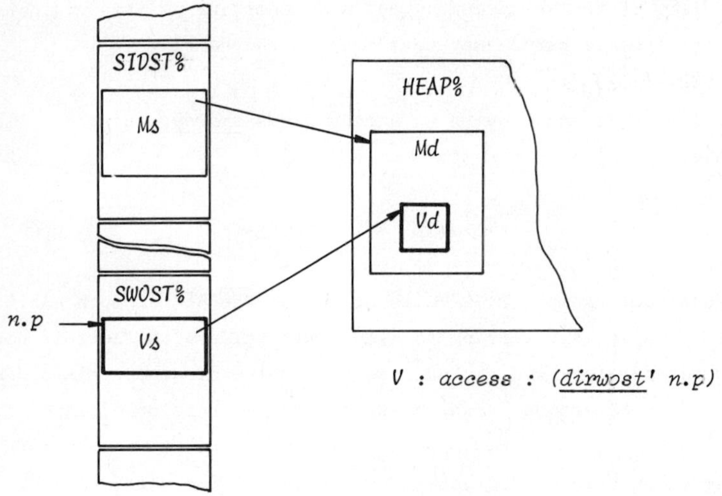

fig. 2.16

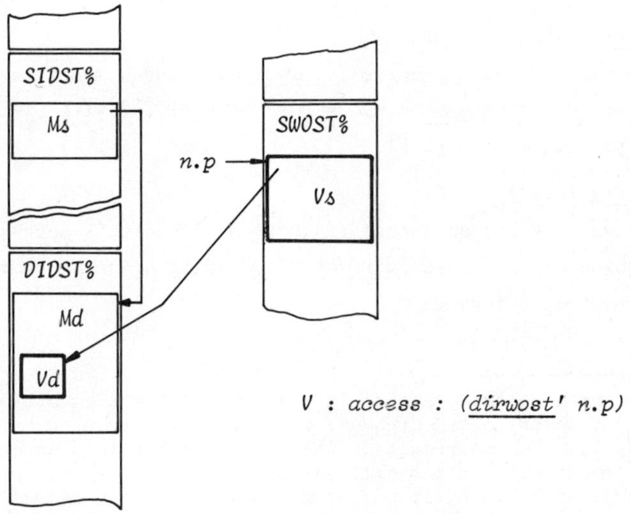

fig. 2.17

d) the access class of *V* is *indwost* and according to its mode, it contains a name *N* (fig. 2.18).

e) the access class of the value is *indwost* and according to its origin, the value itself (or its dynamic part) may be stored on the *HEAP%* .

Example 2.13 (fig. 2.19)

Suppose a value *V*(*Vs* and *Vd*) with an access class *indwost* has the following *origin* properties :

- *kindo* = *var*
- *derefo* = *1*
- *flexo* = *1*

As it was the case for example 2.12, *Vd* is stored on the *HEAP%*. Such a situation may result from a variable referring to a multiple value with flexible bounds and which is first dereferenced giving rise to a value of access class *diriden* and then involved in an action by which its access is transformed into (*indwost n.p*)(†).

However, if the value *V* were originated from an identifier which is only involved in an action transforming the access (*kindo* = *iden* and *derefo* = *0*), *Vd* would not be stored on the *HEAP%*.

(2) A *HEAP%* value accessible through a *WOST%* value is protected through an *IDST%* value, assuming that no side-effects may occur, if the *kindo* of the *WOST%* value is *iden* or *var* and if its *bno* is smaller or equal to the depth number *bn* of the current *block*.

Example 2.14 (fig. 2.20)(††)

Suppose the value *V* has an access (*dirwost n.p*) and comes from a copy of an *IDST%* value *V'* (*kindo* = *iden* or *kindo* = *var*) of a *BLOCK%* with *bn*≤n (*bno*=*bn*≤n).
Clearly *Vh* is protected through *V'*.

Example 2.15 (fig. 2.21)

Suppose the value *V* has an access (*indwost n.p*) and this access comes from the transformation of an access (*diriden n'.p'*) with *n'*≤*n* (*bno* = *n'*≤ *n*).
Clearly *Vh* is protected through *V*.

(†) This may happen when a choice action is translated, the elements of the choice being e.g. all of access class *diriden*. In order to be able to translate the action which applies to the result of the choice action in a unique way, this result must be provided with a single access whichever the result of the choice would be. In section I.2.3.4, it has been explained how to manage when the result fits into a register : the unique access is (*dirwost n.p*); when the value does not fit in a register it is more efficient to deal with an access (*indwost n.p*), giving rise to the situation of the present example (see II.14).

(††) From now on, the arrow ➡ appearing in the figures means that the value pointed to is protected.

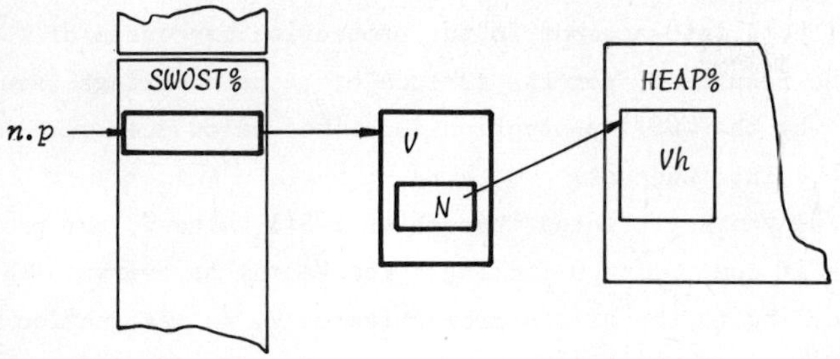

V : access : (<u>indwost</u> n.p)

<u>fig</u>. 2.18

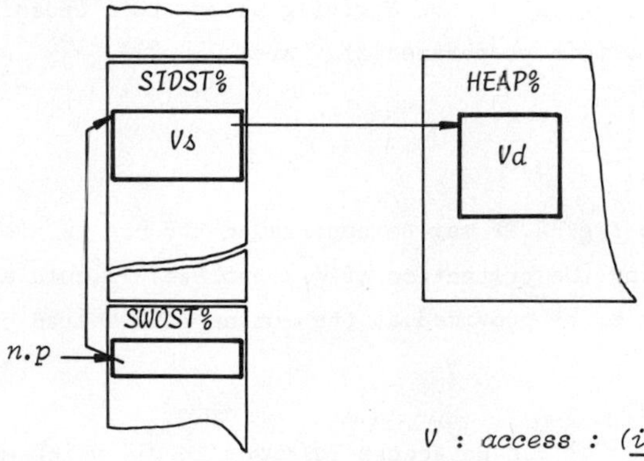

V : access : (<u>indwost</u> n.p)

<u>fig</u>. 2.19

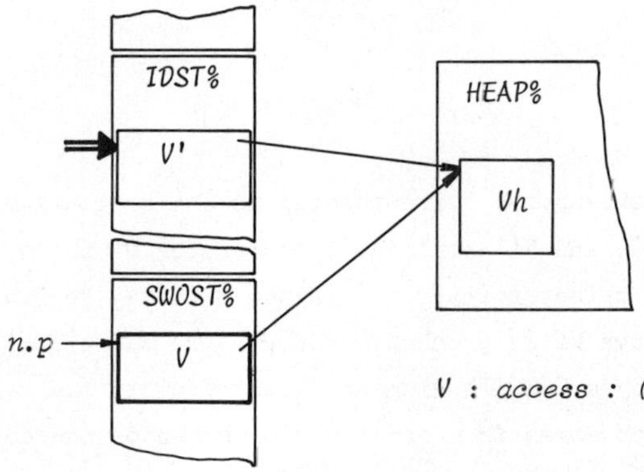

V : access : (<u>dirwost</u> n.p)

<u>fig</u>. 2.20

(3) Side-effects are legal in only three cases in ALGOL 68 (see I.2.3.3) but in practice, wrong programs may have side-effects everywhere. The consequences of not taking such side-effects into account in the protection mechanism of *WOST%* values are similar to those resulting from the absence of scope checkings (see I.2.5.1). This is the reason why the *WOST%* protection described below does take even disallowed side-effects into account.

Suppose a *HEAP%* value *Vh* is protected through an *IDST%* value *V*, the protection may become obsolete if some pointer linking *V* and *Vh* may be overwritten. This may happen if, according to the *origin* properties of *V*, an assignation may take place, by which pointers corresponding to names or to offsets of flexible descriptors involved in the link may be overwritten.

Example 2.16 (fig. 2.22)

Suppose a value *V* is stored on *WOST%* with an access *(dirwost n.p)* ; suppose moreover that this value contains a name *N* giving access to a (possible *HEAP%*) value *V1*, and that the *origin* properties of *V* are

- *kindo* = *var*
- *bno* ⩽ n
- *derefo* = 1

The name pointer (1) in fig. 2.22 may be superseded through an assignation to the variable, thus making the protection of V_1 obsolete. In such a case, a *GCWOST%* protection has to be provided at the moment *V* is stored on *WOST%*.

Example 2.17 (fig. 2.23)

Suppose a value *V*(*Vs* and *Vd*) has an access *(dirwost' n.p)*, which means that only the static part of the value is stored on *SWOST%* and that its dynamic part is stored in another part of the memory, possibly the *HEAP%* ; suppose moreover that for this value

- *kindo* = *var*
- *bno* ⩽ n
- *derefo* = 1
- *flexo* = 1

According to *flexo* = 1, the name *N* corresponding to the original variable is *flexible* (see I.2.5.2.a), and *Vs'* contains a descriptor *D'* the offset of which points to the *HEAP%*. The offset pointer (1) in fig 2.23 may be changed by an assignation to *N* and although *Vd* is protected through the variable, it must also be protected through *Vs* by a *GCWOST%* element. Note that, if the value *V* has an access class *indwost* which comes from the transformation of the class *diriden*, the protection remains valid, whether *kindo* is *iden* or *var* (fig. 2.24).

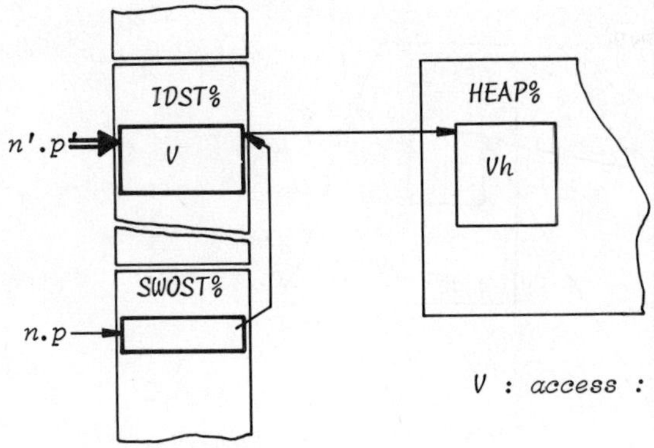

V : *access* : (<u>*indwost*</u> *n.p*)

<u>fig</u>. 2.21

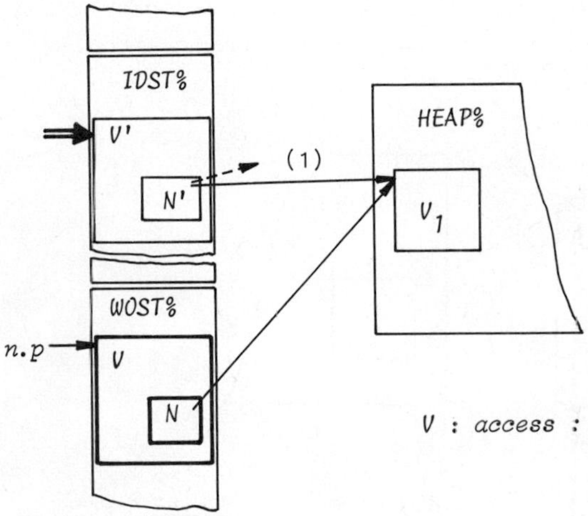

V : *access* : (<u>*dirwost*</u> *n.p*)

<u>fig</u>. 2.22

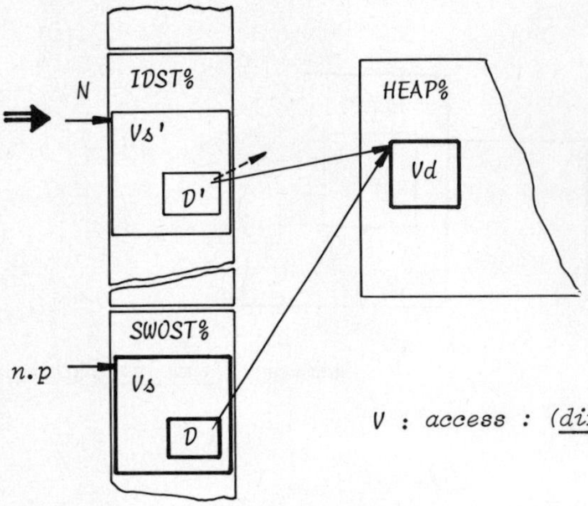

V : access : (<u>dirwost'</u> n.p)

<u>fig</u>. 2.23

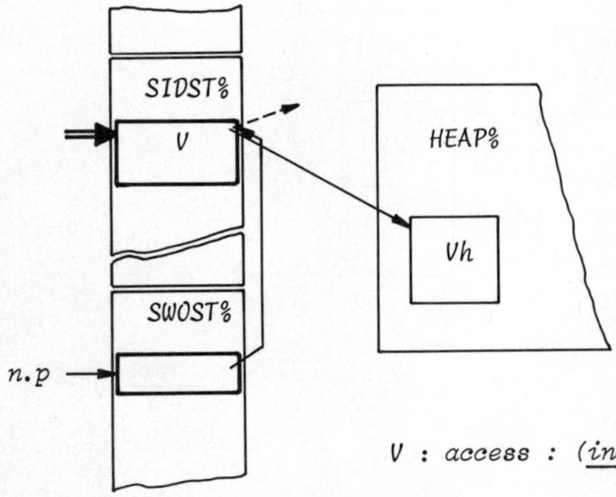

V : access : (<u>indwost</u> n.p)

<u>fig</u>. 2.24

Remark 1.

Local optimization may cause a value, considered to be stored on *WOST%* in the intermediate code, never to be actually stored at run-time on this stack but only to appear in a register ; theoretically, if such a *WOST%* value, a name for example, is protected, the protection should take the local optimization into account i.e. protect the name in the register and not on *WOST%*. Actually, not taking local optimizations into account is of no consequence if the garbage collector is not called before the protection of the value has been erased from *GCWOST%*. If the latter condition is not fulfilled, it is always possible to inhibit the local optimization by the generation of a special object instruction between the copy of the name and its use. In this respect, an exhaustive study of ALGOL 68 actions on register values can be found in PART II.

Example 2.18

Suppose a name *N* has to be stored on *WOST%* and to be protected through a *GCWOST%* element. In practice, the object instruction by which the name is protected may be generated before the instruction storing the name on *WOST%*. Suppose that the instruction by which the name is used is generated thereafter and that finally the instruction cancelling the protection of the name on *WOST%* is generated.

Intermediate code	Machine code
Protection of *N*	Protection of *N*
Copy of *N* on *WOST%*	LDA *N* STA w
Use of *N*	LDA w
⋮	⋮
Cancelling of the protection	Cancelling of the protection

Clearly, without precautions, the local optimization will eliminate the sequence STA w, LDA w and the name will never be stored on *WOST%*. Although the protection applies to the cell w, the process remains valid if the instruction by which the name is used never cause the call of the garbage collection (see also Remark 2).

Remark 2.

We have explained how to minimize the run-time garbage collection information on the base of static properties of values. When a value has to be protected, the following conceptual sequence of instructions appears :

- Protect the value
- ... use the value ...
- Cancel the protection.

If during the machine code generation it appears that between the setting up of the protection and its cancelling, the garbage collector can never be called, the protection and the corresponding cancelling may be ignored.

Remark 3.

Suppose we have to translate an action with a number of parameters stored on *WOST%* and protected via *GCWOST%* and suppose the result of the action is a value which has to be stored on *WOST%* and also to be protected. There are several strategies allowing to construct the result on *WOST%* while controlling the protection of *WOST%* values, in order to avoid the destruction of *HEAP%* values accessible through the result of the action :

1) The protection management may be taken in charge by the routine translating the action. More precisely, information is furnished to the routine about the necessity of protecting the parameters and the result, instead of storing the protection on *GCWOST%* systematically. When the garbage collection is called from inside the routine, necessary precautions are taken in order to ensure the protection of the parameters still needed and the partial result already constructed. This strategy has the disadvantage of sensibly complicating the translation of some actions.
2) The second solution has been explained in example 2.6, it consists in avoiding the overwriting of the parameters by the result, thus leaving the protection of the parameters valid until the result has been completely constructed. Clearly, in this way, the result cannot give access to non-protected *HEAP%* values. Thereafter the protections of the parameters are cancelled and replaced by the protection of the result.
3) The third solution is used when a *WOST%* value has to be copied in another location of the *WOST%* and when the copy risks to overwrite either the static part of the original value or its protection. It consists in copying the static part of the value first, without modifying the offset pointers and in protecting this static part ; the dynamic parts are copied thereafter and the offset pointers modified accordingly one by one.
   Such a problem appears when the result of a block has an access class *dirwost'*, when it is protected and when it has a *bno* equal to the *bn* of the block left (hence it has to be copied in the calling block with an access class *dirwost*).

   Example 2.19 (fig. 2.25)

   Suppose a value *V* (*Vs* and *Vd*) with an access class *dirwost'* is protected through $GCWOST\%_i$ and is the result of $BLOCK\%_i$. When this result is copied in the calling $BLOCK\%_{i-1}$, the copy *Vd'* of *Vd* risks to overwrite *Vs* and its protection.
4) A last solution which can be used without restriction consists in several dynamic actions :

   - to evaluate the size of the dynamic part of the value to be copied.

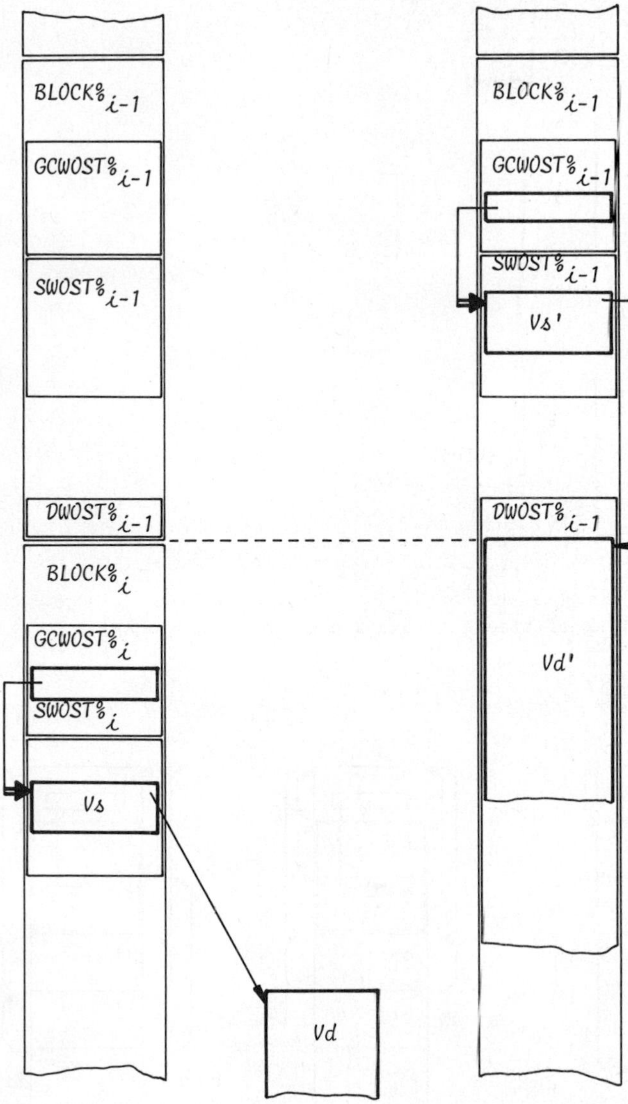

a. before exit from BLOCK%$_i$ *b*. after exit from BLOCK%$_i$

<u>fig</u>. 2.25

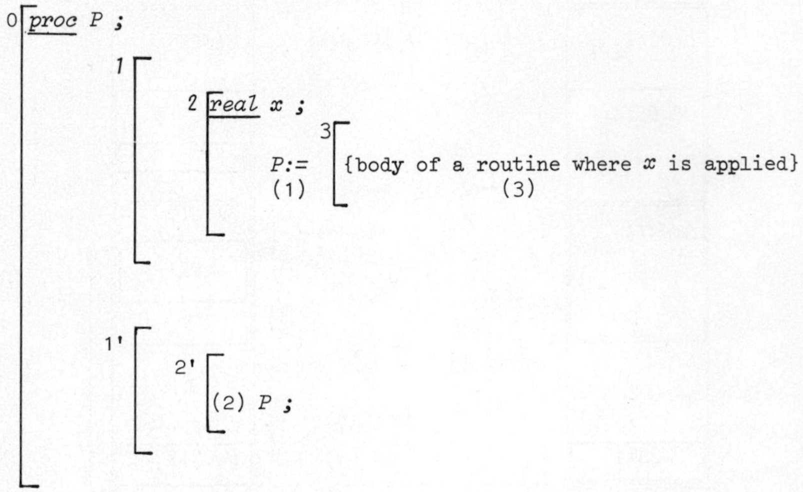

a. Nesting of blocks {*1* and *2* are retained blocks}

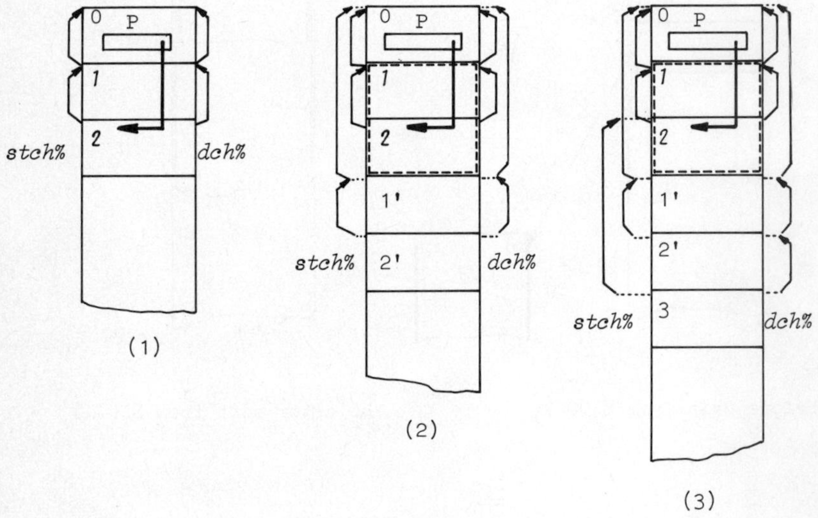

b. *RANST%* at the execution points (1), (2) and (3)

fig. 2.26

- to call the garbage collection if there is not space enough, and to stop if this call does not free enough space.
- to copy the value without precaution, given we are sure the garbage collection will no more be called during the copy.

Remark 4.

For languages allowing, unlike ALGOL 68, *block retention* on the stack, the dynamic chain does not link all blocks present on *RANST%*. Retained blocks fall outside the dynamic chain but only those blocks which are accessible must be taken into account by the garbage collector. The access to such blocks necessarily passes through accessible instances of routines the memory representation of which contains the address of the *H%* of the inner *BLOCK%* accessible from inside the routine. Such *H%* addresses of instances of routines are used by the garbage collector to take accessible retained blocks into account (fig. 2.26).

2.5 DYNAMIC CHECKS

The language ALGOL 68 requires a number of checks ensuring program security. These checks impose a steady control of stored values avoiding wrong interpretations of the contents of the memory, in particular of pointers. Such misinterpretations could have disastrous effects on :

(1) the execution of compiled programs to the point of overwriting important data and perhaps the system itself.

(2) the garbage collector marking memory locations falling outside the *HEAP%* or belonging to the garbage.

The checks which are imposed by the language ALGOL 68 are the checks of mode, of bounds, of scope and the checks of flexibility(†). Remark however that full security is only obtained if the compiler protects itself against side-effects and controls the use of non-initialized locations.

The most catastrophic effect of not performing the above checks is clearly the destruction of the system, but this can easily be solved on computers with a memory protection. However, even when a memory protection is available, implementing the above checks is useful because it allows to inform the programmer of an error with more precision.

The checks of mode are completely static, they are treated in the ALGOL 68 syntax. The checks of bounds are generally dynamic ; it does not seem worthwhile to detect the rare (and uninteresting) cases where these checks can be made at compile-time. The problem of initialization of locations is solved by generating appropriate

---

(†) The revised report includes the flexibility into the mode and hence the corresponding checks are completely static [8].

object code initializing the pointers contained in the static parts of the locations reserved at the elaboration of generators, and in the static part of the identifier stack of each block. Control of disallowed side-effects (collateral elaborations leading to undefined results) has influenced the management of garbage collection information (see I.2.4.3.b). The checks of scope and flexibility are in principle performed at run-time, however, in the present section, it is shown how, by means of static properties associated to values, it is possible to replace dynamic checks of scope and flexibility by static ones in a large number of cases, thus increasing the run-time efficiency.

2.5.1 SCOPE CHECKING

a. Generalities

In ALGOL 68, *scopes* are defined as *ranges* i.e. parts of program ; however this definition has a dynamic aspect because it includes ranges resulting from the dynamic copies of routines in the call (and deproceduring) mechanism.

The goal of scope checking is to prevent two types of situations :

(1) where use is made of values supposed to be stored in locations of names which are lost, i.e. which have been recovered thanks to the stack mechanism (and possibly used for other purposes). This first case involves scopes associated to names.

Example 2.20

```
(ref real xx ;
     xx := (real x ; x := 3.14) ;
     ...   {use of xx dereferenced} ...)
```

Example 2.21

```
(ref real xx ;
     (real x ; xx := x := 3.14) ;
     ... {use of xx dereferenced} ...)
```

In the above programs, the name possessed by *x* ceases to exist after the inner *block* has been left ; the further use of *xx* dereferenced would lead to the contents of the location of *x*, which has been recovered as soon as the inner *block* has been left.

(2) where use is made of the value possessed by identifiers or variables declared in a *block* which has been left, hence which is no more represented on *RANST%*. This second case involves scopes associated to routines and formats.(†)

(†) In the sequel, when "scope of routines" appears in the text, it includes "scope of formats" as well.

Example 2.22

(*proc* *P* ;

(*real* *x* ;

...

P := {procedured coercend where *x* is used} ;

...)

...

{call of} *P* ;

...)

The call (dereferencing + deproceduring) of *P* involves the elaboration of the routine (procedured coercend) which uses *x*, i.e. a variable declared in a *block* which has been left.

To prevent undesired effects in both situations (1) and (2), it is sufficient to perform scope checking each time a block is left and each time an assignation is elaborated.

In principle, scope checking is performed at run-time ; such dynamic scope checking lies on dynamic scope information (representation) associated to values and *blocks*. In practice, in many cases, scope checking can be performed at compile-time. Such static scope checking lies on a static scope property associated to values and on *bn* of *blocks*.

b. Dynamic scope checking

In *range oriented implementations* (see I.1.3), *block*'s exactly correspond to ranges which are relevant as far as scope checking is concerned ; only these ranges will be considered as *scopes*. One can say that, at a given run-time moment, to each *scope* there corresponds a *BLOCK%*. Hence, a *scope* can be dynamically represented by the address of the heading *H%* of the corresponding *BLOCK%*. If now *RANST%* grows in the direction of increasing machine addresses, to an inner scope corresponds a higher *H%* address and vice-versa ; clearly, dynamic scope checking is reduced to *H%* addresses comparisons.

The problem is to be able to make dynamic scope information available when required by dynamic scope checking. The solution consists in associating *H%* addresses to *blocks* and their resulting values, and to values of the left and right parts of assignations.

At the elaboration of a *block* its dynamic scope information is the contents of the *DISPLAY%* element of the depth number of that *block*.

For values containing neither names nor routines, there is no scope checking implied : they may always be the result of a *block* or be assigned (but of course never be assigned to).

With each name and routine, a dynamic scope indication, i.e. a *H%* address, is associated ; this makes part of their memory representation. The scope of the values some of whose components are containing names or routines, can be deduced from the scope of these components through a dynamic interpretation. Associating such values with a dynamic scope is of no help because these values may be referred to by names and subsequently their components can be assigned to ; this could change the scope of both the components and the value itself.

The dynamic scope checking itself is quite simple

(1) If the dynamic scopes of a *block* and its result are h_b and h_r respectively, the scope checking requires $h_b > h_r$

(2) If the dynamic scopes of the left and right parts of an assignation are h_l and h_r respectively, the scope checking requires $h_l \geq h_r$.

Remark 1.

One could think of another solution for dynamic scope representation of names which avoids to store a scope information in their memory representation ; it would consist in using the address of the location of the name itself as its dynamic scope representation. The trouble is that on the one hand, dynamic scope checking is no longer reduced to comparisons because this could lead to wrong error messages when names of the same *BLOCK%* are concerned, on the other hand scope checking involving local names, the locations of which are on the *HEAP%* for reasons of flexibility, would not be valid.

Remark 2.

In *procedure oriented implementations,* there is not a *block* for each relevant *scope* ; instead of using a *H%* address as dynamic scope information, we may for example use the *IDST%* address of the value of the first identifier (variable) of a relevant *scope*, and when such a *scope* does not contain identifier (variable) declarations, the address of a dummy cell reserved for this purpose on *IDST%*.

Remark 3.

The technique of *linked stack* implies a more complicated dynamic scope representation, for example a numbering of the *blocks*, representative of the tree structure of the "stack" (see I.1.5). The checks consist in controlling that no access is given from a *block* on the top of the tree to a value of a *block* on its bottom ; this automatically controls that no access is given from a *block* to a value of a *block* of a parallel branch.

c. Static scope checking

In many cases, it is possible to associate with values a static property called *static scope* ; it consists of two fields : the *inner scope (insc)* and the *outer scope (outsc)*, representing the smaller limits between which at compile-time we are sure the scope of the value will lie. It is on such limits that the static scope checking is based ; this avoids the necessity of dynamic scope checking in many cases.

The problem here is how to represent *insc* and *outsc* at compile-time. Clearly, depth numbers of *block*'s may play this part, as far as they grow like the corresponding *H%* addresses, i.e. as far as the dynamic mechanism of copy of routines is not involved. More precisely, the static scope representation of the value of a formal parameter of a routine denotation can generally nct be based on the *insc* and *outsc* of the corresponding possible actual parameters.

<u>Example</u> 2.23

Suppose the following program structure where the brackets represent *block*'s and are numbered according to their depth numbers :

```
0 [
    proc P =   1' [ {Routine denotation with a formal parameter
                     x of mode ref μ}
                    ref μ xx ; ...
                        xx := x ; ...
                  ]
               1  [
                    2 [
                        μ v ;
                        ...
                        P(v)
                        ...
                      ]
                  ]
  ]
```

The *RANST%* situation, after *blocks* 0,1,2 have been entered, after *P* has been called and the assignation *xx:=x* has been elaborated, is pictured in <u>fig</u>. 2.27.

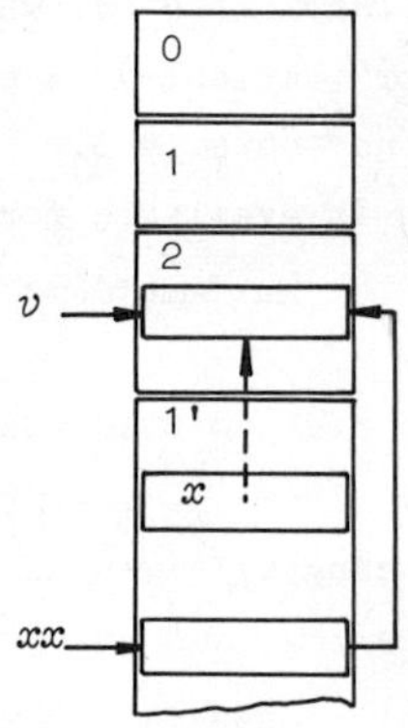

<u>fig</u>. 2.27

The assignation *xx:=x*, leading to the bold faced arrow, is obviously allowed, but using for *x* the *insc* and *outsc* of *v*, which are both equal to 2 (see *d*), would lead to a wrong error message, considering that *insc* and *outsc* of *xx* are both equal to 1. In practice, the *insc* and *outsc* of the formal parameters will be made equal to N_r and 0 respectively, where N_r is the depth number of the block where the routine appears (however see *d*(1) below).

The algorithm of static scope checking can now be written :

(1) When a *block* of depth *bn* and delivering a result with $insc=bn_1$ and $outsc=bn_2$, is left :

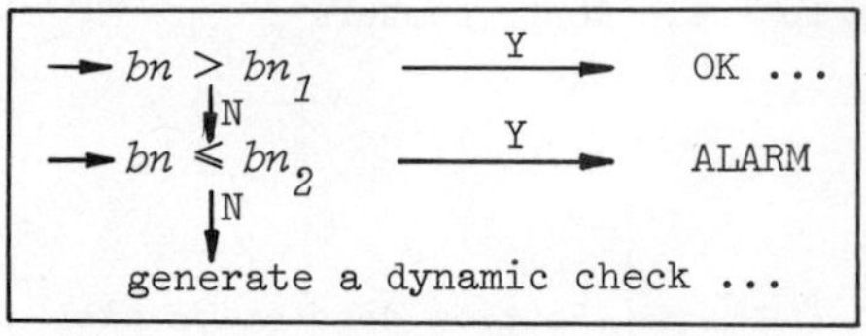

(2) When a value with $insc=bn_1$ and $outsc=bn_2$ is assigned to a name with $insc=bn_1'$ and $outsc=bn_2'$:

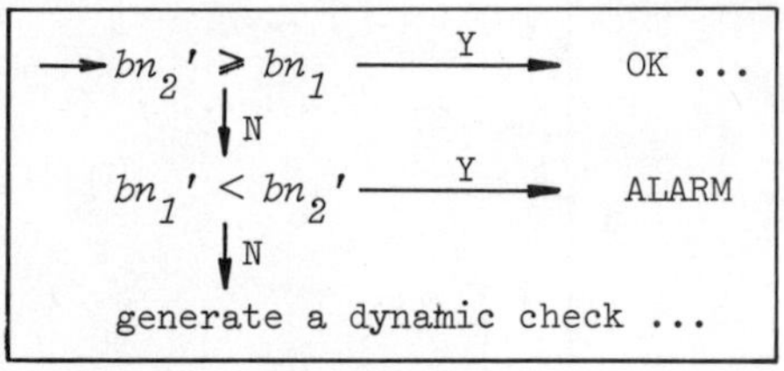

d. Static management of inner and outer scopes

An exhaustive study of the static scope management can be found in PART II, only a few examples are given here :

(1) if the mode of the value shows that it contains neither names nor routines, *insc=outsc* = 0, i.e. the whole program.

(2) for a generator (or a variable) *insc=outsc=bn*, where *bn* is the depth number of the *block* where the generator (variable) is elaborated (declared) if this generator is local, otherwise *insc=outsc* = 0.

(3) when no static scope indication is available for a value, *insc*=N, *outsc*=0, where N is an integer equal to the maximum *block* depth number admitted by the compiler.

(4) choice and display actions give rise to *insc* and *outsc* based on those of their elements.

(5) a value obtained by a dereferencing is given an *insc* equal to the *insc* of the name which has been dereferenced, and an *outsc* equal to 0.

(6) The *insc* of the result of a call is equal to the depth number of the *block* where the call appears ; its *outsc* is equal to 0.

(7) The *insc* of a formal parameter of a routine is the depth of the *block* where the routine appears ; its *outsc* is equal to 0.

Example 2.24

```
(real x ;
 ref real xx ;
    (ref real yy;
         real y ;
    xx { insc =0, outsc =0}  := yy {1,0}
                                   {dynamic check} ;
    yy {1,1} :=y {1,1}   {OK}   ;
    xx {0,0} :=y {1,1}   {ALARM}  ;
    ...) ...)
```

2.5.2 CHECKS OF FLEXIBILITY

a. Generalities

The memory locations of the elements of a multiple value with flexible bounds and referred to by a name may either disappear or change place in memory.

Example 2.25

```
([ 1:4 flex] int x :=(1,2,3,4) ;
  ... x[ 3] ...
  x:=(10,20) )
```

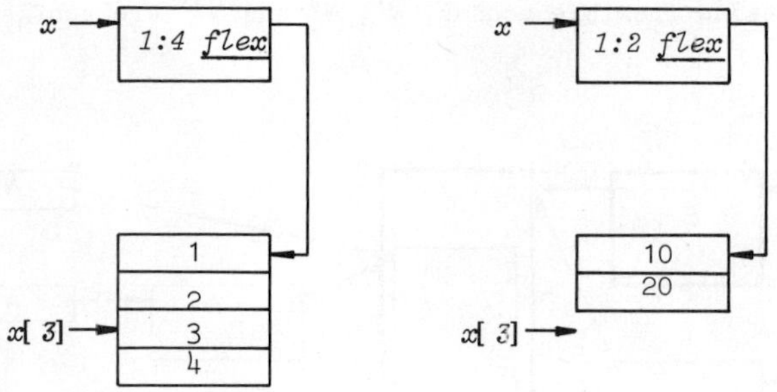

{after the declaration of *x*} fig. 2.28.a

{after the assignation *x:=(10,20)*} fig. 2.28.b

The consequences are twofold :

(1) The security of ALGOL 68 programs may suffer in the following sense : names giving access to elements of flexible multiple values (these names are defined as subflexible names in the sequel) may become conceptually meaningless.

(2) Effects analogous to those of not checking the scopes may arise in some implementations in which, when an assignation to a flexible name is performed, the hole possibly created on the *HEAP%* is connected to a list of holes in order to be

used to store further *HEAP%* values, and this, without checking whether locations of such holes are accessible through subflexible names.

In order to avoid such consequences, the accesses of subflexible names must be strongly restricted. The checks of flexibility are intended to control these accesses. Their precise description implies the introduction of a number of definitions :

- a *refselection* is a selection applied to a value of mode <u>*ref*</u> <u>*struct*</u> *(...)*
- a *refslice* is a slice applied to a value of mode <u>*ref*</u> [...] μ, giving rise to a value of mode <u>*ref*</u> μ or <u>*ref*</u> [...] μ
- a *refrowing* is a rowing applied to a value of mode <u>*ref*</u> μ or <u>*ref*</u> [...] μ, giving rise to a value of mode <u>*ref*</u> [...] μ
- a *refrowrowing* is a rowing applied to a value of mode <u>*ref*</u> [...] μ, giving rise to a value of mode <u>*ref*</u> [...] μ
- a *flexible name* is a name which refers to a stored value which is a multiple value with flexible bounds.
- a *subflexible action* is either a *refslice* or a *refrowrowing*
- a *subflexible name* is a name resulting from a subflexible action applied to a flexible name or from a refselection, a refslice or a refrowing applied to a subflexible name.

In the fig. 2.29, *N* is a name referring to a multiple value *M* with a descriptor *D* and elements *E*. *N'* results from a *refrowrowing* of *N*, *N"* and *N"'* from a *refslice* applied to *N*. If *D* contains flexible bounds, *N'*, *N"* and *N"'* are subflexible names.

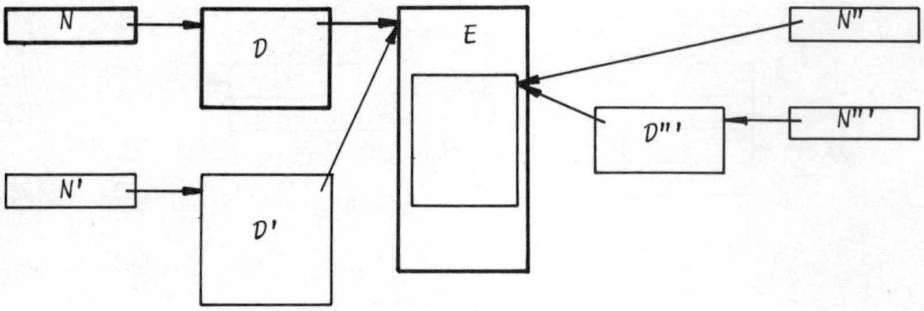

<u>fig</u>. 2.29

Subflexible names are characterized by the fact that they give access to locations which may, by assignation, either disappear or change place in memory. It is the accesses to subflexible names which are controlled by the checks of flexibility.

We distinghuish two kinds of accesses :

- *remanent accesses* which are provided by the elaboration either of an *assignation* or of an *identity declaration*(†) ; these actions will be called *remanent access actions ;*

- *temporary accesses* which are provided by the elaboration of actions only furnishing an access through an intermediate result, such are *slices, rowings, selections, unitings* and *display actions* (actions by which a value is made a component of a row or structure *display*) ; these actions will be called *temporary access actions.*

Eventually, it is useful to introduce the following two classes of actions :

- *remdisp access actions* grouping remanent access and display actions ;
- *component access actions* which are temporary access actions at the exclusion of display actions.

remanent access actions	assignation	*remdisp access actions*
	identity declaration	
temporary access actions	display	
	slice	*component access actions*
	selection	
	rowing	
	uniting	
subflexible actions	refslice	
	refrowrowing	

In practice we shall forbid a *remdisp access action* to apply neither to subflexible names(††), nor to multiple values with an element which is a subflexible name. Note that this way of doing slightly differs from what is required by [1]:

(1) [1] forbids refrowing actions but not refslices to apply to flexible names, which is inconsistent.

(2) [1] allows a temporary and by transitivity a remanent access to be given to a subflexible name through a rowing of such a name giving rise to a value of mode [ ] **ref** μ ; this is obviously an oversight.

b. Static and dynamic checks of flexibility(†††)

The properties of flexibility and subflexibility are dynamic properties of names ; the checks by which it is controlled that no remdisp access is given to a subflexible name are generally dynamic too, though in many cases these checks can be perfor-

(†) Identity declarations also contain those resulting from the copy rule in calls and formulas.

(††) No assignation changing the size of the value referred to by a considered flexible name may take place between a subflexible action creating a given subflexible name of the considered flexible name and a remdisp access action to a subflexible name issued from the given one, at least when no disallowed side-effects appear.

(†††) In the revised ALGOL 68, checks of flexibility are completely static.

med at compile-time. The checks of flexibility may take place at two levels : at the level of the *subflexible actions* or at the level of the *remdisp access actions*.

α. *Checks at the level of subflexible actions.*

The information about the existence of a remdisp access action must be transmitted from top to bottom, i.e. through the component access actions towards the subflexible actions. In case of assignation, the transmission is made through its left part, but it is reinitialized for its right part(†).

Thanks to this transmission, it is known, at the level of the subflexible action whether a check of flexibility must be performed, check forbidding this action to apply to a flexible name.

Let us consider the multiple values referred to by a name to which a subflexible action applies, action which results in a name to which a remdisp access will be given ; the dynamic check of flexibility reduces itself to checking whether the descriptors of those multiple values have flexible bounds.

The static management has to deal with two problems : the flexibility of names and the top-down transmission.

(1) The flexibility will be dealt with by means of the static property *flexbot* associated to values. This property is 0, 1 or 2 :
  - 0 if it is known at compile-time that the value is not a flexible name,
  - 1 if the contrary is known at compile-time,
  - 2 if the information is not available at compile-time.

(2) The transmission can be performed by means of the static prevision mechanism on *TOPST*. However, we cannot avoid a dynamic action in the transmission when a call process takes place : it can generally not be decided at compile-time whether the result of a routine will be given a remdisp access or not. A dynamic transmission is then performed by means of the field *flex%* stored in the heading *H%* of the *BLOCK%*'s of the routines ; it is set up at the call and indicates dynamically whether the result will be given a remdisp access or not ; clearly this dynamic transmission is transitive when calls are nested. *Flex%* is equal to 1 when a remdisp access is given to the result of the call, and to 0 otherwise. The dynamic check of *flex%* must be provided with an access to the *H%* of the routine where this *flex%* can be found, which access reduces itself to the *bn* of the routine. How this *bn* will be made available is explained in I.3 ; let us just say here that for each subflexible action we have a static (top) property at our disposal : *flextop* which has the values : *(<u>stat</u> 0)*, *(<u>stat</u> 1)* and *(<u>dyn</u> bnrout)* :

(†) This method does generally not work for the conforms-to-and-becomes relation where the information about the actual existence of an assignation is generally dynamic and only known <u>after</u> the right part of the relation has been elaborated. In this case the second method has to be applied, but given this last one is less efficient, its use will be avoided wherever possible.

- *(<u>stat</u> 0)* when it is known at compile-time that no remdisp access will be given to the result of the subflexible action,
- *(<u>stat</u> 1)* when the contrary is known,
- *(<u>dyn</u> bnrout)* when this information is not available, in which case *bnrout* gives access to *flex%*.

We can now write the algorithm which takes place at the translation of a subflexible action on a name (<u>fig</u>. 2.30).

β. *Checks at the level of remdisp access actions*

The property of *subflexibility* must be transmitted from subflexible actions to remdisp access actions (bottom-up transmission) ; this transmission of a dynamic property generally implies a dynamic action. This can be done by associating to *WOST%* values a new dynamic property *subflexbot%* which can be stored on *FLEXWOST%* similar to *DMRWOST%* or *GCWOST%* ; clearly, the static management of a static property *subflexbot* stored on *BOST* can minimize the dynamic management of *subflexbot%*. As said above, this method, because less efficient than the first one, is only used in case of conforms-to-and-becomes relations. The existence of such a relation must now be transmitted from top to bottom generally at compile-time and at run-time when a call process takes place. This transmission can be performed by refining the properties *flextop* and *flex%*. We do not enter into further details here.

c. Static management of the bottom property of flexibility

The property *flexbot* associated to generators and variables is 0 or 1 according the actual declarers (the elaboration of which creates the corresponding name) begin with a bounds bracket (†) with direct constituent flexible bounds or not ; for the value of other actions using values of generators or variables, a mechanism of transitivity on *BOST* is used.

<u>Remark</u> 1.

In addition to ensuring the checks of flexibility, the property *flexbot* is used to update the property *flexo*. When a dereferencing is translated, the property *flexo* is made equal to the property *flexbot* of the dereferenced name.

<u>Remark</u> 2.

Dynamic checks which are generated are provided with error diagnostic information; this information is deduced from *diago*.

<u>Remark</u> 3.

The checks of flexibility are rather heavy ; clearly, they could be sensibly alleviated at the price of small restrictions to [1], introduced in [8], i.e. we could
(1) require that the result of a routine does not give access to a subflexible name.
(2) consider a conforms-to-and-becomes action as a remdisp access action.

(†) NOTION bracket : sub symbol, NOTION, bus symbol.
bounds : VICTAL ROWS rower.

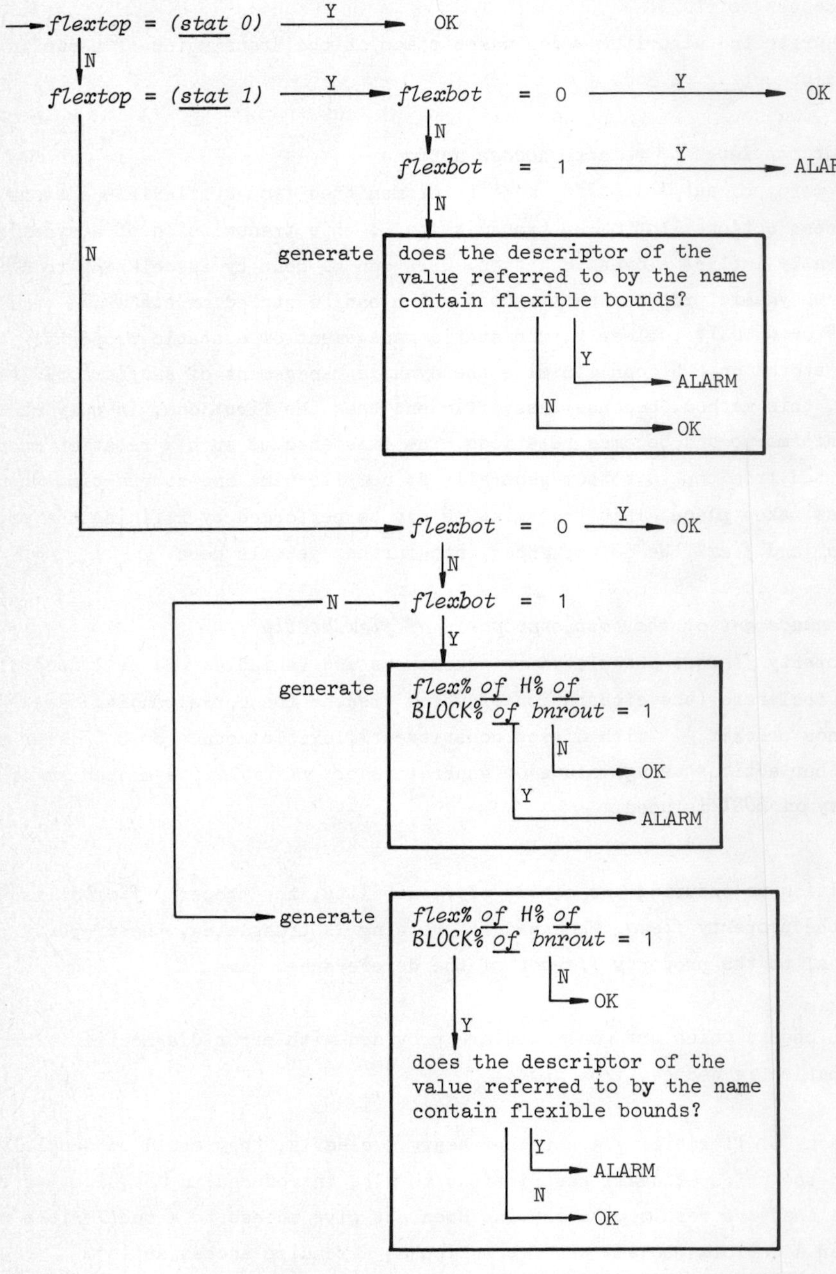
flextop = (stat 0)
Y
OK
N
flextop = (stat 1)
Y
flexbot = 0
Y
OK
N
flexbot = 1
Y
ALARM
N
N
generate
does the descriptor of the value referred to by the name contain flexible bounds?
Y
ALARM
N
OK
flexbot = 0
Y
OK
N
N
flexbot = 1
Y
generate
flex% of H% of BLOCK% of bnrout = 1
N
OK
Y
ALARM
generate
flex% of H% of BLOCK% of bnrout = 1
N
OK
Y
does the descriptor of the value referred to by the name contain flexible bounds?
Y
ALARM
N
OK

fig. 2.30

3. *STUDY OF THE PREVISION MECHANISM*

As explained in I.0, the prevision mechanism is based on *TOPST* which contains, at each compile-time moment, the sequence of actions the prefix markers of which have been scanned, but which have not yet been completely translated. The top element of *TOPST* is the action currently translated ; the other elements are the future actions in which the result of the current action may be involved.

The study of the static properties of values has shown how profit can be taken of preexisting stored values, but in a number of cases, the resulting value of an action does not exist in memory and hence, it has to be constructed somewhere. It will be shown in this section how *TOPST* may be used to foresee the future use of the result of the current action and possibly to reduce the number of run-time manipulations of this result (copies for instance). In addition, it will be shown how *TOPST* allows to deal with the transmission of the property *flextop* used in the checks of flexibility (I.2.5).

3.1 *MINIMIZATION OF COPIES*

The generation of the most optimal object code is the one which would take the whole *TOPST* into account. However the number of different situations grows in a combinatorial way with the number of *TOPST* elements ; on the other hand, the gain in efficiency provided by a complete analysis of *TOPST* is not proportional to the corresponding effort made in writing the compiler. For these reasons, the present study of the prevision mechanism is far from exhaustive : we shall limit ourselves to a number of considerations on the most interesting previsions.

The first considerations are based on the penultimate *TOPST* element which is an action called the *next action* as opposed to the top element of *TOPST* called the *current action,* i.e. the action currently translated.

(1) Suppose the current action delivers a result which does not preexist and suppose the next action is a remanent access action (assignation or identity declaration) implying the storage of the result of the current action in a specific part of the memory. Clearly, instead of constructing this result on *WOST%* (providing it with a temporary access) and copying it thereafter, it is more efficient to construct it directly where it has to be stored anyway, i.e. in the location of the name which is assigned to or in the *IDST%* memory space reserved for the value of the actual parameter of the identity declaration.
When an action by which a value has to be constructed on *WOST%* is translated, the translation routine of the action is parametrized with the *RANST%* address

of *SWOST%* where the static part of the value has to be constructed ; the dynamic part of the value is constructed on *DWOST%* starting from *ranstpm%* The same routine may be used when the value, according to the previsions, is directly constructed on *IDST%*;the only difference is that the *RANST%* address is an *IDST%* address instead of a *WOST%* address. For the identity declaration, the subsequent checks of the bounds of the constructed value with the values of the formal bounds are made in a straightforward way. However, when the value is constructed in the location where it has to be assigned, there are two main differences :
(a) instead of overwriting the non flexible bounds of the location, they have just to be checked for equality with the bounds of the assigned value.
(b) the dynamic part of the value has to be constructed from run-time addresses obtained by a dynamic interpretation of the descriptors of the location and not from *ranstpm%*. Clearly, the translation routine of actions constructing a value could be split in order to take this into account, this would complicate the compiler.

(2) Suppose two successive actions have to be applied to the result of the current action, namely *rowing* and *actual parameter* respectively. The rowing will cause either the creation of a descriptor or the extension of an existing descriptor. In both cases it can be foreseen where the descriptor will ultimately be stored, and hence it is possible to construct it directly there. The complications implied by combining a rowing with an assignation are obvious.

(3) Another kind of previsions saving copies of values is related to the creation of an overhead to *WOST%* values. Each time a value has to be constructed on *WOST%*, an analysis of *TOPST* may show whether the value will be provided with an overhead (rowing or uniting) or not ; in the affirmative, space is reserved in front of the value on *WOST%* for the overhead.
Note that overheads may accumulate and they have to be transmitted through a number of actions. Instead of analyzing *TOPST* each time instructions storing the result of an action on *WOST%* have to be generated, a property called *Δmem* can be transmitted as a field of each *TOPST* element ; this *Δmem* contains the size of the memory space to be reserved in front of the result of the corresponding action, if it appears that it has to be stored on *WOST%* at run-time.
The static management of *Δmem* consists in
(1) initializing to 0 the *Δmem* of the actions,the value of the parameters of which are not, as such, involved in the result of the action (identity declaration for example) ,
(2) transmitting *Δmem* unchanged, from top to bottom [(†)] (i.e. from outer actions to

(†) On *TOPST* the transmission of *Δmem* goes from the bottom to the top of the stack.

inner actions) through actions the result of which is or is a part of one of their parameter (slice and selection for example),

(3) associating to a rowing or uniting action a *Δmem* which is the sum of the *Δmem* of the next action and the overhead size of the current rowing or uniting.

3.2 THE TOP PROPERTIES OF FLEXIBILITY

flextop has been defined in I.2.5.2, we now briefly explain its management on *TOPST*.

- *flextop* is initialized :

  to *(stat 1)* at remdisp access actions i.e. assignation and identity declaration ,

  to *(dyn bnrout)* at the actions by which a value is made the result of a routine (body of routine actions) ; *bnrout* is the *bn* of the routine,

  to *(stat 0)* otherwise.

- *flextop* is transmitted through component access actions.

Clearly, at call actions, instructions must be generated for filling *flex%* in the *H%* of the routine at run-time.

PART II : DETAILS OF TRANSLATION INTO INTERMEDIATE CODE

0. INTRODUCTION

0.1 GENERALITIES

In PART I, we have described the basic principles for the design of the intermediate code generation. In PART II we shall now describe how these principles have been implemented. This description is intended to be a complete documentation where all technical solutions can easily be accessed. An overview of this description can be found in [19] and [20] .

Here, we have tried to be as close to the actual implementation as possible, at the price of being sometimes less orthogonal than what could be ; this was the surest way for not misleading the reader. Moreover, we have tried to motivate the solutions which are implemented, to point out their advantages and drawbacks, and to propose better solutions when known to us but not implemented for historical or practical reasons.

As far as the description method is concerned, we have been confronted with several alternatives :

- the first alternative consists in giving the design of the compiler in a completely formalized form. We abandoned this solution because in such a description important points are not sufficiently prominent, which makes the algorithm difficult to grasp.
- the second alternative consists in being completely informal. This would make it impossible to control the bulk of information.
- the solution we have adopted is a compromise where a strict formalism is only used when necessary, where unessential features are pointed out once for all and taken for granted thereafter.

The primitives used in the description are summarized in II.0.2, they are as far as possible ALGOL 68 like, although better primitives could have been used.

As we shall see, the description covers the translation process proper as well as the run-time actions meant by the generated intermediate code. General conventions related to these descriptions are explained in sections II.0.4 and II.0.3, respectively ; moreover, a summary of the notations can be found in APPENDIX 4.

In section II.1 to II.17 the translation of the ALGOL 68 constructions is described. They have been ordered as logically as possible in order to introduce the problems progressively.

One important construction is the 'block', i.e. a construction causing the creation of a new data area (*BLOCK%*) on the run-time stack (*RANST%*). We distinguish blocks which are entered and left in a lexicographical order from blocks which are entered by a call mechanism. The former are referred to as lexicographical blocks, abbreviated 'lblocks', whereas the latter are called procedure blocks, abbreviated 'pblocks'. Unlike lblocks, pblocks have their definition and application at different places in the program.

Section II.1 deals with lblocks, while sections II.2 to II.4 deal with constructions directly related to lblocks, namely, mode identifiers, generators and label identifiers.

Sections II.5 to II.9 deal with pblocks i.e. nonstandard routines with or without parameters, dynamic bounds of mode declarations and dynamic replications of format denotations.

Section II.10 treats the terminal constructions not directly related to block constructions, while II.11 treats another important set of constructions : the kernel invariant constructions. Indeed, their actions consist of the selection of a part (kernel) of a parameter value.

Confrontations and calls of standard routines are then treated (II.12 and II.13).

Section II.14 deals with choice constructions, i.e. those involving a balancing of static properties.

Finally section II.15 treats collateral clauses, where row and structure displays cause the main problems, and sections II.16 and II.17 describe the constructions not fitting in the above classification.

0.2 METHOD OF DESCRIPTION

The sections related to detailed descriptions are divided into three parts : 'syntax', 'translation scheme' and 'semantics'.

The '<u>Syntax</u>' is kept very simple, it describes the essential context-free structure of the constructions ; in fact, the syntax is the syntax of the output of the syntactic analyzer [11] where source functions are made explicit by means of prefix markers. As a convention, denotations for prefix markers end with '∇', terminals consist of small letters and nonterminals consist of capital letters (APPENDIX 2 gives a review of the whole syntax). In a way, this syntax is an abstract ALGOL 68 syntax ; it is not concerned with detailed program representations and hence it is in general applicable to the revised version of ALGOL 68 and to other related languages.

The '<u>Translation scheme</u>' is not essential ; it is just intended to give the reader an overview of the successive steps and cases in the semantics.

The '<u>Semantics</u>' is described by means of a 'pseudo-formalism' where the following rules are applied :

- english sentences replace intricate formulas when this seems to improve clarity without being prejudicial to precision.
- accessory features such as current pointer incrementations are dropped.
- motivations for each choice are made as explicit as possible.

Some precisions are now given on the formal part of the description which involves both the specification of the compiler actions (translation proper) and of the run-time actions of the generated intermediate code instructions.

a. Description tools

The description tools used in the semantics are very few, they can be summarized as follows :

(1) Data structures : integers, booleans, characters, procedures, one-dimensional arrays, records, one level references.

(2) Operations on data structures : integral and boolean calculations, procedure calls, indexings, selections, assignations.

(3) Control structures : pure sequence, goto, conditional-, case- and for-clauses.

It is to be noted that a complete study of these tools and in particular of the possibility of producing efficient machine code from the description language is outside the scope of this book.

b. Description of the translation proper

The translation into intermediate code is organized in different Steps ; a step may be subdivided in different Cases [8]. 'Steps' are introduced to group compiler actions in logical blocks. 'Cases' are introduced in order to differentiate strategies in steps, according to some criteria generally based on fundamental access classes (I.2.3.1 and II.0.4.5). The description uses compile-time devices, variables and procedures which will be introduced in II.0.4. Two particular procedures deserve a special mention here : ρ and *GEN*.

- ρ(N) where 'N' is a non-terminal of the syntax means that the translation of the construction N is activated.
- *GEN*(I), where 'I' is an intermediate code instruction (ICI), means that instruction I is generated.

c. Description of run-time actions

A full understanding of the translation process necessitates the knowledge of the run-time actions corresponding to the ICI's which are generated. In the text, the specification of these actions for an ICI follows its generation *GEN*(I). This makes the information available at the place it is needed, but it gives some problems of description. Indeed, no confusion may exist between denotations for data accessible at the moment of the generation and denotations for data accessible by the run-time actions. The method used to avoid these confusions is based on precise conventions which are now described.

(1) In fact an ICI generation is the generation of a function call where the function and the actual parameters have to be specified. For reasons of readability the formal parameters are also recalled in each generation such that the generation of an ICI has the following form :

$$GEN(\underline{\phi}\ f_1\S : a_1, \ldots f_i\S : a_i, \ldots f_n\S : a_n) \qquad \{k\}$$

- $\underline{\phi}$ denotes the function of the ICI, it is underlined,
- $f_i\S$ denotes the formal parameters of the ICI ; all these denotations end with §,
- a_i are expressions which deliver the values of the actual parameters of the function call i.e. of the ICI generated.
  Clearly, a_i's use denotations for compile-time devices, variables and procedures currently available during translation. They are calculated during translation ,
- k is an entry point in the list of ICI's given in APPENDIX 5.

Example : *GEN(<u>assign</u> mode§ : <u>int</u>,*
cadds§: (<u>constant</u> 3),
caddd§: (<u>variden</u> n.p)) {85}

(2) After the generation of an ICI and before its actions are described, some precisions about its formal parameters and the table informations available through them are generally given. The table information is found either in compile-time tables or in run-time tables. The contents of the compile-time tables vary during translation ; it is the contents of such tables at the end of the intermediate code translation which are available through formal parameters. In the notations for compile-time tables, a suffix § is used when we want to specify that it is the state of a compile-time table at the end of the ICI-translation which is meant (e.g. *CONSTAB*§). In contrast with this, run-time tables are suffixed with % (e.g. *RANST*%). Table information can be accessed through selections and indexings : in order to avoid repetitions of such operations along the description of run-time actions, identifiers are generally defined for each piece of table information used in the run-time actions. These identifiers are suffixed with § or with % according they correspond to compile-time or run-time information.

(3) The run-time actions are then described ; they are introduced by <u>Action</u> 1, <u>Action</u> 2 ... instead of steps. These descriptions use constants, denotations ending with § and denotations for run-time devices, variables and procedures.

The latter denotations are introduced in II.0.3, they all end with %. {ICI actions can be retrieved thanks to cross-references of appendix 5.}

Remark. In practice, a translation phase into machine code takes place after IC-translation and before run-time execution. This machine code translation has at its disposal all values corresponding to denotations ending with § and hence calculations on such values and on constants may take place during machine code generation : they do not imply run-time actions. In this report, this level of calculation has been merged with the description of the run-time actions, but it can easily be recovered thanks to the notational conventions : all calculations appearing in the description of run-time actions and applying to constants and/or denotations ending with § can be performed during machine code generation. All calculations involving denotations ending with % are pure run-time calculations. For example, in the expression

DISPLAY% [*bn§+1*] := *ranstpm%*

the sum *bn§+1* is performed during machine code generation but the indexing and the assignation are pure run-time actions.

Some peculiarities of the formalism.

In principle, we use the syntax of ALGOL 68 to express operations on data, however, some peculiarities have to be mentioned :

(1) For filling a record, ALGOL 68 provides for two means :
   - assignation field by field
   - structure displays

   the first notation is heavy, the second one is unclear ; we have used the following compromise :
   the access to the record is mentioned once in prefix, and assignations to field selectors follow ; for example the filling of all fields *sidsz*, *dmrsz*, ... of a record stored at the entry *BLOCKTAB*[*bnc*] , is written :

```
( of  BLOCKTAB[ bnc]   : sidsz := ... ,
                         dmrsz := ... ,
                         ...          )
```

(2) The description of some table contents is easily formalized by vectors of records ; for example, to *BLOCKTAB* corresponds the declaration :

   [*0* : ...] struct(int *sidsz*, *dmrsz*, ...) *BLOCKTAB* ;

   However, the contents of other tables consist of different sorts of records and their formalization using the union feature is unnatural and leads to inefficiencies. We consider such tables as vectors of memory cells ; for example, with

   mode cellval = co the mode of any value which can be stored in a memory cell co ;

   we assume the declaration

   [*0* : ...] cellval *RANST%* ;

such that *RANST%* entry points can be defined by indexing :

RANST% [*ranstpm%*]

or *RANST%* [*DISPLAY%* [*bn$*]] .

However, when it is known that a particular data structure is stored in the table from this entry, we allow a selection ; but for avoiding ambiguities, the mode of the data structure assumed to be stored at the entry of the table is specified between parentheses in the selection :

stch% of (h%) RANST% [*i%*]

here *h%* represents the mode characterizing a *BLOCK%* heading, *stch%* is a selector defined in this mode (see II.0.3.1).

(3) Records may be nested. When it is not ambiguous, the selection of a field corresponding to an inner level of nesting appears as one single selection without expliciting all intermediate steps : e.g. *tadd of cadd* is used instead of *tadd of add of cadd*, in the context of *cadd cadd* and *mode cadd = struct (char class, struct(int hadd, tadd)add)*.

(4) Boolean constants are denoted *true* and *false* or *0* and *1* indifferently.

(5) Finally, some liberty is sometimes taken in the English text with respect to the distinction between static management and run-time execution : a static property π is updated at compile-time ; each updating corresponds to a specific run-time action α (e.g. block entry, storage or deletion of a value on *RANST%*). When this is not ambiguous, the following sentence in the semantics of the translation process : "*the static property* π *is updated during the static management corresponding to the run-time action* α" is shortened into : "π *is updated at* α".

0.3 DECLARATIONS FOR RUN-TIME ACTIONS

The following sections play the part of the declarations for the run-time devices, variables and procedures presupposed in the description of the ICI actions. The memory of the computer is considered an uninterrupted sequence of cells :

[*0* : ...] *cellval* MEM%.

At run-time the memory is partitioned into a part of fixed size and two parts of varying size.

The part of fixed size consists of the object program *OBPROG%*, the run-time routines, a constant table *CONSTAB%* (see II.0.4.1) and a mode table *DECTAB%* (see II.0.4.2).

HEAP% is the first part of varying size. Its first free cell is characterized by a pointer[(†)] *heappm%* ; the *HEAP%* grows towards decreasing addresses. All *HEAP%* values are accessed through *RANST%*. *HEAP%* memory recovery is made by the garbage collector.

RANST% is the second part of varying size ; it consists of a number of data areas denoted *BLOCK%*'s. Each time a block (program text) is elaborated, a new *BLOCK%* is created on *RANST%*. The first free cell of *RANST%* is characterized by a pointer *ranstpm%*. On *RANST%*, *BLOCK%*'s are accessed through a *DISPLAY%* which is, at each run-time moment, the list of the addresses of all active *BLOCK%*'s. The *DISPLAY%* address corresponding to the last entered *BLOCK%* is characterized by *rtbn% ; rtbn%* is also the lexicographical depth number of the program block currently elaborated.

More formally, we can write :

```
[0: ...] cellval RANST%  ;
[0: ...] cellval HEAP%   ;
[0: N-1] int DISPLAY%; co  N=57 in the X8 implementation co
 int ranstpm%, heappm%, rtbn% .
```

0.3.1 BLOCK% CONSTITUTION

Each *BLOCK%* is organized in specific parts (devices) :

H% with static size *h*.

This is the heading of *BLOCK%*, containing link data.

SIDST% with static size *sidsz*.

This part contains the static parts of values possessed by identifiers (operators) through identity (operator) declarations.

DMRWOST% with static size *dmrsz*.

This part contains information for dynamic memory recovery of *WOST%* values.

GCWOST% with a static size *gcsz*.

This part contains garbage collection information for *WOST%* values.

SWOST% with static size *swostsz*.

This part contains static parts of intermediate results.

DIDST+LGST% with a dynamic size.

This part contains dynamic parts of values possessed by identifiers through identity declarations, and locations reserved through local generators.

DWOST% with a dynamic size.

This part contains dynamic parts of intermediate results.

In a *BLOCK%* :

H%, *SIDST%*, *DMRWOST%*, *GCWOST%* and *SWOST%* constitute *SBLOCK%*, while *DIDST+LGST%* and *DWOST%* constitute *DBLOCK%*.

In fact, all the above devices are introduced to facilitate informal decriptions.

(†) This pointer is actually an index ; a similar remark holds for other devices.

Formally, these devices are accessed through *DISPLAY%* and *RANST%* and their contents is accessed through indexings and selections : e.g. *stch% of (h%) RANST% [i%]* where the mode *h%* defines the structure of *H%* (see II.0.3.2).

When a *BLOCK%* is set up, *SIDST%* and *GCWOST%* have to be initialized ; the following procedures are used for this purpose (assume the declaration *int io%*) :

```
proc NILSIDST% = (int bn%, sidsz%, δ%) :
  (:io%:= DISPLAY% [bn%] +h+δ% ;
   for i% from io% to io% + sidsz%-1
   do RANST% [i%] := nil od)
   co In practice, not all cells of SIDST% have to be initialized but only those
      corresponding to
        - pointers of names
        - descriptor offsets
        - union overheads
        - dynamic routine representations.
        Information for this can be gathered during the translation of declara-
        tions in the same way SIDST% garbage collection information is gathered
        in gcid (see II.0.4.4). This gathering is not described in this book.
        The reason for initializing the above cells is to avoid desastrous conse-
        quences, when they are used (through a program error) before actual ini-
        tialization co.
proc NILGCWOST% = (int bn%, rgchp%, gcsz%) :
  (:io%:= DISPLAY% [bn%]+ rgchp% ;
   for i% from io% to io% + gcsz%-1
   do RANST% [i%]:= nil od)
co under some circumstances, it is the following procedure which is used to initia-
   lize GCWOST% (see II.5) co.
proc NILGCWOST1% = (int gchp%, gcsz%) :
   for i% from gchp% to gchp% + gcsz%-1
   do RANST% [i%]:= nil od.
```

GCWOST% is used to protect the *WOST%* values of the *BLOCK%* ; in other words, *GCWOST%* is a guide for the garbage collector for tracing *HEAP%* values accessible through *SWOST%*. It is clear that the garbage collector would be misled when called with a non-significant *GCWOST%* contents.

When pblocks are entered and left, it is generally necessary to update the *DISPLAY%* to recover the conditions of the declaration and of the call of the pblock respectively. This is performed by means of the following procedure (see fig. 0.1) :

```
proc UPDDISPLAY% = (int bnsc%, scope%) :
   co  scope%  is a pointer to H% of a BLOCK% where a static chain stch% is found
      co
   (:int stch% := scope%,
         bn% := bnsc%,
LO:if stch% ≠ DISPLAY%[bn%]
     then DISPLAY%[bn%]  := stch%;
         stch% := stch% of (h%) RANST% [stch%];
         bn% -:= 1;
         LO
   fi).
```

In the above procedure, the conditional clause introduces a shortcut in *DISPLAY%* updating. This is only valid if irrelevant *DISPLAY%* elements are always *nil*. *DISPLAY%* elements are set to nil by means of the following procedure :

```
proc NILDISPLAY% = (int bn1%, bn2%) :
   for i% from bn1% to bn2%
   do DISPLAY% [i%] := nil od.
```

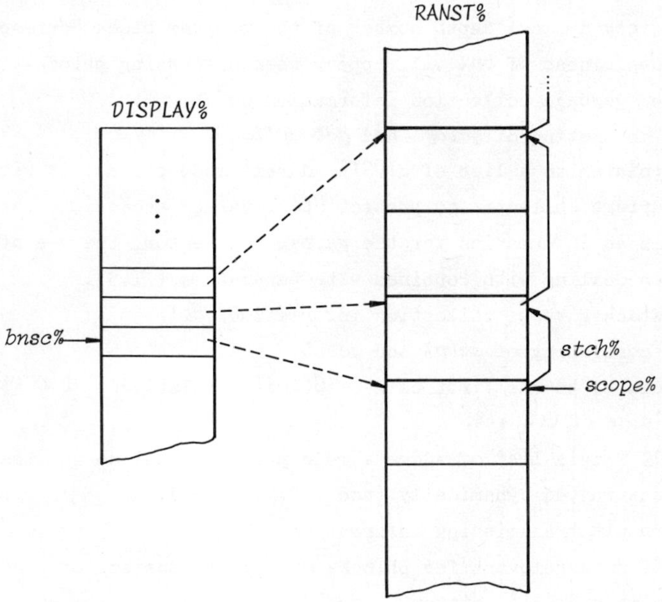

fig. 0.1 *DISPLAY%* updating

0.3.2 H% INFORMATION

Each *BLOCK%* corresponds to a program block. This program block is activated (called) from inside another program block, its calling block '$block_c$' ; it is defined (declared) in another block, its scope block '$block_s$'. When *BLOCK%* is set up, there corresponds to it on *RANST%* a $BLOCK\%_c$ and a $BLOCK\%_s$ which in turn correspond to the program $block_c$ and $block_s$ respectively. In case block is a lblock, $block_c$ and $block_s$ are identical, and so are $BLOCK\%_c$ and $BLOCK\%_s$.

The *H%* of a *BLOCK%* contains the following information :

- the static chain *stch%*.
  It links its *BLOCK%* with the corresponding $BLOCK\%_s$.
- the dynamic chain *dch%*.
  It links its *BLOCK%* with the corresponding $BLOCK\%_c$.
- the working pointer *wp%*.
  It points to the first cell of *DWOST%*. This information is useful in case of jump into a block, in order to recover *RANST%* memory space up to *DIDST+LGST%*.
- the block number *bn%*.
  It is the lexicographical depth number of the program block corresponding to *BLOCK%*. The usefulness of *bn%* will appear when discussing pblocks.
- the identifier garbage collection information *gcid%*.
  It is a pair consisting of *gcidp%* and *gcbodyflag%*.
  gcidp% is a pointer to a list of *SIDST%* address-mode pairs ; it will be interpreted by the garbage collector to protect *HEAP%* values accessible through *SIDST%*.
  gcbodyflag% is an information for the garbage collector, the use of which will be explained when dealing with routines with parameters (II.5).
- the working stack garbage collection information *gcw%*.
  It is a pair consisting of *gchp%* and *gcsz%*.
  gchp% is a pointer to the first cell of *GCWOST%*, relative to *BLOCK%*.
  gcsz% is the size of *GCWOST%*.
  In fact, *GCWOST%* is a list of address-mode pairs but unlike the list *gcid%*, *GCWOST%* is constructed dynamically (see I.2.4.3.a(2)).
- the routine result transmission information *result%*.
  This information is relevant for pblocks only ; it consists of :
  swostp% which is a *SWOST%* pointer.
  gcp% which is a *GCWOST%* pointer.
  dmrp% which is a *DMRWOST%* pointer.
  flex% which gives information for the checks of flexibility.
  prevflag% which gives information on previsions.
- the routine return jump *retjump%*.
  this information is relevant for *pblocks* only.

Formally, we can write a mode corresponding to the *H%* structure :

```
mode h% = struct (int  stch%,
                       dch%,
                       wp%,
                       bn%,
                  struct (int gcidp%,
                          bool gcbodyflag%) gcid%,
                  struct (int gchp%, gcsz%)gcw%,
                  struct (int swostp%,
                              gcp%,
                              dmrp%,
                              flex%,
                          bool prevflag%) result%,
                  int retjump%).
```

0.3.3 DYNAMIC VALUE REPRESENTATION

The principles guiding the memory representation of the values can be found in [12]. Here, we give further precisions on the memory representation of names, multiples values and values of mode union. Memory representation of routines, formats and tamrof values will be described in II.5 and II.9.

- A name which does not refer to a multiple value consists of two fields, namely *pointer%* and *scope%*.
  pointer% is the address of the location of the name,
  scope% is represented by the machine address of the *BLOCK%* to which the name is local ; *scope%* of global names is the address of the first cell of *RANST%*.
- A name which refers to a multiple value consists of *pointer%* and *scope%* and also of space for a descriptor [14].
- A multiple value consists of a descriptor and elements.
  The descriptor consists of the following fields :
  the *offset%* which is a pointer to the first element,
  the *states%*,
  the *iflag%* (interstice flag) indicating whether elements are contiguous in memory or not,
  the total stride *do%* which is the memory size between the static part of the first and the last element, including these elements. For each dimension i, we have the bounds *li%* and *ui%*, and the stride *di%*.
  Note that *iflag%* and *do%* have been introduced for the sake of efficiency when manipulating multiple values.
- Union values consist of an *overhead%* and the value itself.
  The overhead characterizes the actual mode of the value : it is a *DECTAB%* pointer *dectabp%*.
  For more details see section II.0.4.2.

Formally we have :

mode *name%* = *struct* (*int* *pointer%*, *scope%*) ;

mode *rowname%* = *struct* (*int* *pointer%*, *scope%*, *descr%* *descr%*) ;

mode *descr%* = *struct* (*int* *offset%*,
[ ]*bool* *states%* ,
bool *iflag%* ,
int *do%* ,
[*1:* ...] *struct* (*int* *l%*, *u%*, *d%*) *bounds%*);

mode *union%* = *struct* (*int* *overhead%*, [*1:* ...] *cellval* *value%*).

0.4 DECLARATIONS FOR COMPILE-TIME ACTIONS

The translation makes use of a number of tables and stacks. Some of the tables contain information gathered during syntactic analysis ; this information may be used at any moment of the translation. Moreover, table information is completed during translation in order to be available when machine code will be generated or even at run-time.

0.4.1 THE CONSTANT TABLE : CONSTAB

CONSTAB is a table which is filled during syntactic analysis;it contains values of denotations. Moreover, this table will be completed during translation, for example with information on routines (II.5 to II.9) or with data structures that can be constructed at compile-time. During translation into machine code, CONSTAB is also used to pass on parameters to run-time procedures. Clearly CONSTAB must be available at run-time. The state of the constant table at the end of IC generation will be referred to as CONSTAB§ while its run-time instance will be referred as CONSTAB%. During translation, *constabpm* represents the pointer to the first free cell of CONSTAB and *constabp* will be used as current pointer to some piece of information.
Constabpm must be incremented each time a new information is added to CONSTAB ; this incrementation is implicit in the algorithms of translation. Formally we can write :

[*0:*...]*cellval* CONSTAB ;

int *constabpm*, *constabp*.

0.4.2 THE DECLARER TABLE : DECTAB

DECTAB is a table which is filled during syntactic analysis, it contains modes together with bounds and flexibility information. Modes are stored under the form of linked lists. DECTAB consists of an initialized part and possibly of a part specific to the program being translated. The initialized part is meant to recognize current modes easily (which allows to perform optimizations) and to contain modes defined in the standard prelude. For more details see [11] .

In principle *DECTAB* is complete after syntactic analysis ; its information is referred to from the program resulting from the syntactic analysis (*SOPROG*). Modes and declarers will be manipulated as *DECTAB* pointers denoted *dectabp* or simply *mode*. *DECTAB* pointers are used as parameters of ICI's to mean a mode or a declarer. Such information will be used among other things to decompose the IC functions into machine instructions. For reasons of uniformity, the state of *DECTAB* after IC generation will be denoted *DECTAB§*.

DECTAB is also used to calculate different kinds of information during IC generation, information influencing the parameters of the storage allocation. This information is obtained through procedure calls having a *DECTAB* entry as a parameter. Like modes these procedures are recursive. They are described here in an informal way :

<u>*proc*</u> *STATICSIZE = (<u>int</u> dectabp) <u>int</u> :*

<u>*co*</u> the size of the static part *(staticsize)* of a value of mode *dectabp* is the result of this procedure <u>*co*</u>

The result of this procedure in the X8 implementation is summarized below :

<u>mode</u>	<u>staticsize</u>(nb of words)
<u>*int*</u>	1
<u>*bool*</u>	1
<u>*char*</u>	1
<u>*bits*</u>	1
<u>*bytes*</u>	1
<u>*real*</u>	2
<u>*name*</u> (non row)	2
<u>*name*</u> (row)	2 + descriptor size
<u>*row*</u> (n dim)	3 + 3 n
<u>*proc*</u> ...	2
<u>*format*</u>	2
<u>*struct*</u> *(...)*	Σ field staticsize
<u>*union*</u> *(...)*	1 + max (field staticsize)

<u>*proc*</u> *DMRRELEVANT = (<u>int</u> dectabp) <u>struct</u>(<u>int</u> class, spec) :*

<u>*co*</u> a data structure indicating which kind of dynamic memory recovery property (*dmr*) is needed for a value of mode *dectabp*. The result has the form *(<u>stat</u> 0.α)*, *(<u>dyn</u> 0.0)* or <u>*nil*</u>. In case of <u>*stat*</u>, α is the relative address of the first offset in the value <u>*co*</u>.

proc *GCRELEVANT* = (*int* *dectabp*)*bool* :

co the result of this procedure indicates whether a value of mode *dectabp*, stored on *WOST%* risks to give access to *HEAP%*, in which case the value must be protected through *GCWOST%* *co*.

proc *SCOPERELEVANT* = (*int* *dectabp*) *bool* :

co the result of this procedure indicates whether, according to the mode *dectabp*, the scope of a value of this mode is always the whole program or not *co* .

proc *NONREF* = (*int* *mode*)*bool* :

co *false* if *mode* begins with *ref*, *true* otherwise *co*.

proc *NONROW* = (*int* *mode*)*bool* :

co *false* if *mode* begins with *row*, *true* otherwise *co*.

proc *UNION* = (*int* *mode*)*bool* :

co *true* if *mode* begins with *union*, *false* otherwise *co*.

proc *DEREF* = (*int* *mode*)*int* :

co *mode* begins with *ref* ; the result is the *DECTAB* pointer of *mode* without the *ref* *co*.

proc *DEROW* = (*int* *mode*)*int* :

co *mode* begins with *rows* ; the result is the *DECTAB* pointer of *mode* without the *rows* *co*.

proc *NBDIM* = (*int* *mode*)*int* :

co *mode* begins with *rows* or *ref* *rows* ; the result is the number of dimensions of the *rows* *co*.

proc *RESULT* = (*int* *mode*)*int* :

co *mode* begins with *proc* ; the result is the *DECTAB* pointer of the mode of the result of the procedure *co*.

In principle, *DECTAB§* can be completely interpreted during machine code generation : it is not necessary to have it available at run-time. However, in order to shorten our compiler project we were compelled to have a run-time instance *DECTAB%*. This one is used in two cases :

a. During manipulation of values of mode *union* : the *overhead%* of such a value is a *DECTAB%* pointer *dectabp* specifying the actual mode of the value. When constructions involving union values are translated, sets of instructions are generated for the manipulation of a value of each possible actual mode. The choice between all sets of instructions is performed thanks to a switch which is generated on the basis of mode comparisons between the *overhead%* and each constituent mode of the union ; DECTAB% is used for this purpose. Note that this run-time DECTAB% use could be avoided at the price of having a precise ordering of the constituent modes in each union.

b. During garbage collection : the tracing of a value is based on its address and its mode ; DECTAB% has to be used to guide the tracing. Note that run-time routines for the tracing can be generated from the mode and from the access to the value without difficulty. In such a case the use of DECTAB% at run-time is avoided.

Formally we can write :

[*0:...*] *cellval* DECTAB ;

At each DECTAB entry point, a two field record is stored :

mode dec = struct(char class, int spec).

Class is *int, real, bool,...,struct,row, union, ref, proc*. *Spec* is usually a DECTAB pointer where the next part of the mode is found.

If *class* is *ref*, the pointer gives access to a *dec* record.

If *class* is *struct, row,union,proc*, the pointer gives access to a specific data structure describing the mode [11] .

0.4.3 THE MULTIPURPOSE STACK : MSTACK

During translation all sorts of information have to be saved and/or passed on from one part of a construction to another part. Due to the recursive nature of ALGOL 68, the information must generally be handled by means of stacks. Several stacks are specialized (BOST, TOPST), but it is very useful to have a multipurpose stack at one's disposal, this will be denoted MSATCK :

[*0:...*] *cellval* MSTACK;

The current pointer to the first free cell of MSTACK is denoted *mstackpm*. MSTACK is accessed through the following procedures :

```
proc INMSTACK = (cellval x) :
   (MSTACK [mstackpm] :=x;
   mstackpm+:=1);
proc OUTMSTACK = (ref cellval y) :
   (mstackpm -:=1;
   y:=MSTACK [mstackpm] );
```

0.4.4 THE BLOCK TABLE : BLOCKTAB

In order to generate appropriate code for the run-time RANST% organization at block entry and exit, a number of static informations for each block must be gathered during the translation of that block ; these informations are : *sidsz*, *dmrsz*, *gcsz*, *swostsz*, *gcid* and *bn*. These informations are calculated in a table BLOCKTAB in which there is an entry for each block. Therefore, all blocks are statically differenciated by means of a cumulative block number. In contrast with the usual block number which represents the static nesting of blocks, the cumulative block number is different for each block. During translation, *bn* and *bnc* will be two integral variables corresponding respectively with the block number and with the cumulative block number of the block currently translated.

Formally :

[*0:...*] *struct(int sidsz, dmrsz, gcsz, swostsz, gcid, bn)* BLOCKTAB ;

int bn, bnc.

BLOCKTAB will be used for machine code generation ; its state after ICI generation will be denoted BLOCKTAB§. When, during the description of the actions of an ICI, fields of a BLOCKTAB§ element are used, selections like *sidsz of* BLOCKTAB§ [*i*] are not repeated everywhere ; notations such as *sidsz§* for *sidsz of* BLOCKTAB§ [*i*] are introduced.

The management of *bn* and *bnc*

At each block entry and exit, the *bn* and *bnc* management is performed by the compiler routines *INBLOCK1* and *OUTBLOCK1* respectively.

INBLOCK1 is called with a parameter bn_{sc} i.e. the *bn* of the scope block of the block entered. The actions of *INBLOCK1* and *OUTBLOCK1* are described now :

```
proc INBLOCK1 = (int bn_sc) :
   (INMSTACK(bnc) ;
    bn:=bn_sc+1 ;
    bnc:=bncmax +:=1)
    co bncmax is initialized by -1 co.

proc OUTBLOCK1 =
   (:OUTMSTACK(bnc);
     bn:=bn of BLOCKTAB[ bnc] ).
```

The management of the sizes *sidsz*, *dmrsz*, *gcsz* and *swostsz*

The above sizes have been defined in II.0.3.1, they represent sizes of static parts of run-time devices in a BLOCK% : SIDST%, DMRWOST%, GCWOST% and SWOST%. These sizes are calculated in BLOCKTAB during the translation of each block. They are accessed thanks to the entry *bnc*.

At each block entry, the different BLOCKTAB fields and in particular the sizes are initialized by means of the procedure *INBLOCK2* :

```
proc INBLOCK2 = (int bn_sc) :
     (of BLOCKTAB[bnc] : sidsz:=0,
                         dmrsz:=0,
                         gcsz:=0,
                         swostsz:=0,
                         gcid:=0,
                         bn:=bn_sc+1).
```

The sizes in *BLOCKTAB* are the current maximum sizes of the corresponding *RANST%* parts at each moment of translation. These sizes are updated each time an action is translated in which a new value or new information is stored on *SIDST%*, *DMRWOST%*, *GCWOST%* or *SWOST%*, respectively.
Since the last three devices are stack controlled within a given block, we need current *dmrc*, *gcc* and *swostc*, representing the relative addresses of the first free cells within their corresponding device. These counters have to be updated each time code is generated for storing an information on, or deleting an information from *DMRWOST%*, *GCWOST%*, and *SWOST%* respectively. This is done by means of the following procedures :

```
proc INCREASEWOST = (int n) :
                  (swostc+:= n;
                   if swostc>swostsz of BLOCKTAB[bnc]
                      then swostsz of BLOCKTAB[bnc]:=swostc
                   fi).
proc DECREASEWOST = (int n) :
                    swostc -:= n.
```

Analogously, we can write the following compiler routines :
INCREASEDMR, DECREASEDMR, INCREASEGC, DECREASEGC.

Inside a block, a value is never erased from *SIDST%*, the field *sidsz* of BLOCKTAB may be used as current(†) counter. The following procedure is used for the static management of *sidsz* in BLOCKTAB :

```
proc INCREASESIDST = (int n) :
                     sidsz of BLOCKTAB[bnc] +:=n.
```

In the detailed description, increase and decrease operations are implicit.

The sizes *dmrsz*, *gcsz* and *swostsz* characterize a block, with the exclusion of all inner blocks. Therefore, each time an inner block is entered, the counters *dmrc*, *gcc* and *swostc* have to be saved on MSTACK and they are restored when the inner block is left. This is performed by means of the following procedures :

(†) However, in the descriptions, the notation *sidc* will be used instead of *sidsz* *of* BLOCKTAB[*bnc*] , by analogy with *dmrc*, *gcc* and *swostc*.

```
proc INBLOCK3 =
      (:INMSTACK(dmrc) ;
        INMSTACK(gcc) ;
        INMSTACK(swostc) ;
        dmrc:=gcc:=swostc:=0) .
proc OUTBLOCK3 =
      (:OUTMSTACK(swostc) ;
        OUTMSTACK(gcc) ;
        OUTMSTACK(dmrc)).
```

The *BLOCKTAB* property *gcid*.

For a given lblock, *gcid* represents a pointer to *SIDST%* garbage collection information. The form of this garbage collection information is a list of identifier address-mode pairs which will have to be interpreted.
Gcid is initialized at block entry by *INBLOCK2* and it is updated each time a declaration is translated, declaration which at run-time gives rise to the storage of a value on *IDST%*, which risks to give access to the *HEAP%*.

0.4.5 RECALL OF STATIC PROPERTIES

In this section static properties of values are briefly recalled ; this also serves as interface between the principles described in I and the actual implementation.

a. The mode.

The *mode* has the form of a *DECTAB* pointer, its use has already been explained (II.0.4.2).

b. The access.

The access is a static property of stored values. It indicates how to access such values at run-time. A number of new conventions are defined here :

α. From now on, the property *access* will be denoted *cadd*, (for complete address).
Formally :

mode cadd = struct(char class, add add) ;
mode add = struct (int hadd, tadd) ;
co hadd and *tadd* stand for head and tail address respectively *co*.

For *cadd* representations we use structure displays with some notational simplifications :

(variden n.p) is used instead of *(variden, n,p)*
(constant 5) is used instead of *(constant, 0,5)*
co when *hadd* is not significant, it is formally 0, but it is omitted in the *cadd* denotation *co*.

β. As explained in I.1.4, each information or value in *SBLOCK%* is statically addressable through a doublet *n.p*. Since during the intermediate code generation the static management of addresses is done relatively to each particular device, we have not the *p*'s of the doublets at our disposal but addresses relative to each device. Therefore, instead of *n.p* doublets we have an intermediate form *bnc*.α where α is a relative pointer *(sidc, dmrc, gcc, swostc)* within a particular device(†).

The transformation of the intermediate form to the final *n.p* doublets will be done during a further pass (machine code generation, see III).

As an example, consider *gcc* which is a relative address in *GCWOST%* (see fig. 0.2). To transform this into a *n.p* address, we need the sizes *h*, *sidsz* and *dmrsz*. Although the latter two are static, they are only available at the end of the translation of the block ; they are retrieved from *BLOCKTAB§* at the entry *bnc*. In our example we have the intermediate doublet *bnc.gcc*.

During a further pass, this doublet is easily transformed into a n.p doublet as follows :

n := *bn* <u>of</u> BLOCKTAB§[*bnc*] ;
p := *h*+*sidsz* <u>of</u> BLOCKTAB§[*bnc*]
+*dmrsz* <u>of</u> BLOCKTAB§[*bnc*]
+*gcc*

To which device a particular doublet belongs is deduced from the access class associated to it (see below).

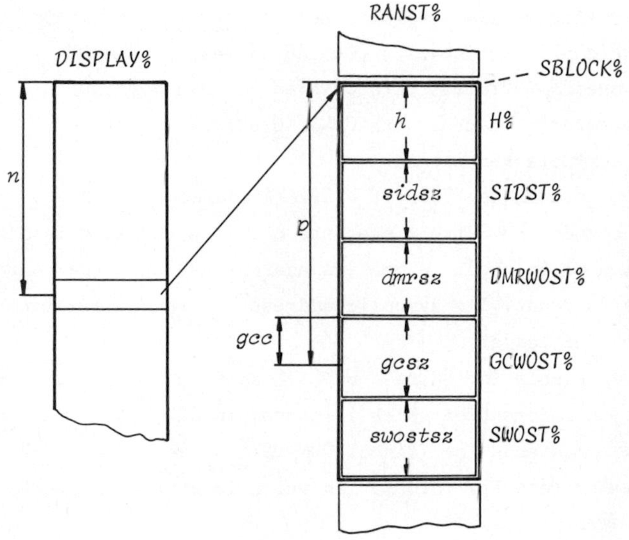

fig. 0.2 RANST% *accesses*

(†) The same remark holds for all doublets *n.p* appearing in the other static properties *smr*, *dmr* and *gc*.

γ. There exists nine fundamental classes of accesses already discussed in I.2.3. During the *static management*, different cases have to be distinguished ; this distinction is precisely based on these nine classes of accesses. These are the following :

(constant v) stands for "constant (literal) of value *v*".

(dircttab constabp) stands for "direct *CONSTAB* address a".

(diriden bnc.sidc) stands for "direct *IDST%* address *bnc.sidc*".

(variden bnc.sidc) stands for "variable *IDST%* address *bnc.sidc*".

(indiden bnc.sidc) stands for "indirect *IDST%* address *bnc.sidc*".

(dirwost bnc.swostc) stands for "direct *WOST%* address *bnc.swostc*".

(dirwost' bnc.swostc) is similar to *(dirwost bnc.swostc)* but is used for values which have only their static part on *WOST%*.

(indwost bnc.swostc) stands for "indirect *WOST%* address *bnc.swostc*".

(nihil 0) indicates that no value *(void)* is involved.

δ. In addition to the above fundamental access classes, the following accessory classes are used in the description of IC generation :

- Four accessory classes are special cases of *(constant v)* :
  - *(intct v)* "integer constant *v*"
  - *(boolct v)* "Boolean constant *v*"
  - *(bitsct v)* "bits constant *v*"
  - *(charct v)* "character constant *v*"
- Three accessory classes are special cases of *(dircttab constabp)* :
  - *(routct constabp)* "routine with *CONSTAB* address *constabp*"
  - *(formatct constabp)* "format with *CONSTAB* address *constabp*"
  - *(tamrofct constabp)* "tamrof with *CONSTAB* address *constabp*"
- The other accessory classes are new :
  - *(ddisplay bn)* stands for "direct *DISPLAY%* address *bn*"
  - *(dirabs a)* stands for "direct absolute *a*", it says that *a* is a symbolic representation of an absolute machine address and that the contents of this address is meant. The symbolic address is transformed into absolute address by the loader.

(dirgcw bnc.gcc) stands for "direct *GCWOST%* address *bnc.gcc*". It means the garbage collection information which is stored in *GCWOST%* at the address *bnc.gcc*.

(dirdmrw bnc.dmrc) stands for "direct *DMRWOST%* address *bnc.dmrc*". It means the dynamic memory recovery information which is stored in *DMRWOST%* at the address *bnc.dmrc*.

(varabs a) stands for "variable absolute *a*". It means that *a* is the symbolic representation of a value considered a literal constant ; it is used to facilitate easy modification of some machine representations, nil for example.

(varwost bnc.swostc) stands for "variable *WOST%* address *bnc.swostc*". It means the address corresponding to the *SWOST%* address *bnc.swostc*.

(i2iden bnc.sidc) stands for "double indirect *IDST%* address *bnc.sidc*". This access is similar to *(indiden bnc.sidc)* but with one more level of indirection.

(i2wost bnc.swostc) stands for "double indirect *WOST%* address *bnc.swostc*". This access is similar to *(indwost bnc.swostc)* but with one more level of indirection.

ε. The following procedure is used :

proc DEREFCADD = (cadd $cadd_s$*)cadd :*

co $cadd_s$ is an access to a name ; the result is the access to the value referred to by the name *co*

$(cadd_s$ = *(diriden* α) | *(indiden* α)

|: " = *(variden* α) | *(diriden* α)

|: " = *(indiden* α) | *(i2iden* α)

|: " = *(dirwost* α) | *(indwost* α)

|: " = *(indwost* α) | *(i2wost* α)).

c. The static memory recovery : smr.

Smr is a property allowing to recover the memory space occupied by the static parts of *WOST%* values. It has the form of a *SWOST%* doublet : *bnc.swostc*. Formally, the mode of *smr* is *add*.

d. The dynamic memory recovery : dmr.

Dmr is a property allowing to recover the memory space occupied by the dynamic part of *WOST%* values. It has one of the following forms :

(stat bnc.swostc)

(dyn bnc.dmrc)

or *(nil 0.0)* shortened *nil*.

Formally, the mode of *dmr* is *cadd*.

e. The garbage collection property : gc.

Gc is a property allowing to protect *HEAP%* values accessible through *WOST%*. It has one of the following forms :

bnc.gcc

or *0.nil* shortened *nil*.

Formally, the mode of *gc* is *add*.

The management of the static property *gc* is somewhat intricate ; it is expressed by means of formulas based on the principles explained in I.2.4.3. *Gc* management is influenced by the properties *flexbot* and *flexo* as it will appear in the formulas. However, for the sake of simplicity, the static management of *flexbot* and *flexo* is not explicit in this book.

Both *flexbot* and *flexo* are integral values :

- *flexbot* is 1,0 or 2 according it is known at compile-time that the corresponding value is or not a flexible name, or if this information is not known at compile-time.
- *flexo* is 1,0 or 2 according it is known at compile-time that the lastly dereferenced name in the past story of the value, was or not flexible or if this is not known at compile-time.

The following procedures are used :

<u>proc</u> *GENSTANDGC* =

    (: *GEN* (<u>stgcwost</u> *mode§* : $mode_o$,
                              cadd§ : $cadd_o$,
                              caddgc§ : (<u>dirgcw</u> gc_o)).   {6}

Action :

a gc-protection for the *WOST%* value characterized by *mode§-cadd§* is set up at the *GCWOST%* address *caddgc§*.

<u>proc</u> *NOOPT* =

    (: (gc_o≠ <u>nil</u> | *GEN*(<u>nooptimize</u>)))   {102}

<u>co</u> <u>nooptimize</u> is a command which is generated in order to inhibit local optimizations at the interface between two modules (see I.2.4.3, <u>remark</u> 1) <u>co</u>.

<u>Example</u> :

This example is intended to show how formulas for gc-management are established.

Suppose (II.11.3) the static properties of the primary of a slice are $mode_s$, $cadd_s$ ..., those of the reuslt of the slice are $mode_o$, $cadd_o$ ... . Suppose also $class_s$=<u>indwost</u> <u>and</u> *NONREF*($mode_s$) <u>and</u> *NONROW*($mode_o$). In this case, the translation of the slice is such that an indirect address to the selected element of the multiple value is stored on *WOST%* and is used to access the result of the slice. Let D_s and E_s denote the descriptor and the elements of the multiple value V_s on which the slice applies and let V_o denote the value resulting from the slicing.

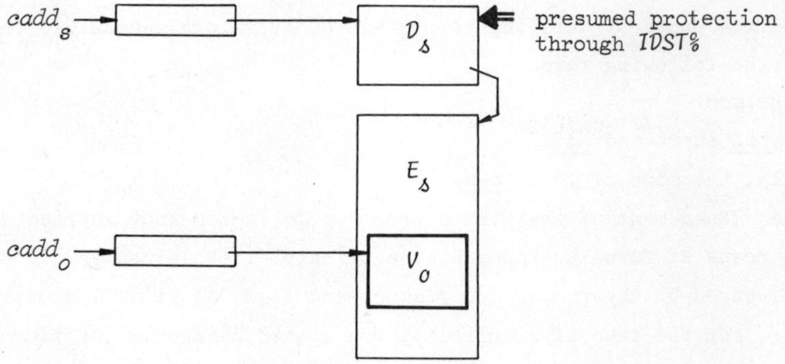

<u>fig</u>. 0.3

We make the following considerations :

a. If the whole value V_s was protected through *GCWOST%*, the resulting value V_o which is an element of V_s and which is also accessible through an indirect address, has also to be protected through *GCWOST%*.

b. In the other case, V_s is not protected through *GCWOST%* either because it gives not access to *HEAP%* or because it is already protected through *SIDST%* (see fig. 0.3).

These last two alternatives cannot be differenciated by means of the actual static properties at our disposal ; the worst case will be taken into consideration i.e. V_s is protected through *SIDST%*. The question is, is this protection valid for V_o. The answer is yes if no-side effect may supersede the offset of D_s, and this through a program error. Such a superseding may only appear if two conditions are fulfilled :

$derefo_s$=<u>*true*</u> : there has been a dereferencing since the origin of the value

$flexo_s \neq 0$: the lastly dereferenced name might be flexible.

The above considerations give rise to the following formula :

```
gc_o := (gc_s ≠ nil | gc_s
         |:derefo_s and | flexo_s ≠0   |bnc.gcc
                                       |nil).
```

If a protection for V_o is needed, an ICI establishing the dynamic protection has to be generated :

(gc$_o$ ≠ <u>nil</u> | GENSTANDGC).

<u>N.B.</u> Through the static management of *gc*, particular attention must be paid on that non relevant *GCWOST%* protections must be overwritten either by a new protection or by <u>*nil*</u> *(GEN(<u>stgcnil</u> ...))*. For making this precaution more clear, *gcc* management by means of *INCREASEGC (gcelemsz)* or *DECREASEGC (gcelemsz)* is sometimes explicit ; *gcelemsz* represents the size of a *GCWOST%* protection.

f. The origin property : or.

Or allows to keep track of the past story of a value, it consists of 6 fields :

kindo : <u>*iden*</u>, <u>*var*</u>, <u>*gen*</u> or <u>*nil*</u>

bno is a block number related to the *kindo* <u>*iden*</u>, <u>*var*</u> or <u>*gen*</u>.

derefo keeps track of dereferencings

geno keeps track of the presence of local generators

flexo keeps track of flexible names.

diago keeps information useful for error diagnostics.

The static management of the *flexo* and *diago* on *BOST* is implicit in the sequel.

Formally, we can write :

```
mode origin = struct(char kindo,
                     int  bno,
                     bool derefo,
                          geno).
```

g. The scope property : scope.

Scope consists of two informations on the scope of the value : the inner scope *insc* and the outer scope *outsc*. Both *insc* and *outsc* are block numbers *bn*. *N* which is an integer greater than the maximum value of *bn* is sometimes used as *insc* and/or *outsc* value, to mean a scope which is empty. Formally :

<u>mode</u> <u>scope</u> = <u>struct</u> (<u>int</u> *insc, outsc*).

h. The bottom property of flexibility : flexbot.

Flexbot is used to reduce the number of dynamic checks of flexibility ; as already stated the management of this property is not explicit in this book.

<u>Remarks</u>

1. In order to diversify static properties, they are indexed. As a rule, for one pameter constructions, static properties of the parameter are indexed with '*s*' (source) and static properties of the result are indexed with '*o*' (object).

ex : $cadd_s$, $cadd_o$.

2. In order to simplify the notations :

$class$ <u>of</u> $cadd_x$ is denoted $class_x$,
add <u>of</u> $cadd_x$ is denoted add_x,
$hadd$ <u>of</u> $cadd_x$ is denoted $hadd_x$,
$tadd$ <u>of</u> $cadd_x$ is denoted $tadd_x$.

Similar conventions hold for other static properties when this is not ambiguous.

ex : $insc_x$, $outsc_x$, $kindo_x$, $geno_x$ ... {*scope* is shortened into *sc*}

0.4.6 THE SYMBOL TABLE : SYMBTAB

SYMBTAB is a table which is intended to perform the links between definition and applications of declared objects. This is obtained by associating to each declaration and application of a declared object the same *SYMBTAB* entry in the program resulting from the syntactic analysis. At this entry, static properties deduced from the declaration are stored and they are available at each application.

A special problem arises when an application of a declared object lexicographically preceeds its corresponding declaration. This problem is treated extensively in the detailed descriptions ; it is partially solved by having a number of properties filled in *SYMBTAB* during syntactic analysis.

The static properties which are stored in *SYMBTAB* are *mode*, *cadd* and *scope*. Moreover, two flags *flagdecl* and *flagused* are stored in *SYMBTAB*. They indicate whether the declaration *(flagdecl)* or an application *(flagused)* of the declared object have already been met during translation. Formally :

[*0:...*] <u>struct</u> (<u>int</u> *mode*, <u>cadd</u> *cadd*, <u>scope</u> *scope*,
<u>bool</u> *flagdecl, flagused*)*SYMBTAB*.

SYMBTAB is no longer needed after IC generation. In practice and for historical reasons, *SYMBTAB* is split up into an identifier table *IDENTAB* and an indication table *INDTAB* (see [11]).

0.4.7 THE BOTTOM STACK : BOST

BOST is a stack used to perform the bottom-to-top transmission of static properties of values. When a construction has to be translated, we assume that the static properties of its parameters appear at the top of *BOST* ; one of the static effects of the translation is to replace on *BOST* the static properties of the parameters by those of the result of the construction. Deletion of *BOST* elements must generally be accompanied by compile-time actions related to memory management. There are two types of such actions :

- updating of static *RANST%* pointers. This is done by compiler-routines : *DECREASEWOST, DECREASEDMR* and *DECREASEGC.*
- generation of object instructions for dynamic memory management :
  a. *DWOST%* memory recovery implies a run-time updating of *ranstpm% :*
  Case A : *dmr* of the deleted set of *BOST* properties is of the form *(stat bnc.α)* : the following generation takes place :
  GEN (stword cadds§ : (dirwost bnc.α),
  caddo§ : (dirabs ranstpm%)) {4}
  Action : *ranstpm%* := *RANST%* [*co* an index corresponding to *cadds§ co*].
  Case B : *dmr* of the deleted set of *BOST* properties is of the form *(dyn bnc.β)* ; the following generation takes place :
  GEN (stword cadds§ : (dirdmrw bnc.β),
  caddo§ : (dirabs ranstpm%)) {4}
  b. If a gc-protection *bnc.γ* is present in the deleted set of static properties, the corresponding *GCWOST%* element must be nilled ; the following generation takes place :
  GEN (stgcnil caddgc§ : bnc.γ) {13}

  Action :
  RANST% [*co* an index resulting from an access *(dirgcw caddgc§) co*]
  := nil.

All these actions will remain implicit in the sequel.

Each *BOST* element consists of a complete set of static properties ; formally :

```
[ 0:...] struct (int mode,
                 cadd cadd,
                 add smr,
                 cadd dmr,
                 add gcc,
                 origin or,
                 scope scope,
                 int obprogp {see II.14}) BOST ;
```

int bostpm *co* the pointer to the first free *BOST* element ;
bostpm management is implicit in the sequel *co*.

The following procedure is used :

proc NEWBOST = (cadd caddx) :

co a new element is created at the top of *BOST* ; the field *cadd* of this *BOST* element is initialized with *caddx* *co*.

0.4.8 THE TOP STACK : TOPST

TOPST is a stack used to collect information for long range previsions. The use of *TOPST* makes it possible to detect, during the translation of an action, that its result will be used as the parameter of another specific action.

A new *TOPST* element is set up each time the translation of a parameter π_α of an action α is activated ; it is deleted at the completion of this translation(†). In the description of the translation process, the translation of π_α will be represented by $\rho(\pi_\alpha)$ (see II.0.2). In addition, we suppose that $\rho(\pi_\alpha)$ implicitly contains the setting up and the deletion of the corresponding *TOPST* element. Sometimes, however, for the sake of clarity, the setting up of a *TOPST* element is explicitly stated by means of the routine *NEWACTION* :

proc NEWACTION = (char action) :

co a new *TOPST* element is set up with *action* as its first field. *co*.

In this case, a call $\rho'(\pi_\alpha)$ may appear in the text, it has the same meaning as $\rho(\pi_\alpha)$ except that it does not hide any *TOPST* management.

When reference is made to *Δmem of TOPST[topstpm-1]* , the short notation *Δmem* is sometimes used.

In general, the management of *TOPST* properties will remain implicit except when it appears to be essential for the description, in particular for the description of the checks of flexibility.

In APPENDIX 3, a complete review of *TOPST* properties for each π_α is given. Each *TOPST* element consists of the following information :

action having, in principle, the form of a non-terminal π_α.

flextop being used to control the checks of flexibility ;
it has three forms :
(stat 0) which means that no check is required
(stat 1) which means that a check is required
(dyn bn) which means that the information on the necessity of a check is found in the *H%* of the active *BLOCK%* with a block number *bn*.

Δmem being a prevision information allowing to foresee, in front of some values, space for storing an overhead (rowing and uniting).

bal being a field used in choice constructions handling (II.14).

(†) This is equivalent to the principle of I.0 and I.3 where instead of π_α, a prefix marker is stored on *TOPST*.

Formally :

```
    [0:...] struct (char action,
                    struct (int class,
                                spec) flextop,
                    struct (int countbal,
                                countelem,
                            bool flagbal) bal,
                            int Δmem) TOPST ;
int topstpm  co the pointer to the first free TOPST element ;
               topstpm management is implicit in the sequel co.
```

0.4.9 OBJECT PROGRAM ADDRESS MANAGEMENT

Entry points into the object program are represented by labels which must be transformed into actual machine addresses by the loader after machine code has been generated. For this purpose, loader commands are inserted in the object program under the form of label definitions. Two kinds of labels have to be distinguished : program defined labels and compiler defined labels.

- For program defined labels the correspondence between defined and applied occurrences is obtained through *SYMBTAB* as for any other identifier.
- For compiler defined labels, needed in the translation of e.g. conditional clauses, the correspondence between defined and applied occurrences is obtained through *MSTACK*, given the recursive aspect of the ALGOL 68 programs. For this purpose, procedure calls *INMSTACK(L)* and *OUTMSTACK(L)* are used ; for the sake of simplicity these calls will remain implicit in the sequel.

Actually *L* is a particular value of a counter *labnb* which is incremented by 1 each time a new label is needed. The value 1 of this counter always corresponds to the standard label *exit*.
A special kind of access is sometimes used in the descriptions : *(label bnc.labnb)* ; in this access *bnc* corresponds to the block where the label is declared.

Labels do not only appear in the object program but we shall also be led to store labels in *CONSTAB* in order to make the corresponding program address available at run-time through an entry point in *CONSTAB%* (see II.5.4). Clearly, the loader must also transform labels of *CONSTAB§* into machine addresses ; for this purpose, each time a label is stored in *CONSTAB* at compile-time, a loader command is also generated in the object program.

The commands which are generated have the following form :

```
  (labid labnb§)      {35} for program defined labels
  (labdef labnb§)     {28} for compiler defined labels
  (updconstab mode§,
              constabp§) {33} for labels stored in CONSTAB.
```

0.4.10 THE SOURCE PROGRAM : SOPROG

SOPROG results from the syntactic analysis. It is in principle a prefixed form of the program tree and is described by means of a syntax. It consists of elements which correspond either to prefix markers or to terminals. Each element consists of two fields *class* and *spec*. *Spec* is generally a table pointer allowing to connect nodes of the tree to tables : *CONSTAB, DECTAB* and *SYMBTAB*. *Spec* is also used to specify scopes of routines and formats. In *SOPROG*, we suppose the coercions are made explicit (in fact coercions appear in a separate table *COERTAB* but this is without importance). For more details see [11].

Formally :

[*0:...*] <u>*struct*</u> *(<u>char</u> class, <u>int</u> spec) SOPROG.*

Sometimes, the strategy of translation depends on right context in *SOPROG*. Such a context is checked by means of the following procedure :

<u>*proc*</u> *CONTEXT = (<u>char</u> class)<u>bool</u> :*

class <u>of</u> SOPROG [soprogpm] = class ;

Soprogpm is the current pointer in *SOPROG* to the first element not yet involved in the translation ; its static management is implicit, but this does not hamper the correct interpretation of *CONTEXT* calls.

0.4.11 THE OBJECT PROGRAM : OBPROG

OBPROG consists of the ICI's generated. These instructions are independent modules, to be elaborated sequentially except when explicit breaks of sequence appear. In case of choice constructions (conditional, case, serial clauses) a special problem arises : a common interface must be ensured between each alternative and the instructions applying to the result of the choice construction ; the optimal interface can only be determined in the light of the static properties of the results of all alternatives. For this reason, ICI performing the interface cannot be generated in the normal sequence, they are generated in a separate table *BALTAB* (balancing table). The connection between *SOPROG* and *BALTAB* is obtained in the following way :

After each alternative a 'hole' is left in *OBPROG* ; if it appears thereafter that ICI's take place in the hole, these ICI's are generated in *BALTAB* and the hole in *OBPROG* is replaced by a link to *BALTAB*.

Formally :

[*0:...*] <u>*cellval*</u> *OBPROG ;*

[*0:...*] <u>*cellval*</u> *BALTAB.*

Patterns of object instructions are generally different but they all have the same first field representing the function of the ICI. It is the interpretation of this field which allows to reach the parameters particular to each function. *OBPROG* is filled by means of *GEN* described above.

1. LEXICOGRAPHICAL BLOCKS

Lexicographical blocks (lblocks) are 'programs' and 'serial clauses' ; however, for reasons of efficiency, only serial clauses with 'identity-', 'operator-', 'mode-', 'label-declarations' and/or 'local generators' are considered lblocks, i.e. give rise to a *BLOCK%* device at run-time. Considering a serial clause with label declarations a lblock allows, when a jump is performed, to use the normal block mechanism for recovering space for dynamic parts of intermediate results. As already stated, lblocks are caused to be executed by the normal lexicographical program elaboration.

As opposed to lblocks, procedure blocks (pblocks) are caused to be executed by a call mechanism ; they are 'non-standard-routines', 'dynamic bounds of mode declarations' and 'dynamic replications of formats'. This section deals with lblocks only. Their implementation is 'block oriented', as opposed to the 'procedure oriented' technique described for ALGOL 60 in [5] ; this means that a new *BLOCK%* is created each time a lblock is entered. Application of the 'procedure oriented' techniques to ALGOL 68 is not investigated in this book.

<u>Syntax</u>

LBLOCK → lblock∇ BLOCKBODY

{BLOCKBODY corresponds to serial clause ; see II.14.2}.

<u>Translation scheme</u>

1. Block entry :
   1.1 Static block entry
   1.2 *GEN(<u>inblock</u> ...)*
2. ρ(BLOCKBODY)
3. Block exit :
   3.1 Static block exit
   3.2 *GEN(<u>stadd</u> ... ranstpm%)*
   3.3 *GEN(<u>stword</u> ... rtbn%)*
   3.4 *GEN(<u>checkscblock</u> ...)*
   3.5 Result transmission
   3.6 *GEN(<u>stword</u> <u>nil</u> ... DISPLAY% ...).*

Semantics

Step 1 : Block entry :

Step 1.1 : Static block entry :

At block entry, *INBLOCK1(bn)*, *INBLOCK2(bn)* and *INBLOCK3* are activated, calculating a new *bn* and initializing a number of compile-time locations.

Step 1.2 :

GEN(inblock bnc§ : bnc) {42}

-*bnc§* gives an entry to *BLOCKTAB§* where all static lblock informations can be found to perform the necessary run-time actions at the entry of the new block. These informations are : *sidsz§*, *dmrsz§*, *gcsz§*, *swostsz§*, *gcid§* and *bn§*. The run-time actions of *inblock* are :

Action 1 :

DISPLAY% [*bn§*] *:=ranstpm%*

{a new *DISPLAY%* element is set up}.

Action 2 :

ranstpm% +:=h+ sidsz§+dmrsz§+gcsz§+swostsz§

{Space is reserved on *RANST%* for *SBLOCK%* of the new *BLOCK%* ; the garbage collector may be called}.

Action 3 :

rtbn%:=bn§

{*rtbn%* is a run-time variable containing the *bn* of the current block. This variable is not strictly necessary, but it reduces the number of parameters of object instructions, especially those that risk to call the garbage collector.}

Action 4 : Filling in of *BLOCK%* heading *H%* :

stch%:=dch%:=DISPLAY%[bn§-1]

wp%:=ranstpm%

bn%:=bn§

gcid%:=(gcid§,0)

gcw%:=(h+sidsz§+dmrsz§,gcsz§).

Action 5 :

NILSIDST%(bn§, sidsz§,0)

{*SIDST%* is initialized}.

Action 6 :

NILGCWOST%(bn§,h+sidsz§+dmrsz§,gcsz§)

{*GCWOST%* is initialized in its whole}.

Step 2 :

ρ(BLOCKBODY)

{At run-time, BLOCKBODY results in a value possibly of mode void. After the translation ρ(BLOCKBODY), the static properties of this result appear on *BOST*. In the next steps, these static properties will be suffixed with $result_s$, where *s* stands for source. E.g. $caddresult_s$ is the notation for the static access of the value resulting from BLOCKBODY.}

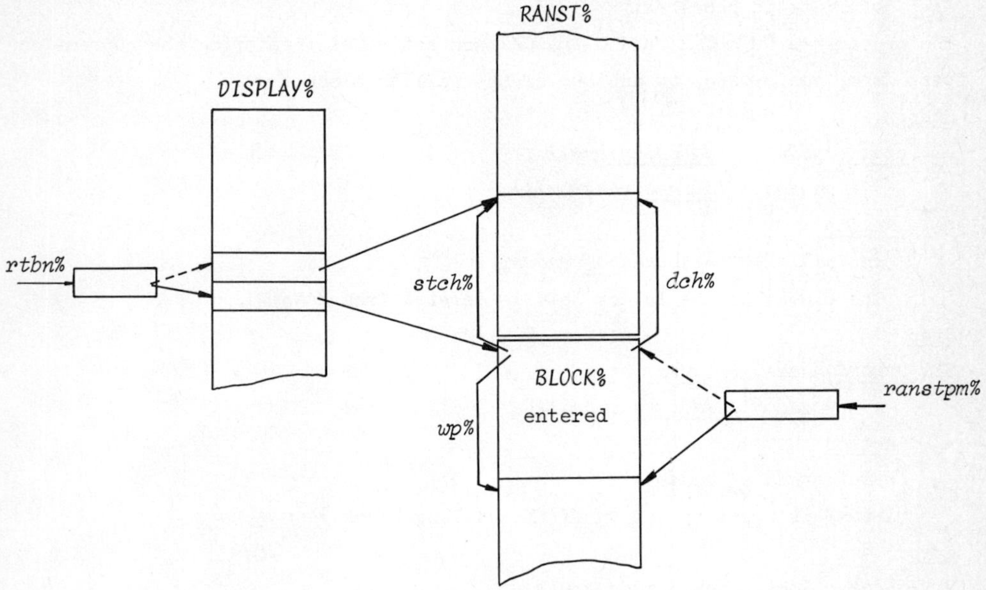

fig. 1.1 Block entry.

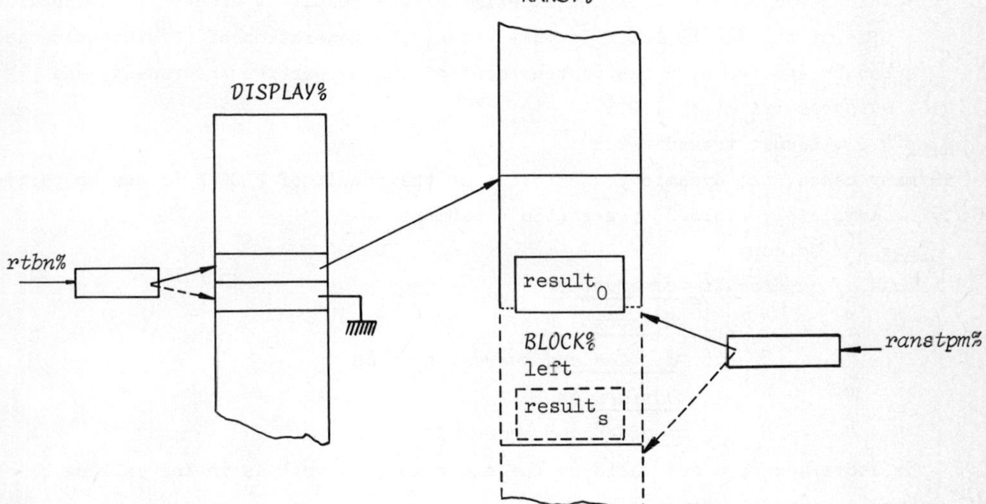

fig. 1.2 Block exit.

Step 3 : Block exit :

Step 3.1 : Static block exit :

The procedures *OUTBLOCK3* and *OUTBLOCK1* are activated, restoring the current counters *dmrc*, *gcc*, *swostc*, *bn* and *bnc* of the calling block.

Step 3.2 :

GEN(stadd cadds§ : (ddisplay bn+1) ,
caddo§ : (dirabs ranstpm%)) {5}

Action :

ranstpm%:=DISPLAY%[tadd of cadds§]

{The *BLOCK%* of the lblock left is deleted from *RANST%*}.

Step 3.3 :

GEN(stword cadds§ : (intct bn),
caddo§ : (dirabs rtbn%)) {4}

Action :

rtbn%:=tadd of cadds§

{*rtbn%* is reset to the *bn* of the calling block.}

Step 3.4 :

GEN(checkscblock mode§ : $moderesult_s$,
cadd§ : $caddresult_s$,
bn§ : bn) {90}

Action :

This ICI checks whether the lifetime of the result is greater than the lifetime of the *BLOCK%* left. In many cases, the generation of this dynamic check can be avoided by a static treatment of the properties $inscresult_s$ and $outscresults_s$ (see I.2.5.1).

Step 3.5 : Result transmission :

In many cases, the dynamic transmission of the result of BLOCKBODY can be partially or completely avoided by a static treatment :

Case A : No copy :

class of $caddresult_s$*=constant or*
" " " *=dirctab or*
" " " *=diriden and* $bnoresult_s \leq bn$ *or*
" " " *=variden or*
" " " *=indiden and* $bnoresult_s \leq bn$.

The above accesses are valid in the block left as well as in the calling block ; thus no copy is generated.

On *BOST*, the static properties of the result remain unchanged.

Case B : Copy static part :

class of $caddresult_s$*=dirwost' and* $bnoresult_s \leq bn$ *and* $kindoresult_s \neq$ *nil*

The dynamic part of the result is stored outside *BLOCK%* left, only the static part has to be copied in the calling *BLOCK%* :

GEN(<u>ststatwost</u> mode§ : moderesult$_s$*,*
cadds§: caddresult$_s$*,*
caddo§: caddresult$_0$*)* {12}

-*caddresult*$_0$ is the access to the location where the static part of the result of BLOCKBODY is copied : *caddresult*$_0$ = *(<u>dirwost</u>' bnc.swostc)* where *swostc* has been restored by *OUTBLOCK3*.

<u>Action</u> :

The static part of the value of *mode§* is copied from *cadds§* to *caddo§*.

On *BOST*, the static properties of the result are as follows :

cadd:=caddresult$_0$ {i.e. *(<u>dirwost</u>' bnc.swostc)*}

smr:=bnc.swostc

gc management is based on the following statement :

if *gcresult*$_s$*=<u>nil</u>* then *gcresult*$_0$*:=<u>nil</u>* ,

otherwise *gc:=bnc.gcc* and a run-time gc-protection must be set up in the calling *BLOCK%* :

GEN(<u>stgcwost</u> mode§ : moderesult$_s$*,*
cadd§ : (<u>dirwost</u>' bnc.swostc) ,
caddgc§ : (<u>dirgcw</u> bnc.gcc)) {6}

All other static properties of the result remain unchanged.

<u>Case</u> C : Copy address :

class <u>of</u> caddresult$_s$*=<u>indwost</u> <u>and</u> bnoresult*$_s$ *≤bn <u>and</u> kindoresult*$_s$*≠<u>nil</u>*.

The indirect address has to be copied :

GEN(<u>stadd</u> cadds§ : (<u>dirwost</u> spec <u>of</u> caddresult$_s$*),*
caddo§ : (<u>dirwost</u> bnc.swostc)) {5}

-*cadds§* and *caddo§* are the accesses of the direct address to be copied, before and after copy respectively.

On *BOST* :

cadd:=(<u>indwost</u> bnc.swostc)

smr:=bnc.swostc

gc remains *<u>nil</u>* or becomes *bnc.gcc* analoguously to case B.

Other static properties are unchanged.

<u>Case</u> D : No result :

class <u>of</u> caddresult$_0$*=<u>nihil</u>*.

The result is void ; nothing has to be copied.

On *BOST*, all static properties are unchanged.

<u>Other cases</u> : Copy whole value :

The whole value (static and dynamic part, if it exists) has to be copied :

GEN(<u>stwosti</u> mode§ : moderesult$_s$*,*
cadds§: caddresult$_s$*,*
caddo§: (<u>dirwost</u> bnc.swostc)) {1|2|3}

On *BOST* :

cadd:=(dirwost bnc.swostc)

smr:=bnc.swostc

dmr:=nil, stat or dyn according to $moderesult_s$;

for this purpose, *DMRRELEVANT*($moderesult_s$) is used.

In case *dmr* is *dyn*, an object instruction is generated :

GEN(stdmrwost cadd§ : (dirabs ranstpm%),

cadddmr§ : (dirdmrw bnc.dmrc)) {7}

Clearly, this object instruction when it exists must be generated before *stwosti* which may modify *ranstpm%*.

Action :

ranstpm% is copied in the location of *DMRWOST%* with an access (*dirdmrw cadddmr§*).

gc is treated as follows :

-in case *class of* $caddresult_s$=*dirwost and* $bnoresult_s$ ⩽*bn* then *gc:=bnc.gcc* if and only if $gcresult_s$≠*nil* ; *gc* remains *nil* otherwise.

-in the other cases, *gc:=bnc.gcc* or *gc:=nil* according to $moderesult_s$. *GCRELEVANT*($moderesult_s$) is used for this purpose. When *gc≠nil*, a gc-protection is set up in the calling *BLOCK%* :

GEN(stgcwost mode§ : $moderesult_s$,

cadd§ : (dirwost bnc.swostc),

caddgc§ : (dirgcw bnc.gcc)) {6}

As explained in I.2.4.3, remark 3, different strategies exist for copying a value. It is the strategy explained under 3 which is used here. The suffix *i* in the ICI *stwosti* is related to the garbage collector activation : *i* is 1 when the garbage collector does not risk to be activated i.e. when the result has no dynamic part or when it is completely stored on *RANST%* in the *BLOCK%* left ; no run-time check controlling whether enough space is available is necessary. Suffix *i* is 3 in the other cases ; then, it should be clear that the generation of *stgcwost* must take place before the generation of *stwost3*.

Step 3.6 : Nilling of *DISPLAY%* :

GEN(stword cadds§ : (varabs nil),

caddo§ : (ddisplay bn+1)) {4}

Action :

NILDISPLAY% (tadd of caddo§, tadd of caddo§)

{The *DISPLAY%* element of the *BLOCK%* left is nilled.}

Previsions

(1) The analysis of *TOPST* allows to group successive block exits avoiding repetitive copies of results. Moreover, if it appears that the result will be assigned after block exit, the *assignation* may be performed before block exit ; then, the static properties of the value of the *assignation* are put on *BOST* instead of those of the result ; no extra copy of the result is needed. If the result of the block is used as *actual parameter*, a similar solution holds.

(2) When the result is copied in the calling *BLOCK%* (see case B and other cases), the static part of the result is actually copied from *swostc+Δmem*, where *Δmem* may be 0 (see I.3.1 (3)). *Δmem* takes into account the fact that in the calling block the value may be provided with an overhead (rowing or uniting). *Δmem* is available at the top of *TOPST*.

2. MODE IDENTIFIERS

2.1 IDENTITY DECLARATION

Syntax

IDEDEC → idedec∇ FDECLARER iden = ACPAR

OPDEC → opdec∇ FDECLARER oper = ACPAR

- FDECLARER specifies the mode of the identifier and possibly formal bounds together with flexibility information.
- iden(oper) is the declared object characterized by a *SYMBTAB* entry, there *flagused*, denoted here *flagusediden*, is found.
- ACPAR is the actual parameter delivering the run-time value which is made to be possessed by the declared object.

Translation scheme

1. ρ(FDECLARER)
2. ρ(ACPAR)
3. Establishment of the relation of possession
4. Identifier garbage collection protection
5. *GEN(checkformal)*.

Semantics

Case A :

Flagusediden=0. i.e. the declaration is met before all applications.

Step 1 :

ρ(FDECLARER)

All bounds, possibly through mode indications (see II.8), are translated. Suppose there are n bounds, after the translation ρ(FDECLARER), their static properties appear on *BOST*. They will be denoted *cadd1, smr1,..., cadd2 , smr2,...* .

Step 2 :

ρ(ACPAR)

At run-time ACPAR results in a value. After the translation ρ(ACPAR), the static properties of this value appear on *BOST*. They will be denoted : $modeacpar_s$, $caddacpar_s$, $smracpar_s$, ...

Step 3 : Establishment of the relation of possession :

This step performs the relation of possession between identifier (operator) and actual parameter value. This is done by making the value available at each use of the identifier (operator). It may imply a run-time action by which the value is stored on *IDST%*. Statically, in *SYMBTAB*, the identifier is characterized by a set of properties according to the cases below.

<u>Case</u> A': No copy :

class <u>*of*</u> $caddacpar_s$ = <u>*constant*</u> <u>*or*</u>
" " " = <u>*dircttab*</u> <u>*or*</u>
" " " = <u>*diriden*</u> <u>*and*</u> $kindoacpar_s$=<u>*iden*</u> <u>*or*</u>
" " " = <u>*variden*</u>.

No run-time action is implied : the access to the ACPAR stored value remains valid as long as the possession relation exists. It is that stored value which will be used at each application of the declared object. The static management consists in copying the static properties of the ACPAR value from *BOST* to *SYMBTAB* :

In *SYMBTAB* :

$mode:=modeacpar_s$
$cadd:=caddacpar_s$
$scope:=scopeacpar_s$
flagdecl:=1

<u>Case</u> B' : Copy static part :

class <u>*of*</u> $caddacpar_s$=<u>*dirwost*</u>.

Only the static part of the ACPAR value is copied on *SIDST%* :

GEN(<u>*ststatacpar*</u> *mode§* : $modeacpar_s$,
cadds§: $caddacpar_s$,
caddo§: (<u>*diriden*</u> *bnc.sidc*)) {108}

- *hadd* <u>*of*</u> *caddo§*, through *BLOCKTAB§* , gives access to *bn§*.

<u>Action</u> :

The static part of the value characterized by *cadds§-mode§* is copied on *SIDST%* at the access *caddo§*.

The dynamic part, if it exists, is on *DWOST%* ; it is just considered a part of *DIDST%* by updating *wp%* in *H%* of the current *BLOCK%* :

wp% <u>*of*</u> (<u>*h%*</u>) *RANST%*[*DISPLAY%*[*bn§*]] *:=ranstpm%*.

In *SYMBTAB*, the static properties of the declared object are the following :

$mode:=modeacpar_s$
cadd:=(<u>*diriden*</u> *bnc.sidc)*
$scope:=scopeacpar_s$
flagdecl:=1.

<u>Other cases</u>' : Copy whole value :

The whole value is copied on *IDST%* of the current *BLOCK%* :

GEN(<u>*stacpar*</u> *mode§* : $modeacpar_s$,
cadds§: $caddacpar_s$,
caddo§: (<u>*diriden*</u> *bnc.sidc*)) {8}

Action :

The value characterized by *cadds§-mode§* is copied on *IDST%* of the current *BLOCK%*. If this value has a dynamic part, *wp%* of the current *BLOCK%* is updated ; in this case, the garbage collector may be called.

Static properties of the declared object in *SYMBTAB* are as in case B below.

Step 4 : Identifier garbage collection protection :

Let *modeiden, caddiden, scopeiden* be the static properties of the value possessed by the identifier and stored in *SYMBTAB*.

The static management of *gcid* in *BLOCKTAB* consists in adding the pair *caddiden-modeiden* to the chain *gcid of BLOCKTAB[bnc]*, but this, only in the cases where the identifier gives rise to a stored value on *IDST%* and where, according to *modeiden*, this value risks to give access to the *HEAP%*. *GCRELEVANT(modeiden)* is used for this purpose.

Step 5 :

```
GEN(checkformal : mode§ : modeiden,
                  cadd§ : caddiden,
                  n§    : n,
                  cadd1§: cadd1,
                   ...     ...
                  caddn§: caddn)                    {60}
```

-*modeiden* is a *DECTAB* pointer where static information about the declarer is stored. This information is the mode and for each dimension of a row mode it is indicated whether the bounds are 'flexible' or 'either'.

-*cadd1* ... are the accesses of the integers which are the values of the non virtual bounds calculated in step 1.

Action :

The bounds of the value characterized by *cadd§-mode§* are compared with the integers corresponding to *cadd1§*... .

Case B :

Flagusediden = 1.

This case is identical to case A except step 3 because it must take into account the fact that some static management has already taken place at the level of the first use of the identifier :

Step 3 :

```
GEN(stacpar mode§ : modeacpar_s,
            cadds§: caddacpar_s,
            caddo§: caddiden   )                    {8}
```

caddiden is issued from *SYMBTAB*.

On *SYMBTAB*

scope := scopeacpar$_s$

flagdecl := 1.

Remark on flexibility

Strictly speaking a check of flexibility is expected here, but we recall the *TOPST* mechanism allows to perform such a check at a syntactically lower level, i.e. at the level of slices and rowed coercends, see I.2.5.2.

What has to be done here, is

flextop of TOPST[topstpm-1] := (stat α)

where α is 1 or 0 according the actual parameter is a name or not. This takes place at the beginning of ρ(ACPAR).

At the level of 'refslices' and 'refrowrowings' (II.11.3 and II.11.5) the generation

GEN (checkflex cadd§ : cadd) {61}

takes place, and this, when

flextop of TOPST[topstpm-1] = (stat 1)

indicating that the result is a name which will be given a remanent access.

In *checkflex*, *cadd§* is the address of the name on which the action refslicing or refrowrowing applies : *checkflex* provides for a run-time error message if the name appears to be flexible.

2.2 LOCAL VARIABLE DECLARATION

Syntax

LOCVARDEC → locvardec∇ ADECLARER variable |
locvardec∇ ADECLARER variable := SOURCE

{-ADECLARER specifies the mode of the value referred to by the variable and possibly actual bounds together with flexibility information.
-variable is the declared object characterized by a *SYMBTAB* entry where *flagused*, denoted here *flagusedvar*, is found.}

Translation scheme

1. ρ(ADECLARER)
2. Location reservation and initialization
3. Establishment of the relation of possession
4. Variable garbage collection protection
5. Variable initialization :
   5.1 ρ(SOURCE)
   5.2 Assignation.

Semantics

Case A :

Flagusedvar=0.

Step 1 :

ρ(ADECLARER)

All bounds are translated. Their static properties appear on *BOST* ; they will be denoted *cadd1, smr1,...* .

Step 2 : Location reservation and initialization :

GEN(locvargen mode§ : ref mode of ADECLARER,
cadd§ : (variden bnc.sidc),
n§ : n,
cadd1§: cadd1,
... ...
caddn§: caddn) {87}

-*add of cadd§* is the *SIDST%* address where the location has to be reserved. Space reservation for the static part of the location is obtained through the static management of *sidsz of BLOCKTAB[bnc]* ; it implies no dynamic action.

Action 1 : Dynamic space reservation :

For dynamic space reservation, values of bounds the access of which are *cadd1§,...,caddn§,* are used. This space reservation is done either on *DIDST+LGST%* or on *HEAP%*. The *HEAP%* is used when *union(...row...)* or *flex* is involved in *mode§ ;* then *heappm%* is updated. In the other case, *ranstpm%* and *wp%* in *H%* of the current *BLOCK%* are updated (see I.2.3.2, rule b4). In both cases, the garbage collection may be called.

Action 2 : Location initialization :

Descriptors are filled with their appropriate offset, states, iflag, bound values and strides. Moreover, in order to avoid disastrous use of uninitialized locations, union overheads, name-and routine-pointers are initialized with *nil*(†).

{Both action 1 and action 2 are based on the same data structure characterized by *mode§* ; they can be handled simultaneously by the same routine such that the data structure is passed through only once}.

Step 3 : Establishment of the relation of possession :

The static properties of the variable are put in *SYMBTAB* :

mode := ref mode of ADECLARER
cadd := (variden bnc.sidc)
scope := (bn,bn)
flagdecl := 1

These static properties of the variable will be denoted *modevar, caddvar,...*

(†) Actually, in case of local variable, the initialization of the static part of the location is performed at block entry.

Step 4 : Variable garbage collection protection :

The pair *caddvar-modevar* is added to the chain *gcid* of BLOCKTAB[*bnc*] , but only in the case the variable risks to give access to the HEAP%. *GCRELEVANT(mode* of ADECLARER) is used for this purpose.

Step 5: Variable initialization :

If the variable declaration contains an initialization, the following steps are executed :

Step 5.1 :

ρ(SOURCE)

At run-time, SOURCE delivers the value to be assigned. After the translation ρ(SOURCE), its static properties appear on BOST ; they will be denoted *modes*, *cadds* ... .

Step 5.2 : Assignation :

```
GEN(assign mode§ : modes,
           cadds§: cadds,
           caddd§: caddvar)                    {85}
```

Action :

The value characterized by *cadds§-mode§* is assigned to the name with the access *caddd§*. No scope checking is required.

Case B :

Flagusedvar = 1.

This case is very similar to case A except for steps 2 and 3 which must take into account the fact that some static management has already been performed at the first use of the variable :

Step 2 : Location generation and initialization :

Static properties of the variable are already on SYMBTAB, they are denoted *modevar*, *caddvar* ...

```
GEN(locvargen mode§ : modevar,
              cadd§ : caddvar,
              n§    : n,
              cadd1§: cadd1,
               ...     ...
              caddn§: caddn)                   {87}
```

No static space reservation takes place.

Step 3 :

In SYMBTAB :

flagdecl := 1.

Remark on dynamic space reservation

(1) Dynamic space reservation on RANST%, as it is implemented, is done step by step. The figure below illustrates how space is reserved for a value V with static part Vs and dynamic part Vd. First space is reserved for Vs, then for the static

part Vds of Vd, then for the static part Vdd1s of the dynamic part of the first element, then (recursively) its dynamic part Vdd1d, then Vdd2...Vddn are treated analogously. During this stepwise reservation process, all pointers, linking static parts with their corresponding dynamic parts, and other descriptor information are set up.

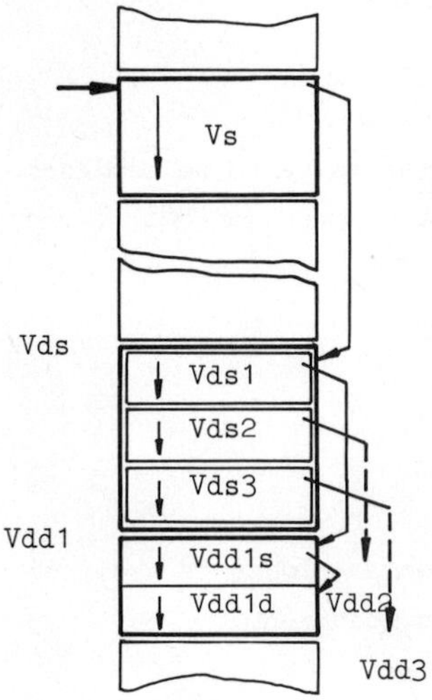

<u>fig</u>. 2.1 *RANST%* space reservation

(2) Stepwise dynamic space reservation on *HEAP%* requires a strategy which is somewhat different from that on *RANST%*. The reason is that *RANST%* grows towards increasing addresses, whereas *HEAP%* grows towards decreasing addresses. Moreover, for reasons of selection, indexing and for reasons of hardware (in our computer, a real value takes two cells), fields within a static part and elements within a dynamic part must be stored in one same order, i.e. the order of increasing addresses.

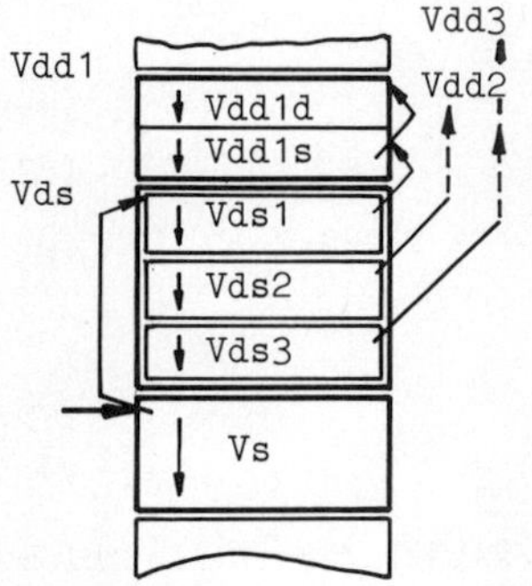

<u>fig</u>. 2.2 *HEAP%* space reservation

(3) Instead of this stepwise space reservation , one could imagine a global space reservation where space is reserved at once for the whole value. However, this would demand a run-time precalculation of the total size of V, followed by a stepwise process for setting up pointers and descriptor information.
This means that the data structure is passed through twice.
Note that step by step space reservation is also advantageous when copying values from one part of the memory to another. However, the advantage is based on another reason, namely a reason of *gc*-protection. More precisely, our *gc*-protection mechanism is such that during the step by step copy process, already copied parts of the old value become unprotected (see I.2.4.3.b, Remark 3.3). The space for these parts can be freed by the garbage collector before the completion of the copy of the whole value. This would not be the case with a global copy process.

2.3 HEAP VARIABLE DECLARATION

Syntax

HEAPVARDEC → heapvardec∇ ADECLARER variable |
heapvardec∇ ADECLARER variable := SOURCE.

Translation scheme

1. ρ(ADECLARER)
2. Location reservation and initialization
3. Establisment of the relation of possession
4. Variable garbage collection protection
5. Variable initialization
   5.1 ρ(SOURCE)
   5.2 Assignation.

Semantics

Case A :

Flagusedvar = 0.

Step 1 :

ρ(ADECLARER)

Bounds of ADECLARER are translated. Their static properties appear on *BOST* ; they will be denoted *cadd1, smr1* ... .

Step 2 : Location reservation and initialization :

```
GEN(heapvargen mode§ : ref mode of ADECLARER,
               cadd§ : (diriden bnc.sidc),
               n§    : n,
               cadd1§: cadd1,
               ...     ...
               caddn§: caddn)                    {88}
```

Action : Space reservation :

The whole location (static and dynamic part) characterized by *mode§*, is reserved on *HEAP%*. The garbage collector may be called. Clearly, if the location has a dynamic part, values of bounds the access of which are *cadd1§, cadd2§,...,* are used.

The name created is stored on *SIDST%* at the access *cadd§*, its two fields are :

pointer% := HEAP% pointer of the location

scope% := DISPLAY%[0] .

Step 3 : Establishment of the relation of possession :

The static properties of the name stored on *SIDST%* are put in *SYMBTAB* :

mode := ref mode of ADECLARER

cadd := (diriden bnc.sidc)

scope := (0,0)

flagdecl := 1

The static properties will be denoted *modevar, caddvar* ... .

Step 4 : Variable garbage collection protection :

The pair *caddvar-modevar* is added to the chain *gcid of BLOCKTAB[bnc]* .

Step 5 : Variable initialization :

See II.2.2, step 5.

Case B :

Flagusedvar = 1.

See II.2.2 case B with heapvargen instead of locvargen.

2.4 APPLICATIONS OF MODE IDENTIFIERS

Syntax

'Iden' is terminal with which a *SYMBTAB* entry is associated. The static properties stored at this entry will be denoted *modeiden, caddiden* ... . When *class of caddiden = diriden or variden*, through *BLOCKTAB*, *hadd of caddiden* gives access to *bniden*, i.e. the bn of the identifier declaration.

Semantics

Case A :

Flagdecliden = 1.

A new *BOST* element is set up :

mode := modeiden

cadd := caddiden

smr, dmr and *gc* are irrelevant

or := (iden, bniden,0,0), (var, bniden,0,0) or (nil,0,0,0) according to *class of caddiden (diriden - variden - constant or dircttab).*

scope := scopeiden

ASSLICE (caddiden)

with <u>proc</u> *ASSLICE=(<u>cadd</u> cadd) :*

(action <u>of</u> TOPST [*topstpm-1*] = *"DESTINATION"*

| MSTACK [*mstackpm-2*] := *cadd*

|: *action <u>of</u>* TOPST [*topstpm-1*] = *"SOURCE"*

<u>and</u> action <u>of</u> TOPST [*topstpm-2*] = *"DEREFCOERCEND"*

| MSTACK [*mstackpm-2*] := *cadd)*

<u>co</u> This routine is intended to avoid, in certain cases the copy on WOST% of slice result, copy needed when overlappings in assignation may occur as in *(A[2:3] := A[1:2])*
(see II.12.1)

<u>co</u> .

<u>Case</u> B :

Flagdecliden = 0 <u>and</u> flagusediden = 0.

We shall suppose that the syntactic analyzer has partially filled the *SYMBTAB* entry of the identifier :

mode = mode issued from the declaration

cadd = (<u>variden</u> bnciden.0) for a local variable

(<u>diriden</u> bnciden.0) otherwise

scope = (bniden,bniden) for a local variable,

(0,0) for a heap variable,

(bniden,0) otherwise

flagused = 0

flagdecl = 0

with *bniden* and *bnciden* for the *bn* and *bnc* of the block of the declaration of the identifier.

The above *SYMBTAB* information is easily accessible at the level of the syntactic analyzer, it just implies a *bn-bnc* counting.

On *SYMBTAB*

tadd <u>of</u> cadd := sidsz <u>of</u> BLOCKTAB [*bnciden*]

flagused := 1

Static space is reserved on *SIDST%* by updating *sidsz <u>of</u>* BLOCKTAB [*bnciden*] . The situation is now the one of <u>case</u> A.

Remark that in case of a variable, no efficiency is lost ; in the other cases, optimizations resulting from the analysis of the static properties of the actual parameter of the identity declaration, unavailable here, are lost.

ASSLICE (caddiden).

<u>Case</u> C :

Flagusediden = 1.

{see <u>case</u> A}.

3. GENERATORS

3.1 LOCAL GENERATOR

Syntax

LOCGEN → loc∇ ADECLARER.

Translation scheme

1. ρ(ADECLARER)
2. Location reservation and initialization
3. Static management.

Semantics

Step 1 :

ρ(ADECLARER)

{All bounds are translated, their static properties appearing on *BOST* are denoted *caddl, smr1 ... caddn ...*}

Step 2 : Location reservation and initialization :

GEN(locgen mode§ : ref mode of ADECLARER,
cadd§ : (dirwost bnc.swostc),
caddgc§: (dirgcw bnc.gcc),
n§ : n,
cadd1§ : cadd1,
... ...
caddn§ : caddn) {93}

-In *BLOCKTAB*, *hadd of cadd§* gives access to *bn§*.

Action 1 : Space reservation :

The location in its whole is reserved on *DIDST+LGST%* i.e. from *ranstpm%* . However locations for elements of flexible arrays and for array elements involved in values of mode *union* are reserved on *HEAP%* from *heappm%* ; *wp%* of the current *BLOCK%* must be updated. The garbage collector may be called.

The name created is stored on *SWOST%* at *cadd§*, its two fields are :

pointer% := RANST% pointer of the location {*ranstpm%*}

scope% := DISPLAY% [*bn§*] .

Action 2 : Location initialization :

See II.2.2, case A, step 2, action 2.

Action 3 : Location garbage collection protection :

If according to *mode§* (including flexibility information), the location risks to give access to *HEAP%*, a gc-protection is stored on *GCWOST%* at the access *caddgc§*. Such a gc-protection consists of *cadd§-mode§*.

Step 3 : Static management :

The static properties of the name created are stored on *BOST* :

mode := *ref mode of* ADECLARER

cadd := (*dirwost bnc.swostc*)

smr := *bnc.swostc*

dmr := *nil*

gc := *bnc.gcc* or *nil* according to *mode of* ADECLARER

or := (*gen*,*bn*,*0*,*1*)

scope := (*bn*,*bn*).

3.2 HEAP GENERATOR

Syntax

HEAPGEN → heap∇ ADECLARER.

Translation scheme

1. ρ(ADECLARER)
2. Location reservation and initialization
3. Static management.

Semantics

Step 1 :

ρ(ADECLARER).

Step 2 : Location reservation and initialization :

```
GEN(heapgen mode§  : ref mode of ADECLARER,
            cadd§  : (dirwost bnc.swostc),
            caddgc§: (dirgcw bnc.gcc),
            n§     : n,
            cadd1§ : cadd1,
             ...      ...
            caddn§ : caddn)                          {94}
```

Action 1 : Space reservation :

The location in its whole is reserved on *HEAP%* from *heappm%*.

The name created is stored on *SWOST%* at *cadd§* :

pointer% := *HEAP%* pointer of the location

scope% := *DISPLAY%*[*0*]

Action 2 : Location initialization :

See II.2.2, case A, step 2, action 2.

Action 3 : Location garbage collection protection :

A gc-protection consisting of *cadd§-mode§* is stored on *GCWOST%* at *caddgc§*.

<u>Step</u> 3 : Static management :

On *BOST* :

mode := <u>*ref*</u> *mode* <u>*of*</u> ADECLARER

cadd := (<u>*dirwost*</u> *bnc.swostc*)

smr := *bnc.swostc*

dmr := <u>*nil*</u>

gc := *bnc.gcc*

or := (<u>*gen*</u>, 0, 0, 0)

scope := (0, 0).

4. LABEL IDENTIFIERS

4.1 GENERALITIES

Program defined labels allow to jump from some parts to other parts of programs by means of goto's. In ALGOL 68 jumps can be performed from an inner to an outer block and also from inside an expression to outside this expression. The problem of the *goto* is a problem of memory recovery of the *BLOCK%*'s left and/or of the partial results of the expression left. However, it is to be noted that ALGOL 68 dissalows dynamic label transmission (assignation of labels, labels transmitted as procedure parameters) as such. Hence, a block into which a *goto* is performed is always active, i.e. accessible through *DISPLAY%*.

But on the other hand, the effect of dynamic label transmission is obtained through 'procedured jumps' : like many other constructions, jumps may be procedured, thus giving rise to a routine ; routines can be transmitted dynamically. The implementation of procedured jumps enters the frame of the proceduring-deproceduring mechanism ; however, if no precautions are taken, the general mechanism gives rise to inefficiencies. In II.7, we explain how these inefficiencies are avoided.

4.2 LABEL DECLARATION

Syntax

LABELDEC → labeldec∇ label :

{with label a *SYMBTAB* entry is associated}.

Translation scheme

1. *GEN(labid labnb)*
2. Label static properties.

Semantics

Step 1 :

GEN(labid labnb§ : labnb) {35}

Step 2: Label static properties :

The *SYMBTAB* element associated with 'label' is filled :

mode := void
cadd := (label bnc.labnb)
flagdecl := 1.

Note that this filling may take place during syntactic analysis as well, thus avoiding problems of declared object applications appearing lexicographically before their declaration.

4.3 GOTO STATEMENT

Syntax

GØTØ → goto∇ label

{with label, a *SYMBTAB* entry is found ; there *bnc* of the block of the label declaration and *labnb* are found. They will be denoted *bncid* and *labnbid* respectively}.

Translation scheme

1. *GEN(goto ... labnbid ...)*
2. Goto static properties.

Semantics

Step 1 :

```
GEN(goto bnc§ : bnc,
         bncid§: bncid,
         labnbid§: labnbid,
         swostc§ : swostc)                    {31}
```

-*bnc§*, through *BLOCKTAB§*, gives access to *bn§*

-*bncid§*, through *BLOCKTAB§*, gives access to *sidszid§*, *dmrszid§*, *gcszid§*, *swostszid§* and *bnid§*.

Action 1 :

(bncid§ ≠ bnc§ | rtbn% := bnid§) ;

(swostszid§ ≠ 0 | ranstpm% := wp% of (h%) RANST% [DISPLAY%[bnid§]]).

Action 2 :

NILGCWOST% (bnid§,h+sidszid§+dmrszid§,gcszid§).

Action 3 :

NILDISPLAY% (bnid§+1,bn§).

Action 4 :

goto labnbid§.

Step 2 : Goto static properties :

Goto delivers no value, this will be characterized on *BOST* by the following properties

mode := void

cadd := (nihil 0)

other static properties are irrelevant.

These properties are useful at block exit for example, where they characterize the absence of result. They will be deleted from *BOST* at the level of semicolons in serial clauses.

Remark

In our implementation, label declarations cause a serial clause to be a block. The only reason for this is, when a jump is performed, to let the normal block mechanism (*wp%*) recover space for the dynamic parts of intermediate results.

In the following example,

(.....a+(.....;l:b(B |c| goto l)))*

the values '*a*' and '*b*' are supposed to have dynamic parts and the operators '*' and '+' are supposed to be defined on operands of the appropriate mode. When a jump is performed the dynamic part of '*a*' must remain on *DWOST%*, but that of value '*b*' must disappear.

Note that a slight increase of compiler organization could avoid label declarations to be taken into account in the definition of lblocks.

5. NON-STANDARD ROUTINES WITH PARAMETERS

5.1 GENERALITIES

Non-standard routines with parameters are pblock's i.e. blocks, the definition and the application of which are generally at different places in the program. Before entering into the translation details of this type of routines, it is convenient to discuss some general ideas about four important subjects related to non-standard routine definition-application mechanisms :

- static pblock information,
- strategy of parameter transmission,
- strategy of result transmission,
- static and dynamic routine transmission.

5.1.1 STATIC PBLOCK INFORMATION

As for a lblock the static pblock informations are calculated in BLOCKTAB during block translation at an entry bnc_b (†). These informations are : $sidsz_b$, $dmrsz_b$, $gcsz_b$, $swostsz_b$, $gcid_b$ and bn_b.

The management of *bn* and *bnc* at each pblock entry and exit is performed by the same compiler-routines *INBLOCK1* and *OUTBLOCK1* as for lblocks. *INBLOCK1* is activated with the parameter bn_{sc}, i.e. the *bn* of the scope block of the pblock entered. This bn_{sc} has been explicitely attached to pblock's by the syntactic analyzer. Also, the compiler-routines *INBLOCK2*, *INBLOCK3* and *OUTBLOCK3* as defined in II.0.4.4 are used in pblocks. A pblock, which is a non-standard routine with parameters, consists of formal parameters and a body of routine. The formal parameters play the role of declarations in the pblock. The body of routine is the body of the pblock and it may be translated as such : however, in order to increase efficiency, when the body of routine is itself a block, this lblock is combined with the pblock of the routine. In such a case :

- $sidsz_b$ and $gcid_b$ take into account not only the formal parameters but also the identifiers (operators) declared in the lblock of the body. More precisely,

$$sidsz_b = sidsz_{b1} + sidsz_{b2}$$

where $sidsz_{b1}$ corresponds to the formal parameters and $sidsz_{b2}$ to the lblock of the body of routine.

- $gcid_b$ points to the following structure :
  - the address-mode pair list for the protection of the formal parameters

---

(†) The suffix '*b*' is used for pblocks properties in order to distinguish them from the properties of actual parameter blocks (II.5.1.2), suffixed with '*a*'.

- a flag *'gcbodyflag'* which usefulness will appear later.
- the address-mode pairs for the protection of the identifiers of the lblock of the body of the routine, if it exists.
- the end of chain for address-mode pair lists.

- $dmrsz_b$, $gcsz_b$, $swostsz_b$ take into account the elaboration of the formal parameters (strict bounds) and of the body of the routine, if this body is combined with the routine pblock.

5.1.2 STRATEGY OF PARAMETER TRANSMISSION

The main problem is that actual parameters have to be elaborated in the environment of the calling block but at the same time the resulting values of these parameters are possessed by the formal parameters (through *SIDST%*) of the pblock of the routine called.

The idea is then to consider the actual parameters forming a fictitious lblock where identifiers corresponding to the formal parameters would be declared. To this lblock, we associate a pseudo-$BLOCK\%_a$ for the elaboration of the actual parameters in their environment. The value of the actual parameters are made to be possessed by the identifiers of the pseudo-$BLOCK\%_a$ by storing them on $SIDST\%_a$ of the pseudo-$BLOCK\%_a$. To the pseudo-$BLOCK\%_a$ correspond static properties calculated during its translation and stored at the entry bnc_a of BLOCKTAB : $sidsz_a$, $gcsz_a$, $swostsz_a$, $gcid_a$ and bn_a.

A high efficiency for parameter transmission is obtained by organizing the pseudo-$BLOCK\%_a$ in such a way it can easily be transformed into the $BLOCK\%_b$ of the routine without moving the values of the actual parameters. This is automatically obtained for the static parts of these parameters : thanks to the mode of the routine available at the call, $SIDST\%_a$ can be given the same structure as $SIDST\%_{b1}$. The solution for the dynamic parts lies in reserving the same amount *totsz* of cells for the static part of pseudo-$BLOCK\%_a$ and of $BLOCK\%_b$

$$totsz = h + sidsz_a + max\ (dmrsz_a + gcsz_a + swostsz_a,\ sidsz_{b2} + dmrsz_b + gcsz_b + swostsz_b)$$

according to <u>fig</u>. 5.1.

The transformation of pseudo-$BLOCK\%_a$ into $BLOCK\%_b$ will be performed at the call once the actual parameters have been calculated in their environment and stored on $SIDST\%_a$. This transformation will in particular change the environment of the actual parameters into the one of the routine. It will affect $H\%_a$ and *DISPLAY%*.

At this point *gcid%* deserves a special attention. In $H\%_a$, $gcid\%_a$ must protect the actual parameters, i.e. $SIDST\%_a$ only ; in $H\%_b$, $gcid\%_b$ must protect $SIDST\%_{b1}$ ($\equiv SIDST\%_a$) and $SIDST\%_{b2}$. The list pointed to by $gcid\%_b$ has the structure explained in II.5.1.1 ; *gcbodyflag* incorporated in this list makes it possible to use the first part of the list $gcid\%_b$ for protecting both $SIDST\%_a$ and $SIDST\%_{b1}$. Hence, $gcid\%_a$ is made equal to $gcid\%_b$; however, the garbage collector must know where to stop the list analysis, either at *gcbodyflag* when it has been called from the pseudo-$BLOCK\%_a$ or at the normal list end, when it is called from $BLOCK\%_b$. For this purpose, *gcbodyflag%* <u>*of*</u> *gcid%* in *H%* of $BLOCK\%_a$ ($BLOCK\%_b$) is used : *gcbodyflag%* is 1 during pseudo-$BLOCK\%_a$ elaboration and it is 0 otherwise.

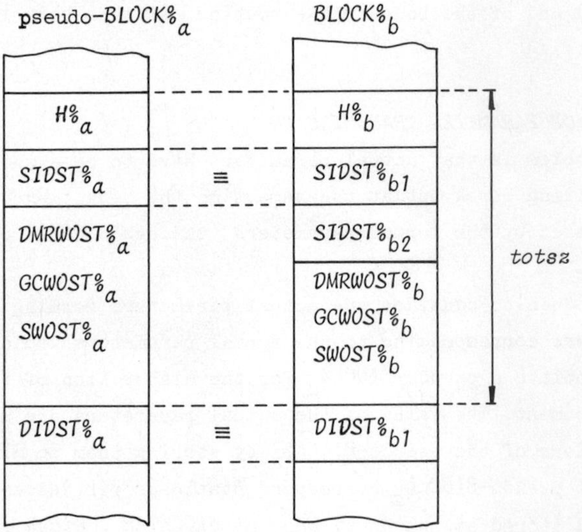

<u>fig</u>. 5.1 Pseudo-*BLOCK%* organization

5.1.3 STRATEGY OF RESULT TRANSMISSION

The definition of a routine and its calls are generally at different places in the program. The routine must be translated independently from the places where it is called. This causes a problem of interface as far as result transmission is concerned. This interface problem is solved by transmitting informations dynamically between the call and the body of the routine. If the result transmission takes place at the call translation, then information is passed on from the body of routine to the call. This information is e.g. the address of the result, saved in a memory cell or a register. If on the other hand the result transmission takes place at the body of routine translation, then informations are passed on from the call to the body of routine. It is the second strategy that has been adopted here. Hence, in addition to the return jump, the informations which are passed on dynamically from the call to the body of routine are :

(1) the current counters *gcc, dmrc, swostc* just before the call is translated ; these counters indicate where to store the result of the routine together with a *dmr* dynamic information and a *gc* protection if necessary.

(2) previsions which, as will be explained later, allow to avoid the copy of the result of a routine in the calling *BLOCK%*, in a number of cases (see II.5.5).

The transmission of run-time information from call to routine is performed by means of the *H%* fields already mentioned in II.0.3.2 : *swostp%, gcp%, dmrp%, flex%, prevflag%* and *retjump%*.

The case of *flex%* is now briefly recalled.

If the result of the routine is a name, information on the use of the name must be transmitted from the call to the body of the routine in order to be able to perform checks of flexibility inside the body. Therefore, at the call, the field *flex%* in *H%* is filled with a flag indicating whether a remanent access will be given to that name or not. When a remanent access will be given (*flex%* = 1), the name must not be subflexible, see I.2.5.2.

Flex% is checked at the level of refslices and refrowings (II.11.3 and II.11.5), for this purpose, the instruction

GEN(<u>checkflexr</u> bncrout§: bncrout,
cadd§ : cadd) {62}

is generated when it appears that the resulting value is a name which might be subflexible and which, according to *TOPST* is involved in the result of a routine : *(flextop <u>of</u> TOPST[topstpm-1] = (<u>dyn</u> bnrout))*. In the instruction *<u>checkflexr</u> :*

-*bncrout§* through *BLOCKTAB%* furnishes *bnrout§* i.e. the bn of the routine. At run-time, *DISPLAY%[bnrout§]* gives access to *flex%* in the *H%* of the routine.

-*cadd§* is the access of the name on which the refslice or refrowrowing applies.

<u>Action</u> :

If *flex% = 1*, this means that the result of the routine will be given a remanent access at the call ; then a run-time alarm is provided if it appears that the name of access *cadd§* is flexible.

5.1.4 STATIC AND DYNAMIC ROUTINE TRANSMISSION

During the translation, the body of routine will be represented in *CONSTAB* by a number of static properties necessary for translating its calls. This *CONSTAB* routine representation consists of :

l_o	address of the translated routine ; l_o is symbolic at translation-time, it must be transformed into a machine address by the loader. For this reason, loader commands are generated in the object code.
bnsc	*bn* of the scope block of the routine
$sidsz_b$ $dmrsz_b$ $gcsz_b$ $swostsz_b$	sizes related to the body of the routine

gcid$_b$ — *gc* information for *SIDST%* of the routine block.

flagstand — telling whether the routine is standard or not.

flagjump — telling whether the routine is a simple jump or not (see deproceduring). Both flags (standard and jump) are used to generate more optimized code during the call of standard routines and procedured jumps.

Formally, the static *CONSTAB* routine representation is characterized by

<u>mode</u> <u>rout</u> = <u>struct</u> (<u>label</u> *lo*,
<u>int</u> *bnsc*, *sidsz*$_b$ *dmrsz*$_b$, *gcsz*$_b$, *swostsz*$_b$, *gcid*$_b$,
<u>bool</u> *flagstand*, *flagjump*).

Dynamically transmitted routines must be dynamically represented in memory (on *RANST%* or on *HEAP%*). The static property *cadd* of such a routine will be of the form ($\underline{\alpha}$ *doublet*) where α is of one of the classes <u>*diriden*</u>, <u>*indiden*</u>, <u>*dirwost*</u> etc ... and the doublet is *bnc.sidc* or *bnc.swostc*. This depends on the way the routine is obtained and the place where it is stored in memory. The memory representation of a routine consists of :

-a pointer to *CONSTAB%* making all *CONSTAB%* information dynamically available at the call.

-a scope information which is the dynamic address of the *BLOCK%* of the scope of the routine. This address is *DISPLAY%*[*bnsc*] calculated at a moment the *BLOCK%* of the scope of the routine is accessible, i.e. at the moment the *cadd* of the routine of the form (<u>*routct*</u> *constabp*) is transformed into the corresponding dynamic routine representation (III.5.4.2).

Formally, the dynamic routine representation is characterized by

<u>mode</u> <u>rout%</u> = <u>struct</u> (<u>int</u> *constabp%*, *scope%*).

5.2 CALL OF STATICALLY TRANSMITTED ROUTINES

<u>Syntax</u>

CALL → call∇ PRIMCALL (ACPAR1 , ACPAR2 , ... , ACPARn)

FORMULA → dformula∇ operator OPERAND1 OPERAND2 |
mformula∇ operator OPERAND

{CALLS and FORMULAS are quite similar : PRIMCALL and operator deliver a routine ; ACPARi and OPERANDi deliver the values of the parameters of the routine. In contrast with PRIMCALL which needs a preelaboration, operator is a terminal giving access to a *SYMBTAB* element where static properties of the routine are found. Below, the translation is based on the syntax of CALL only}.

Translation scheme

1. ρ(PRIMCALL)
2. Prefix actual parameter translation :
   2.1 Static block entry
   2.2 *GEN (inacpar ...)*
3. Actual parameter translation :
   for i to n do
   3.1 ρ(ACPARi)
   3.2 Establishment of the relation of possession
   od
4. *GEN (call ... lreturn)*
5. *GEN (labdef lreturn)*
6. Static block exit
7. Result static properties.

Semantics

Step 1 :

ρ(PRIMCALL)

{At run-time, PRIMCALL results in the routine to be called. After the translation ρ(PRIMCALL), the static properties of the routine appear on *BOST*. They will be denoted *moderout*, *caddrout* ... . In this section we suppose that *caddrout* is of the form *(routct constabp)*. All properties stored within the routine representation in *CONSTAB* are available at compile-time. We also suppose that, according to these properties, the routine is not standard *(flagstand = 0)* ; standard routine calls are treated in II.13.}.

Step 2 : Prefix actual parameter translation :

Step 2.1 : Static block entry :

First of all, the current counters of the calling block are saved in order to be available in step 2.2 :

savebnc := bnc
saveswostc := swostc
savegcc := gcc
savedmrc := dmrc.

INBLOCK1(bn) calculates the *bnc* i.e. bnc_a of the fictitious actual parameter block. During the actual parameter translation (step 3) the block informations $sidsz_a$, $dmrsz_a$, $gcsz_a$ and $swostsz_a$ are calculated in *BLOCKTAB* at the entry bnc_a. These calculations are initialized by *INBLOCK2(bn)* and *INBLOCK3*. $Gicd_a$ is not calculated : as explained above, it is $gcid_b$ which will be used for the gc-protection of $SIDST\%_a$ thanks to *gcbodyflag*.

Step 2.2 :

GEN (inacpar bnca§ : bnc {i.e. bnc_a},
flex§ : flextop of TOPST[topstpm-1],
caddrout§: caddrout,
caddres§ : (dirwost savebnc.savewostc),
gccres§ : savegcc,
dmrcres§ : savedmrc) {50}

-*bnca§* through BLOCKTAB§ gives access to : *sidsza§, dmrsza§, gcsza§, swostsza§* and *bna§*.

-*flex§* has two possible forms :

-(stat 1) or (stat 0) which means that *flex%* of H% of the BLOCK% entered must be set to 1 or 0 respectively.

-(dyn bn) which means that *flex% of* H% of the BLOCK% entered must be set to the value of *flex% of (h%)* RANST%[DISPLAY%[*bn*]] .

-*caddrout§ = (routct constabp§)* ; it gives access in CONSTAB§[*constabp§*] to the static properties of the routine : *lo§, bnsc§, sidszb§, dmrszb§, gcszb§, swostszb§, gcidb§, flagstand§* (here supposed to be 0) and *flagjump§*.

From there :

totsz§ := h + max(sidsza§ + dmrsza§ + gcsza§ + swostsza§,
sidszb§ + dmrszb§ + gcszb§ + swostszb§)

-*caddres§, gccres§* and *dmrcres§* indicate where to copy the result of the call together with a *gc* and *dmr* information if necessary.

- fig. 5.2 illustrates the following actions.

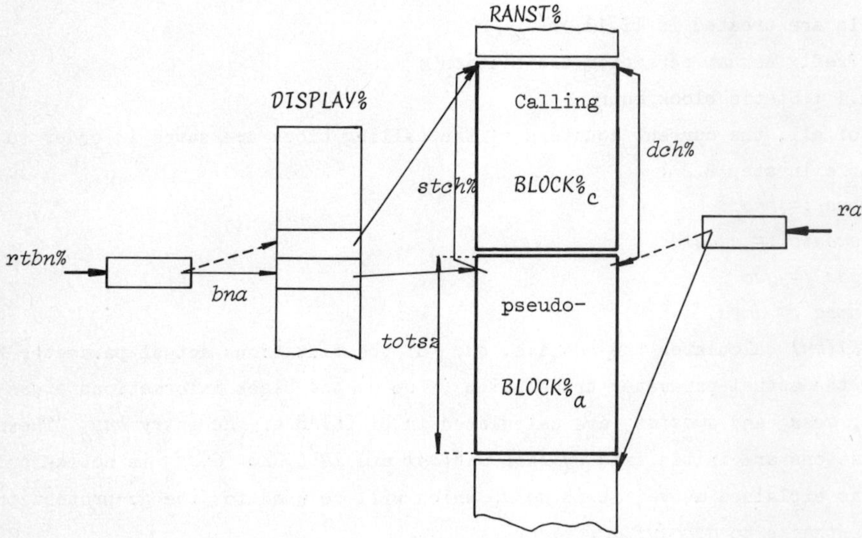

fig. 5.2 Action *inacpar*.

Action 1 :

DISPLAY%[bna§] := ranstpm%.

Action 2 :

ranstpm% +:= totsz§.

{the garbage collector may be called}

Action 3 :

rtbn% := bna§.

Action 4 : Filling in of pseudo-*BLOCK%* heading *H%* :

stch% := dch% := DISPLAY%[bna§-1]

wp% := ranstpm%

bn% := bna§

swostp% := tadd of *caddres§* *gcp% := gccres§* *dmrp% := dmrcres§*	{transformed into absolute addresses through *DISPLAY%[bna§-1]* }

flex% := (class of *flex§* = stat
|*spec* of *flex§*
|*flex%* of *(h%)* RANST%[*DISPLAY%[spec* of *flex§*]]

gcid% := (gcidb§,1)

gcw% := (h + sidsza§ + dmrsza§, gcsza§).

Action 5 :

NILSIDST% (bna§, sidsza§,0).

Action 6 :

NILGCWOST% (bna§, h + sidsza§ + dmrsza§, gcsza§).

Step 3 : Actual parameter translation :

for *i* to *n* do

Step 3.1 :

ρ(ACPARi)

Each parameter is translated in turn. At the end of the translation of a given actual parameter, its static properties appear on *BOST* ; these will be denoted $modeacpar_s$, $caddacpar_s$, $smracpar_s$,... .

Step 3.2 :

Establishment of the relation of possession :

This step performs the relation of possession formal parameter-actual parameter value through the pseudo-$BLOCK\%_a$ mechanism. This is performed by copying the value of the actual parameters in $IDST\%_a$ of the pseudo-$BLOCK\%_a$ which later will be considered $IDST\%_{b1}$. Here, *sidsz* of BLOCKTAB[*bnc*] is controlled thanks to $modeacpar_s$ (it is denoted simply *sidc*).

Case A :

Class of $caddacpar_s$ = dirwost.

Only the static part is copied :

GEN (<u>*ststatacpar*</u> *mode§ : modeacpar*$_s$,
cadds§ : caddacpar$_s$,
caddo§ : (<u>*diriden*</u> *bnc.sidc))* {108}

{see II.2.1, step 3, case B'}

<u>Other cases</u> :

The whole of the value has to be copied :

GEN (<u>*stacpar*</u> *mode§ : modeacpar*$_s$,
cadds§ : caddacpar$_s$,
caddo§ : (<u>*diriden*</u> *bnc.sidc))* {8}

{see II.2.1, step 3, other cases'}

<u>*od*</u>

<u>Step</u> 4 :

After the values of the actual parameters have been stored in *IDST%*$_a$ of the pseudo-*BLOCK%*$_a$, this one is transformed into the *BLOCK%*$_b$ of the routine. This is performed by changing its environment which is the one of the actual parameters into the environment of the routine. Thereafter a jump to the routine body is performed :

GEN (<u>*call*</u> *lreturn§ : lreturn,*
caddrout§: caddrout,
bnca§ : bnc) {52}

-*caddrout§* is here of type *(*<u>*routct*</u> *constabp)*, it gives access at compile-time to the *CONSTAB* routine representation :

-*lo§, bnsc§, sidszb§, dmrszb§, gcszb§, swostszb§, flagstand§, flagjump§,* and *gcidb§*. Here, *flagstand§* and *flagjump§* are supposed to be 0.

-*bnca§* gives access to the pseudo-*BLOCK%*$_a$ information in *BLOCKTAB§ : sidsza§, dmrsza§, gcsza§, swostsza§,* and *bna§*.

<u>Action</u> 1 :

DISPLAY% [*bnsc§+1*] := *DISPLAY%*[*bna§*] .

<u>Action</u> 2 :

rtbn% := bnsc§+1.

<u>Action</u> 3 : Modification of pseudo-*BLOCK%*$_a$ heading *H%*$_a$:

stch% := DISPLAY%[*bnsc§*]
bn% := bnsc§+1
gcw% := (h + sidszb§ + dmrszb§, gcszb§)
retjump% := lreturn§
gcbodyflag% := 0.

<u>Action</u> 4 : Nilling of *SIDST%*$_{b2}$

We recall that *SIDST%*$_b$ = *SIDST%*$_a$ + *SIDST%*$_{b2}$ and that *SIDST%*$_a$ is filled with the actual parameter values ; only *SIDST%*$_{b1}$ has to be nilled :

NILSIDST% (bnsc§+1, sidszb2§, sidsza§).

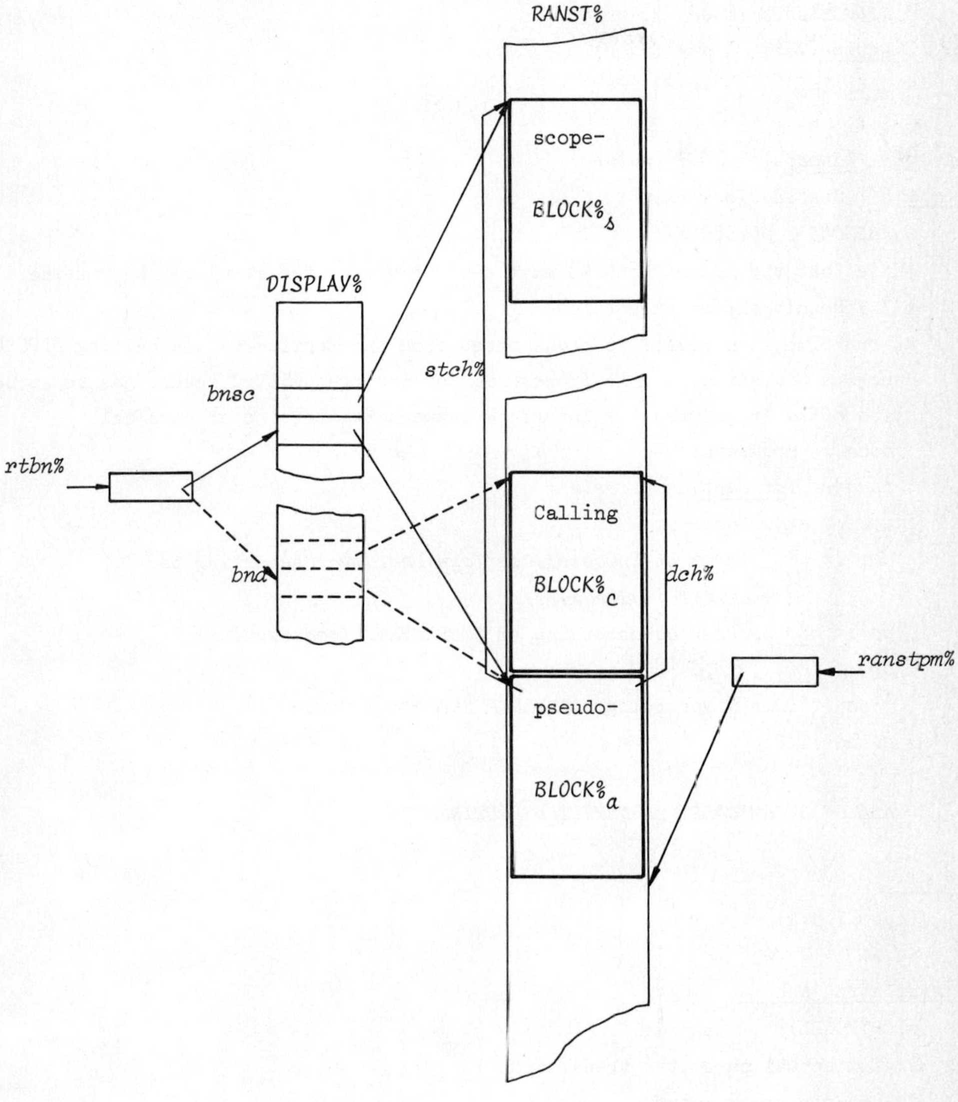

fig. 5.3 Action *call*.

Action 5 :

NILGCWOST% (bnsc§+1, h+sidszb§ + dmrszb§, gcszb§).

Action 6 :

NILDISPLAY% (bnsc§+2, bna§).

Action 7 :

goto lo§.

Step 5 :

GEN (labdef labnb§ : lreturn). {28}

Step 6 : Static block exit :

OUTBLOCK3 ; OUTBLOCK1.

{Note that the dynamic *BLOCK%* exit takes place at the level of the routine.}

Step 7 : Result static properties :

At run-time, the result is transmitted from the routine to the calling *BLOCK%*. Hence, a new set of static properties for the transmitted result has to be set up on *BOST*. It ensures the interface between the routine and the call.

mode := moderesult

cadd := (dirwost bnc.swostc)

smr := bnc.swostc

dmr := nil, (stat bnc.swostc') or (dyn bnc.dmrc) according to *DMRRELEVANT (moderesult)*

gc := nil or bnc.gcc according to *GCRELEVANT (moderesult)*

or := (nil ,0,0,0)

insc := 0 or N according to *SCOPERELEVANT (moderesult)*

outsc := 0 .

5.3 CALL OF DYNAMICALLY TRANSMITTED ROUTINES

Syntax

{see II.5.2}.

Translation scheme

1. ρ(PRIMCALL)
2. Prefix actual parameter translation :
   2.1 Static block entry
   2.2 *GEN (inacpar ...)*
3. Actual parameter translation :
   for i to n do
   3.1 ρ(ACPARi)
   3.2 Establishment of the relation of possession
   od

4. *GEN (checkstand ... ls ...)*
5. *GEN (call ... lreturn ...)*
6. *GEN (labdef ls)*
7. *GEN (standcall1 ... lreturn ...)*
8. *GEN (labdef lreturn)*
9. Static block exit
10. Result static properties.

Semantics

Step 1 :

ρ(PRIMCALL)

{At run-time, PRIMCALL results in the routine to be called ; its static properties appear on *BOST* after the translation ρ(PRIMCALL). These properties will be denoted *moderout, caddrout*, ... In this section, we assume that *caddrout* is not of the form *(routct constabp)*. This means that which routine will be called is not known at compile-time. The *CONSTAB* routine representation is not available. Instructions must be generated to interpret at run-time this *CONSTAB%* routine representation.}

N.B : According to [1] the elaborations of PRIMCALL and ACPARi are serial ; hence side-effects destroying the dynamic routine representation may take place during the elaboration of ACPARi ; this may invalidate the use of *caddrout* for accessing the routine. Clearly, such a destruction may only appear if the dynamic routine representation is superseded by an assignation, which is not possible if *class of caddrout = dirwost* or if *dereforout = 0*. In the other cases the routine has to be copied on *WOST%* in order to avoid side-effects :

```
GEN (stwost3 mode§  : moderout,
             cadds§ : caddrout,
             caddo§ : (dirwost bnc.swostc))      {3}
```

Step 2 : Prefix actual parameter translation :

Step 2.1 : Static block entry :

{see II.5.2 step 2.1}

Step 2.2 :

```
GEN (inacpar bnca§     : bnc,
             flex§     : flextop of TOPST[ topstpm-1],
             caddrout§: caddrout,
             caddres§ : (dirwost savebnc.saveswostc),
             gccres§  : savegcc,
             dmrcres§ : savedmrc)                  {50}
```

-The actions of *inacpar* have been described in II.5.2, step 2.2 for *caddrout§* of the form *(routct constabp)*. Here, *caddrout§* is not of this form, hence, it is through *CONSTAB%*, i.e. at run-time, that *caddrout§* gives access to *lo%*, *bnsc%, sidszb%, dmrszb%, gcszb%, swostszb%* and *gcidb%* ; from there

totsz% := h + max (sidsza§ + dmrsza§ + gcsza§ + swostsza§,

sidszb% + dmrszb% + gcszb% + swostszb%).

Action 1 :

DISPLAY%[bna§] := ranstpm%.

Action 2 :

ranstpm% +:= totsz%.

Action 3 :

rtbn% := bna§.

Action 4 :

stch% := dch% := DISPLAY%[bna§-1]

wp% := ranstpm%

bn% := bna§

swostp% := tadd of caddres§ |

gcp% := gccres§ | {transformed into absolute addresses through *DISPLAY%[bna§-1]* }

dmrp% := dmrcres§ |

flex% := {see II.5.2}

gcid% := (gcidb%,1)

gcw% := (h + sidsza§ + dmrsza§, gcsza§).

Action 5 :

NILSIDST% (bna§, sidsza§,0).

Action 6 :

NILGCWOST% (bna§, h + sidsza§ + dmrsza§, gcsza§).

Step 3 : Actual parameter translation :

for i to n do

Step 3.1 :

ρ(ACPARi).

{see II.5.2, step 3.1}.

Step 3.2 : Establishment of the relation of possession :

{see II.5.2, step 3.2}.

od.

Step 4 :

GEN (checkstand labnb§ : ls,

cadd§ : caddrout) {34}

-*cadd§*, at run-time, gives access to the *CONSTAB%* routine representation where *flagstand%* is found.

-Action :

flagstand% is checked ; if it is 1, a jump to *labnb§* is performed. This is necessary because, for obvious reasons of efficiency, standard routines are not entered through the general call mechanism.

Step 5 :

GEN (call lreturn§ : lreturn,
caddrout§: caddrout,
bnca§ : bnc) {52}

The action of *call* has been described in II.5.2, step 4, for *caddrout = (routct constabp)*. Here *caddrout* is not of this form ; this has two implications :

- it is through CONSTAB%, at run-time, that *caddrout* gives access to *lo%* ...
- the DISPLAY% is not necessarily representative of the environment of the routine, it must be updated.

Action 1 :

DISPLAY%[bnsc%+1] := DISPLAY%[bna§].

Action 2 :

rtbn% := bnsc%+1.

Action 3 :

UPDDISPLAY% (bnsc%, scope%).

{*scope%* is the dynamic scope found in the dynamic routine representation ; it is a pointer to *H%* of the scope *BLOCK%* of the routine, in other words, *scope%* characterizes the environment of the routine}.

Action 4 : Modifications of pseudo-$BLOCK\%_a$ heading $H\%_a$:

stch%:= DISPLAY% [bnsc%]
bn% := [bnsc%+1]
gcw%:= (h + sidszb% + dmrszb%, gcszb%)
retjump% := lreturn§
gcbodyflag% := 0.

Action 5 : Nilling of $SIDST\%_{b2}$:

NILSIDST% (bnsc%+1, sidszb2%, sidsza§).

Action 6 :

NILGCWOST% (bnsc%+1, h + sidszb% + dmrszb%, gcszb%).

Action 7 :

NILDISPLAY% (bnsc%+2, bna§).

Action 8 :

goto lo%.

Step 6 :

GEN (labdef labnb§ : ls). {28}

Step 7 :

GEN (standcall1 lreturn§ : lreturn,
n§ : n,
bnca§ : bnc,
caddrout§ : caddrout,
cadd1§ : cadd1,
... ...
caddn§ : caddn) {55}

-*cadd1, ..., caddn* are the addresses of the actual parameters stored on $IDST\%_a$, they have the form *(diriden, bnc.sidc)*.

-Action :

standcall1 action is similar to *standcall* action explained in II.13 ; the main differences are

-the parameter information is more dynamic here

-after the standard call, the pseudo-$BLOCK\%_a$ must be deleted and the result transmitted to the calling *BLOCK%*.

Step 8 :

GEN (labdef labnb§ : lreturn) {28}

Step 9 : Static block exit :

{see II.5.2, step 6}.

Step 10 : Result static properties :

{see II.5.2, step 7}.

5.4 ROUTINE DENOTATION

Syntax

ROUTDEN → routden∇ (FORPAR1, ... , FORPARn) : ROUTBODY

FORPARi → FDECLARERi fideni

{With fideni, a *SYMBTAB* entry is associated ; with routden∇, *bnsc* is associated, it represents the static scope of the routine made explicit by the syntactic analyzer}.

Translation scheme

1. *GEN (jump l)*
2. *GEN (labdef lo)*
3. Static block entry
4. *for i to n do*
   - 4.1 ρ(FORPARi)
   - 4.2 Formal parameter static properties
   - 4.3 *GEN (checkformal ...)*

   od
5. ρ(ROUTBODY)
6. *GEN (return ...)*
7. *GEN (labdef l)*
8. Static block exit
9. Routine static properties
   - 9.1 *CONSTAB* routine representation
   - 9.2 *BOST* routine properties.

Semantics

Step 1 :

GEN (jump labnb§ : l) {27}

Action :

An absolute jump around the routine is performed ; this is only necessary if the text of the translated routine is stored in the same stream as the text of the translated program where it appears.

Step 2 :

GEN (labdef labnb§ : lo) {28}

{*lo* represents the entry point of the routine}.

Step 3 :

INBLOCK1(bnsc) ; INBLOCK2(bnsc) ; INBLOCK3.

Step 4 :

for i to n do

Step 4.1 :

ρ(FORPARi)(†)

Each formal parameter is translated in turn. At the end of ρ(FORPARi) the static properties of the bounds of the corresponding formal declarer appear on *BOST*. They will be denoted *caddl, smrl, ... caddn, smrn, ...* .

Step 4.2 : Formal parameter static properties :

Conceptually, the situation is analogous to identity declaration except that here actual parameters have been elaborated at the call and their values are already stored on *SIDST%* of the routine *BLOCK%*. According to this, the following static properties of the formal parameters are stored in *SYMBTAB* :

mode := mode of FDECLARER

cadd := (diriden bnc.sidsz of BLOCKTAB[*bnc*] *)*

scope := (bn,0) or (0,0) according to *SCOPERELEVANT (mode of* FDECLARER)

{see I.2.5.1.d (7)}.

These properties will be referred to as *modefiden, caddfiden, ...* . The static management of *gcid* in *BLOCKTAB* consists in adding the pair *caddfiden-modefiden* to the chain if, according to *GCRELEVANT (modefiden)*, the formal identifier risks to give access to the *HEAP%*. After the last formal parameter has been treated, *gcbodyflag* is added at the end of the chain.

Step 4.3 :

```
GEN (checkformal mode§  : modefiden,
                 cadd§  : caddfiden,
                 n§     : n,
```

(†) For reasons of simplicity, the implementation of gommas is not described ; note however that the pseudo-block mechanism allows to make this implementation in an efficient way. Gommas do no longer exist in ALGOL 68 revised.

caddl§ : caddl,

...

caddn§ : caddn) {60}

{see II.2.1, step 5}

od .

Step 5 :

ρ(ROUTBODY)

{The body of the routine is translated as a normal unitary clause, with the exception that if this clause is a lblock, it is merged with the pblock (body of routine) and this for reasons of efficiency. The merging is easily obtained by inhibiting in the lblock translation all steps except ρ(BLOCKBODY). After the translation ρ(ROUTBODY), the static properties of the result of the routine appear on *BOST*. They will be denoted *moderes, caddres* ... .

Step 6 :

GEN (return moderes§ : moderes,
caddres§ : caddres,
bnbody§ : bn) {53}

-*bnbody§*, at run-time and through *DISPLAY%*[*bnbody§*] gives access to the *H%* of the *BLOCK%* of the routine. In this *H%*, information set up at the call is found : *swostp%, dmrp%, gcp%, retjump%* and *dch%*. The first three indicate where to copy the result in the calling *BLOCK%* ; *dch%* gives access to *H%* of this calling *BLOCK%* and hence to *bn%* of this *BLOCK%*.

Action 1 : Scope checking :

If the scope of the value is smaller or equal to the scope of the routine, an error message is printed ; note that this action can be avoided in many cases by a static analysis of the property *scoperes* (I.2.5.1).

Action 2 : Result transmission :

The result of the routine, if it exists, is copied from the routine *BLOCK%* into the calling *BLOCK%* at the address *swostp%*. At the end of the copy, *ranstpm%* points to the first free cell in the calling *BLOCK%*. Whether a *gc* and/or *dmr* information has to be constructed in the calling *BLOCK%* from *gcp%* and/or *dmrp%* is based on the mode of the result *(GCRELEVANT, DMRRELEVANT)* ; this ensures the interface with the call.

Action 3 : *DISPLAY%* updating :

DISPLAY% is reset to the state it had just before the routine was called. This can be done thanks to the *dch%* of the *BLOCK%* of the routine which gives access to the *stch%* of the calling *BLOCK%*. *Rtbn%* is reset to the *bn%* of that *BLOCK%*. Note that it is possible to avoid *bn%* to be stored in *H%* of *BLOCK%*'s, but in such a case the *bn* of the calling block is no longer accessible from the body of routine. Then, *DISPLAY%* updating must be delayed up to the level of the call, after the return jump has been elaborated. For this purpose an object instruction

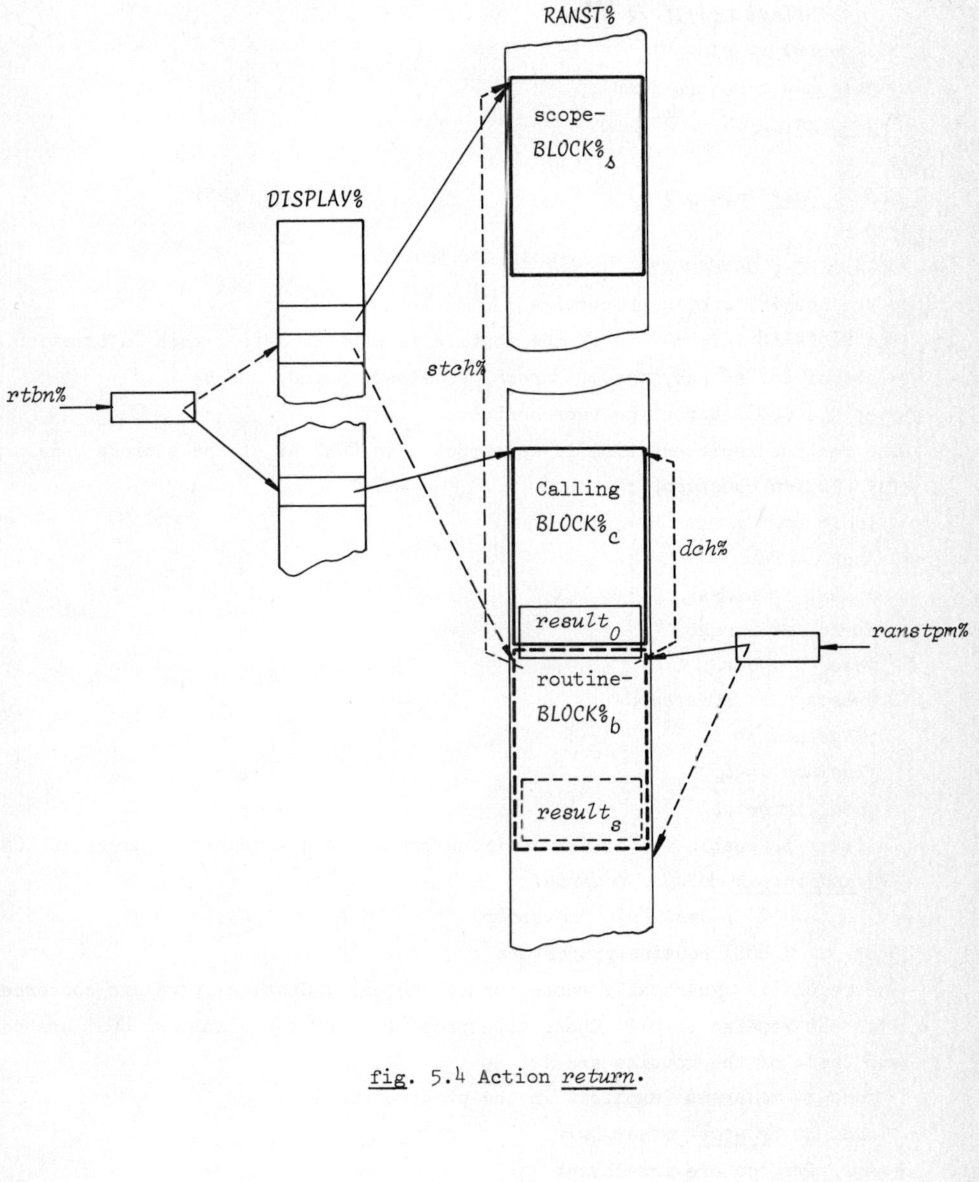

fig. 5.4 Action *return*.

having the *bn* of the calling block as a parameter must be generated at the call.

x% := dch% __of__ (h%) RANST%[DISPLAY%[bnbody§]]

g% := bn% __of__ (h%) RANST%[x%]

UPDDISPLAY% (g%, x%)

DISPLAY% [g%+1] := __nil__

rtbn% := g%.

__Action__ 4 : Return jump :

__goto__ retjump%.

__Step__ 7 :

GEN (__labdef__ labnb§ : l) {28}

__Step__ 8 :

OUTBLOCK3 ; OUTBLOCK1.

__Step__ 9 : Routine static properties :

The BLOCKTAB information of the routine is now complete ; this information consists of *lo, sidszb, gcszb, dmrszb, swostszb, gcidb,* and *bnb.*

__Step__ 9.1 CONSTAB routine representation

The routine representation is constructed in CONSTAB at the address *constabp :*

(__of__ CONSTAB[constabp] :

lo := lo,

bnsc := bnsc,

$sidsz_b$:= sidszb,

$dmrsz_b$:= dmrszb,

$gcsz_b$:= gcszb,

$swostsz_b$:= swostszb,

flagstand := 0,

flagjump := 0,

$gcid_b$:= gcidb)

In order to enable the loader to transform *lo* into a machine address in CONSTAB§ :

GEN(__updconstab__ mode§ : moderout,

constabp§ : constabp) {33}

__Step__ 9.2 : BOST routine properties :

The result is dynamically passed on to the call. Statically we are concerned here with the routine itself. The static properties of the result on BOST are deleted and those of the routine are set up :

mode := moderout {explicit in the program text}

cadd := (__routct__ constabp)

smr, dmr, gc are irrelevant

or := (__nil__, 0,0,0)

scope := (bnsc, bnsc).

5.5 PREVISIONS

As it has been said in II.5.2 (strategy of result transmission), a solution has been chosen where result transmission takes place at the translation of body of routine. Information on result transmission is passed on dynamically from call to body of routine using *H%*. Previsions for the result can be implemented by transmitting the flag *prevflag%* from the call to the routine through *H%* of the routine ; at the translation of the routine, this flag is dynamically retrieved. Several cases have to be considered :

(1) *prevflag%* = 1, this indicates that the result will be directly assigned or used as an actual parameter after the call.

(1.1) The result is such that it cannot enter into a register. In this case, instead of copying the result in the calling *BLOCK%*, only the address of this result is copied. At the call, the access management gives rise, for the result, to the access *(indwost bnc.swostc)* ; it is this indirect access which will be used to copy the result directly in its final location thus avoiding an extra copy. What the storage of the indirect address in the calling *BLOCK%* is concerned, *swostp%* *dmrp%* and *gcp%* of the *H%* of the routine *BLOCK%* are used as for storing the result itself.

(1.2) The result is such that it can enter into a register. The copy of the result is as quick as the one of its address ; *prevflag%* is disregarded, the result is copied in the calling *BLOCK%*.

(2) *prevflag%* = 0, i.e. the handling of the result after the call is not a simple copy ; the result is copied in the calling *BLOCK%* where it can be handled without further precautions.

Remark on the use of registers for result transmission

The handling of results of routines has similarities with the handling of values furnished by choice constructions (conditional clause ...) : such constructions furnish one value which may however result from several different functions ; which function is elaborated and furnishes the result, is not known at compile-time. In I.2.3.4 it has been shown how, in case of choice constructions, the generation of special instructions *loadreg* and *storereg* allows to reintroduce the use of registers when they are available. The same is true in case of routine calls :

(1) When the result can enter into a register, the instruction *(loadreg caddresult)* is generated in the routine after result calculation and the instruction *(storereg caddresult)* is generated at each call just after the return label. In this way, when a register is available, the result transmission is performed through this register without extra storage.

(2) When an indirect address is transmitted, the same process applies to the indirect address, such that the address transmission is performed through a register without extra storage.

5.6 COMPARISON BETWEEN LBLOCKS AND PBLOCKS

In this section, the object programs for lblocks and pblocks are compared. The lblock contains a list of declarations and the block body BLOCKBODY. For the sake of simplicity only identity declarations IDEDECi are considered and these declarations are supposed to be grouped at the beginning of the lblock. An IDEDECi consists of a formal declarer FDECLARERi, an identifier IDENi and an actual parameter ACPARi. For pblocks, the four constituents BLOCKBODY, FDECLARERi, IDENi and ACPARi are divided among the call and the routine denotation.

In the call we find ACPARi, whereas in the routine denotation we find FORPARi (which plays exactly the role of FDECLARERi and IDENi in lblocks) and ROUTBODY (which is analogous to BLOCKBODY). Clearly, the constituent PRIMCALL has not its counterpart in lblocks where the definition and application of the block is the same construction. Below, the object programs (in the form of skeletons) of both lblocks and pblocks are displayed. This may give a deeper insight into the object code generation of blocks.

Lblock	Pblock	

<u>Syntax</u>
LBLOCK → lblock∇ IDEDEC1 ...
    IDEDECn BLOCKBODY
IDEDECi → idedec∇ FDECLARERi
    IDENi = ACPARi
<u>Semantics</u>
GEN (<u>*inblock*</u> ...)
 	
<u>*for*</u> *i* <u>*to*</u> *n* <u>*do*</u>
ρ(FDECLARERi)
ρ(ACPARi)
GEN (<u>*stacpar*</u> ...)
GEN (<u>*checkformal*</u>)
<u>*od*</u>
ρ(BLOCKBODY)
 	
GEN(<u>*outblock*</u>)
	<u>Syntax</u>
	CALL → call∇ PRIMCALL (
	    ACPAR1, ACPAR2, ...,
	    ACPARn)
	<u>Semantics</u>
	GEN (<u>*inacpar*</u>)
	
	<u>*for*</u> *i* <u>*to*</u> *n* <u>*do*</u>
	    ρ(ACPARi)
	    GEN (<u>*stacpar*</u> ...)
	<u>*od*</u>
	GEN (<u>*call*</u> ...)
	
	GEN (<u>*labdef*</u> *lreturn*)
		<u>Syntax</u>
		ROUTDEN → routden∇ (FORPAR1,
		FORPAR2, ..., FORPARn) : ROUTBODY
		FORPARi → FDECLARERi fideni
		
		<u>Semantics</u>
		    GEN (<u>*jump*</u> *l*)
		    GEN (<u>*labdef*</u> *lo*)
		
		        <u>*for*</u> *i* <u>*to*</u> *n* <u>*do*</u>
		            ρ(FORPARi)
		        GEN (<u>*checkformal*</u>)
		        <u>*od*</u>
		        ρ(ROUTBODY)
		    GEN (<u>*return*</u>)
		    GEN (<u>*labdef*</u> *l*)

6. *NON-STANDARD ROUTINES WITHOUT PARAMETERS*

6.1 *DEPROCEDURING OF STATICALLY TRANSMITTED ROUTINES*

Syntax

DEPROC → deproc∇ DEPROCCOERCEND

{deproc∇ represents the prefix marker corresponding to the coercion 'deproceduring' made explicit by the syntactic analyzer} .

Translation scheme

1. ρ(DEPROCCOERCEND)
2. *GEN (deproc ... lreturn ...)*
3. *GEN (labdef ... lreturn ...)*
4. Result static properties.

Semantics

Step 1 :

ρ(DEPROCCOERCEND).

{At run-time, DEPROCCOERCEND results in a routine without parameters. After the translation ρ(DEPROCCOERCEND), the static properties of the routine appear on *BOST*. They will be denoted *moderout, caddrout* ... . In this section we suppose *caddrout* is of the form *(routct constabp)*. All properties stored within the routine representation in *CONSTAB* are available at compile-time. We also suppose that according to these properties the routine is neither standard *(flagstand* = 0*)* nor a procedured jump *(flagjump* = 0*)*. Standard routines are treated in II.13 and procedured jump in II.7}.

Step 2 :

{What has been said about non standard routines with parameters remains valid here except that no pseudo-*BLOCK%* will be organized for actual parameters. The routine *BLOCK%* will be directly organized by the call step}.

```
GEN (deproc lreturn§  : lreturn,
            caddrout§ : caddrout,
            caddres§  : (dirwost bnc.swostc),
            gccres§   : gcc,
            dmrcres§  : dmrc,
            flex§     : flextop of TOPST[ topstpm-1] )  {56}
```

-*caddrout§* = *(routct constabp§)*, it gives access in *CONSTAB§*[*constabp§*] to the static properties of the routine :

lo§
bnsc§
sidszb§
dmrszb§
gcszb§
swostszb§
flagstand§ {here supposed to be 0}
flagjump§ {here supposed to be 0}
gcidb§

-*caddres§*, *gccres§* and *dmrcres§* indicate where to copy the result together with a *gc* and *dmr* information if necessary. Note that through BLOCKTAB, *hadd* <u>of</u> *caddres§* gives access to *bn* of the calling block denoted *bn§*.

-*flex§* : see II.5.2, step 2.2

<u>Action</u> 1 :

savedispbn% := DISPLAY%[bn§]

DISPLAY% [bnsc§+1] := ranstpm%.

<u>Action</u> 2 :

ranstpm%+:= h + sidszb§ + dmrszb§ + gcszb§ + swostszb§

{the garbage collector may be called}.

<u>Action</u> 3 :

rtbn% := bnsc§+1.

<u>Action</u> 4 : Filling of routine BLOCK% heading H% :

stch% := DISPLAY%[bnsc§]
dch% := savedispbn%
up% := ranstpm%
bn% := bnsc§+1
gcid% := (gcidb§,0)
gcw% := (h + sidszb§ + dmrszb§, gcszb§)
swostp% := tadd <u>of</u> *caddres§* | {transformed into
gcp% := gccres§ | absolute addresses
dmrp% := dmrcres§ | through *DISPLAY%[savedispbn%]* }
flex% {see II.5.2}
retjump% := lreturn§.

<u>Action</u> 5 : Nilling of *SIDST%*

{see II.5.2, step 4, action 4 with *sidsza§* = 0 and *sidszb§* = *sidszb2§*.}

NILSIDST% (bnsc§+1, sidszb§,0).

<u>Action</u> 6 :

NILGCWOST% (bnsc§+1, h + sidszb§ + dmrszb§, gcszb§).

<u>Action</u> 7 :

NILDISPLAY% (bnsc§+2, bn§).

<u>Action</u> 8 :

<u>goto</u> *lo§.*

Step 3 :

GEN (labdef labnb§ : lreturn) {28}

Step 4 : Result static properties :

{see II.5.2, step 7}.

6.2 DEPROCEDURING OF DYNAMICALLY TRANSMITTED ROUTINES

Syntax

{see II.6.1}.

Translation scheme

1. ρ(DEPROCCOERCEND)
2. *GEN(checkstand ... ls ...)*
3. *GEN(checklab ... lg ...)*
4. *GEN(deproc ... lreturn ...)*
5. *GEN(labdef ls)*
6. *GEN(standdeproc ... lreturn ...)*
7. *GEN(labdef lg)*
8. *GEN(callab ...)*
9. *GEN(labdef lreturn)*
10. Result static properties.

Semantics

Step 1 :

ρ(DEPROCCOERCEND)

{comment similar to II.5.3, step 1 excluding NB}.

Step 2 :

GEN(checkstand labnb§ : ls,
cadd§ : caddrout) {34}

{see II.5.3, step 4}.

Step 3 :

GEN(checklab labnb§ : lg,
cadd§ : caddrout) {36}

-*cadd§*, at run-time, gives access to the *CONSTAB%* routine representation where *flagjump%* is found.

Action :

flagjump% is checked ; if it is 1, a jump to *labnb§* is performed. The reason of this is that, for the sake of efficiency, procedured jumps are treated in a special way {II.7}.

<u>Step</u> 4 :

GEN(<u>deproc</u> lreturn§ : lreturn,
caddrout§ : caddrout,
caddres§ : (<u>dirwost</u> bnc.swostc),
gccres§ : gcc,
dmrcres§ : dmrc,
flex§ : flextop <u>of</u> TOPST[topstpm-1]) {56}

-The action of <u>deproc</u> has been described in II.6.1, step 2 for *caddrout* = *(<u>routct</u> constabp)*. Here *caddrout* is not of this form, this has two implications :

-it is at run-time, through *CONSTAB%* that *caddrout§* gives access to *lo%* ...

-the *DISPLAY%* is not necessarily representative of the environment of the routine ; it must be updated.

<u>Action</u> 1 :

savedispbn% := DISPLAY%[bn§]
DISPLAY%[bnsc%+1] := ranstpm%.

<u>Action</u> 2 :

ranstpm% +:= h + sidszb% + dmrszb% + gcszb% + swostszb%
{the garbage collector may be called}.

<u>Action</u> 3 :

rtbn% := bnsc%+1.

<u>Action</u> 4 :

UPDDISPLAY% (bnsc%, scope%)
{ *scope%* is the scope of the routine available in its dynamic representation}.

<u>Action</u> 5 : Filling of routine *BLOCK%* heading *H%* :

stch% := DISPLAY%[bnsc%]
dch% := savedispbn%
wp% := ranstpm%
bn% := bnsc%+1
gcid% := (gcidb%,0)
gcw% := (h+sidszb%+dmrszb%, gcszb%)
swostp% := tadd <u>of</u> caddres§
gcp% := gccres§
dmrp% := dmrcres§

{ transformed into absolute addresses through *DISPLAY%[savedispbn%]* } (applies to the three lines above)

flex% := {see II.5.2}
retjump% := lreturn§.

<u>Action</u> 6 :

NILSIDST% (bnsc%+1, sidszb%,0).

<u>Action</u> 7 :

NILGCWOST% (bnsc%+1, h+sidszb%+dmrszb%, gcszb%).

<u>Action</u> 8 :

NILDISPLAY% (bnsc%+2, bn§).

<u>Action</u> 9 :

<u>goto</u> lo%.

<u>Step</u> 5 :

GEN(<u>labdef</u> labnb§ : ls) {28}

<u>Step</u> 6 :

GEN(<u>standdeproc</u> lreturn§ : lreturn,
caddrout§: caddrout,
caddres§ : (<u>dirwost</u>, bnc.swostc),
gccres§ : gcc,
dmrcres§ : dmrc,
flex§ : {see II.5.2}) {57}

{A standard routine without parameters is called, this will be described in II.13}.

<u>Step</u> 7 :

GEN(<u>labdef</u> labnb§ : lg) {28}

<u>Step</u> 8 :

GEN(<u>callab</u> bnc§ : bnc,
caddrout§ : caddrout) {58}

{This instruction is explained in II.7.3}.

<u>Step</u> 9 :

GEN(<u>labdef</u> labnb§ : lreturn). {28}

<u>Step</u> 10 : Result static properties :

{see II.5.2, step 7}.

6.3 PROCEDURING (BODY OF ROUTINE WITHOUT PARAMETERS)

<u>Syntax</u>

PROC → proc∇ ROUTBODY

{proc∇ represents the prefix marker corresponding to the coercion 'proceduring' made explicit by the syntactic analyzer}.

<u>Translation scheme</u>

1. *GEN(<u>jump</u> l)*
2. *GEN(<u>labdef</u> lo)*
3. Static block entry
4. ρ(ROUTBODY)
5. *GEN(<u>return</u> ...)*
6. *GEN(<u>labdef</u> l)*
7. Static block exit
8. Routine static properties :
   8.1 *CONSTAB* routine representation
   8.2 *BOST* routine properties.

Semantics

{The translation is identical to the one of II.5.4 on routine denotation, except that step 4 on formal parameters is absent here.}

6.4 ANOTHER TRANSLATION SCHEME

One may easily make the following remark about the actual translation scheme of non-standard routines without parameters. A number of informations about the body of routine (such as $sidsz_b$, $dmrsz_b$, $gcsz_b$, *bnsc* etc ...) may only be dynamically accessible at the call while they are statically accessible at the body of routine. The question is then : is it possible to defer all run-time actions from the call to the body of routine, where all these routine informations are statically accessible? Thus, one would increase the run-time efficiency of the call-body of routine interface. The answer is positive, but only in the case of routines without parameters. If parameters are involved then e.g. the calculation of *totsz* is necessary at the level of the call, to be able to store dynamic parts of actual parameters.
In case of routines without parameters, the only routine informations which may be dynamically accessible and which use may not be deferred to the body of routine are :

lo
bnsc
flagstand
flagjump

Thus, the *CONSTAB* routine representation may reduce to these four informations. Besides an increase of run-time efficiency in the case of dynamically transmitted routines without parameters, the new translation scheme optimizes the size of the object program, since more run-time actions are associated with the body of routine and are not repeated at each call.

In the description of II.6.1 to II.6.3, the handling of routine-call without parameters has been treated as a particular case of routine-call with parameters, by analogy. Below a skeletal description of a second translation scheme for routines without parameters is given where the handling of dynamically accessible information at the call is deferred to the body of routine.
Note that the run-time actions as such are not different from those used in the actual translation of non-standard routines without parameters. What is different is the way the actions are divided among the call and the body of routine.

Actually, this scheme is not implemented for proceduring and deproceduring only for historical reasons.
It is however used in the translation of bounds of mode declarations (II.8) and dynamic replications in formats (II.9).

6.4.1 DEPROCEDURING1 OF STATICALLY TRANSMITTED ROUTINES

Syntax

{see II.6.1}.

Translation scheme

1. ρ(DEPROCCOERCEND)
2. *GEN(deproc1 ... lreturn ...)*
3. *GEN(labdef lreturn)*
4. Result static properties.

Semantics

The translation is exactly the one of II.6.1 except that *GEN(deproc ...)* is replaced by *GEN(deproc1 ...)* :

Step 2 :

GEN(deproc1 : lreturn§ : lreturn,
caddrout§: caddrout,
caddres§ : (dirwost bnc.swostc),
gccres§ : gcc,
dmrcres§ : dmrc,
flex§ : flextop of TOPST[topstpm-1]) {109}

The action of this instruction limits itself to fill *H%* of the *BLOCK%* of the routine with information available at the call and to jump to the routine body :
-*hadd of caddres*, through *BLOCKTAB§*, gives access to *bn§*, ... i.e. the *bn* of the calling block.

Action 1 :

ranstpm% +:= h

{the garbage collector may be called}.

Action 2 : Filling of *BLOCK%* heading *H%* :

dch% := DISPLAY%[bn§]
swostp% := tadd of caddres§
gcp% := gccres§
dmrp% := dmrcres§
{transformed into absolute addresses through *DISPLAY%[bn§]* }
flex% := {see II.5.2}
retjump% := lreturn§.

Action 3 :

goto lo§.

6.4.2 DEPROCEDURING1 OF DYNAMICALLY TRANSMITTED ROUTINES

Syntax

{see II.6.1}.

Translation scheme

1. ρ(DEPROCCOERCEND)
2. *GEN(checkstand ... ls ...)*
3. *GEN(checklab ... lg ...)*
4. *GEN(deproc1 ... lreturn ...)*
5. *GEN(labdef ls)*
6. *GEN(standdeproc ... lreturn ...)*
7. *GEN(labdef lg)*
8. *GEN(callab ...)*
9. *GEN(labdef lreturn)*
10. Result static properties.

Semantics

The translation is exactly the one of II.6.2 except that *GEN(deproc ...)* is replaced by *GEN(deproc1 ...) :*

Step 4 :

```
GEN(deproc1 lreturn§  : lreturn,
            caddrout§ : caddrout,
            caddres§  : (dirwost bnc.swostc),
            gccres§   : gcc,
            dmrcres§  : dmrc,
            flex§     : flextop of TOPST [ topstpm-1] )  {109}
```

-The action of *deproc1* has been described in II.6.4.1 for *caddrout = (routct constabp)*. Here *caddrout* is not of this form ; this has two implications :

-the *CONSTAB* routine representation is now available through *CONSTAB%* i.e. at run-time. Note that only the properties *lo%* and *bnsc%* are needed here.

-the *DISPLAY%* is not necessarily representative of the environment of the routines ; it must be updated.

Action 1 :

ranstpm% +:= h

{the garbage collector may be called}.

Action 2 : Filling *BLOCK%* heading *H%* :

dch% := DISPLAY%[bn§]

swostp% := tadd of caddres§

gcp% := gccres§

dmrp% := dmrcres§

flex% := {see II.5.2}

retjump% := lreturn§ .

Action 3 :

UPDDISPLAY% (bnsc%, scope%).

Action 4 :

goto lo%.

6.4.3 PROCEDURING1

Syntax

{see II.6.3}.

Tanslation scheme

1. *GEN(jump l)*
2. *GEN(labdef lo)*
3. Static block entry
4. *GEN(inbody ...)*
5. ρ(ROUTBODY)
6. *GEN(return ...)*
7. *GEN(labdef l)*
8. Static block exit
9. Routine static properties :
   9.1 *CONSTAB* routine representation
   9.2 *BOST* routine properties.

Semantics

Compared with II.6.3, only step 4 is new ; it completes the actions of *deproc1* with respect to those of *deproc* :

Step 4 :

GEN(inbody bncbody§: bnc) {110}

-*bncbody§* is a *BLOCKTAB§* entry where the following information is found : *sidszb§, dmrszb§, gcszb§, swostszb§, gcidb§* and *bnb§*{*bnsc§ = bnb§-1*}.

-*inbody* has the same actions as *deproc* (II.6.1, step 2) except for actions which have been performed by *inproc1* at the call.

Action 1 :

save% := ranstpm% - h

ranstpm% +:= sidszb§ + dmrszb§ + gcszb§ + swostszb§

{The garbage collector may be called}.

Action 2 :

NILDISPLAY (bnsc§+2, rtbn%).

Action 3 :

DISPLAY%[bnsc§+1] := save%.

Action 4 :

rtbn% := bnsc§ + 1.

Action 5 :

(of (h%) RANST%[DISPLAY%[bnsc§+1]] :
stch% := DISPLAY%[bnsc§],
wp% := ranstpm%,
bn% := bnsc§+1,
gcid% := (gcidb§, 0),
gcw% := (h + sidszb§ + dmrszb§, gcszb§)).

Action 6 :

NILSIDST% (bnsc§ +1, sidszb§, 0)

Action 7 :

NILGCWOST% (bnsc§+1, h + sidszb§ + dmrszb§, gcszb§).

7. PROCEDURED JUMPS

7.1 GENERALITIES

As mentioned in II.4, the dynamic label transmission passes through the proceduring-deproceduring mechanism. Implementing this mechanism without precaution would lead to the creation of a *BLOCK%* for the body of a routine which reduces to a jump. Such a *BLOCK%* is useless, it is left as soon as it is created. Procedured jumps are easily detected at compile-time, and when the corresponding routine is transmitted dynamically, the *flagjump* of the *CONSTAB%* routine representation can be interpreted dynamically. Actually when deproceduring a routine which is a procedured jump, the only thing to do is to jump to the label definition of the procedured jump while performing the necessary actions of memory management. These actions differ from those of the normal jump explained in II.4 in that the *BLOCK%* into which the jump is performed is not necessarily active. As for return from dynamically transmitted procedures, it is the scope associated with the dynamic routine representation (which gives access to the *H%* of the label declaration *BLOCK%*) which allows to update the *DISPLAY%* properly.

What concerns the translation of the procedured jump, it reduces to constructing on *CONSTAB* the static routine representation in which this time *lo* is the label to which the jump must be performed, and no longer the entry point of the routine. Clearly no result is involved.

7.2 CALL OF STATICALLY TRANSMITTED PROCEDURED JUMPS

Syntax

DEPROC → deproc∇ DEPROCCOERCEND.

Translation scheme

1. ρ(DEPROCCOERCEND)
2. *GEN(callab ...)*
3. Result static management.

Semantics

Step 1 :

ρ(DEPROCCOERCEND).

At run-time DEPROCCOERCEND results in a routine without parameters. After the translation ρ(DEPROCCOERCEND), the static properties of the routine appear on *BOST*. They will be denoted *caddrout* ... . In this section we suppose that *caddrout* is of the form *(<u>routct</u> constabp)* : the *CONSTAB* routine representation is available at compile-time. In this section, we suppose moreover that in *CONSTAB*, *flagjump*=1; this means that the routine is a procedured jump. This procedured jump is characterized in *CONSTAB* by *lo*, the program entry point of the label involved, and by *bnsc*, the *bn* of the block of the label declaration.

<u>Step</u> 2 :

GEN(<u>callab</u> bnc§ : bnc,
caddrout§ : caddrout) {58}

-*caddrout§*, in *CONSTAB§*, gives access to *lo§* and *bnsc§* ; it is to be noted that in case of statically transmitted routines, the *BLOCK%* of the routine declaration is active and hence, it is accessible through *DISPLAY%[bnsc§]* . In the *H%* of this *BLOCK%*, at run-time, *wp%* and *gcw%* are found. These informations will be used in the actions of <u>*callab*</u>, they will be denoted *wplab%* and *gcwlab%* = *(gchplab%, gcszlab%)* respectively. The actions of <u>*callab*</u> are quite similar to those of the jump (see II.4.3).

<u>N.B.</u> If in *CONSTAB§* the information would have contained *bncsc§* instead of *bnsc§*, through *BLOCKTAB§* the static information of the block of the label declaration would have been available. In such a case, *gcwlab%* information is no longer needed and the description of the actions of <u>*callab*</u> are identical to those of <u>*goto*</u>. For historical reasons it is the first approach which is implemented.

-*bnc§*, through *BLOCKTAB§*, gives access to *bn§*, i.e. the bn of the block in which the deproceduring takes place.

<u>Action</u> 1 :

ranstpm% := wplab% {space is recovered on *RANST%*}

rtbn% := bnsc§.

<u>Action</u> 2 :

NILGCWOST1% (gchplab%, gcszlab%).

<u>Action</u> 3 :

NILDISPLAY% (bnsc§+1, bn§).

<u>Action</u> 4 :

<u>goto</u> lo§.

<u>Step</u> 3 : Result static management :

On *BOST*, the static properties of DEPROCCOERCEND are deleted, they are replaced by a set of properties characterizing the result of the deproceduring :

mode := <u>void</u>

cadd := (<u>nihil</u> 0).

7.3 CALL OF DYNAMICALLY TRANSMITTED PROCEDURED JUMPS

This case is exactly the one described in II.6.2 (Deproceduring of dynamically transmitted routines). The actions of <u>*callab*</u> in case *caddrout* ≠ *(<u>routct</u> constabp)* are still to be explained.

<u>Step</u> 8 :

GEN (<u>callab</u> bnc§ : bnc,

caddrout§ : caddrout) {58}

-caddrout§, through *CONSTAB%*, gives access to *lo%* and *bnsc%*. The *BLOCK%* of *bnsc%* is not necessarily active : the *DISPLAY%* must be updated. Thereafter, *DISPLAY%* [*bnsc%*] gives access to *wplab%* and *gcwlab% = (gchplab%, gcszlab%)*.

-The dynamic routine representation contains *scope%* which is the pointer to the *BLOCK%* of the label declaration.

-bnc§, through *BLOCKTAB§*, gives access to *bn§*.

<u>Action</u> 1 :

UPDDISPLAY% (bnsc%, scope%).

<u>Action</u> 2 : Space recovery :

ranstpm% := wplab% ; rtbn% := bnsc§.

<u>Action</u> 3 :

NILGCWOST1% (gchplab%, gcszlab%).

<u>Action</u> 4 :

NILDISPLAY% (bnsc%+1, bn§).

<u>Action</u> 5 :

<u>goto</u> lo%.

7.4 JUMP PROCEDURING

<u>Syntax</u>

JPROC → jproc∇ label

{With label, a *SYMBTAB* entry is associated, giving access to *bnclab* and *labnblab*}.

<u>Translation scheme</u>

1. *CONSTAB* procedured jump representation
2. *BOST* procedured jump representation.

<u>Semantics</u>

No object code is generated for the procedured jump, only a static management is necessary :

<u>Step</u> 1 : *CONSTAB* procedured jump representation :

Through *BLOCKTAB*, *bnclab* gives access to *bnlab*.

The routine representation is constructed in *CONSTAB* at the entry *constabp* :

lo := labnblab

bnsc := bnlab

flagjump := 1

In order to enable the loader to transform *lo* into a machine address in *CONSTAB§* :

GEN(<u>updconstab</u> mode§ : <u>label</u>,

constabp§: constabp) {33}

<u>Step</u> 2 : *BOST* procedured jump representation :

Dynamically, a jump is performed. Statically, we are concerned with the value consisting of the procedured jump ; the corresponding static properties are stored on *BOST* :

mode := <u>*proc*</u> <u>*void*</u>

cadd := (<u>*routct*</u> *constabp*)

smr, *dmr* and *gc* are irrelevant

or := (<u>*nil*</u>, *0*,*0*,*0*)

scope := (*bnlab*, *bnlab*).

8. BOUNDS OF MODE DECLARATIONS

8.1 GENERALITIES

As for non-standard routines, the definition of a mode-indication and its applications are at different places in the program. Here, the whole of the bounds contained in a mode declaration is considered the routine without parameters.

Its access is restricted to *(routct constabp)* since these routines cannot be transmitted dynamically neither by assignation nor as actual parameter. As a consequence, the scope block bn_{sc} can always be considered the block where the declaration appears. Furthermore, the run-time address of the scope *BLOCK%* will always be available on *DISPLAY%* at the moment of the call.

This means that bounds in mode declarations can be elaborated in the environment of the call except when the bounds contain blocks. Then the normal routine-call mechanism is implied, i.e. *BLOCK%* and *DISPLAY%* organization. The reason for this is that addressing inside blocks of bounds is based on the lexicographical structure of the program. In the actual implementation the routine-call mechanism is used for mode indications containing bounds which are not integral denotations. The result of the routine consists here of the list of all the calculated bounds. It is this list that will be transmitted to the calling block at the return of the routine. Integral denotation bounds are treated statically. The translation scheme for the call-body of routine will be that of II.6.4.1 and II.6.4.3.

Bound routine representation

As for other routines, static information must be collected in order to be able to translate the call properly. However the situation here is somewhat different :

(1) The routine is always statically accessible, hence no *CONSTAB%* representation, available at run-time, is needed.

(2) The result of the routine is a number of integers corresponding to the number of bounds *nbbds*, delivered by the mode indication (i.e. recursively through other mode indications!) ; *nbbds* represents the static size of the result of the routine, it must be available at the call for *SWOST%* space reservation.

The static routine representation will consist of the following informations :

-*mode*, a *DECTAB* pointer where the mode of the actual declarer of the mode declaration together with bounds and flexibility information is found. In particular *nbbds*, i.e. the number of the bounds which are not simple integer denotations can be deduced from *mode*.

-*lo*, the label of the body of the bound routine

-bnsc, the block number of the block where the mode indication is declared.

This routine representation is so simple that it can easily be calculated during syntactic analysis, thus avoiding problems of mode indications appearing lexicographically before the corresponding declaration. In the sequel, we suppose that this routine representation is available in *SYMBTAB* at the entry corresponding to the mode indication :

mode = *mode* <u>*of*</u> ADECLARER

cadd = (<u>*label*</u> bn_{sc}.*lo*).

8.2 CALL OF MODE INDICATION

<u>Syntax</u>

CALLMODIND → callmodind∇ modind

{With modind, a *SYMBTAB* entry is associated where *modind (nbbdsind)*, *bnscind* and *loind* are found}.

<u>Translation scheme</u>

1. *GEN(<u>callmind</u> ... lreturn)*
2. *GEN(<u>labdef</u> lreturn)*
3. Bounds static properties.

<u>Semantics</u>

<u>Case</u> A :

nbbdsind=0, i.e. all actual bounds, if any, reduce to integral denotations : *modind* is a *DECTAB* entry where the declarer is stored together with bounds integral denotations.

<u>Step</u> :

<u>*for*</u> *all bounds of DECTAB*[*modind*]

<u>*do*</u> a new *BOST* element is set up with the static properties of the integral denotation :

mode := <u>*int*</u>

cadd := (<u>*intct*</u> *v*) where *v* is the value of the integral denotation of the bound.

smr, *dmr* and *gc* are irrelevant

or := (<u>*nil*</u>, 0,0,0)

scope := (0,0)

<u>*od*</u>.

<u>Case</u> B :

nbbdsind ≠ 0.

<u>Step</u> 1 :

GEN(<u>callmind</u> lreturn§ : lreturn,
bncres§ : bnc,
swostcres§: swostc,
lbody§ : loind) {43}

-*bncres§*, through *BLOCKTAB§* gives access to *bnres§*.

-The actions of *<u>callmind</u>* are similar to the actions of *<u>deprocl</u>* (II.6.4.1).

<u>Action</u> 1 :

ranstpm% +:= h

{The garbage collector may be called}.

<u>Action</u> 2 : Filling in of *BLOCK%* heading :

dch% := DISPLAY%[bnres§]

swostp% := swostcres§ {transformed into absolute address}

gcp% and *dmrp%* and *flex%* are irrelevant

retjump := lreturn§.

<u>Action</u> 3 :

<u>goto</u> loind§.

<u>Step</u> 2 :

GEN(<u>labdef</u> labnb§ : lreturn). {28}

<u>Step</u> 3 : Bounds static properties :

Static properties of all bounds of the mode indication are stored on *BOST* ; *modind* is the guide for this storage; it indicates the values *v* of the bounds which are simple integral denotations ; the corresponding static properties are :

mode := <u>int</u>

cadd := (<u>intct</u> v)

On the other hand, the ith bound which is transmitted as result of the routine has the properties

mode := <u>int</u>

cadd := (<u>dirwost</u> bnc.swostc+i-1)

This *cadd* ensures the interface between the call and the routine.

8.3 MODE DECLARATION (BODY OF ROUTINE)

<u>Syntax</u>

MODEDEC → modedec∇ modind = ADECLARER

{-Modind is characterized by an entry in *SYMBTAB* where *modind (nbbdsind), bnscind* and *loind* are found.

-The actual declarer ADECLARER specifies the mode of the mode indication and possibly actual bounds.}

Translation scheme

1. *GEN(jump l)*
2. *GEN(labdef loind)*
3. Static block entry
4. *GEN(inmind ...)*
5. ρ(ADECLARER)
6. *GEN(outmind ...)*
7. *GEN(labdef l)*
8. Static block exit
9. Static management.

Semantics

Case A :

nbbdsind = 0.

The translation is complete.

Case B :

nbbdsind ≠ 0.

Step 1 :

GEN(jump labnb§ : l). {27}

Step 2 :

GEN(labdef labnb§ : loind). {28}

Step 3 : Static block entry :

INBLOCK1 (bnscind) ; INBLOCK2 (bnscind) ; INBLOCK3.

Step 4 :

GEN(inmind bncbody§ : bnc) {45}

{see II.6.4.3, actions of *inbody*}.

Step 5 :

ρ(ADECLARER)

All bounds are translated. Suppose there are *n* bounds involved, their static properties appear on *BOST* after the translation ρ(ADECLARER) ; they will be denoted *cadd1, smr1 ...*

```
GEN(outmind bnbody§ : bn,
            n§       : n,
            cadd1§   : cadd1,
             ...        ...
            caddn§   : caddn)                {44} (†)
```

{The actions are similar to the actions of *return* (II.5.4, step 6) ; here, the result consists of *n§* integers with source accesses *cadd1§ ... caddn§*

(†) Actually, amongst the *n* bounds only those which do not correspond to integral denotations have to be transmitted as parameters of *outmind*.

which have to be copied into *n§* consecutive cells in the calling *BLOCK%* from the address *swostp%* ; *swostp%* is found in *H%* of the current *BLOCK%* accessible through *DISPLAY%[bnbody§]* }.

Step 7 :

GEN(labdef labnb§ : l) {28}

Step 8 : Static block exit :

OUTBLOCK3 ; OUTBLOCK1.

Step 9 : Static management :

Routine static properties have been stored in *SYMBTAB* during syntactic analysis; given the mode declaration in itself delivers no value, the only thing to do is to delete the static properties of the *n* bounds from *BOST*.

9. DYNAMIC REPLICATIONS IN FORMATS

9.1 GENERALITIES

As for non-standard routines, the definition of a format (format denotation) and its applications (transformat) are at different places in the program. Here the whole of the dynamic replications contained in a format denotation is considered a routine without parameters. As for non-standard rcutines, formats may be transmitted dynamically. The result of the routine is a set of integers, corresponding to the values of the dynamic replications ; unlike the number of dynamic bounds of a mode indication, the number of dynamic replications resulting from the application of a format in not known at compile-time, hence this result has to be handled like a dynamic array of integers. Moreover, the association of a format with a file gives rise to some problems discussed below.

From the above considerations, there are four different objects to be distinguished for handling formats :

- -the routine and its representation in *CONSTAB*.
- -the memory representation of the routine.
- -the memory representation of the result of the routine (tamrof value).
- -the storage of a tamrof value in files.

(1) The routine is the text consisting of the dynamic replications of the format. The static representation of a format routine consists of :
-lo : the label generated in front of the body of the routine,
-ndrep : the number of dynamic replications in the format,
-bnsc : the static representation of the scope of the format,
-formstringp : a pointer to format denotation string in memory.
As for non-standard routines, such a format representation must be stored in *CONSTAB%* in order to be available at run-time when a dynamically transmitted format is called. The access to the format in *CONSTAB* has the form: *(formatct constabp).*
Formally, the *CONSTAB* format representation is characterized by
mode routform = struct (label lo,
int ndrep, bnsc, formstringp).

(2) Given formats may be dynamically transmitted (i.e. assigned or used as actual parameter), they must have a dynamic representation which will be stored on *RANST%* or *HEAP%*. This dynamic representation, as for non-standard routines, consists of a *CONSTAB%* pointer *constabp%* to the static format representation and of a dynamic scope information, *scope%*. Actually *scope%* = *DISPLAY%*[bn_{sc}] in the environment of the format, i.e. at the moment a format of access *(formatct constabp)* is caused to be stored on *RANST%* or on *HEAP%* (III.5.4.2).

Formally,

mode routform% = struct (int constabp%, scope%)

(3) The result of a call of a routine of type dynamic replication is of the mode *tamrof*.

The tamrof value has a memory representation which is analogous to that of an integer array, i.e. it has a descriptor (static part) and a number of elements (dynamic part). The reason for this is that the number of dynamic replications resulting from the call of a format is generally not known at compile-time. The memory representation of a *tamrof* value is as follows :

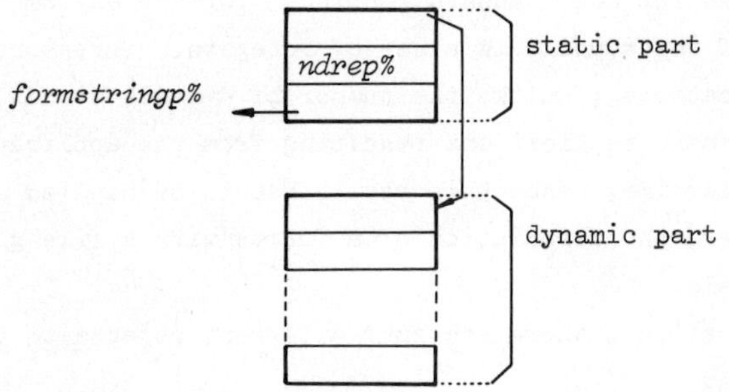

The body of routine results in a set of integers, which must be transmitted in the calling *BLOCK%* in the form of a tamrof value. Formally, the descriptor of a tamrof value is characterized by :

mode tamrofd% = (int offset%, ndrep%, formstringp%)

(4) A tamrof value has to be included in a file. Given its size is not only dynamic, but also not known at the creation of a file, space for storing the dynamic part of the tamrof value cannot be reserved at file creation.

Given the inclusion of the (tamrof) value into a file does not necessarily take place at the level of the block of the file, dynamic bounds may not be stored on *RANST%* and, thus, they must be on the *HEAP%*, like the elements of a flexible array. Another solution would consist in reserving at the creation of each file enough space for storing the maximum number of dynamic replications associated with each format in the whole of the program.

9.2 CALL OF STATICALLY TRANSMITTED FORMATS

Syntax

TRANSFORMAT → transformat∇ FORMATCOERCEND

{transformat∇ is the prefix marker corresponding to the coercion by which dynamic replications of a format are elaborated.}

Translation scheme

1. ρ(FORMATCOERCEND)
2. *GEN(<u>calldynrep</u> ... lreturn ...)*
3. *GEN(<u>labdef</u> lreturn)*
4. Result static properties.

Semantics

<u>Step</u> 1 :

ρ(FORMATCOERCEND)

{At run-time, FORMATCOERCEND results in a value of mode *<u>format</u>*. After the translation ρ(FORMATCOERCEND), the static properties of the format appear on *BOST*. They will be denoted *caddformat* ... . In this section we suppose *caddformat* is of the form *(<u>formatct</u> constabp)*. All properties stored within the format representation in *CONSTAB* are available at compile-time. In particular *ndrep* is known}.

<u>Step</u> 2 :

<u>Case</u> A :

ndrep ≠ 0.

GEN(<u>calldynrep</u> lreturn§ : lreturn,
bncres§ : bnc,
swostcres§ : swostc,
caddformat§ : caddformat) {46}

-*bncres§*, through *BLOCKTAB§* gives access to *bnres§* ...

-*caddformat§* gives access to *loformat§* and *bnscformat§* in *CONSTAB§*.

<u>Action</u> 1 :

ranstpm% +:= h

{The garbage collector may be called}.

<u>Action</u> 2 : Filling of *BLOCK%* heading *H%* :

dch% := DISPLAY%[bnres§]

swostp% := swostcres§ {transformed into absolute address.}

retjump := lreturn§.

<u>Action</u> 3 :

<u>goto</u> loformat§.

<u>Case</u> B :

ndrep = 0.

no action is taken.

<u>Step</u> 3 :

<u>Case</u> A :

ndrep ≠ 0.

GEN(<u>labdef</u> labnb§ : lreturn) {28}

<u>Case</u> B :

ndrep = 0.

No action is taken.

Step 4 : Result static properties :

Static properties of the transformat are put on *BOST* :

Case A :

ndrep ≠ 0.

mode := tamrof

cadd := (dirwost bnc.swostc)

smr := bnc.swostc

dmr := (stat bnc.swostc)

gc := nil

or := (nil,0,0,0)

scope := (0,0)

{These properties ensure the interface of result transmission between the routine and the call}.

Case B :

ndrep = 0.

mode := tamrof

cadd := (tamrofct constabp)

smr, *dmr* and *gc* are irrelevant

or := (nil,0,0,0)

scope := (0,0).

9.3 CALL OF DYNAMICALLY TRANSMITTED FORMATS

Syntax

{see II.9.2}.

Translation scheme

1. ρ(FORMATCOERCEND)
2. *GEN(checkdynrep ... l ...)*
3. *GEN(calldynrep ... lreturn ...)*
4. *GEN(labdef l)*
5. *GEN(initdynrep ...)*
6. *GEN(labdef lreturn)*
7. Result static properties.

Semantics

Step 1 :

ρ(FORMATCOERCEND)

{see II.9.1, step 1 but this time, *caddformat ≠ (formatct constabp)* ; the *CONSTAB* static properties of the format are not available at compile-time}.

Step 2 :

GEN(checkdynrep labnb§ : l,
caddformat§: caddformat) {51}

Action :

If *ndrep%* of the *CONSTAB%* format representation accessible through the dynamic format representation is 0 then goto *l*.

Step 3 :

GEN(calldynrep lreturn§ : lreturn,
bncres§ : bnc,
swostcres§ : swostc,
caddformat§: caddformat) {46}

The actions of calldynrep have been explained in II.9.2 for *caddformat§ = (formatct constabp)*. Here *caddformat§* is not of this form, at run-time it gives access to the dynamic format representation : *constabp%* and *scope%*, denoted here *constabpformat%* and *scopeformat%* ; in turn, *constabpformat%* through *CONSTAB%*, gives access to *loformat%* and *bnscformat%*

Action 1 :

ranstpm% +:= h

{the garbage collector may be called}.

Action 2 : Filling *BLOCK%* heading

dch% := DISPLAY%[bnres§]
swostp% := swostcres§
retjump% := lreturn§.

Action 3 :

UPDDISPLAY% (bnscformat%, scopeformat%).

Action 4 :

goto *loformat%*.

Step 4 :

GEN(labdef labnb§ : l) {28}

Step 5 :

GEN(initdynrep caddformat§ : caddformat,
caddrep§ : (dirwost bnc.swostc)) {49}

The aim of this instruction is to ensure the dynamic interface between the cases where *ndrep% = 0* and ≠ *0*.

Action :

A tamrof value with 0 element is stored on *WOST%*.

Step 6 :

GEN(labdef labnb§ : lreturn) {28}

Step 7 : Result static properties :

Static properties of the transformat are put on *BOST* :

mode := *tamrof*
cadd := (*dirwost* *bnc.swostc*)
smr := *bnc.swostc*
dmr := (*stat* *bnc.swostc*)
gc := *nil*
or := (*nil*,0,0,0)
scope := (0,0).

9.4 DYNAMIC REPLICATIONS (BODY OF ROUTINE)

FORMAT → format∇ DYNREP

{With format∇, a *CONSTAB* pointer *formatstringp* is associated ; it points to the format string (at the exclusion of dynamic replications) ; *bnscformat* is supposed to be explicit in the source text. DYNREP is the program text of the dynamic replications}.

Translation scheme

1. *GEN(jump l)*
2. *GEN(labdef loformat)*
3. Static block entry
4. *GEN(indynrep ...)*
5. ρ(DYNREP)
6. *GEN(outdynrep)*
7. *GEN(labdef l)*
8. Static block exit
9. Format static properties :
   9.1 *CONSTAB* format representation
   9.2 *BOST* format properties.

Semantics

Step 1 :

GEN(jump labnb§ : l) {27}

Step 2 :

GEN(labdef labnb§ : loformat) {28}

Step 3 : Static block entry :

INBLOCK1 (bnscformat) ; INBLOCK2 (bnscformat) ; INBLOCK3

{*bnsc* is the static scope of the format made explicit by the syntactic analyzer}.

Step 4 :

GEN(indynrep bncbody§ : bnc) {47}

{see II.6.4.3 actions of *inbody*}.

Step 5 :

ρ(DYNREP)

{At run-time DYNREP results in n integers ; after the translation ρ(DYNREP) the static properties of these n integers appear on *BOST* ; they will be denoted *cadd1, smr1 ...*}.

Step 6 :

GEN(outdynrep bnbody§ : bn,
n§ : n,
cadd1§ : cadd1,
... ...
caddn§ : caddn,
formatstringp§ : formatstringp) {48}

{see II.5.4, step 6, but here it is a *tamrof* value which has to be transmitted, it consists of the *n§* integers of access *cadd1§ ... caddn§* and *formatstringp§.*}.

Step 7 :

GEN(labdef labnb§ : l) {28}

Step 8 :

OUTBLOCK3 ; OUTBLOCK1.

Step 9 : Format static properties :

Step 9.1 : *CONSTAB* format representation :

The format representation is constructed in *CONSTAB* at the address *constabp* :

lo := loformat
ndrep := n
bnsc := bnscformat
formstringp := formatstringp.

Step 9.2 : *BOST* format properties :

The static properties are erased from *BOST*, they are replaced by those of the format :

mode := format
cadd := (formatct constabp)
smr, dmr and *gc* are irrelevant
or := (nil,0,0,0)
scope := (bnsc,bnsc)

In order to enable the loader to transform *lo* into a machine address in *CONSTAB§*, a command is generated : *GEN(updconstab mode§ : format,*
constabp§: constabp) {33}.

10. OTHER TERMINAL CONSTRUCTIONS

Terminal constructions are applications of declared objects, denotations with the exception of routine and format denotations, generators, *skip*, *nil* and *empty*.

Declared objects and generators are treated in II.2 and II.3 respectively . Here, we explain how to translate the other terminal constructions.

10.1 DENOTATIONS

In this section we deal with *int*, *real*, *bool*, *char*, *bits* and *string* denotations. These denotations specify particular values and consequently also their intrinsic static properties, in particular their mode and their scope.

The accesses created for denotations are of two kinds :

(1) *(constant v)* for small integers {*(intct v)*}, booleans {*(boolct v)*}, characters {*(charct v)*} or small bits {*(bitsct v)*} in which case *v* specifies the value itself.

(2) *(dircttab constabp)* in the other cases ; then the value is stored in CONSTAB at the entry *constabp*.

The translation of a denotation reduces to store on BOST the corresponding set of static properties and possibly to store in CONSTAB the value of the denotation.

Moreover, remark that strings are stored in CONSTAB under the form of a descriptor and elements. CONSTAB relocation implies the generation of a loader command, the effect of which is to update the offset of the decriptor :

GEN(updconstab mode§ : string,
constabp§ : constabp). {33}

10.2 SKIP

Skip stands for some value of a particular mode ; it can be handled in different ways.

(1) A special access could be created (*skip 0*) in such a way all decisions about *skip* handling are postponed to the constructions using it.

(2) Some value of the mode specified by the context is stored on CONSTAB thus giving rise to a value of access *(dircttab constabp)*. Which value is chosen is without importance except when a misuse of *skip* could lead to desastrous consequences. For this reason, names of such values are initialized with *nil*, descriptors are such that they correspond to 0 element, union overheads and procedures are initialized with some special flag.

(3) For historical reasons, the elaboration of <u>*skip*</u> corresponds, in the X8-implementation, to the storage of some value of the specified mode on *WOST%* at run-time. This value is initialized as under (2). This implementation of <u>*skip*</u> is now described.

<u>Syntax</u>

'*Skip*' is a terminal with which a particular mode, *modeskip* has been associated by the syntactic analyzer.

<u>Translation scheme</u>

1. *BOST* management
2. *GEN(<u>stskip</u> ...)*.

<u>Semantics</u>

<u>Step</u> 1 : *BOST* management :

$cadd_0$:= (<u>*dirwost*</u> *bnc.swostc* + Δ*mem*)
$mode_0$:= *modeskip*
smr_0 := *bnc.swostc*
dmr_0 := <u>*nil*</u>
gc_0 := <u>*nil*</u>
or_0 := (<u>*nil*</u>, 0, 0, 0)
$scope_0$:= (0,0)

<u>Step</u> 2 :

GEN(<u>stskip</u> mode§ : $mode_0$,
cadd§ : $cadd_0$) {99}

<u>Action</u> :

The cells which have been statically reserved at the address *cadd§* for the static part of a value of *mode§* are initialized as explained above (2).

10.3 NIL

<u>*Nil*</u> stands for a name which must be distinguishable from other names ; as <u>*skip*</u>, it could be handled in different ways :

(1) a special access could be created (<u>*nil*</u> *0*), but this would increase the static management without significant gain.

(2) a dynamic <u>*nil*</u> representation could be stored on *CONSTAB* with an access (<u>*dirctab*</u> *constabp)*.

(3) For historical reasons the elaboration of <u>*nil*</u> corresponds to the storage of the dynamic representation of <u>*nil*</u> on *WOST%* at run-time. It is this strategy which is described below(†).

(†) This solution for <u>*nil*</u> and <u>*skip*</u> is not optimal as far as run-time is concerned ; however it allows to state that a name is never stored in *CONSTAB*, which lightens the static management in a number of cases.

Syntax

'*nil*' is a terminal with which a particular mode *modenil* has been associated by the syntactic analyzer.

Translation scheme

1. *BOST* management
2. *GEN(stnil ...)*.

Semantics

Step 1 : *BOST* management :

$cadd_o$:= (*dirwost* *bnc.swostc* + Δ*mem*)
$mode_o$:= *modenil*
smr_o := *bnc.swostc*
dmr_o := *nil*
gc_o := *nil*
or_o := (*nil*, 0, 0, 0)
$scope_o$:= (0, 0).

Step 2 :

GEN(stnil cadd§ : $cadd_o$) {98}

Action :

The dynamic representation of *nil* is stored at the address *cadd§* :

pointer% := 0

scope% := address of the first cell of RANST%.

Remark

A number of constructions require a dynamic check on *nil*. These constructions are 'assignation', 'refselection', 'refslice', 'refrowing', 'dereferencing' and operations combined with assignations (*+:=*, *-:=*, *×:=*,...). With the static properties which have been described, the dynamic check on *nil* is avoided in case the name to be checked has an access class *variden*. The addition of a new field *nilo* to the static property *or* would allow to decrease the number of dynamic checks on *nil* a step further. For a given stored value, *nilo* would indicate whether all constituent names of the value are *nil* or not, or if this is not known at compile-time.

10.4 EMPTY

Empty stands for a multiple value with 0 element ; three solutions similar to those explained for *skip* and *nil* are possible here. Again, for historical reasons it is the third solution which has been implemented and which is described.

Syntax

'*Empty*' is a terminal with which a particular mode *modeempty* has been associated by the syntactic analyzer.

Translation scheme

1. *BOST* management
2. *GEN(<u>rowingempty</u> ...).*

Semantics

<u>Step</u> 1 : *BOST* management :

$cadd_o$:= (<u>dirwost</u> *bnc.swostc* + *Δmem*)
$mode_o$:= *modeempty*
smr_o := *bnc.swostc*
dmr_o := <u>nil</u>
gc_o := <u>nil</u>
or_o := (<u>nil</u>, 0, 0, 0)
$scope_o$:= (0, 0)

<u>Step</u> 2 :

GEN(<u>rowingempty</u> mode§ : modeempty,
cadd§ : $cadd_o$) {77}

-*mode§* gives access to the number *n§* of dimensions and to the staticsize *staticsize§* of the potential elements.

<u>Action</u> :

The dynamic representation of a multiple value with *n§* dimensions and 0 element is stored at the address *cadd§* :

```
offset% := 0
states% := (1,...1)
iflag% := 0
do%    := 0
for i to n§-1 do
li% := 1
ui% := 0
di% := 0
od
ln% := 1
un% := 0
dn% := staticsize§.
```

11. KERNEL INVARIANT CONSTRUCTIONS

'Kernel invariant constructions' are constructions the result of which is just a value or a part of a value accessible through one of its parameters. Hence, the result of such constructions always preexists in memory ; it will be used for the result of the construction as far as rules a1 to b4 of I.2.3.2 are not violated.
These constructions are : 'selection', 'dereferencing', 'slice', 'uniting' and 'rowing'.

11.1 SELECTION

There are two kinds of selections : those applying to non-name values (non-ref-selections) and those applying to names (ref-selections). They must be treated with different strategies.

Syntax

SELECTION → selection∇ selector of SECONDARYSEL.

Translation scheme

1. ρ(SECONDARYSEL)
2. A(†) Non-ref-selection

1. $class_s$ = *dircttab* or	In each case
" = *diriden*	1. *BOST* static properties
2. " = *indiden*	2. Generation of run-time actions {*GEN*}
3. " = *indwost*	1. *gc*
4 " = *dirwost*	2. *dmr*
	3. *copy*

3. B Ref-selection
   1. Check of *nil*
   2.

1. $class_s$ = *diriden*	
2. " = *indiden*	1. *BOST*
3. " = *variden*	2. *GEN*
4. " = *dirwost*	
5. " = *indwost*.	

Semantics

Step 1 :

ρ(SECONDARYSEL)

(†) Underlined numbering stands for a Case.

{the static properties of the value on which the selection applies appear on *BOST* ; they are denoted $mode_s$, $cadd_s$ ... ; 'selector' and $mode_s$ give access to $mode_o$ of the selected field and to *reladd* i.e. the relative address of the selected field in the static part of the structured value.}.

Step 2 :

A number of cases based on $mode_o$ are distinguished ; through all these cases, the storage of $mode_o$ on *BOST* will be implicit.

Case A : Non-ref-selection :

NONREF($mode_s$).

A number of subcases, 'case A.i' of case A are distinguished, they are based on $class_s$; through these cases, the static properties or_o and $scope_o$ are treated the same way :

$or_o := or_s$

$scope_o :=$ (*SCOPERELEVANT*($mode_o$) | $scope_s$
| (0,0)) .

Their storage on *BOST* will remain implicit.

Case A.1 :

$class_s$ = dircttab or
" = diriden.

On *BOST* :

$cadd_o := (class_s, hadd_s.tadd_s + reladd)$

smr_o, dmr_o and gc_o are irrelevant.

No dynamic action is implied.

Case A.2 :

$class_s$ = indiden.

{Instead of copying the value of the field on *WOST%*, an indirect address to its preexisting instance is stored}.

Step A.2-1 : *BOST* static properties :

$cadd_o :=$ (indwost *bnc.swostc* + Δmem)

$smr_o :=$ *bnc.swostc*

$dmr_o :=$ nil

$gc_o := (kindo_s$ = "iden" | nil
| *bnc.gcc*).

Step A.2-2 : Generation of run-time actions :

Step A.2-2.1 : Gc :

GENSTANDGC.

Step A.2-2.2 : Copy :

```
GEN(stplus cadd1§ : (diriden adds),
           cadd2§ : (intct reladd),
           caddo§ : (dirwost bnc.swostc + Δmem))  {18}
```

Action :

The indirect address of access *cadd1§*, incremented by the integer of access *cadd2§* is stored in the memory cell of access *caddo§*.

Step A.2-2.3 :

NOOPT.

Case A.3 :

$class_s$ = indwost.

{The strategy consists in superseding on *WOST%* the indirect address of the structure by the one of the selected field}.

Step A.3-1 : *BOST* static properties :

$cadd_o := cadd_s$

$smr_o := smr_s$

$dmr_o :=$ nil

$gc_o := gc_s$.

Step A.3-2 : Generation of run-time actions :

Step A.3-2.1 : Gc :

($gc_o \neq$ nil | GENSTANDGC).

Step A.3-2.2 : Copy :

GEN(plus cadds§ : (intct reladd),
caddo§ : (dirwost add_s)) {14}

Action :

The contents of the cell of address *caddo§* is incremented by the integer of access *cadds§*.

Step A.3-2.3 :

NOOPT.

Case A.4 :

$class_s$ = dirwost.

{The field preexists on *WOST%*, it is that instance which is used as result. There may be some dynamic action related to *gc* and *dmr*}.

Step A.4-1 : *BOST* static properties :

$cadd_o :=$ (dirwost bnc.$tadd_s$+reladd)

$smr_o := smr_s$

$dmr_o :=$ (DMRRELEVANT($mode_o$) $\neq$ nil | dmr_s
| nil)(†)

$gc_o :=$ (GCRELEVANT($mode_o$) and $gc_s \neq$ nil | gc_s
| nil).

Step A.4-2 : Generation of run-time actions :

(†) Here, even when the field has a dynamic part, we can imagine a process recovering *DWOST%* memory space of the next fields in the structured value.

Step A.4-2.1 : Dmr :

$(dmr_s$ = (stat α) and dmr_o = nil
|GEN(stword cadds§ : (dirwost α),
caddo§ : (dirabs ranstpm%)) {4}
|:dmr_s = (dyn β) and dmr_o = nil
|GEN(stword cadds§ : (dirdmrw β),
caddo§ : (dirabs ranstpm%))). {4}

Step A.4-2.2 : Gc :

$(gc_s \neq$ nil and gc_o = nil
|GEN(stgcnil caddgc§ : (dirgcw gc_s))

Action :

the gc-protection is cancelled.

|:$gc_o \neq$ nil | GENSTANDGC).

Case B : Ref-selection :

∼NONREF ($mode_s$).

Through subcases B.i, the static properties or_o, $scope_o$ and dmr_o are treated in the same way : $or_o := or_s$
$scope_o := scope_s$
$dmr_o :=$ nil.

Their storage on BOST remains implicit.

Step B.1 : Check of nil :

(class of $cadd_s \neq$ variden
|GEN(checknil cadd§ : $cadd_s$)) {106}

Action :

A run-time error message is provided if the name of access cadd§ is nil.

Step B.2 :

Case B.1 :

$class_s$ = diriden.

{The subname is constructed on WOST%}.

Step B.1-1 : BOST static properties :

$cadd_o$:= (dirwost bnc.swostc + Δmem)
smr_o := bnc.swostc
gc_o := ($derefo_s$ = 1 | bnc.gcc
| nil).

Step B.1-2 : Generation of run-time actions :

Step B.1-2.1 : Gc :

$(gc_o \neq$ nil | GENSTANDGC).

Step B.1-2.2 : Copy :

GEN(stnameincr cadds§ : $cadd_s$,
incr§ : reladd,
caddo§ : $cadd_o$) {20}

Action :

A name is stored at the address *caddo§* ; it is a copy of the name stored at *cadds§* but with *pointer%* incremented by *incr§*.

Step B.1-2.3 :

NOOPT.

Case B.2 :

$class_s$ = *indiden*.

This case is identical to case B.1 except for gc_o :

gc_o := *bnc.gcc*.

Case B.3 :

$class_s$ = *variden*.

Step B.3-1 : *BOST* management :

$cadd_o$:= (*variden* $hadd_s$.$tadd_s$ + *reladd*)

smr_o and gc_o are irrelevant

No dynamic action is implied.

Case B.4 :

$class_s$ = *dirwost*.

{The pointer of the name is incremented on *WOST%*}

Step B.4-1 : *BOST* management :

$cadd_o$:= $cadd_s$

smr_o := smr_s

gc_o := gc_s.

Step B.4-2 : Generation of run-time actions :

Step B.4-2.1 : Gc :

(gc_o ≠ *nil* | *GENSTANDGC*).

Step B.4-2.2 : Copy :

GEN(*plus* *cadds§* : (*intct* *reladd*),

caddo§ : $cadd_o$) {14}

Step B.4-2.3 :

NOOPT.

Case B.5 :

$class_s$ = *indwost*.

{the subname is constructed on *WOST%*}.

Step B.5-1 : *BOST* static properties :

$cadd_o$:= (*dirwost* *bnc.tadd* *of* smr_s + Δ*mem*)

smr_o := smr_s

gc_o := (gc_s ≠ *nil* | gc_s

|:$derefo_s$ | *bnc.gcc*

| *nil*).

Step B.5-2 : Generation of run-time actions :

Step B.5-2.1 : Gc :

(gc_o ≠ *nil* | *GENSTANDGC*).

Step B.5-2.2 : Copy :

GEN(stnameincr caddss : $cadd_s$,
incr§ : reladd,
caddo§ : $cadd_o$). {20}

Step B.5-2.3 :

NOOPT.

Remark 1

In case of non-ref-selection, and when $class_s$ = indiden or indwost, an indirect address is stored on *WOST%*. However, if the selected field does fit into a register, it is as efficient to store the value itself instead of its address on *WOST%*.

Let X be the address of the cell where the address of the source structure is stored, and Y the address of the result on *WOST%*.

Case 1 : the address of the result is stored at Y :

```
LDB X
ADB =  reladd
STB Y
LDB Y          {use of the result}
LDA 0,B
```

Case 2 : the value itself is stored at Y :

```
LDB X
ADB =  reladd
LDA 0,B
STA Y
LDA Y          {use of the result.}
```

After local optimizations, the machine instructions produced with the two strategies are identical. However, the second solution may be more efficient as far as gc-protection is concerned : a value on *WOST%* must be protected less often than if it is accessed through an indirect address.

Remark 2

Thanks to *TOPST*, it is easy to control whether the subname resulting from a ref-selection will be immediately dereferenced or not. In case of the affirmative, the dereferencing can be combined with the selection ; this allows to avoid an intermediate construction of the subname and reduces the number of gc-protection actions. The above remarks though not described here in whole details have been implemented in the X8-compiler.

Remark 3

A new field *Δadd* associated with the indirect access *(indiden n.p)* and *(indwost n.p)* would allow to avoid any dynamic action to translate a selection of a field of a structured value with one of these above accesses. *Δadd* would be an increment to the indirect address, and the selection would correspond to *Δadd+:=reladd*.

In most of machine codes, loading in register A the contents of a word of access *(__indiden__ n.p, Δadd)* (using the index register B), would correspond to :

LDB *n.p*
LDA *Δadd, B*

11.2 DEREFERENCING

__Syntax__

DEREF → deref∇ DEREFCOERCEND.

__Translation scheme__

1. ρ(DEREFCOERCEND)
2. Check of *__nil__*
3. __A__. $class_s$ = *__diriden__*
   __B__. " = *__indiden__*
   __C__. " = *__variden__*
   __D__. " = *__dirwost__ __and__ NONROW*($mode_o$)
   __E__. " = *__dirwost__ __and__ ∼NONROW*($mode_o$)
   __F__. " = *__indwost__.*

| 1. *BOST*
| 2. *GEN*

__Semantics__

__Step__ 1 :

ρ (DEREFCOERCEND)

{The static properties of the value on which the dereferencing applies, appear on *BOST* ; they are denoted $mode_s$, $cadd_s$ ...}.

__Step__ 2 : Check of *__nil__ :*

(class __of__ $cadd_s$ ≠ *__variden__*
   |*GEN(__checknil__ cadd§ :* $cadd_s$*))*   {106}

__Step__ 3 :

A number of cases essentially based on $class_s$ are distinguished ; through all the cases, the static properties $mode_o$, or_o and $scope_o$ are treated in the same way :

$mode_o$:= *DEREF*($mode_s$)
or_o := or_s
derefo __of__ or_o := *1*
$scope_o$:= *(SCOPERELEVANT*($mode_o$) | ($insc_s$, 0)
   | (0,0)).

__Case__ A :

$class_s$ = *__diriden__.*

__Step__ A-1 : *BOST* static properties :

$cadd_o$:= (*__indiden__* add_s)

smr_o, dmr_o and gc_o are irrelevant.

No dynamic action is implied.

Case B :

$class_s$ = indiden.

{the address of the resulting value is copied on *WOST%*}

Step B-1 : *BOST* static properties :

$cadd_o$:= (indwost bnc.swostc + Δmem)

smr_o := bnc.swostc

dmr_o := nil

gc_o := bnc.gcc.

Step B-2 : Generation of run-time actions :

Step B-2.1 : Gc :

GENSTANDGC.

Step B-2.2 : Copy :

GEN(stword cadds§ : (indiden add_s),
caddo§ : (dirwost add_o)). {4}

Step B-2.3 :

NOOPT.

Case C :

$class_s$ = variden.

Step C-1 : *BOST* static properties :

$cadd_s$:= (diriden add_s)

smr_o, drm_o and gc_o are irrelevant

No dynamic action is implied.

Case D :

$class_s$ = dirwost and *NONROW* ($mode_o$).

Step D-1 : *BOST* static properties :

$cadd_o$:= (indwost add_s)

smr_o := smr_s

dmr_o := nil

gc_o := gc_s.

Step D-2 : Generation of dynamic actions :

Step D-2.1 : Gc :

(gc_o ≠ nil | *GENSTANDGC*).

Case E :

$class_s$ = dirwost and ∿*NONROW*($mode_o$).

{This distinction between the cases *NONROW*($mode_o$) and ∿*NONROW*($mode_o$) is implied by the solution adopted to treat local names [14] . Indeed, the descriptor of the multiple value may be stored on *WOST%* behind the name, but this information is dynamic. In order to be able to proceed in the static management with one single static property, an instruction has to be generated in order to force the copy of the descriptor on *WOST%* if it is not already there}.

Step E-1 : *BOST* static properties :

$cadd_o$:= (dirwost' bnc.tadd$_s$ + staticszname)

{*staticszname* means" staticsize of a name referring to a non-row value "; in our case it is 2.}

smr_o := smr_s

dmr_o := nil

gc_o := ($gc_o \neq$ nil | gc_s
 |:flexbot$_s \neq 0$ | bnc.gcc
 | nil).

Step E-2 : Generation of run-time actions :

Step E-2.1 : Gc :

($gc_o \neq$ nil | GENSTANDGC).

Step E-2.2 : Copy :

GEN(stndescrwost mode§ : $mode_o$,
 cadd§ : $cadd_o$) {15}

Action :

If the descriptor pointed to by the name of access $cadd_o$ and mode $mode_o$ is not stored in a location just after the name, then a copy of the descriptor in this location is performed and the name *pointer%* is made equal to the address of the new instance of this descriptor.

Case F :

$class_s$ = indwost.

{the pointer of the name is stored on *WOST%*}.

Step F-1 : *BOST* static properties :

$cadd_o$:= (indwost bnc.tadd of smr_s + Δmem)

smr_o := smr_s

dmr_o := nil

gc_o := ($gc_s \neq$ nil | gc_s
 |:derefo$_s$ | bnc.gcc
 | nil).

Step F-2 : Generation of dynamic actions :

Step F-2.1 : Gc :

($gc_o \neq$ nil | GENSTANDGC).

Step F-2.2 : Copy :

GEN(stword cadds§ : (indwost add_s),
 caddo§ : (dirwost add_o)). {4}

Remark

In case of $class_s$ = indiden or indwost a remark similar to remark 1 of II.11.1 holds. It has been implemented in the X8 compiler.

11.3 SLICE

Different translation strategies have to be implemented according the slice applies to a name or not, and according the result is of mode *row/ref row* or not.

Syntax

SLICE → slice∇ PRIMSLICE INDEXERS

INDEXERS → [INDEXER1 , ..., INDEXERn]

INDEXERi → TRIMMER|
INDEX

{with slice∇ the *DECTAB* pointer $mode_o$ corresponding to the value resulting from the slice, is associated}.

Translation scheme

1. ρ(PRIMSLICE)
2. Check of *nil*
3. Check of *flex*
4. Descriptor space reservation
5. ρ'(INDEXERS)
6. Initializations
7. *for i to NBDIM* ($mode_s$)
   do A" *GEN(trimmer ...)*
   B" *GEN(index ...)*
   od
8. *GEN(fillstrides...)*
9. A *NONREF*($mode_s$) *and* ~*NONROW*($mode_o$)
   B *NONREF*($mode_s$) *and NONROW*($mode_o$)
   C ~ *NONREF*($mode_s$) *and* ~*NONROW(DEREF*($mode_o$))
   D ~ *NONREF*($mode_s$) *and NONROW(DEREF*($mode_o$)).

Semantics

Step 1 :

ρ(PRIMSLICE)

{The static properties of the value on which the slice applies appear on *BOST* ; they are denoted $mode_s$, $cadd_s$ ...}

ASSLICE ($cadd_s$) (see II.2.4 and II.12.1).

Step 2 : Check of *nil* :

(~ *NONREF*($mode_s$) *and* $cadd_s \neq$ *variden*
|*GEN(checknil cadd§ :* $cadd_s$)) {106}

Step 3 : Check of *flex* :

(∼ *NONREF*($mode_s$) *and flextop of* TOPST[*topstpm-1*] = (*stat 1*)

|*GEN*(*checkflex cadd§* : $cadd_s$) {61}

{Action :

A run-time alarm is provided if the name with access *cadd§* is flexible.}

|: ∼*NONREF*($mode_s$) *and class of flextop of* TOPST[*topstpm-1*] = *dyn*

|*GEN*(*checkflexr bncrout§* : *spec of flextop of* TOPST[*topstpm-1*],

cadd§ : $cadd_s$)) {62}

{Action :

(*flex% of* (*h%*) RANST%[DISPLAY%[*bncrout§*]] = 1.}

|*co* if the name with access *cadd§* is flexible then a run-time alarm is provided *co*))

Step 4 : Descriptor space reservation :

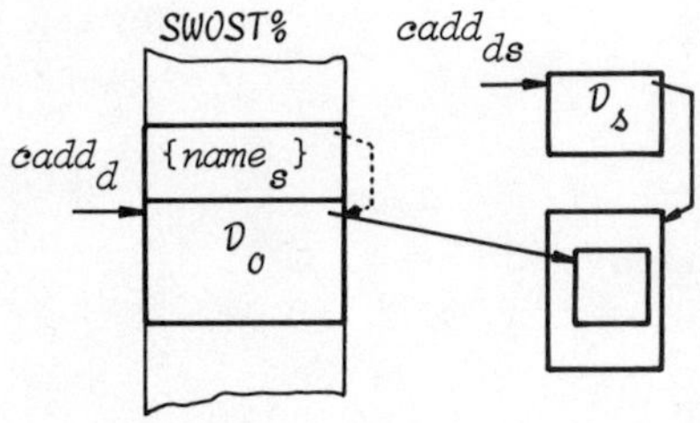

Case A' :

NONREF($mode_s$).

$mode_d$:= $mode_o$

$cadd_d$:= (*dirwost bnc.swostc* + Δ*mem*)

smr_d := *bnc.swostc*

{$cadd_d$ and smr_d are properties related to the descriptor of the resulting value ; it is constructed in the first free cell of *SWOST%* (see remark 2)}

$cadd_{ds}$:= $cadd_s$.

{$cadd_{ds}$ is the address of the source descriptor}.

Case B' :

∼ *NONREF*($mode_s$).

$mode_d$:= *DEREF*($mode_o$)

$cadd_d$:= (*dirwost bnc.swostc* + Δ*mem* + *staticsznrname*)

smr_d := *bnc.swostc*

{Here space is reserved from the first free cell of *SWOST%* for the resulting name and the descriptor, if any, referred to by this name}.

$cadd_{ds}$:= *DEREFCADD*($cadd_s$).

Step 5 :

ρ'(INDEXERS)

{All tertiaries of the indexers are translated, their properties including those of the default tertiaries appear on *BOST* and this together with a flag allowing their correct interpretation (trimmer or index). For a trimmer in the ith dimension, we have three sets of static properties denoted $cadd_{li}$ ... $cadd_{ui}$ ... and $cadd_{l'i}$ ... respectively.

For an index in the ith dimension we have one set denoted $cadd_i$ ...}.

Step 6 : Initializations :

reladd := relative address of the field *bounds%* of the first dimension in the descriptor of access $cadd_d$, to be constructed.

GEN(stword cadds§ : $cadd_{ds}$,
caddo§ : $cadd_d$) {4}

{the offset is copied}.

Step 7 :

for i to NBDIM($mode_s$)

do

Case A" :

The indexer is a trimmer.

GEN(trimmer n°dim§ : i,
cadds§ : $cadd_{ds}$,
caddl§ : $cadd_{li}$,
caddu§ : $cadd_{ui}$,
caddl'§ : $cadd_{l'i}$,
caddoff§: $cadd_d$,
caddt§ : (dirwost bnc.$tadd_d$ + reladd)) {63}

-*cadds§* and *n°dim§* give access to the current triplet *bounds%* in the source descriptor. Let l_i%, u_i% and d_i% be the corresponding three integer values.

-*caddl§*, *caddu§* and *caddl'§* give access to the three integers resulting from the corresponding indexer ; they are denoted *l%*, *u%* and *l'%*.

-*caddoff§* gives access to the object offset denoted off_o%.

-*caddt§* is the access to the location where the current triplet *bounds%* has to be stored in the object descriptor ; the corresponding fields are denoted l_t%, u_t% and d_t%.

Action :

(li% ≤ l% and u% ≤ u_i%
*| off_o% +:= (l%-l_i%) * d_i% ;*
l_t% := l'% ;
u_t% := (l'%-l%) + u% ;
d_t% := d_i%
| co an error message is provided co)

reladd +:= co the size of an element of the field *bounds% co*.

Case B" :

The indexer is an index .

GEN(index n°dim§ : i,
cadds§ : $cadd_{ds}$,
caddi§ : $cadd_i$,
caddoff§ : $cadd_d$) {64}

-*cadds§* and *n°dim§* give access to $l_i\%$, $u_i\%$ and $d_i\%$ (see step 7, case A).

-*caddi§* gives access to the offset denoted here *k%*.

-*caddoff§* gives access to the offset of the object descriptor denoted $off_o\%$.

Action :

$(l_i\% \leqslant k\% \leqslant u_i\%$
$|off_o\% +:= (k\%-l_i\%) * d_i\%$
$|$ co an error message is provided co)

od.

Step 8 :

GEN(stfillstrides mode§ : $mode_d$,
caddescr§: $cadd_d$) {66}

Action :

The descriptor characterized by *mode§-caddescr§* is completed i.e., the fields (with *n=NBDIM(mode§)*)

states% := (1,1,...,1)

iflag% := 1

for i to n

do $(l_i\% > u_i\% \mid d_o\% := 0 ; L)$

od ;

$d_o\% := \sum_{i=1}^{n} d_i\% * (u_i\%-l_i\%) + STATICSIZE\ (DEROW(mode\S))$

L :.

Step 9 :

A number of cases based on $mode_s$ and $mode_o$ are now distinguished ; through these cases the static properties $mode_o$, or_o and $scope_o$ on *BOST* are treated in the same way :

$mode_o := mode_o$ explicit in the source text.

$or_o := or_s$

$sc_o := sc_s$

Their storage on *BOST* will remain explicit.

Case A :

$NONREF(mode_s)$ and $\sim NONROW(mode_o)$.

Case A.1 :

$class_s$ = *dircttab.*

<u>Step</u> A.1-1 : *BOST* static properties :

$cadd_o$:= (<u>*dirwost*</u>'*add*$_d$)

smr_o := smr_d

dmr_o := <u>*nil*</u>

gc_o := <u>*nil*</u>

No other run-time action is implied.

<u>Case</u> A.2 :

$class_s$ = <u>*diriden*</u>.

See case A.1 except for gc_o :

gc_o := (*derefo*$_s$ <u>*and*</u> *flexo*$_s$ ≠ 0 |*bnc.gcc*
|<u>*nil*</u>)

(gc_o ≠ <u>*nil*</u> | *GENSTANDGC*).

<u>Case</u> A.3 :

$class_s$ = <u>*indiden*</u>.

See case A.1 except gc_o :

gc_o := (*kindo*$_s$ = <u>*var*</u> <u>*or*</u> *flexo*$_s$ ≠ 0 |*bnc.gcc*
|<u>*nil*</u>)

(gc_o ≠ <u>*nil*</u> | *GENSTANDGC*).

<u>Case</u> A.4 :

$class_s$ = <u>*dirwost*</u>.

<u>Step</u> A.4-1 : *BOST* static properties :

$cadd_o$:= (<u>*dirwost*</u> *add*$_d$)

smr_o := smr_s

dmr_o := dmr_s

gc_o := gc_s.

<u>Step</u> A.4-2 : Generation of run-time actions :

<u>Step</u> A.4-2.1 : Gc :

(gc_o ≠ <u>*nil*</u> |*GENSTANDGC*).

<u>Case</u> A.5 :

$class_s$ = <u>*dirwost'*</u>.

See case A.1 except smr_o and gc_o :

smr_o := smr_s

gc_o := gc_s

(gc_o ≠ <u>*nil*</u> | *GENSTANDGC*).

<u>Case</u> A.6 :

$class_s$ = <u>*indwost*</u>.

See case A.1 except gc_o

gc_o := (gc_s ≠ <u>*nil*</u> |gc_s
|:*derefo*$_s$ <u>*and*</u> *flexo*$_s$ ≠ 0 |*bnc.gcc*
|<u>*nil*</u>)

(gc_o ≠ <u>*nil*</u> | *GENSTANDGC*).

Case B :

NONREF($mode_s$) and *NONROW*($mode_o$).

{The descriptor constructed at $cadd_d$ reduces to its offset ; this one is used as indirect address of the result of the slice}.

Case B.1 :

$class_s$ = dircttab.

Step B.1-1 : BOST static properties :

$cadd_o$:= (indwost add_d)
smr_o := smr_d
dmr_o := nil
gc_o := nil

No dynamic action is implied.

Case B.2 :

$class_s$ = diriden.

See case B.1 except for gc_o :

gc_o := ($derefo_s$ and $flexo_s \neq 0$ | bnc.gcc
| nil)
($gc_o \neq$ nil | GENSTANDGC).

Case B.3 :

$class_s$ = indiden.

See case B.1 except gc_o :

gc_o := ($kindo_s$ = var or $flexo_s \neq 0$ | bnc.gcc
| nil)
($gc_o \neq$ nil | GENSTANDGC).

Case B.4 :

$class_s$ = dirwost.

{Remember I.2.3.2, rule b1 : no indirect addressing from WOST% to WOST% ; the copy of the static part of the result is forced on SWOST%.}

Step B.4-1 : BOST static properties :

$cadd_o$:= (dirwost bnc.$tadd_s$)
smr_o := smr_s
dmr_o := (dmr' := DMRRELEVANT($mode_o$) ;
class of dmr' = nil | nil
|:class of dmr_s = stat | $tadd_o$ +:=1 ; {avoid offset superseding}
dmr_s
| dmr_s)
gc_o := ($gc_s \neq$ nil and GCRELEVANT($mode_o$) | gc_s
| nil).

Step B.4-2 : Generation of dynamic actions :

Step B.4-2.1 : Dmr :

$(dmr_o$ = nil and class of dmr_s = stat
  |GEN(stword caddsS : (dirwost add of dmr_s),
      caddo§ : (dirabs ranstpm%))   {4}

| : dmr_o = nil and class of dmr_s = dyn
  |GEN(stword cadds§ : (dirdmrw add of dmr_s),
      caddo§ : (dirabs ranstpm%))   {4}

{Memory is recovered on DWOST%}.

Step B.4-2.2 : Gc :

$(gc_s \neq$ nil and gc_o = nil
  |GEN(stgcnil caddgc§ : (dirgcw bnc.gc_s)))   {13}

$(gc_s \neq$ nil | GENSTANDGC).

Step B.4-2.3 : Copy :

GEN(ststatwost mode§ : $mode_o$,
  cadds§: (indwost add_d),
  caddo§: $cadd_o$).   {12}

Step B.4-2.4 :

NOOPT.

Case B.5 :

$class_s$ = dirwost'.

See case B.1 except smr_o and gc_o :

  $smr_o := smr_s$
  $gc_o := gc_s$
  $(gc_o \neq$ nil | GENSTANDGC).

Case B.6 :

$class_s$ = indwost.

see case B.1 except gc_o which is treated as gc_o in case A.6 and $smr_o := smr_s$.

Case C :

∿NONREF($mode_s$) and ∿NONROW(DEREF($mode_o$)).

{The result is a name for which space has been reserved in front of the descriptor. This name has to be constructed}.

GEN(stname caddpointer§ : (varwost add_d),
  caddscope§ : $cadd_s$,
  caddo§ : (dirwost bnc.$tadd_d$ - staticsznrname))   {67}

Action :

A name is stored at the address caddo§ :

pointer% := address corresponding to caddpointer§

scope% := copy of the scope of the name with address caddscope§.

Case C.1 :

$class_s$ = diriden.

Step C.1-1 : *BOST* static properties :

$cadd_o$:= (dirwost bnc.$tadd_d$ - staticsznrname)

smr_o := smr_d

dmr_o := nil

gc_o := ($derefo_s$ or $flexbot_s$ = 0 |bnc.gcc
|nil)

($gc_o \neq$ nil | GENSTANDGC)

NOOPT.

Case C.2 :

$class_s$ = indiden .

See case C.1 except gc_o :

gc_o := bnc.gcc

GENSTANDGC.

Case C.3 :

$class_s$ = variden.

See case C.1 except gc_o :

gc_o := ($flexbot_s \neq 0$ |bnc.gcc
|nil)

($gc_o \neq$ nil |GENSTANDGC).

Case C.4 :

$class_s$ = dirwost.

See case C.1 except smr_o and gc_o :

smr_o := smr_s

($gc_s \neq$ nil |gc_s
|:$flexbot_s \neq 0$ |bnc.gcc
|nil)

($gc_o \neq$ nil | GENSTANDGC).

Case C.5 :

$class_s$ = indwost.

See case C.1 except smr_o and gc_o :

smr_o := smr_s

gc_o := ($gc_s \neq$ nil |gc_s
|:$flexbot_s \neq 0$ or $derefo_s$ |bnc.gcc
|nil)

($gc_o \neq$ nil | GENSTANDGC).

Case D :

∿ NONREF($mode_s$) and NONROW(DEREF($mode_o$)).

{No descriptor is involved, the offset stored at $cadd_d$ is used as name pointer ; the dynamic action reduces to store the scope}

GEN(stscope cadds§ : $cadd_s$,
caddo§ : $cadd_d$) {69}

Action :

The field *scope%* of the name stored at *cadds§* is stored in the field scope of the name stored at the address *caddo§*.

The management is identical to case C except

$cadd_o$:= (<u>*dirwost*</u> *bnc.tadd*$_d$).

Remark 1

If according to *TOPST* it appears that the subname resulting from a refslice will be immediately dereferenced, dereferencing is combined with slicing ; this allows to avoid the name construction on *WOST%*.

Remark 2

In the above descriptions, space for the resulting descriptor is reserved at the top of *WOST%* ; it would be more efficient, as far as *WOST%* space consumption is concerned to overwrite the source descriptor when this one is on *WOST%*.

Remark 3

The *iflag%* of the descriptor is systematically set to 1, which indicates that the elements of the multiple value are not necessarily contiguous ; this causes less efficient algorithms to be used at run-time, to manipulate (copy for example) the multiple value. Clearly in some cases easily detectable, *iflag%* could be set to 0 given the elements are contiguous ; this would increase for these cases the run-time efficiency.

Remark 4

Each indexer gives rise to a new ICI (<u>*trimmer*</u> or <u>*index*</u>). All the ICIs could be grouped in a single one, thus causing less redundancy in the ICI parameters and leaving more liberty for generating machine instructions.

Remark 5

The revised version of ALGOL 68 allows selections to be performed through rows. This is easily implemented : the resulting descriptor has an offset which is the one of the source descriptor incremented by the relative address of the selected field inside the structured value.

Remark 6

If array elements are stored in machine bits or bytes instead of words the above algorithms have to be reconsidered.

11.4 UNITING

Syntax

UNITED → uniting∇ UNCOERCEND

{With uniting∇, the mode of the result of uniting, $mode_0$, is associated}.

Translation scheme

1. ρ(UNCOERCEND)
2. A. Uniting union

   B. Uniting not-union

1. $class_s$ = constant or	
" = dircttab	
2. " = diriden	1. *BOST*
3. " = indiden	2. *GEN*
4. " = variden	
5. " = dirwost	
6. " = dirwost'	
7. " = indwost.	

Semantics

The solution described below supposes that the union overheads are *DECTAB* pointers specifying the actual mode of the union value. For a given mode union, the order of the constituent modes is not fixed ; hence handling of union values requires a dynamic check on equality of modes. Two main cases have to be considered according *UNION*($mode_s$) *is* true or not.

Step 1 :

ρ(UNCOERCEND)

{The static properties of the value to be united appear on *BOST* ; they are denoted $mode_s$, $cadd_s$ ... . The *TOPST* management of *Δmem* ensures space reservation for the overhead on *WOST%*}.

Step 2 :

Case A : Uniting union :

UNION($mode_s$).

Only the mode has to be modified on *BOST* ; no dynamic action is implied given the overhead has the form of a *DECTAB* pointer where the actual mode of the value is specified.

Case B : Uniting not union :

∼ *UNION*($mode_s$) .

{An overhead has to be created ; if the source value is on *WOST%*, space for this overhead has been foreseen in front of the value thanks to *Δmem* of the *TOPST* element set up at ρ(UNCOERCEND). *Δunion* represents the size of the overhead in memory words, in practice *Δunion = 1*}.

A number of subcases are now distinguished, they are based on $class_s$. Through these cases the static properties $mode_o$, or_o and $scope_o$ are treated in the same way :

$mode_o$:= mode of the coercend after uniting (see syntax).

$or_o := or_s$

$sc_o := sc_s$

Their storage on *BOST* will remain implicit.

Case B.1 :

$class_s$ = constant or

" = dircttab.

{The resulting value could be constructed in *CONSTAB* ; here a solution where the value is constructed on *WOST%* is described}.

Step B.1-1 : *BOST* static properties :

```
caddo := (dirwost bnc.swostc + Δmem)
smro  := bnc.swostc
dmro  := (dmr' := DMRRELEVANT(modes) ;
           (class of dmr' = stat  |(stat
                                    bnc.tadd of dmr' + taddo + Δunion)
           |:class of dmr' = dyn  |(dyn bnc.dmrc)
                                  |nil))
gco := nil.
```

Step B.1-2 : Generation of run-time actions :

Step B.1-2.1 : Dmr :

```
(class of dmro = dyn
         |GEN(stdmrwost cadd§   : (dirabs ranstpm%),
                        cadddmr§: (dirdmrw bnc.add of dmro))   {7}
```

Step B.1-2.2 : Copy :

```
GEN(stoverhunion mode§ : modes,
                 cadd§ : caddo).                               {17}
```

Action :

An overhead corresponding to $mode_s$ is stored at the address $cadd_o$.

```
GEN(stwost3 mode§ : modes,
            cadds§: cadds,
            caddo§: (dirwost bnc.taddo + Δunion))              {3}
```

Action :

The value characterized by *mode§-cadds§* is stored at the address *caddo§* (see II.1).

N.B This last copy could be avoided, see remarks.

Step B.1-2.3 :

NOOPT.

<u>Case</u> B.2 :

$class_s$ = <u>*diriden*</u>.

See case B.1 except for gc_o and the corresponding IC generation :

```
gc_o := (GCRELEVANT(mode_s) and derefo_s |bnc.gcc
                                         |nil)
(gc_o ≠ nil | GENSTANDGC).
```

<u>Case</u> B.3 :

$class_s$ = <u>*indiden*</u>.

See case B.1 except for gc_o and the corresponding IC generation :

```
gc_o := (GCRELEVANT(mode_s) |bnc.gcc
                            |nil)
(gc_o ≠ nil | GENSTANDGC).
```

<u>Case</u> B.4 :

$class_s$ = <u>*variden*</u>.

See case B.1 except for drm_o and the corresponding IC generation :

dmr_o := <u>*nil*</u>.

<u>Case</u> B.5 :

$class_s$ = <u>*dirwost*</u>.

<u>Step</u> B.5-1 : *BOST* static properties :

```
cadd_o := (dirwost bnc.tadd_s - Δunion)
smr_o := smr_s
dmr_o := {it must be checked whether the overhead does supersede a dmr informa-
        tion, in which case this information must be saved on DMRWOST%}
        (class of dmr_s = stat and
        tadd_o ≤ tadd of dmr_s < tadd_s
          |flag := 1 ; (dyn bnc.dmrc)
          |flag := 0 ; dmr_s)
gc_o := gc_s.
```

<u>Step</u> B.5-2 : Generation of run-time actions :

<u>Step</u> B.5-2.1 : Dmr :

```
(flag=1 | GEN(stdmrwost cadd§ : (dirwost add of dmr_s),
                         cadddmr§ : (dirdmrw dmr_o))     {7}
```

<u>Step</u> B.5-2.2 : Copy :

```
GEN(stoverhunion mode§ : mode_s,
                 cadd§ : cadd_o)                 {17}
```

<u>Case</u> B.6 :

$class_s$ = <u>*dirwost'*</u>.

{an overhead is created and the copy of the dynamic part is forced on *WOST%*}

<u>Step</u> B.6-1 : *BOST* static properties :

$cadd_o$:= (<u>dirwost</u> bnc.$tadd_s$ − Δunion)

smr_o := smr_s

dmr_o := (dmr' := DMRRELEVANT($mode_s$) ;

(class <u>of</u> dmr' = <u>stat</u> |(<u>stat</u> bnc.tadd <u>of</u> $cadd_s$ + tadd <u>of</u> dmr')

|:class <u>of</u> dmr' = <u>dyn</u> |(<u>dyn</u> bnc.dmrc)

| <u>nil</u>)

gc_o := gc_s.

<u>Step</u> B.6-2 : Generation of run-time actions :

<u>Step</u> B.6-2.1 : Dmr :

(class <u>of</u> dmr_o = <u>dyn</u>

|GEN(<u>stdmrwost</u> cadd§ : (<u>dirabs</u> ranstpm%),

cadddmr§: (<u>dirdmrw</u> bnc.add <u>of</u> dmr_o)) {7}

<u>Step</u> B.6-2.2 : Copy :

GEN(<u>stoverhunion</u> mode§ : $mode_s$,
cadd§ : $cadd_o$) {17}

GEN(<u>stdynwost3</u> mode§ : $mode_s$,
cadd§ : $cadd_s$) {11}

<u>Action</u> :

The dynamic part of the stored value characterized by mode§-cadd§ is stored on RANST% from ranstpm%.

<u>Case</u> B.7 :

$class_s$ = <u>indwost</u>.

{an overhead is created and the copy of the whole value is forced on WOST%}

See case B.6 except $cadd_o$ and the corresponding IC generation for the copy :

$cadd_o$ = (<u>dirwost</u> bnc.tadd <u>of</u> smr_s + Δmem)

GEN(<u>stwost3</u> mode§ : $mode_s$,
cadds§: $cadd_s$,
caddo§: (<u>dirwost</u> bnc.$tadd_o$ + Δunion)) {3}

<u>Remark 1</u>

The use of DECTAB at run-time for handling values of mode <u>union</u> can be avoided at the price of some additional compile-time actions : in DECTAB the constituent modes of all union modes must be ordered consistently. In this way the run-time overhead can be replaced by the number of the constituent mode in the ordering. It is to be noted that now, a uniting of a united mode may imply a run-time modification of the source overhead. Suppose we have to translate an action (copy for example) on a union value, and suppose T1,T2,...Tn are the IC to be generated for translating the action applied to the values of the n constituent modes of the union. With the strategy described in this report, we generate :

(overhead% = mode1 $|T_1$
$|$*:overhead% = mode2* $|T_2$
...
$|$*:overhead% = moden* $|T_n$ *)*

With the strategy avoiding the use of *DECTAB* we would generate *(overhead%* $|$*T1,T2,...Tn).*

Remark 2

The above translation of uniting is not optimal ; it could be improved in two ways :

(1) By accepting to have values of mode union with an access class ***dirwost'***, which would avoid the copies of the dynamic parts of united values.

(2) By having a new access class ***unionwost*** meaning that only the overhead of a union value is stored on *WOST%* together with a pointer to the actual value.
An alternative solution of (2) would consist in keeping the source access unchanged but in having another property on *BOST* telling whether the value has been united and in this case, indicating which is the overhead. In this way the run-time representation will only be constructed when the union value will have to be copied. Note that this solution becomes redundant if previsions are implemented.

11.5 ROWING

Syntax

ROWING → rowing∇ ROWCOERCEND

{Consecutive rowings are supposed to be grouped ; with rowing∇, the mode of ROWCOERCEND ($mode_s$) and the mode after rowing ($mode_o$) are associated ; Δrow is defined as the space needed for extending the static part of the source value according to all consecutive rowings to be performed}.

Translation scheme

1. Prefix translation
2. ρ(ROWCOERCEND)
3. Check of *nil*
4. Check of *flex*
5. A *NONREF*($mode_o$) and ~*NONROW*($mode_s$)

1. $class_s$ = *dircttab*	1. *BOST*
2. " = *diriden*	2. *GEN*
3. " = *indiden*	
4. " = *dirwost*	
5. " = *dirwost'*	
6. " = *indwost*	

5. B *NONREF*($mode_o$) <u>and</u> *NONROW*($mode_s$)

1. $class_s$ = <u>*constant*</u>	
2. " = <u>*dircttab*</u> <u>*or*</u>	
" = <u>*diriden*</u>	1. *BOST*
3. " = <u>*indiden*</u>	2. *GEN*
4. " = <u>*variden*</u>	
5. " = <u>*dirwost*</u>	
6. " = <u>*dirwost'*</u>	
7. " = <u>*indwost*</u>	

5. C ∿*NONREF*($mode_o$) <u>and</u> ∿*NONROW*(*DEREF*($mode_s$))

1. $class_s$ = <u>*diriden*</u>	
2. " = <u>*indiden*</u>	1. *BOST*
3. " = <u>*variden*</u>	2. *GEN*
4. " = <u>*dirwost*</u>	
5. " = <u>*indwost*</u>	

5. D ∿*NONREF*($mode_s$) <u>and</u> *NONROW*(*DEREF*($mode_s$))

1. $class_s$ = <u>*diriden*</u>	
2. " = <u>*indiden*</u>	
3. " = <u>*variden*</u>	1. *BOST*
4. " = <u>*dirwost*</u>	2. *GEN*
5. " = <u>*indwost*</u>.	

<u>Semantics</u>

<u>Step</u> 1 : Prefix translation :

(*NONREF*($mode_o$) <u>and</u>
NONROW($mode_s$) <u>and</u>
class <u>*of*</u> *DMRRELEVANT*($mode_s$) ≠ <u>*nil*</u>
 | *GEN*(<u>*incrrtwostpm*</u> *caddincr§* : (<u>*intct*</u> *STATICSIZE*($mode_s$)) {25}
  <u>Action</u> :
  Let *i* be the integer of access *caddincr§* ;
  ranstpm% +:= *i*
  {The garbage collector may be called}
)

This step takes into account I.2.4.2, Remark 2. According to what, when a rowing applies to a nonrow value, the static part of the source value, if stored on *SWOST%*, must be copied on *DWOST%*. Here space is foreseen for such a copy.

<u>Step</u> 2 :

ρ(ROWCOERCEND)

{We recall here that at the entry of ρ calls, the management of *TOPST* is performed. In case of ROWCOERCEND, *Δmem* in the new *TOPST* element is the *Δmem* of the subjacent *TOPST* element incremented by *Δrow*. In this way, after the translation ρ(ROWCOERCEND), if its result is on *WOST%*, there is always space enough, in front of the static part of the value to extend the descriptor according to the number of rowings *nrow*. Also, after this translation, the static properties of ROWCOERCEND appear on *BOST*. They are denoted $mode_s$, $cadd_s$ ...}.

Step 3 : Check of *nil* :

(∼ *NONREF*($mode_o$).
 | *GEN*(*checknil cadd§* : $cadd_s$)) {106}

Step 4 : Check of *flex* :

(∼*NONREF*($mode_o$) *and* ... (see II.11.3, step 3)).

Step 5 :

A number of cases based on $mode_s$ and $mode_o$ are now distinguished ; through these cases, the static properties $mode_o$, or_o and $scope_o$ on *BOST* are treated in the same way :

$mode_o$:= $mode_o$
or_o := or_s
sc_o := sc_s.

Case A :

NONREF($mode_o$) *and* ∼*NONROW*($mode_s$).

Case A.1 :

$class_s$ = *dirctab*.

Step A.1-1 : *BOST* static properties :

$cadd_o$:= (*dirwost' bnc.swostc* + Δ*mem*)
smr_o := *bnc.swostc*
dmr_o := *nil*
gc_o := *nil*.

Step A.1-2 : Generation of run-time actions :

Step A.1-2.1 : Copy :

GEN(*rowingrow modes§* : $mode_s$,
 modeo§ : $mode_o$,
 cadds§ : $cadd_s$,
 caddo§ : $cadd_o$) {74}

Action :

A descriptor is constructed at the address *caddo§*. This descriptor is the descriptor of the multiple value stored at $cadd_s$, rowed a number of times according to *modes§* and *modeo§*.

Case A.2 :

$class_s$ = *diriden*.

See case A.1 except for gc_o :

gc_o := ($derefo_s$ *and* $flexo_s$ ≠ 0
 | *bnc.gcc*
 | *nil*)

(gc_o ≠ *nil* | *GENSTANDGC*).

<u>Case</u> A.3 :

$class_s$ = <u>indiden</u>.

See case A.1 except gc_o :

gc_o := ($kindo_s$ = <u>var</u> <u>or</u> $flexo_s \neq 0$
| bnc.gcc
| <u>nil</u>)

($gc_o \neq$ <u>nil</u> | GENSTANDGC).

<u>Case</u> A.4 :

$class_s$ = <u>dirwost</u>.

<u>Step</u> A.4-1 : BOST static properties :

$cadd_o$:= (<u>dirwost</u> bnc.$tadd_s$ − Δrow)

smr_o := smr_s

dmr_o := see II.11.4 step B.5-1

gc_o := gc_s.

<u>Step</u> A.4-2 : Generation of run-time actions :

<u>Step</u> A.4-2.1 : Dmr :

See II.11.4 step B.5-2.1.

<u>Step</u> A.4-2.2 : Gc :

($gc_o \neq$ <u>nil</u> | GENSTANDGC).

<u>Step</u> A.4-2.3 : Copy :

See case A.1, but here, source bound%'s have not to be copied.

<u>Case</u> A.5 :

$class_s$ = <u>dirwost</u>'.

<u>Step</u> A.5-1 : BOST static properties :

$cadd_o$:= (<u>dirwost</u>' bnc.$tadd_s$ − Δrow)

smr_o := smr_s

dmr_o := <u>nil</u>

gc_o := gc_s.

<u>Step</u> A.4-2 : Generation of run-time actions :

<u>Step</u> A.5-2.1 : Gc :

($gc_o \neq$ <u>nil</u> | GENSTANDGC).

<u>Step</u> A.5-2.2 : Copy :

see step A.4-2.3.

<u>Case</u> A.6 :

$class_s$ = <u>indwost</u>.

<u>Step</u> A.6-1 : BOST static properties :

$cadd_o$:= (<u>dirwost</u>' bnc.tadd <u>of</u> smr_s + Δmem)

smr_o := smr_s

dmr_o := <u>nil</u>

gc_o := ($gc_s \neq$ <u>nil</u> | gc_s
|: $derefo_s$ <u>and</u> $flexo_s \neq 0$ | bnc.gcc
| <u>nil</u>).

Step A.6-2 : Generation of run-time actions :

Step A.6-2.1 : Gc :

(gc_o ≠ nil | GENSTANDGC).

Step A.6-2.2 : Copy :

see step A.1-2.1.

Case B :

NONREF($mode_o$) and NONROW($mode_s$).

Case B.1 :

$class_s$ = constant.

Step B.1-1 : *BOST* static properties :

$cadd_o$:= (dirwost bnc.swostc + Δmem)
smr_o := bnc.swostc
dmr_o := (stat $tadd_o$)
gc_o := nil.

Step B.1-2 : Generation of run-time actions :

Step B.1-2.1 : Copy :

```
GEN(stliteralrow mode§  : mode_o,
                 cadds§ : cadd_s,
                 caddo§ : cadd_o)              {83}
```

Action :

A multiple value of *mode§* and with one element of access *cadds§* (which corresponds to a literal) is stored on *WOST%* at the access *caddo§*. The element is stored on *DWOST%* which implies to increment *ranstpm%* ; hence, the garbage collector may be called.

Case B.2 :

$class_s$ = dircttab or
" = diriden.

Step B.2-1 : *BOST* static properties :

$cadd_o$:= (dirwost' bnc.swostc + Δmem)
smr_o := bnc.swostc
dmr_o := nil
gc_o := nil

Step B.2-2 : Generation of run-time actions :

Step B.2-2.1 : Copy :

```
GEN(rowingscades modeo§ : mode_o,
                 cadds§ : cadd_s,
                 caddo§ : cadd_o)              {70}
```

Action :

The descriptor of a multiple value of *modeo§* and with one element of address *cadds§* is constructed on *SWOST%* at the address *caddo§*.

Case B.3 :

$class_s$ = *indiden*.

See case B.2 except for gc_o :

gc_o := (kindo_s = var |gcc |nil)

($gc_o \neq$ nil | GENSTANDGC).

Case B.4 :

$class_s$ = *variden*.

See case B.1 except copy :

GEN(rowingvar modeo§ : $mode_o$,
cadds§ : $cadd_s$,
caddo§ : $cadd_o$) {71}

Action :

The multiple value of *modeo§* and with an element of access $cadd_s$ = *(variden x.y)* is constructed on *WOST%* at the address $cadd_o$. The element is stored on *DWOST%* ; *ranstpm%* has to be incremented and the garbage collector may be called. The name has the following form :

pointer% := DISPLAY% [bn of BLOCKTAB§ [x]] +h+y

scope% := DISPLAY% [bn of BLOCKTAB [x]].

Case B.5 :

$class_s$ = *dirwost*.

Step B.5-1 : *BOST* static properties :

$cadd_o$:= (dirwost bnc.tadd of smr_s + Δmem)

smr_o := smr_s

dmr_o := (stat $tadd_o$)

gc_o := gc_s.

Step B.5-2 : Generation of run-time actions :

Step B.5-2.1 : Gc :

($gc_o \neq$ nil | GENSTANDGC).

Step B.5-2.2 : Copy :

GEN(rowingscal2 modeo§ : $mode_o$,
cadds§ : $cadd_s$,
caddo§ : $cadd_o$,
dmrcs§ : dmr_s) {73}

Action 1 :

{*class of dmrs§ ≠ nil*}, *dmrs§* gives access to the *RANST%* pointer of the first cell of the dynamic part of the value. Step 1 has reserved space in front of this dynamic part for storing the static part. This static part of *cadds§* is copied in this space. In this way, rule b2 of I.2.3.2 is respected.

Action 2 :

A descriptor for a multiple value of *modeo§* with one element, the static part of which has been copied on *DWOST%* by action 1, is constructed at the address *caddo§*.

Case B.6 :

$class_s$ = dirwost'.

Step B.6-1 : BOST static properties :

$cadd_o$:= (dirwost bnc.tadd of smr_s + Δmem)
smr_o := smr_s
dmr_o := (stat $tadd_o$)
gc_o := ($gc_s \neq$ nil and GCRELEVANT($mode_o$) | gc_s
|: $derefo_s$ and GCRELEVANT($mode_o$) | bnc.gcc
| nil).

Step B.6-2 : Generation of run-time actions :

Step B.6-2.1 : Gc :

($gc_s \neq$ nil $\wedge$ gc_o = nil | GEN(stgcnil caddgc§ : (dirgcw gc_s)) {13}
|: $gc_o \neq$ nil | GENSTANDGC).

Step B.6-2.2 : Copy :

GEN(rowingscall modeo§ : $mode_o$,
caddS§ : $cadd_s$,
caddo§ : $cadd_o$) {72}

Action 1 :

The whole of the source value with access cadds§ is copied on DWOST% at the address :

ranstpm%-STATICSIZE($mode_s$)

{see step 1 and I.2.3.2, rule b4}.

Action 2 :

A descriptor for a multiple value of modeo§, with one element which has been copied on DWOST% by action 1 is constructed at the address caddo§.

Case B.7 :

$class_s$ = indwost.

Step B.7-1 : BOST static properties :

$cadd_o$:= (dirwost' bnc.smr_s + Δmem)
smr_o := smr_s
dmr_o := nil
gc_o := gc_s.

Step B.7-2 : Generation of run-time actions :

Step B.7-2.1 : Gc :

($gc_o \neq$ nil | GENSTANDGC).

Step B.7-2.2 : Copy :

GEN(rowingscades modeo§ : $mode_o$,
cadds§ : $cadd_s$,
caddo§ : $cadd_o$) {70}

Action :

A descriptor for a multiple value of modeo§ and with one element of access cadds§ is constructed on SWOST% at the address caddo§.

<u>Case</u> C :

$\sim$ *NONREF*$(mode_o)$ <u>and</u> $\sim$*NONROW*(*DEREF*$(mode_s)$).

<u>Case</u> C.1 :

$class_s$ = <u>*diriden*</u>.

<u>Step</u> C.1-1 : *BOST* static properties :

$cadd_o$:= (<u>*dirwost*</u> *bnc.swostc* + Δ*mem*)

smr_o := *bnc.swostc*

dmr_o := <u>*nil*</u>

gc_o := ($derefo_s$ <u>or</u> $flexbot_s \neq 0$ | *bnc.gcc*
| <u>*nil*</u>).

<u>Step</u> C.1-2 : Generation of run-time actions :

<u>Step</u> C.1-2.1 : Gc :

($gc_o \neq$ <u>*nil*</u> | *GENSTANDGC*).

<u>Step</u> C.1-2.2 : Copy :

GEN(<u>*rowingrefrow*</u> *modes§* : $mode_s$,
modeo§ : $mode_o$,
cadds§ : $cadd_s$,
caddo§ : $cadd_o$) {76}

<u>Action</u> 1 :

A descriptor for a multiple value of mode *DEREF(modeo§)* and resulting from the rowing of a multiple value of mode *DEREF(modes§)* and referred to by a name of access *cadds§* is constructed on *SWOST%* at the address (<u>*dirwost*</u> *hadd* <u>*of*</u> *caddo§.tadd* <u>*of*</u> *caddo§* + *staticsznrname*).

<u>Action</u> 2 :

A name referring to the descriptor created by action 1 and with a scope equal to the scope of the name of access *cadds§* is constructed at the address *caddo§*.

<u>Case</u> C.2 :

$class_s$ = <u>*indiden*</u>.

See case C.1 except gc_o :

gc_o := *bnc.gcc*

GENSTANDGC.

<u>Case</u> C.3 :

$class_s$ = <u>*variden*</u>.

See case C.1 except gc_o :

gc_o := ($flexbot_s \neq 0$ | *bnc.gcc* | <u>*nil*</u>)

($gc_o \neq$ <u>*nil*</u> | *GENSTANDGC*).

<u>Case</u> C.4 :

$class_s$ = <u>*dirwost*</u>.

See case C.1 except $cadd_o$, smr_o and gc_o

$cadd_o$:= (__dirwost__ bnc.$tadd_s$ - Δrow)
smr_o := smr_s
gc_o := (gc_s ≠ __nil__ | gc_s
|: $flexbot_s$ ≠ 0 | bnc.gcc
| __nil__)

(gc_o ≠ __nil__ | GENSTANDGC).

__Case__ C.5 :

$class_s$ = __indwost__.

See case C.1 except $cadd_o$, smr_o and gc_o :

$cadd_o$:= (__dirwost__ bnc.smr_s + Δmem)
smr_o := smr_s
gc_o := (gc_s ≠ __nil__ | gc_s
|: $derefo_s$ __or__ $flexbot_s$ ≠ 0 | bnc.gcc
| __nil__)

(gc_o ≠ __nil__ | GENSTANDGC).

__Case__ D :

∼ NONREF($mode_o$) __and__ NONROW (DEREF($mode_s$)).

__Case__ D.1 :

$class_s$ = __diriden__.

__Step__ D.1-1 : *BOST* static properties :

$cadd_o$:= (__dirwost__ bnc.swostc + Δmem)
smr_o := bnc.swostc
dmr_o := __nil__
gc_o := ($derefo_s$ | bnc.gcc | __nil__).

__Step__ D.1-2 : Generation of run-time actions :

__Step__ D.1-2.1 : Gc :

(gc_o ≠ __nil__ | GENSTANDGC).

__Step__ D.1-2.2 : Copy :

GEN(__rowingrefsca__ modeo§ : $mode_o$,
cadds§ : $cadd_s$,
caddo§ : $cadd_o$) {75}

__Action__ :

See step C.1-2.2 actions of rowing refrow, but here, the value referred to by the source name is not a multiple value.

__Case__ D.2 :

$class_s$ = __indiden__.

See case D.1 except gc_o :

gc_o := bnc.gcc
GENSTANDGC.

__Case__ D.3 :

$class_s$ = __variden__.

See case D.1 except gc_o :

gc_o := <u>nil</u>.

<u>Case</u> D.4 :

$class_s$ = <u>dirwost</u>.

See case D.1 except $cadd_o$, smr_o and gc_o :

$cadd_o$:= (<u>dirwost</u> bnc.tadd <u>of</u> smr_s + Δmem)

smr_o := smr_s

gc_o := gc_s

(gc_o ≠ <u>nil</u> | GENSTANDGC).

<u>Case</u> D.5 :

$class_s$ = <u>indwost</u>.

See case D.1 except $cadd_o$, smr_o and gc_o :

$cadd_o$:= (<u>dirwost</u> bnc.tadd <u>of</u> smr_s + Δmem)

smr_o := smr_s

```
gc_o := (gc_s ≠ nil  |gc_s
        |:derefo_s   |bnc.gcc
                     |nil)
```

(gc_o ≠ <u>nil</u> | GENSTANDGC).

12. CONFRONTATIONS

12.1 ASSIGNATION

Syntax

ASSIGNATION → assignation∇ DESTINATION := SOURCE.

Translation scheme

1. ρ(DESTINATION)
2. ρ(SOURCE) and check of overlapping
3. Scope checking and generation
   A. *GEN(assign ...)*
   B. Compile-time error message
   C. *GEN(assignscope ...)*
4. *BOST* static management.

Semantics

Step 1 :

INMSTACK((nihil 0)) ;

INMSTACK((nihil 0)) ;

{Two accesses are initialized, they may be superseded at the level of SLICE(c) or IDENTIFIER (II.11.3 and II.2.4)}

ρ(DESTINATION)

{After the translation ρ(DESTINATION), the static properties of the resulting value, which is a name, appear on *BOST* ; they are denoted $mode_d$, $cadd_d$,... .}

Step 2 :

ρ(SOURCE)

{After the translation ρ(SOURCE) the static properties of the resulting value appear on *BOST* ; they are denoted $mode_s$, $cadd_s$ ... .}

OUTMSTACK ($cadd_x$) ;

OUTMSTACK ($cadd_y$) ;

(∼ *NONROW* ($mode_s$)

or class of $cadd_s$ = *dirwost*

or deref of or_s

or class of $cadd_x$ = *variden*

  and class of $cadd_y$ = *variden*

  and add of $cadd_x \neq$ *add of* $cadd_y$

|*goto step3* {overlapping not possible}

|*GEN(<u>checkoverlap</u> mode§ : mode$_s$,*
cadds§: cadd$_s$,
caddo§: cadd$_o$,
labnb§: labnb) {107}

<u>Action</u> :

If the values of *mode§*, on the one hand referred to by the name of access *caddo§*, on the other hand of access *cadds§* may not overlap then <u>goto</u> *labnb*.

(class <u>of</u> cadd$_s$ = <u>dirwost</u>'

|*GEN(<u>stdynwost3</u> mode§ : mode$_s$,*
cadds§: cadd$_s$,
caddo§: cadd$_s$) {11}

|*GEN(<u>stdynwost3</u> mode§ : mode$_o$,*
cadds§: cadd$_s$,
caddo§: (<u>dirwost</u> bnc.swostc)) {11}

on *BOST*, *cadd$_s$* is adjusted according to the generated ICI.

GEN(<u>labdef</u> labnb§ : labnb) {28}

<u>Step</u> 3 : Scope checking and generation

Scope$_d$ and *scope$_s$* are compared (see algorithm I.2.5.1.c(2)) ; this gives rise to the following 3 cases :

<u>Case</u> A :

The static scope checking is relevant and OK.

GEN(<u>assign</u> modes§ : mode$_s$,
cadds§ : cadd$_s$,
caddd§ : cadd$_d$) {85}

<u>Action</u> :

The value characterized by *modes§-cadds§* is assigned to the name with an access *caddd§*. This ICI includes bounds checking. Moreover, as socn as a flexible array or a *<u>union</u>(...<u>row</u>...)* value is passed through in the data structure tree, corresponding source subvalues are stored in new locations on the *HEAP%* and bounds checking are inhibited. In this case, the garbage cc llector may be called. (For more details see PART III).

<u>Case</u> B :

Static scope checking is relevant and NOK.

A compile-time error message is provided.

<u>Case</u> C :

Static scope checking is irrelevant.

GEN(<u>assignscope</u> modes§ : mode$_s$,
cadds§ : cadd$_s$,
caddd§ : cadd$_d$) {86}

<u>Action</u> :

The assignation is performed as in case A, moreover, each time a name, a routine or a format of the data structure is assigned, its dynamic scope $scope\%_{si}$ is compared with the one ($scope\%_d$) of the destination. A run-time error message is provided in case $scope\%_d < scope\%_{si}$.

Step 4 : *BOST* static management :

In principle only the *BOST* properties of the source have to be deleted thus leaving the properties of the destination for characterizing the result of the assignation. However, if according to previsions, the assignation is dereferenced, the dereferencing is combined with the assignation by leaving on *BOST* the static properties of the destination instead of those of the source. This is particularly useful for translating combined assignations, like *x:=y:= ... :=a*, efficiently.

12.2 IDENTITY RELATION

Syntax

IDREL → idrel∇ TERTL $\{:=: \mid :\neq:\}_1^1$ TERTR(†).

Translation scheme

1. ρ(TERTL)
2. ρ(TERTR)
3. *BOST* static properties
4. *GEN(idrel ...)*.

Semantics

Step 1 :

ρ(TERTL)

{After the translation ρ(TERTL), the static properties of the resulting name appear on *BOST* ; they will be denoted $mode_l$, $cadd_l$ ...}.

Step 2 :

ρ(TERTR)

{After the translation ρ(TERTR), the static properties of the resulting name appear on *BOST* ; they will be denoted $mode_r$, $cadd_r$, ...} .

Step 3 : *BOST* static properties :

$mode_o$:= bool

dmr_o := nil

gc_o := nil

or_o := (nil, 0, 0, 0)

sc_o := (0, 0).

(†) The notation $\{...|...\}_i^j$ for alternatives is well known ; i,j indicate the number of repetitions allowed : i=1, j=1 correspond to one occurrence, i=0, j=1 correspond to an option, i=1, j=∞ correspond to a sequence, i=0, j=∞ correspond to a sequence option....

Case A :

$\{class_l \wedge class_r\} \neq \{$<u>dirwost</u> $\wedge$ <u>indwost</u>$\}^{(\dagger)}$.

cadd$_o$:= (<u>dirwost</u> *bnc.swostc* + Δ*mem*)

smr$_o$:= *bnc.swostc*.

Case B :

$class_l$ = {<u>dirwost</u> $\vee$ <u>indwost</u>}.

cadd$_o$:= (<u>dirwost</u> *bnc.tadd* <u>of</u> *smr*$_l$ + Δ*mem*)

smr$_o$:= *smr*$_l$.

Case C :

$class_l \neq$ {<u>dirwost</u> $\wedge$ <u>indwost</u>} <u>and</u> $class_r$ = {<u>dirwost</u> $\vee$ <u>indwost</u>}.

cadd$_o$:= (<u>dirwost</u> *bnc.tadd* <u>of</u> *smr*$_r$ + Δ*mem*)

smr$_o$:= *smr*$_r$.

Step 4 :

GEN(<u>idrel</u>{=|≠} *modesl§* : *mode*$_l$,
caddsl§ : *cadd*$_l$,
caddsr§ : *cadd*$_r$,
caddo§ : *cadd*$_o$) {91|92}

Action :

Case A :

NONROW(DEREF(modesl§)).

The *pointer%'s* of the names of access *caddsl§* and *caddsr§* are compared ; this delivers a boolean value which is stored at *caddo§*.

Case B :

∼ *NONROW(DEREF(modesl§))*.

Case B1

The *pointer%'s* of the names are equal.

The value <u>true</u> is stored at *caddo§*.

Case B2 :

The *pointers%*'s of the names are not equal and the *do%'s* of the descriptors referred to by the names are both equal to 0. The value <u>true</u> is stored at *caddo§*.(††)

Case B3 :

The *pointer%'s* of the names are not equal, *do%'s* are not both equal to 0 and the offsets are not equal.

The value <u>false</u> is stored at *caddo§*.

Other cases :

For each dimension, if *ui%-li%* and *di%* of the two descriptors are respectively equal then <u>true</u> else <u>false</u> is stored at *caddo§*.

(†) This notation stands for $class_l \neq$ <u>dirwost</u> $\wedge\ class_l \neq$ <u>indwost</u> $\wedge\ class_r \neq$ <u>dirwost</u> $\wedge\ class_r \neq$ <u>indwost</u>.

(††) This case is left undefined by the language [1] .

12.3 CONFORMITY RELATION (†)

Syntax

CONFREL → confrel∇ TERTL $\{::= | ::\}_1^1$ TERTR

{With confrel∇, the mode of TERTL is associated, it will be denoted $mode_l$}.

Translation scheme

1. Result static properties
2. ρ(TERTR)
3. A :: 1. *GEN(confto ...)*
   2. *BOST* static properties

   B ::= 1. Static management for TERTR
   2. *GEN(conftobec ...)*
   3. *GEN(jumpno l ...)*
   4. ρ(TERTL)
   5. *GEN(assign(scope)...)*
   6. *BOST* management
   7. *GEN(labdef l)*.

Semantics

Here, we disregard the possibility of performing a number of conformity checks in a static way : although this has been implemented it seems to be of quite relative interests.

Step 1 : Result static properties :

First of all the static properties of the result are put on *BOST* :

$mode_o$:= bool
$cadd_o$:= (dirwost bnc.swostc + Δmem)
smr_o := bnc.swostc
dmr_o := nil
gc_o := nil
or_o := (nil,0,0,0)
sc_o := (0,0)

Space is reserved on *SWOST%* for storing this result.

Step 2 :

ρ(TERTR)(††)

{The static properties of TERTR appear on *BOST* : they are denoted $mode_r$, $cadd_r$, ... }.

(†) Conformity relations do no longer exist is the revised language.

(††)Note that here, *SOPROG* is not scanned in a strict right to left way.

Step 3 :

Case A :

:: .

Step A.1 :

GEN(confto model§ : mode$_l$,
moder§ : mode$_r$,
caddr§ : cadd$_r$,
caddo§ : cadd$_o$) {95}

Action :

A check of conformity is performed between *model§* and the value *moder§-caddr§*. The boolean result is stored at *caddo§*.

Step A.2 : *BOST* static properties :

The static properties of TERTR are deleted from *BOST* (which may cause some dynamic management for *dmr* and *gc*).

Case B :

::= .

Step B.1 : Static management for TERTR* :

The problem is the following : if the result of the relation appears to be *true* then TERTL has to be elaborated serially with TERTR. Hence TERTR has to be prevented against side-effects and its copy must be forced on *WOST%*. However, during the elaboration of the conformity relation, TERTR may be 'deunited' and dereferenced a number of times to give a value of mode *DEREF(mode$_l$)*. According to this, we must define static properties for the value resulting from TERTR after deunitings and dereferencings and copied on *WOST%*. This value will be referred to as the value of TERTR*. The place where the value of TERTR* will be copied on *WOST%* must be chosen carefully ; cases where the value of TERTR or part of it, already stored on *WOST%*, is the value of TERTR* should not involve any extra run-time copy. According to this the static properties of TERTR* are defined and are caused to replace those of TERTR on *BOST*. They are denoted *mode*$*_r$, *cadd*$*_r$, ...

Step B.2 :

GEN(conftobec model§ : mode$_l$,
moder§ : mode$_r$,
caddo§ : cadd$_o$,
caddr§ : cadd$_r$,
gcr§ : gc$_r$,
dmrr§ : dmr$_r$,
*cadd*r§: cadd*$*_r$,
*gc*r§ : gc*$*_r$,
*dmr*r§ : dmr*$*_r$) {96}

Action 1 :

see step 3, case A, *confto*.

Action 2 :

If the result is *true*, the value *moder§-caddr§* after deunitings and dereferencings is copied at the address *cadd*r§* unless it was already there. Also the dynamic management of *gc* and *dmr* has to be performed according, on the one hand to *gcr§* and *dmrr§* for the value deleted and, on the other hand, to *gc*r§* and *dmr*r§* for the value to be stored on *WOST%*.

If the result is *false*, the value *moder§-caddr§* is deleted from *WOST%* ; this means that the *DWOST%* space is recovered thanks to *dmrr§* and the gc-protection is cancelled thanks to *gcr§*.

Step B.3 :

GEN(jumpno labnb§ : l,
cadd§ : $cadd_o$) {29}

Action :

If the boolean value stored at *cadd§* is *false* then *goto l*.

Step B.4 :

ρ(TERTL)

{The static properties of TERTL appear on *BOST*, they are denoted $mode_l$, $cadd_l$ ...}

Step B.5 :

GEN(assignscope mode§ : DEREF($mode_l$),
cadds§ : $cadd*_r$,
caddd§ : $cadd_l$) {86}

-Dynamic scope checking can be avoided in the same way as for assignations.

Action :

see II.12.1.

Step B.6 : *BOST* management :

The static properties of TERTL and TERTR* are deleted from *BOST* possibly together with the generation of run-time actions for *gc* and *dmr* management.

Step B.7 :

GEN(labdef labnb§ : l) {28}

N.B. The static management and the run-time actions of the ICI's generated are such that at this point only the static properties of the boolean result appear on *BOST* ; moreover, at run-time, at label *l*, only the boolean result appears on *WOST%*. In any case,instructions for dynamic management of *gc* and *dmr* corresponding to TERTR or TERTR* have been elaborated.

13. CALL OF STANDARD ROUTINES

Syntax

STDCALL → stdcall∇ (ACPAR1,ACPAR2,...,ACPARn)

{This syntax holds for standard formulas as well asfor standard functions. With stdcall∇ a *SYMBTAB* pointer is associated where the properties of a standard routine are found. They are denoted $mode_r$, $cadd_r$ ...}.

Translation scheme

1. *for* *i* *to* *n* *do*
   ρ(ACPARi) *od*
2. *BOST* static properties
3. *GEN(standcall...)*
4. Gc dynamic actions
5. Static management.

Semantics

The translation scheme which is given here applies to any standard formula. However, in practice, some formulas have to be treated in a particular way in order to increase the efficiency : such are formulas delivering a result in which the value itself of one of its parameters is involved. E.g. *op(int)int +*, *op(real)real +*, *op(compl)compl +*, *op(bool)int abs*, *op(char)int abs*, *op(bits)int abs*, *op(int)char repr* and *op(int) bits bin* ... do not imply any run-time action ; *im*, *re* can be treated as selections, *i* can be treated as a structure display and the run-time action of *conj* may be reduced thanks to an appropriate analysis of the static properties of the parameters. *String* operations may also be treated in a particular way, for example, the dynamic part of the result can directly be constructed on *HEAP%* which allows to avoid its copy when it is assigned thereafter. Finally, operations combined with assignation deserve a special treatment, their result being one of their parameters. When all the parameters of a standard call are denotations, the result can be calculated at compile-time and stored in *CONSTAB*, but one may ask oneself whether this is really worthwhile.

The general translation scheme is as follows :

Step 1 :

for *i* *to* *n* *do*
ρ(ACPARi) *od*

{The static properties of the n parameters appear on *BOST*, they are denoted *mode1*, *cadd1* ... *moden*, *caddn*...}.

<u>Step</u> 2 : *BOST* static properties :

First an analysis of the static properties of the parameters on *BOST* is performed, this results in

- *cadd"* i.e. the address of the first hole between the static parts of two parameters stored consecutively on *SWOST%*, hole with a size ⩾ *STATICSIZE (RESULT* $(mode_r)) + \Delta mem$. In case no hole satisfies the condition, *cadd"* = (<u>*nihil*</u> *0*) {see I.2.4.1, <u>example</u> 2.6 }
- *smr"* i.e. the first *smr*≠<u>*nil*</u> among *smri* ; if all *smri*=<u>*nil*</u>, *smr"*=<u>*nil*</u>
- *dmr"* i.e. the first *dmr*≠<u>*nil*</u> among *dmri* ; if all *dmri*=<u>*nil*</u>, *dmr"*=<u>*nil*</u>
- *dmr"'* i.e. the first *dmr* with a *class*=<u>*dyn*</u> among *dmri* ; if all *class* <u>*of*</u> *dmri*≠<u>*dyn*</u>, *dmr"'*=<u>*nil*</u>.
- *gc"* i.e. the first *gc*≠<u>*nil*</u> among *gci*, if all are <u>*nil*</u>, *gc"*=<u>*nil*</u>
- *insc"* i.e. the highest value of all *insci*.
- *outsc"* i.e. the lowest value of all *outsc*.

On *BOST* :

```
mode_o := RESULT(mode_r)
cadd_o := (mode_o = void | (nihil 0)
          |:cadd" ≠ nil | cadd"
                        | (dirwost bnc.swostc + Δmem))
smr_o := (mode_o = void | nil
         |:smr" ≠ nil   | smr"
                        | bnc.swostc)
dmr_o := (dmr' := (DMRRELEVANT(mode_o) ; flag := 0 ;
         dmr' = nil | nil
        |:class of dmr" = stat
                |(add of dmr" ⩾ tadd_o {I.2.4.2, example 2.11}
                     |flag := 1 ;
                      (dmr"' = nil | (dyn bnc.dmrc)
                                   | dmr"')
                     |dmr")
        |:class of dmr" = dyn
                |dmr"
        |:dmr' = (stat 0.α)
                |(stat bnc.α+tadd_o)
      {|:dmr' = (dyn 0) }
                |(dyn bnc.dmrc))
  (flag=1 | GEN(stdmrwost cadd§ : (dirwost add of dmr"),
                         cadddmr§ : (dirdmrw add of dmr_o)) {7}
gc_o := ( ~GCRELEVANT(mode_o) | nil
        |:gc" ≠ nil           | gc"
                              | bnc.gcc)
```

sc_o := (SCOPERELEVANT($mode_o$) | (insc", outsc")
| (0,0))

or_o := (nil,0,0,0).

Step 3 :

GEN(standcall npar§ : n,
dmrrec§ : dmr",
caddrout§ : $cadd_r$,
caddl§ : caddl,
...
caddn§ : caddn,
caddres§ : $cadd_o$,
dmrres§ : dmr_o,
gcres§ : bnc.gcc,
flex§ : flextop of TOPST[topstpm-1]) {54}

-*dmrrec§* indicates where the dynamic part of the parameters starts on DWOST%, if it exists at all. It has two purposes : in case of routines with a result without dynamic part, it gives information to the routine on how to recover the DWOST% memory of the parameters ; in other cases, it indicates from where the dynamic part of the result might be constructed. It is the task of the routine to prevent early overwriting of dynamic parts of parameters. In case of doubt, *dmrrec§* is disregarded and the dynamic part of the result is constructed from *ranstpm%*.

-*dmrres§* is used in case *dmrrec§=nil* and the result has a dynamic part ; in this case, if *class of dmrres§=dyn, spec of dmrres§* indicates to the routine where on DMRWOST% *dmr* information for the result must be stored.

-*gcres§*:

All parameters are protected before entering the standard routine. Hence, if the garbage collector has to be called from inside the standard routine, this one has not to bother about parameter protection ; clearly, in this case no parameter overwriting may have taken place for the parameters protected from GCWOST% according to *GCRELEVANT(modei)*. However, if the routine has stored some value on HEAP% it must ensure their protection before calling the garbage collector ; *gcres§* indicates where to store such a protection on GCWOST% The gc-protection of the result itself and the cancelling of parameter gc-protection is done outside the routine.

-*flex§*:

In whole generality the result of a standard routine may be a name ; *flex§* provides the routine with information on flexibility, allowing to perform the corresponding checks inside the routine if subnames are created.

Action :

The standard routine with an access *caddrout§* (which is of the form *(dircttab constabp))* and with parameters of access *caddl§,... caddn§* is entered. This routine performs a specific action taking into account the above strategy of *dmr*, *gc* and *flex*.

Step 4 : Gc dynamic actions :

The gc-protection of the parameters must be erased and the result must be protected according to $GCRELEVANT(mode_o)$, corresponding ICI's are generated.

Step 5 : Static management :

Result static properties are already on *BOST*, but the static management of *swostc*, *dmrc* and *gcc* has to be performed :

$$swostc := (mode_o \neq \underline{void} \;|add_o + STATICSIZE(mode_o)$$
$$|:smr'' \neq \underline{nil} \;|smr''$$
$$|swostc)$$

$$dmrc := (class\ \underline{of}\ dmr_o = \underline{dyn} \mid tadd\ \underline{of}\ dmr_o + 1$$
$$|:dmr''' \neq \underline{nil} \;|tadd\ \underline{of}\ dmr'''$$
$$|dmrc)$$

$$gcc := (gc_o \neq \underline{nil} \;|add\ \underline{of}\ gc_o + 1$$
$$|:gc'' \neq \underline{nil} \;|add\ \underline{of}\ gc''$$
$$|gcc).$$

14. CHOICE CONSTRUCTIONS

14.1 GENERALITIES

14.1.1 DEFINITIONS

Choice constructions are 'serial clauses' with 'completers', 'conditional clauses' and 'case clauses'. They are characterized by the fact they have one result of one specific mode but which can be obtained through the elaboration of one out of several subconstructions called *alternatives*. Which alternative is elaborated at run-time is not known at compile-time.

In general, the result of a choice construction is used by another construction, and in order to be able to translate this other construction properly, all alternatives of the choice construction must be characterized by the same static properties; let $mode_b$, $cadd_b$ ... be the denotations of these properties ; they are also referred to as 'a-posteriori' static properties as opposed to 'a-priori' static properties, which are the static properties of the alternatives considered individually. It should be clear that for each alternative, the transformation of its a-priori into the a-posteriori static properties may involve the generation of some run-time actions.

The determination of the a-posteriori properties is the major problem of the choice constructions, it may influence run-time efficiency a great deal. The optimal a-posteriori properties can only be determined in the light of the a-priori properties of all alternatives. We shall now define the principles on which this determination, also called 'balancing process', is based ; but before that, three remarks are needed :

1. Choice constructions may be nested, what we are concerned with here are the alternatives of the inner nesting levels, intermediate levels are disregarded as far as a-priori and a-posteriory static properties are concerned ; e.g. in $(b|x|(i|y,z))$, x, y and z are the three alternatives of the outer conditional clause.
2. Alternatives which are <u>*goto*</u>'s are not taken into consideration in the a-posteriori properties determination.
3. Alternatives which are <u>*skip*</u>'s are translated exactly as required by [1] and their a-priori static properties will result from II.10.2.

14.1.2 BALANCING PROCESS

The strategy defining the a-posteriori static properties of a choice construction from the a-priori static properties of the alternatives is the following :

A. *Mode*

The language definition [1] requires one same a-posteriori mode for all alternatives. The problem is solved at the level of the syntactic analysis [12] where appropriate coercions are generated for each alternative ; consequently, we can consider here that the a-priori modes are always equal to the a-posteriori mode.

B. *Access*

If the a-priori accesses of all alternatives are identical, *(dirwost ...)* for example, this access is the a-posteriori access. Otherwise some dynamic action is required to force a common access ; three cases have to be considered.

Case A : No alternative has an access class which is *dirwost* or *dirwost'*. In this case, a common access *(indwost)* is forced for each alternative, and this by copying the address of the corresponding value on *SWOST%*. Remark that :

- In case the values of the alternatives fit into a register, it is more efficient to use strategy of case C, which, thanks to local optimizations will allow to pass on the result through a register without extra storage (I.2.3.4 Example 2.4).
- Local optimizations also allow to inhibit the actual storage of the indirect address on *SWOST%* by passing on this address in an index register, if available :

Example

$$x := (b|m|n)$$

x,b,m and n are identifiers of access *(diriden* $n_x.p_x$*)*, *(diriden* $n_b.p_b$*)*, *(diriden* $n_m.p_m$*)* and *(diriden* $n_n.p_n$*)* respectively.

Intermediate code :

```
(1)        jumpno (diriden nb.pb), L
(2)        stword (variden nm.pm), (dirwost nw.pw)
(3)        loadreg mode, (indwost nw.pw)
(4)        jump L'
(5) L  :   stword (variden nn.pn), (dirwost nw.pw)
(6)        loadreg mode, (indwost nw.pw)
(7) L' :   storereg mode, (indwost nw.pw)
(8)        assign mode, (indwost nw.pw) (diriden nx.px)
```

Machine code

Before local optimization			After local optimization		
(1)	LDC	$n_b.p_b$	LDC		$n_b.p_b$
	IFJ	L	IFJ		L
(2)	LDB =	$n_m.p_m$	LDB	=	$n_m.p_m$
	STB	$n_w.p_w$			
(3)	LDB	$n_w.p_w$			
(4)	UNJ	L'	UNJ		L'

```
(5) L : LDB    =    n_n.p_n                 L :  LDB    =    n_n.p_n
        STB         n_w.p_w
(6)     LDB         n_w.p_w
(7) L': STB         n_w.p_w                 L':
(8)     LDB         n_w.p_w
        LDA         0,B                          LDA         0,B
        STA         n_x.p_x                      STA         n_x.p_x
```

Case B : No alternative has an access class equal to *dirwost*, but some have an access class equal to *dirwost'*. In this case, only the static part of the values of the alternatives are forced to be stored at the same *SWOST%* address β, giving rise to a common access *(dirwost' β)*. The choice of β is such that it minimizes the number of alternatives resulting in a value with a static part the copy of which has to be forced on *SWOST%*.

Case C : Al least one alternative has an access class *dirwost*. In this case, the values of all alternatives are forced to be completely stored on *WOST%* at the same address γ, giving rise to a common access *(dirwost γ)*. As above, the choice of γ is such that it minimizes the number of alternatives resulting in a value the copy of which has to be forced on *WOST%*.(†)

Remark that case A is not applicable to the situation of case B and C because this would lead to violating rule b2, (I.2.3.2). Disregarding this rule would cause difficulties throughout the whole static management. There is another possibility to turning cases b and c to case a while respecting rule b2 : it consists in copying values of alternatives with access classes *dirwost* or *dirwost'* on *HEAP%*. In some situations, this may be the most efficient solution but it also implies to protect the values stored on the *HEAP%* for reasons of garbage collection.

C. *Smr*

If the a-posteriori access class is *dirwost*, *dirwost'* or *indwost*, *smr:=bnc.swostc* before the choice construction is entered, otherwise it is irrelevant.

D. *Dmr*

In case the choice construction gives rise to an access different from *dirwost* or if *DMRRELEVANT*($mode_b$) = *nil*, then *dmr* := *nil*. Otherwise *dmr* is stat or dyn, according all alternatives with an a-priori access *dirwost* have all a *dmr* class which is stat or not. It is to be noted that a *dmr* transformation from stat to dyn implies a run-time action storing a *RANST%* pointer on *DMRWOST%*. The above strategy for *dmr* is the one which recovers the maximum *DWOST%* space, other strategies can be imagined.

(†) If γ is not the lowest address on *SWOST%*, values which have to be copied from lower to upper *SWOST%* addresses must be copied starting from their last cells.

E. *Gc*

A global analysis based on the a-posteriori mode and access of all alternatives determines the necessity of a protection. Note that if some alternatives are initially stored at the right place on *WOST%* no run-time action is needed for their gc-protection.

F. *Origin*

If all alternatives have the same origin, this is the common origin, otherwise the worst case is chosen, i.e. *kindo* := nil, *derefo* := true if there is one alternative with *derefo* = true ; the same strategy holds for *geno*.

G. *Scope*

Insc is the highest of the *insc* of all alternatives.
Outsc is the lowest of the *outsc* of all alternatives.

14.1.3 GENERAL ORGANIZATION

The fact that a-priori static properties of alternatives must be collected before determining the a-posteriori static properties implies some additional static management :

a. Three new fields are needed on *TOPST* : *countbal*, *countelem* and *flagnextbal*.
   -*countbal* is initialized with 0 when the *TOPST* element is set up, it is increased by 1 each time a new syntactic choice construction is entered and decreased by 1 when it is left. When *countbal* has reached its initial value 0 again, this means that the outer choice construction of the nesting has been left. At that time, static properties of all alternatives are supposed to be stored on *BOST* and the balancing process may take place.
   -*countelem* is intended to count the number of alternatives of the choice construction which are stored on *BOST* ; it is initialized to 0 when the *TOPST* element is set up and increased by one after each alternative has been translated.
   -*flagnextbal* is intended to inhibit the actions which normally take place after the translation of an alternative, when this alternative is in turn a choice clause. Indeed, in such a case, the alternatives are treated at the inner level.
b. A new field is needed on *BOST* : *obprogp*. When a-posteriori properties of alternatives of a choice construction are different from a-priori properties, this may involve the generation of some ICI's. These ICI's must be executed after each corresponding alternative ; however at compile-time they are generated at a moment where the ICI's for all alternatives properly so called have already been generated. The following process is used : after each alternative, a command is generated in *OBPROG* : *GEN* (*hole*) ; it is the *OBPROG* address of this hole which is stored in the field *obprogp* of the corresponding *BOST* element. When, during balancing, instructions have to be generated for an alternative, these instructions are sto-

red in a stream different from *OBPROG*, namely in *BALTAB*. Connection between *OBPROG* and *BALTAB* is obtained by superseding the hole of *OBPROG* by a new command *(baltab baltabp§) ; baltabp§* is the address in *BALTAB* of the balancing instructions which are generated.

c. For each alternative, after the balancing ICI's, if any, have been generated, the ICI *(loadreg* $mode_b$, $cadd_b$*)* is generated. Moreover, the ICI *(storereg* $mode_b$, $cadd_b$*)* is generated at the end of the choice construction. This allows to recover the efficiency of register use for values fitting into such a register (I.2.3.4).

d. At the beginning of the translation of each alternative, the static conditions must be the same, and in particular the current counters *dmrc, gcc* and *swostc*. These are saved on *MSTACK* at the beginning of a choice construction and restored each time the translation of an alternative is entered.

14.1.4 DECLARATIONS RELATIVE TO CHOICE CONSTRUCTIONS

The following procedures perform the general choice construction organization as explained above.

```
proc   INBAL =
           co This procedure is called each time a choice construction is entered
              co
       (:(( countbal of TOPST[ topstpm-1] = 0
               |INMSTACK(dmrc) ;
                INMSTACK(gcc) ;
                INMSTACK(swostc)
          ) ;
          countbal of TOPST[ topstpm-1]  +:=1
       ))
proc   NEXTBAL =
           co This procedure is called after translating an alternative co
       (:(flagnextbal of TOPST[ topstpm-1] = 0
            |countelem of TOPST[ topstpm-1]  +:= 1 ;
             obprogp of BOST[ bostpm-1]  := obprogpm ;
             GEN(hole) {26} ;
             dmrc := MSTACK[ mstackpm-3]  ;
             gcc := MSTACK[ mstackpm-2]  ;
             swostc := MSTACK[ mstackpm-1]
            |flagnextbal of TOPST[ topstpm-1]  := 0
       ))

proc   OUTBAL =
           co This procedure is called when a choice construction is left co
```

(:(countbal *of* *TOPST[topstpm-1] -:=1 ;*
(countbal *of* *TOPST[topstpm-1] = 0*

|*co* countelem determines the number of alternatives, the properties of which are on *BOST*. The common interface of the alternatives is determined (II.14.1.2) ; if necessary, instructions performing this interface are stored in *BALTAB* and connected to *OBPROG* through the holes left by *NEXTBAL*, the addresses of which are stored in the field *obprogp* of *BOST* elements. This gives rise to the a-posteriori set of static properties denoted $mode_b$, $cadd_b$ ... . They replace on *BOST* the a-priori sets of static properties. Moreover, for each alternative the following ICI is generated :

GEN(loadreg mode§ : mode$_b$*,*
cadd§ : cadd$_b$*)*(†) {24}

Action :

Case A :

$class_b$ = *dirwost* *and* there exists a register X into which a value of $mode_b$ fits.

LDX *n.p*{issued from $cadd_b$}

Case B :

$class_b$ = *indwost* *and* there exists an index register Y.

LDY *n.p* {issued from $cadd_b$}

In *OBPROG*, from *obprogpm* the following ICI is generated :

GEN(storereg mode§ : mode$_b$*,*
cadd§ : cadd$_b$*)* {23}

Action :

Case A :

$class_b$ = *dirwost* *and* there exists a register X into which a value of $mode_b$ fits.

STX *n.p*{issued from $tadd_b$}

Case B :

$class_b$ = *indwost* *and* there exists an index register Y.

STY *n.p*{issued from $tadd_b$}

co ;
mstackpm -:= 3
|*flagnextbal* *of* *TOPST[topstpm-1] := 1)).*

(†) At least when $mode_b$ is such that corresponding values fit into a register;this may vary from hardware to hardware.

14.2 SERIAL CLAUSE

General syntax

SERIAL → LBLOCK | NONBLOCK (A)

LBLOCK → lblock∇ BLOCKBODY (B)

BLOCKBODY → NONBLOCK (C)

NONBLOCK → SNONBLOCK | BALNONBLOCK (D)

SNONBLOCK → PRELUDE last∇ LABUNIT (E)

PRELUDE → $\{\{$ DECLA ; | UNITV ;$\}_0^\infty$ DECLA ;$\}_0^1\{$LABUNITVS$\}_0^1$ (F)

BALNONBLOCK → $\{$PRELUDE last∇ LABUNIT . LABELDEC$\}_0^1$
$\{$LABUNITVS last∇ LABUNIT . LABELDEC$\}_0^\infty$
LABUNITVS last∇ LABUNIT (G)

LABUNITV → $\{$LABELDEC$\}_0^\infty$ UNITV (H)

LABUNIT → $\{$LABELDEC$\}_0^\infty$ UNIT (I)

LABUNITVS → $\{$LABUNITV ;$\}_0^\infty$ (J)

DECLA → IDEDEC | LOCVARDEC | HEAPVARDEC | OPDEC | MODEDEC. (K)

Semantics

(A) ρ'(LBLOCK) | ρ'(NONBLOCK)

(B) see II.1

(C) ρ'(NONBLOCK)

(D) ρ'(SNONBLOCK) | ρ'(BALNONBLOCK)

(E) Step 1 :
ρ'(PRELUDE)
Step 2 :
ρ'(LABUNIT)
{The static properties of LABUNIT appear on *BOST*}

(F) Step :
All DECLA, UNITV, LABUNITV are treated :
ρ'(DECLA), ρ(UNITV), ρ'(LABUNITV) ; after each ρ(UNITV), ρ'(LABUNITV), the top element of *BOST* is cancelled; it necessarily corresponds to *void*, *(nihil C)*.

(G) see II.14.2.1

(H) $\{$ρ'(LABELDEC)$\}^\infty$ ρ(UNITV)

(I) $\{$ρ'(LABELDEC)$\}_0^\infty$ ρ'(UNIT)

(J) $\{$ρ'(LABUNITV)$\}_0^\infty$

(K) ρ'(IDEDEC) | ρ'(LOCVARDEC) | ρ'(HEAPVARDEC) | ρ'(OPDEC) | ρ'(MODEDEC)

BALNONBLOCK

Syntax

BALNONBLOCK → $\{$PRELUDE last∇ LABUNIT . LABELDEC$\}_0^1$
$\{$LABUNITVS1 last∇ LABUNIT1 . LABELDEC1$\}_0^1$
...
$\{$LABUNITVSn last∇ LABUNITn . LABELDECn$\}_0^1$
LABUNITVSn+1 last∇ LABUNITn+1.

Semantics

Step 1 :
INBAL.

Step 2 :
{ρ'(PRELUDE)
ρ'(LABUNIT)
NEXTBAL
GEN(jump labnb§ : lc) {27}
ρ'(LABELDEC)$\}_0^1$.

Step 3 :
{*for i to n do*
ρ'(LABUNITVSi)
ρ'(LABUNITi)
NEXTBAL
GEN(jump labnb§ : lc) {27}
ρ'(LABELDEC) *od*$\}_0^1$.

Step 4 :
ρ'(LABUNITVSn+1)
ρ'(LABUNITn+1)
NEXTBAL.

Step 5 :
GEN(labdef labnb§ : lc) {28}

Step 6 :
OUTBAL.

14.3 CONDITIONAL CLAUSE

Syntax

CONDCL → if∇ SERIALB CHOICECL fi.

Semantics

Step 1 :
INBAL.

Step 2 :

ρ(SERIALB)

{on *BOST* the static properties of a boolean value appear : $cadd_c$...}.

Step 3 :

ρ'(CHOICECL).

Step 4 :

OUTBAL.

CHOICE CLAUSE

Syntax

CHOICECL → then1∇ SERIAL | (A)
thef∇ SERIALB CHOICECL | (B)
then2∇ SERIAL1 else∇ SERIAL2 | (C)
then3∇ SERIAL elsf∇ SERIALB CHOICECL. (D)

Translation scheme

A	B	C	D
1. *GEN(jumpno lno)*	←	←	←
2. ρ'(SERIAL)	ρ(SERIALB)	ρ'(SERIAL1)	ρ'(SERIAL)
3. *NEXTBAL*	ρ'(CHOICECL)	*NEXTBAL*	*NEXTBAL*
4. *GEN(jump l)*	←	←	←
5. *GEN(labdef lno)*	←	←	←
6. Elseskip	←	ρ'(SERIAL2)	ρ(SERIALB)
7. NEXTBAL	←	←	ρ'(CHOICECL)
8. *GEN(labdef l)*	←	←	←

Semantics

At the top of *BOST*, the static properties of the condition appear : let $cadd_c$ be the corresponding access.

Case A :

CONTEXT(then1∇).

Step A.1 :

GEN(jumpno labnb§ : lno,
cadd§ : $cadd_c$) {29}

Step A.2 :

ρ'(SERIAL)

{The static properties of SERIAL appear on *BOST* ; they are denoted $mode_s$, $cadd_s$, ...}.

Step A.3 :

NEXTBAL.

Step A.4 :

GEN(jump labnb§ : l) {27}

Step A.5 :

GEN(labdef labnb§ : lno) {28}

Step A.6 : Else skip :

Case A.6.a :

$mode_s$ = *void*.

On *BOST*, the static properties of void are stored :

$mode_o$:= *void*

$cadd_o$:= *(nihil 0)*

Case A.6.b :

$mode_s \neq$ *void*.

Step A.6.b.1 :

GEN(stskip mode§ : $mode_s$,
cadd§ : (dirwost bnc.swostc + Δmem)) {99}

Step A.6.b.2 :

The static properties of *skip* are put on *BOST* :

mode := $mode_s$

cadd := (dirwost bnc.swostc + Δmem)

smr := bnc.swostc

dmr := nil

gc := nil

or := (nil,0,0,0)

sc := (0,0).

Step A.7 :

NEXTBAL.

Step A.8 :

GEN(labdef labnb§ : l) {28}

Case B :

CONTEXT(thef∇).

Step B.1 :

GEN(jumpno labnb§ : lno,
cadd§ : $cadd_c$) {29}

Step B.2 :

ρ(SERIALB).

Step B.3 :

ρ'(CHOICECL).

Step B.4 :

GEN(jump labnb§ : l) {27}

Step B.5 :

GEN(labdef labnb§ : lno) {28}

Step B.6 : Else skip :

see step A.6.

Step B.7 :

NEXTBAL.

Step B.8 :

GEN(labdef labnb§ : l) {28}

Case C :

CONTEXT (then2∇).

Step C.1 :

GEN(jumpno labnb§ : lno,
cadd§ : $cadd_c$*).* {29}

Step C.2 :

ρ'(SERIAL1).

Step C.3:

NEXTBAL.

Step C.4 :

GEN(jump labnb§ : l) {27}

Step C.5 :

GEN(labdef labnb§ : lno) {28}

Step C.6 :

ρ'(SERIAL2).

Step C.7 :

NEXTBAL.

Step C.8 :

GEN(labdef labnb§ : l) {28}

Case D :

CONTEXT(then3∇).

Step D.1 :

GEN(jumpno labnb§ : lno,
cadd§ : $cadd_c$*)* {29}

Step D.2 :

ρ'(SERIAL).

Step D.3 :

NEXTBAL.

Step D.4 :

GEN(jump labnb§ : l) {27}

Step D.5 :

GEN(labdef labnb§ : lno) {28}

Step D.6 :

ρ(SERIALB).

<u>Step</u> D.7 :

ρ'(CHOICECL).

<u>Step</u> D.8 :

GEN(<u>labdef</u> labnb§ : l) {28}

14.4 CASE CLAUSE

<u>Syntax</u>

CASECL → case∇ CASECHOICE in∇ UNIT1, ... UNITn $\{\text{out SERIAL}\}_0^1$ esac

CASECHOICE → UNITC |
CASECONF.

<u>Translation scheme</u>

1. *INBAL*
2. ρ'(CASECHOICE)
3. *GEN(<u>switchcase</u> ...li....,lout,lf...)*
4. *<u>for</u> i <u>to</u> n <u>do</u>*
   4.1 *GEN(<u>labdef</u> li)*
   4.2 ρ'(UNITi)
   4.3 *NEXTBAL*
   4.4 *GEN(<u>jump</u> lf) <u>od</u>*
5. *GEN(<u>labdef</u> lout)*
6. ρ'(SERIAL)
7. *NEXTBAL*
8. *GEN(<u>labdef</u> lf)*
9. *OUTBAL*.

<u>Semantics</u>

<u>Step</u> 1 :

INBAL

<u>Step</u> 2 :

ρ'(CASECHOICE)

{The static properties of an integer appear on *BOST* ; let $cadd_j$ be the correspon-ding access}.

<u>Step</u> 3 :

GEN(<u>switchcase</u> labnb§ : l,
cadd1§ : $cadd_j$,
cadd2§ : (<u>constant</u> n)) {37}

-*labnb§* ... is the first of n+3 labels which will be generated when machine code is produced :

lo=lo§, l1=l1§, ..., ln=ln§, lf=lf§ and *lout=lout§*.

-cadd1§ gives access to an integer *i§*

-cadd2§ gives access to an integer *n§*

Action :

(1 ≤ i§ ≤ n§ | goto address lo§+i§-1

| goto lout§) ;

lo§ : goto l1§ ;

goto l2§ ;

...

goto ln§.

Step 4 :

for i to n do

Step 4.1 :

GEN(labdef labnb§ : li) {28}

Step 4.2 :

ρ'(UNITi)

Step 4.3 :

NEXTBAL

Step 4.4 :

GEN(jump labnb§ : lf) {27}

od.

Step 5 :

GEN(labdef labnb§ : lout) {28}

Step 6 :

Case 6.a :

CONTEXT(out∇)

ρ'(SERIAL)

Case 6.b :

CONTEXT(esac)

see II.14.3.1 step A.6 {Elseskip}.

Step 7 :

NEXTBAL.

Step 8 :

GEN(labdef labnb§ : lf) {28}

Step 9 :

OUTBAL.

14.5 CASE CONFORMITY CLAUSE

Syntax :

CASECONF → caseconf∇ mode1∇ TERTL1...moden∇ TERTLn$\{::|::=\}_1^1$ TERTR

{with modei∇, the mode $mode_{li}$ of TERTLi is associated} (see N.B.2 page 235).

Translation scheme

1. Result static properties
2. ρ(TERTR)
3. A ::.
   1. *for i to n do*
      1.1 *GEN(confto...mode$_{li}$...)*
      1.2 *GEN(jumpno lni)*
      1.3 *GEN(stword...i)*
      1.4 *GEN(jump lf)*
      1.5 *GEN(labdef lnoi)*
      od
   2. *GEN(stword 0)*
   3. *GEN(labdef lf)*
   4. Deletion of TERTR

   B ::=.
   1. Current counters saving
   2. *for i to n do*
      2.1 Static management for copy of TERTR (TERTR*i)
      2.2 *GEN(conftobec...mode$_{li}$...)*
      2.3 *GEN(jumpno lnoi)*
      2.4 ρ(TERTLi)
      2.5 Static scope checking
      2.6 *GEN(assign{scope}...)*
      2.7 *GEN(stword i)*
      2.8 Deletion of TERTLi and TERTR*i
      2.9 *GEN(jump lf)*
      2.10 *GEN(labdef lnoi)*
      2.11 Restoration of current pointers
      od
   3. *GEN(stword 0)*
   4. Deletion of TERTR
   5. *GEN(labdef lf)*
   6. *mstackpm -:=3.*

Semantics

As in conformity relations, a number of static cases can be treated in a special way. Though implemented, they are not described here.

Step 1 : Result static properties :

On *BOST* :

$mode_o$:= <u>int</u>

$cadd_o$:= (<u>dirwost</u> *bnc.swostc*)

smr_o := *bnc.swostc*

dmr_o := <u>nil</u>

gc_o := <u>nil</u>

or_o := (<u>nil</u>,0,0,0)

sc_o := (0,0)

Space is reserved on *SWOST%* for storing the result.

<u>Step</u> 2 :

ρ(TERTR)

{The static properties of TERTR appear on *BOST*, they are denoted $mode_r$, $cadd_r$...}.

<u>Step</u> 3 :

<u>Case</u> A :

::.

<u>Step</u> A.1 :

<u>for</u> *i* <u>to</u> *n* <u>do</u>

<u>Step</u> A.1.1 :

```
GEN(confto model§ : mode_li,
           moder§ : mode_r,
           caddr§ : cadd_r,
           caddo§ : bnc.swostc)                    {95}
```

{see II.12.3}.

<u>Step</u> A.1.2 :

```
GEN(jumpno labnb§ : lnoi,
           cadd§  : bnc.swostc)                    {29}
```

<u>Step</u> A.1.3 :

```
GEN(stword cadds§ : (intct i),
           caddo§ : cadd_o)                        {4}
```

<u>Step</u> A.1.4 :

```
GEN(jump labnb§ : lf)                              {27}
```

<u>Step</u> A.1.5 :

```
GEN(labdef labnb§ : lnoi)                          {28}
```

<u>od</u>.

<u>Step</u> A.2 :

```
GEN(stword cadds§ : (intct 0),
           caddo§ : cadd_o)                        {4}
```

<u>Step</u> A.3 :

```
GEN(labdef labnb§ : lf)                            {28}
```

<u>Step</u> A.4 : Deletion of TERTR :

The static properties of TERTR are deleted from *BOST*, which may cause some dynamic management for *dmr* and *gc*.

Case B :

::=.

Step B.1 : Current counters saving : given only one of TERTLi will be elaborated, current counters must be restored after the translation of each TERTLi, thus restoring the static conditions at the same values. For this reason *dmrc, gcc* and *swostc* are saved :

INMSTACK(dmrc) ;

INMSTACK(gcc) ;

INMSTACK(swostc)

Step B.2 :

for i to n do

Step B.2.1 : Static management for copy of TERTR(TERTR*i) see II.12.3 step B.1, but static properties of TERTR are not overwritten in order to recover them each time the loop is passed through.

Step B.2.2 :

GEN(conftobec model§ : mode$_{li}$*,*
moder§ : mode$_r$*,*
caddo§ : (dirwost bnc.swostc) {bool},
caddr§ : cadd$_r$*,*
gcr§ : gc$_r$*,*
dmrr§ : dmr$_r$*,*
*cadd*r§: cadd**$_{ri}$*,*
*gc*r§ : gc**$_{ri}$*,*
*dmr*r§ : dmr**$_{ri}$*)* {96}

Action :

see II.12.3, step B.2

Step B.2.3 :

GEN(jumpno labnb§ : lnoi,
cadd§ : (dirwost bnc.swostc)) {29}

Step B.2.4 :

ρ(TERTLi)

Step B.2.5 : | see II.12.3 step | B.5
Step B.2.6 : | | B.6

Step B.2.7 : Result saving :

GEN(stword cadds§ : (intct i),
caddo§ : cadd$_o$*)* {4}

Step B.2.8 : Deletion of TERTLi and TERTR*i ;

Static properties of TERTLi and TERTR*i are deleted from *BOST* ; this involves dynamic management for *gc* and *dmr*.

Step B.2.9 :

GEN(jump labnb§ : lf) {27}

<u>Step</u> B.2.10 :

GEN(<u>labdef</u> labnb§ : lnoi) {28}

<u>Step</u> B.2.11 : Restoration of current counters :

dmrc := MSTACK[*mstackpm-3*] ;

gcc := MSTACK[*mstackpm-2*] ;

swostc := MSTACK[*mstackpm-1*]

<u>*od*</u>.

<u>Step</u> B.3 :

GEN(<u>stword</u> cadds§ : (<u>intct</u> 0),

caddo§ : $cadd_o$) {4}

<u>Step</u> B.4 : Deletion of TERTR :

Static properties of TERTR are deleted from *BOST* ; this may cause some dynamic management for *dmr* and *gc*.

<u>Step</u> B.5 :

GEN(<u>labdef</u> labnb§ : lf) {28}

<u>Step</u> B.6 :

mstackpm -:= 3.

<u>N.B.</u>1 : Remark that the above algorithm must be designed very carefully as far the correspondence between static and dynamic management is concerned :

At run-time :

($mode_{li}$ conforms to $mode_r$

|TERTR is transformed into TERTR*i ;

TERTLi is elaborated ;

the assignation takes place ;

TERTR*i and TERTLi are deleted from *WOST%* if they were stored on this stack (this means *dmr* and *gc* management).

|: no $mode_{li}$ conforms to $mode_r$

|TERTR has to be deleted from *WOST%* if it was stored on this stack.)

At compile-time, all situations have to be considered successively, restoring the same conditions (i.e. TERTR, *dmr*, *gcc* and *swostc*) at the beginning of each situation.

<u>N.B.</u>2 : In the revised report a much more simple form of case conformity clause is defined. Its implementation is straightforward : after an expression *E* of union mode has been elaborated, a unit is chosen on the basis of mode comparisons as here. The actual value of *E* is then accessible within each unit through an identifier with a specific mode, element of the union mode. The implementation is performed by giving the identifier an access deduced from the one of the value of *E* available on *BOST*, by deleting the union overhead (this deletion is implemented as a field selection, (section II.11.1) with *reladd*= *Δunion* (size of the union overhead)).

15. COLLATERAL CLAUSES

First of all, the following points must be emphasized : the implementation described here, does not include semaphores ; moreover, the run-time elaboration of collateral clauses is purely left-to-right. There are three kinds of collateral clauses : those which deliver no result, those which deliver a multiple value, they are called 'row displays' and those which deliver a structured value, they are called 'structure displays'.

15.1 COLLATERAL CLAUSE DELIVERING NO VALUE

Syntax

COLLVOID → collvoid∇ (UNITV1,...UNITVn).

Translation scheme

1. *for i to n do*
   1.1 ρ(UNITVi)
   1.2 Deletion from *BOST*
   od
2. Static properties of *void* on *BOST*.

Semantics

par is not considered ; unitary clauses are elaborated serially from left to right.

Step 1 :

for i to n do

Step 1.1

ρ(UNITVi).

Step 1.2

The static properties of *void* are deleted from *BOST*.

od.

Step 2 :

The static properties of *void* are stored on *BOST* :

mode := *void*

cadd := (*nihil 0*).

15.2 ROW DISPLAY

The general strategy for elaborating row displays is the following :

1. Nested row displays are treated at the level of the outer row display in such a

way no descriptors are constructed for the inner levels.

2. Space is reserved on *SWOST%* for the descriptor of the multiple value resulting from the row display before the translation of the display is entered. This freezes some space on *SWOST%* but allows to recover the *SWOST%* space of the row display element(†) at the end of the translation without having to move the descriptor.

3. As opposed to *SWOST%* space reservation for row display result, *DWOST%* space reservation does not take place in prefix. This means that if some elements have a dynamic part on *DWOST%*, the dynamic part of the result will be constructed on top of these dynamic parts of elements. This forbids *DWOST%* space recovery of the dynamic parts of the elements on *DWOST%* up to the moment the result itself is deleted from *WOST%* or, if this space must be recovered, this implies a shift of the dynamic part of the result. It is to be noted that taking point 1 (here above) and the access management into account, situations where row display elements have dynamic parts on *DWOST%* are very rare ; a bit of inefficiency in space or time in these rare situations is not harmful.

N.B. There is a possibility for avoiding to delay *DWOST%* space recovery without implying a shift of the result : as soon as the first unitary clause of the first inner row-display has been elaborated, the complete descriptor of the result can be filled, and hence space can be frozen on *DWOST%* for the static part of the elements of this result. Thereafter, the different unitary clauses are elaborated one by one, and integrated immediately after they have been elaborated in the result of the row display. This solution is somewhat more complicated than the implemented one, as far as static management is concerned. Moreover, at run-time, some mechanism for protecting a partially constructed multiple value would have to be implemented. (see also I.2.3.2, rule b3).

4. Another problem as far as *DWOST%* memory recovery is concerned is due to the presence of local generators in the row display [13] . This presence is detected thanks to *geno* of the elements. When it is 1, for some element, *DWOST%* memory space cannot be recovered using the normal process, which would also recover the location of the generator together with the dynamic space of the result of the row display. In such a case we use *wp%* of the current *BLOCK%* to recover *DWOST%* space ; indeed, *wp%* points behind the location of the lastly elaborated local generator.

5. When a row display consists of denotations only, it can be constructed on *CONSTAB* at compile-time. This last process is not described.

Syntax

COLLROW → collrow∇ (UNITD1,...,UNITDn)

{With collrow∇, *n* and $mode_o$ (the mode of the resulting value) are associated}.

(†) By row display element we mean a value resulting from the elaboration of a constituent unitary clause of the inner row display level.

Translation scheme

1. Initialization
   1.1 *NEWACTION(collrow∇)*
   1.2 *BOST* static properties
   1.3 Element translation
2. Descriptor construction
   2.1 Descriptor initialization
   2.2 Bound filling
3. Value construction
4. *BOST* static properties (finalization)
   4.1 Collection of information
   4.2 Dmr management
   4.3 Gc management
   4.4 Other static properties .

Semantics

Step 1 : Initialization :

Step 1.1 :

NEWACTION (collrow∇).

Step 1.2 : *BOST* static properties :

$mode_0 := mode_0$

$cadd_0 := (\underline{dirwost}\ bnc.swostc + \Delta mem)$

$smr_0 := bnc.swostc$

$dmr_0 := \underline{nil}$

$gc_0 := \underline{nil}$

$or_0 := (\underline{nil}, 0, 0, 0)$

$sc_0 := (0, N)$

Space is reserved on *SWOST%* for the descriptor :

INCREASEWOST(STATICSIZE(mode$_0$*) + ∆mem))* ; this freezes some space during the elaboration of the elements of the collateral clause, but it allows to recover space for all static parts of the elements once the result of the collateral clause has been built up from them. Another strategy would be to reserve no space and to construct the descriptor either in holes between elements or in the first free cell after these elements as it has been explained for standard calls.

Step 1.3 : Element translation :

Procedure *COLROW1* is called, its declaration is the following :

```
proc COLROW1 =
    (: NEWBOST ((collrow  n)) ;
       countelem of TOPST  [topstpm-1] +:= 1 ;
       for i to n do
            (CONTEXT (collrow∇) {collrow∇ gives rise to a new n}
                |COLROW1
                |ρ(UNITDi) ; countelem of TOPST[ topstpm-1] +:=1 ) od)
```

co Static properties of the elements which are not row displays are accumulated on *BOST*, each new level of row display is marked by a *BOST* element *(collrow n)* where *n* is the number of elements of that collateral level. The total number of *BOST* elements thus set up is counted in the field *countelem of TOPST*. This information describes the structure of the multiple value to be constructed from the elements and allows to avoid the construction of descriptors for inner levels of collateral row displays. co

Step 2 : Descriptor construction :

The bounds of the descriptor are defined by the nested structure of the row display, and also by the first UNITD which is met in the inner row display and which is not itself a row-display. Indeed, if this UNITD is a multiple value of m dimensions, the bounds of the last m dimensions of the descriptor of the row display are the bounds of this UNITD. Moreover, once the descriptor has thus been filled, bounds consistency must be checked throughout the rest of the row display. Here a static image of the descriptor can be constructed in order to be able to perform most of checks of bound consistency at compile-time. Strictly speaking, bound consistency must be checked even through structured values involved in row-display elements ; given these checks are no absolutely necessary as far as data structure construction is concerned, they are not mentioned in the descriptions below.

Step 2.1 : Descriptor initialization :

```
GEN(stoverhdescr modeo§: mode_o,
                 states§ : (1,...,1),
                 caddd§ : (dirabs ranstpm%),
                 caddo§ : cadd_o)                    {80}
```

Action :

The overhead of a descriptor is constructed at *caddo§* {for a value of *modeo§*}, with *states§* and with an offset corresponding to *caddd§*.

Step 2.2 : Bound filling :

BOST elements are now analyzed from the 1st element corresponding to the row display. Elements with access *(collrow α)* provide for a new pair of bounds *1:α*. These are stored in the static image of the descriptor and caused to be stored in the descriptor at run-time :

```
GEN(stbounds caddl§ : (intct 1),
             caddu§ : (intct α),
             caddt§ : (dirwost bnc.β))              {79}
```

-β is the access to the field *bounds%* of the current dimension in the descriptor.

Action :

l% and *u%* of the field *bounds%* stored at *caddt§* are filled with the integers of access *caddl§* and *caddu§* respectively.

Suppose the first *BOST* element with an access class ≠ <u>*collrow*</u> is met and let $mode_r$, $cadd_r$,... be the corresponding static properties :

GEN(<u>stfirstcollr</u> modes§ : $mode_r$,
modeo§ : $mode_o$,
cadds§ : $cadd_r$,
caddo§ : $cadd_o$) {81}

<u>Action</u> 1 :

(∼ *NONROW (modes§)*

| <u>*co*</u> The bounds for the last dimensions of the descriptor of *modeo§-caddo§* are filled with those of the descriptor *modes§-cadds§* <u>*co*</u>*)*.

<u>Action</u> 2 :

The strides of the descriptor of *modeo§-caddo§* are filled, including *do%*.

<u>Action</u> 3 :

Space is reserved on *DWOST%* from *ranstpm%* for the static parts of the elements of the multiple value to be constructed (*do%* is the space needed) ; a current pointer in this static part is initialized :

ranstpc% := ranstpm%

ranstpm% +:= do%

{The garbage collector may be called}.

<u>Action</u> 4 :

The elements of the value *modes§-cadds§* or, if *NONROW(modes§)* the value itself, are copied on *RANST%* : their static part from *ranstpc%* and their dynamic part, if any, from *ranstpm%*. In this latter case, the garbage collector may be called.

<u>Step</u> 3 : Value construction :

<u>*For*</u> all remaining *BOST* elements related to the row display <u>*do*</u>

<u>Case</u> A :

A *BOST* element of access (<u>*collrow*</u> α) is met. The static descriptor image is consulted ; if the bounds of the current dimension are filled in this table a static check of bounds may take place.

GEN(<u>checkbounds</u> caddl§ : (<u>intct</u> 1),
caddu§ : (<u>intct</u> α),
caddt§ : (<u>dirwost</u> bnc.β)) {78}

-β is the access of the field *bounds%* of the current dimension of the descriptor.

<u>Action</u> :

l% and *u%* are checked against the bounds of access *caddl§* and *caddu§* respectively. In case of inequality, a run-time error message is provided.

<u>Case</u> B :

A *BOST* element with access class ≠ <u>*collrow*</u> is met.

Let $mode_r$, $cadd_r$ ... be the corresponding static properties.

GEN(<u>stnextcollr</u> modes§ : mode$_r$*,*
modeo§ : mode$_o$*,*
cadds§ : cadd$_r$*,*
caddo§ : cadd$_o$*)* {82}

<u>Action</u> 1 :

If *∿NONROW(modes§)* then a check of bounds is performed between the bounds of the values *modes§-cadds§* and the bounds of the corresponding last dimensions in the descriptor characterized by *modeo§-caddo§*.

<u>Action</u> 2 :

see step 2.2, action 4.

<u>od</u>.

<u>Step</u> 4 : *BOST* static properties (finalization) :

<u>Step</u> 4.1 : Collection of information :

BOST static properties of the collateral display elements are passed through and the following information is deduced from this scanning :

dmr1 : the first *dmr* ≠ *<u>nil</u>*, if any, or *<u>nil</u>* otherwise.

dmr2 : the first *dmr* with a class = *<u>dyn</u>*, if any, or *<u>nil</u>* otherwise.

gc1 : the first *gc* ≠ *<u>nil</u>*, if any, or *<u>nil</u>* otherwise.

geno1 : 1, if at least one of all *geno* is 1, 0 otherwise.

insc1 : the maximum of all *insc*.

outsc1 : the minimum of all *outsc*.

<u>Step</u> 4.2 : Dmr management :

We recall that the UNITD's are all elaborated before the row-display construction proper starts ; their dynamic parts on *DWOST%* appear before the dynamic part of the result of the row display itself. They have to be recovered together with the dynamic part of this result, unless local generators appear among these dynamic parts [13] ; in this case, space can only be recovered up to the location of the lastly elaborated local generator ; *wp%* of the current *BLOCK%* is used for this space recovery.

These considerations give rise to the following algorithm :

(class <u>of</u> dmr1 = <u>nil</u>
|dmr$_o$ *:= (<u>stat</u> tadd*$_o$*)*
|: class <u>of</u> dmr2 ≠ <u>nil</u> | dmrc := tadd <u>of</u> dmr2) ;
(geno1 ≠ 0
|dmr$_o$ *:= (<u>dyn</u> bnc.dmrc) ;*
GEN(<u>stwp</u> bnc§ : bnc,
cadd§ : (<u>dirdmrw</u> bnc.dmrc)) {22}

<u>Action</u> :

The *DMRWOST%* cell of access *cadd§* is superseded by the *wp%* of the current *BLOCK%* characterized by *bnc§*. {Thus *DWOST%* elements above the generator location are not recovered before current *BLOCK%* exit}.

```
    |:class of dmr1 = stat
         |dmr_o := dmr1
   {|:class of dmr1 = dyn}
         |dmr_o := (dyn bnc.dmrc)
    )
```

Step 4.3 Gc management :

During the row display construction, elements stored on *WOST%* have remained protected while no protection was set up for the value being constructed. This has allowed to call the garbage collector, when needed, without further precautions. Now element protections are cancelled and replaced by a protection for the constructed value if necessary.

```
    (gc1 ≠ nil
      |gcc := gc1 ;
       for i from tadd of gc1 to gcc - gcelemsz
       do GEN(stgcnil caddgc§ : (dirgcw bnc.i))        {13}
       od ) ;
    (GCRELEVANT(mode_o)
     |GEN(stgcwost mode§ : mode_o,
                   cadd§ : cadd_o,
                   caddgc§ : (dirgcw bnc.gcc)))       {6}
```

Step 4.4 : Other static properties :

sc$_o$:= (*insc1*, *outsc1*)

geno$_o$:= *geno1*

Static *WOST%* space of the elements is recovered :

swostc := *tadd*$_o$ + *STATICSIZE*(*mode*$_o$)

topstpm -:=1 {collrow∇ is cancelled}.

15.3 STRUCTURE DISPLAY

The strategy of elaboration of structure displays is different from the one of row displays : here it is more interesting to construct the result step by step as the fields are calculated. Indeed when the result of a display element appears on *WOST%*, in most of the cases no run-time action is implied to incorporate it in the structure display. It is also easy to see that we have not to bother about combination of nested structure displays ; in most of the cases, the general recursive process gives the best results automatically.

Note that here no *DWOST%* memory space is frozen unless local generators have been elaborated together with the display elements.

Finally, as for row displays, structure displays consisting of denotations can be constructed on *CONSTAB*.

In the process described below, not only rule a2 of I.2.3.2 is respected (the static part of a value must always appear in consecutive memory cells), but also the dynamic parts of the result of a structure display will always be constructed on *DWOST%* ; hence the access class of the resulting value will never be *dirwost'*. It would be easy to detect cases where such a construction on *DWOST%* can be avoided.

Syntax

COLLSTR → collstr∇ (UNITD1,...,UNITDn)

{With collstr∇ the number of elements *n* and the $mode_0$ of the structured value is associated}.

Translation scheme

1. Initialization :
   1.1 *NEWACTION(collstr∇)*
   1.2 *BOST* static properties
2. Element translation and display construction :

   for i to n do

   2.1 ρ(UNITDi)

   2.2 Integration of the field in the structured value

A $class_{ui}$ = *constant or*	
" = *dircttab or*	
" = *variden*	1. *BOST* {updating}
B $class_{ui}$ = *diriden or*	2. Run-time actions | *dmr*
" = *indiden*	| *gc*
C $class_{ui}$ = *dirwost*	| *copy*
D $class_{ui}$ = *dirwost'*	
E $class_{ui}$ = *indwost*	

   2.3 *Swostcc*

   od

3. *BOST* static properties (finalization)
   3.1 *Dmr* management
   3.2 *Gc* management
   3.3 Other static management.

Semantics

Step 1 : Initialization :

Step 1.1 :

NEWACTION(collstr∇).

Step 1.2 : *BOST* static properties :

$mode_o := mode_o$

$cadd_o :=$ (*dirwost* bnc.swostc + Δmem)

$smr_o :=$ bnc.swostc

$dmr_o :=$ *nil*

$gc_o :=$ *nil*

$or_o :=$ (*nil*, 0, 0, 0)

$scope_o :=$ (0,N)

Here *swostc* is increased by *Δmem* only *(INCREASESWOST (Δmem))*, space for the static parts of the fields is reserved step by step as the elements are translated. A current pointer in this static part is initialized : *swostcc* := $tadd_o$.

Step 2 : Element translation and display construction :

for i *to* n *do*

Step 2.1 :

INMSTACK(swostcc)

ρ(UNITDi)

OUTMSTACK(swostcc)

{The static properties of UNITDi appear on *BOST*, they are denoted $mode_{ui}$, $cadd_{ui}$...}.

Step 2.2 : Integration of the field in the structured value :

Through all cases below, the static properties dmr_o, $geno_o$ and sc_o are treated in the same way :

```
(class of dmr_ui = dyn | dmrc -:= 1) ;
dmr_o := (dmr_o ≠ nil | dmr_o
        |:dmr' := (DMRRELEVANT(mode_ui)) ; dmr' = nil
                  |nil
        |:dmr' = (stat  α)
                  |(stat  bnc.α+swostcc)
                  |GEN(stdmrwost cadd§:(dirabs  ranstpm%),
                              cadddmr§:(dirdmrw bnc.dmrc)) ;   {7}
                  (dyn bnc.dmrc))
geno_o := (geno_ui = 1 | 1
                       | geno_o)
insc_o := (insc_ui < insc_o | insc_ui
                            | insc_o)
outsc_o := (outsc_o < outsc_ui | outsc_ui
                               | outsc_o).
```

Case A :

$class_{ui}$ = *constant or*

" = *dirctab or*

" = *variden*.

Step A.1 : Generation of run-time actions :

GEN(<u>stwost3</u> mode§ : $mode_{ui}$,
cadds§: $cadd_{ui}$,
caddo§: (<u>dirwost</u> bnc.swostcc)) {3}

<u>Case</u> B :

$class_{ui}$ = <u>diriden</u> <u>or</u>
" = <u>indiden</u>.

<u>Step</u> B.1 : *BOST* static properties (updating) :

gc_o := (GCRELEVANT($mode_{ui}$)
|(gc_o = <u>nil</u> | bnc.gcc
| gc_o)
|gc_o)

{It is calculated where to protect the whole structure after it is constructed}.

<u>Step</u> B.2 : Generation of run-time actions :

<u>Step</u> B.2.1 : Gc :

(GCRELEVANT($mode_{ui}$)
|GEN(<u>stgcwost</u> mode§ : $mode_{ui}$,
cadd§ : (<u>dirwost</u> bnc.swostcc),
caddgc§ : (<u>dirgcw</u> gc_o)) {6}

{Elements are protected individually}.

<u>Step</u> B.2.2 : Copy :

see step A.1 and

NOOPT.

<u>Case</u> C :

$class_{ui}$ = <u>dirwost</u>.

<u>Step</u> C.1 : *BOST* static properties :

gc_o := (gc_{ui} = <u>nil</u>
|gc_c
|:gc_o = <u>nil</u>
|gc_{ui}
|gc_o).

<u>Step</u> C.2 : Generation of run-time actions :

<u>Step</u> C.2.1 : Gc :

(gc_{ui} ≠ <u>nil</u> <u>and</u> $tadd_{ui}$ ≠ swostcc
|GEN(<u>stgcwost</u> mode§ : $mode_{ui}$,
cadd§ : (<u>dirwost</u> bnc.swostcc),
caddgc§ : (<u>dirgcw</u> gc_{ui}))) {6}

<u>Step</u> C.2.2 : Copy :

($tadd_{ui}$ ≠ swostcc
|GEN(<u>ststatwost</u> mode§ : $mode_{ui}$,
cadds§ : $cadd_{ui}$,
caddo§ : (<u>dirwost</u> bnc.swostcc))){12}

NOOPT.

Case D :

class$_{ui}$ = *dirwost'*.

Step D.1 : *BOST* static properties :

gc_o := {see step C.1, (refinements can be imagined)}.

Step D.2 : Generation of run-time actions :

Step D.2.1 : Gc :

see step C.2.1 {refinements can be imagined}.

Step D.2.2 : Copy :

```
(tadd_ui = swostcc
        |GEN(stdynwost3 mode§  : mode_ui,
                        cadd§  : cadd_ui)          {11}

        |GEN(stwost3    mode§  : mode_ui,
                        cadds§ : cadd_ui,
                        caddo§ : (dirwost bnc.swostcc))).   {3}
```

Case E :

class$_{ui}$ = *indwost.*

see case B except *gc* :

```
gc_o := ((gc_ui ≠ nil | DECREASEGC(1)) ;
        (GCRELEVANT(mode_ui)
              |co as in case B co
        |:gc_ui ≠ nil
              |GEN(stgcnil caddgc§ : (dirgcw bnc.gcc)) ;        {13}
              gc_o)).
```

Step 2.3 :

swostcc +:= *STATICSIZE*(*mode*$_{ui}$)

od.

Step 3 : *BOST* static properties (finalization) :

Step 3.1 : *Dmr* management :

As soon as a generator local to the current block is involved in the elaboration of the collateral clause (*geno*$_o$=1) memory recovery on *DWOST%* must not eliminate the locations of these generators from *DWOST%* [13] . Space can only be recovered up to the lastly elaborated local generator ; we recall that *wp%* of the current *BLOCK%* points exactly behind all such generators.

```
(geno_o = 1
    |(class of dmr_o = dyn
          |DECREASEDMR(1)) ;
    dmr_o := (dyn bnc.dmrc) ;
    GEN(stwp bnc§  : bnc,
             cadd§ : (dirdmrw bnc.dmrc)))        {22}
```

Step 3.2 : *Gc* management :

Up to now, elements of the structure are protected one by one in such a way *WOST*% protection is steadily controlled during the elaboration of these elements. Now one single protection will replace the field protections :

```
(gc₀ ≠ nil
     |for i from gc₀ + gcelemsz by gcelemsz to gcc - gcelemsz
        do GEN(stgcnil caddgc§ : (dirgcw bnc.i)) {13} od ;
     GEN(stgcwost mode§ : mode₀,
                  cadd§ : cadd₀,
                  caddgc§ : (dirgcw gc₀))).      {6}
```

Step 3.3 :

Other *BOST* properties remain as calculated in step 2.

topstpm -:= 1.

16. MISCELLANEOUS

16.1 WIDENING

Widening can be considered a monadic operator. *Int* to *real* transformation depends on hardware. *Bits* to [] *bool* and *bytes* to [] *char* are special cases of rowing.

16.2 VOIDING

Voiding corresponds to the deletion of a partial result. Statically it corresponds to the deletion of a *BOST* element together with the corresponding ICI generation for static and dynamic memory management ; the deleted *BOST* element is replaced by a new one :

$cadd_o$:= (*nihil* 0)

$mode_o$:= *void*

16.3 FOR STATEMENT

Syntax

FORCL → for∇ $\{$from∇ UNITF$\}_0^1$ $\{$by∇ UNITB$\}_0^1$

to∇ UNITT$\}_0^1$ $\{$foriden$\}_0^1$ $\{$while∇ SERIALW$\}_0^1$

do∇ UNITD

{With foriden, a *SYMBTAB* entry is associated}.

Translation scheme

1. ρ(UNITF)
2. ρ(UNITB)
3. ρ(UNITT)
4. Counter initialization
5. *GEN(forto ...lo...)*
6. 6.1 ρ(SERIALW)
   6.2 *GEN(jumpno ...lf...)*
   6.3 Deletion of *BOST* properties
7. ρ(UNITD)
8. *GEN(plus ...)*
9. *GEN(jump lo)*
10. *GEN(labdef lf)*
11. *BOST* static properties.

<u>Semantics</u>

<u>Step</u> 1 :

<u>Case</u> A :

CONTEXT(from∇).

ρ(UNITF)

{The static properties of UNITF appear on *BOST*, they are denoted $mode_f$, $cadd_f$ ...}.

<u>Case</u> B :

∼ *CONTEXT*(from∇).

The following static properties are stored on *BOST* as default properties for UNITF :

$mode_f$:= <u>*int*</u>

$cadd_f$:= (<u>*intct*</u> 1)

smr_f, dmr_f and gc_f are irrelevant

or_f = (<u>*nil*</u>, 0, 0, 0)

$scope_f$ = (0, 0).

<u>Step</u> 2 :

<u>Case</u> A :

CONTEXT(by∇).

ρ(UNITB)

{The static properties of UNITB appear on *BOST*, they are denoted $mode_b$, $cadd_b$ ...}.

<u>Case</u> B :

∼ *CONTEXT*(by∇).

Default properties for UNITB are put on *BOST* :

see step 1, case B.

<u>Step</u> 3 :

<u>Case</u> A :

CONTEXT(to∇).

ρ(UNITT)

{The static properties of UNITT appear on *BOST*, they are denoted $mode_t$, $cadd_t$ ...}.

<u>Case</u> B :

∼*CONTEXT*(to∇).

A new *BOST* element is created as default for UNITT ; in this element,

$cadd_t$:= (<u>*nihil*</u> 0)

indicating that no upper limit is fixed for the loop.

<u>Step</u> 4 : Counter initialization :

<u>Case</u> A :

CONTEXT(foriden).

The following properties are stored in *SYMBTAB* at the entry associated with foriden :

$mode_i$:= int
$cadd_i$:= (diriden bnc.sidc)
$scope_i$:= (0,0)
$flagdec_i$:= 1

The value of the actual parameter of this implicit identity declaration is furnished by UNICLF :

GEN(stword cadds§ : $cadd_f$,
caddo§ : $cadd_i$) {4}

On BOST, the above static properties stored in SYMBTAB overwrite the static properties of UNITF.

Case B :

∿ CONTEXT(foriden).

If $class_f$ = dirwost, it is the SWOST% cell corresponding to $cadd_f$ which is used as counter of the loop ; otherwise such cell has to be reserved at bnc.swostc :

GEN(stword cadds§ : $cadd_f$,
caddo§ : (dirwost bnc.swostc)) {4}

on BOST the static properties of UNITF are overwritten:

$cadd_f$:= (dirwost bnc.swostc)
smr_f := bnc.swostc.

Step 5 :

Case A :

$class_t \neq$ nihil.

GEN(forto labnb§ : lo,
caddfori§: $cadd_f$,
caddby§ : $cadd_b$,
caddto§ : $cadd_t$) {89}

-caddfori§ gives access to an integer i%
-caddby§ gives access to an integer b%
-caddto§ gives access to an integer t%
-labnb§ is the first of two labels : lo and lf .

Action :

```
(proc(int,int)bool P ;
    (b% > 0 | P:= >
            | P:= <) ;
    lo : (P(i%,t%)
            | lf)
)
```

Clearly, if class of caddby§ is intct, the above algorithm is simplified.

Case B :

$class_t$ = nihil.

GEN(labdef labnb§ : lo) {28}

Step 6 :

Case :

CONTEXT(while∇).

Step 6.1 :

ρ(SERIALW)

{The static properties of SERIALW appear on *BOST*, they are denoted $mode_w$, $cadd_w$ ...}.

Step 6.2 :

GEN(jumpno labnb§ : lf,
cadd§ : $cadd_w$*)* {29}

Step 6.3 : Deletion of *BOST* properties :

The static properties of SERIALW are deleted from *BOST*.

Step 7 :

ρ(UNITD)

{The static properties of UNITD {nihil ...} appear on *BOST* ; they are deleted}.

Step 8 :

Case :

$class_f$ = diriden or $class_t \neq$ nihil.

GEN(plus cadds§ : $cadd_b$*,*
caddo§ : $cadd_f$*)* {14}

Action :

The integral value stored at *caddo§* is incremented by the integral value stored at *cadds§*.

Step 9 :

GEN(jump labnb§ : lo). {27}

Step 10 :

GEN(labdef labnb : lf) {28}

Step 11 : *BOST* static properties :

The three top *BOST* elements are deleted and static space on *SWOST%* is recovered accordingly. A new *BOST* element indicating that no value results from the statement, is set up :

$mode_o$:= void
$cadd_o$:= (nihil 0).

16.4 CALL OF TRANSPUT ROUTINES

Syntax

TRCALL → trcall∇ TRPRIM (UNIT1,...,UNITn).

Translation scheme

1. ρ(TRPRIM)
2. *for* *i* *to* *n* *do*
   ρ(UNITi)
   od
3. *GEN(stdcallinout ...)*
4. *BOST* management.

Semantics

Step 1 :

ρ(TRPRIM)

{The static properties of TRPRIM appear on *BOST*, they are denoted $mode_p$, $cadd_p$ ... . Note that $cadd_p$ is always of class *dircttab* ; hence, we assume that transput routines cannot be dynamically transmitted by a proper program construction}.

Step 2 :

for *i* *to* *n* *do*

Case A :

UNITi → trcoll∇ (UNITi1,...,UNITim).

trcoll∇ is the marker of a collateral clause of

mode [] *union (outtype, proc(file))*
or [] *union (intype, proc(file))*
or [] *outtype*
or [] *intype*

In such a case, the collateral is disregarded, and UNITij are treated at the same level as other UNITk, i.e. their static properties are accumulated on *BOST* :

for *j* *to* *m* *do* ρ(UNITij) *od*

Indeed, it is useless to construct a collateral clause of mode [] *union* ... here, the goal of the transput being to transput actual values.

It is to be noted that this process is only valid if the collateral is directly a parameter of a transput routine. The generalization of the process would imply the possibility of transmitting sets of values as result of blocks or procedures instead of one single value ; this would significantly increase the complexity of the corresponding static management.

Other cases :

ρ(UNITi)

{The static properties of UNITi appear on *BOST*}.

od.

Step 3 :

Suppose we have accumulated the static properties of *t* values on *BOST*, *t* is available for example in the field *countelem* of *TOPST*. Let *mode1*, *cadd1* ..., *mode2*, *cadd2*, ... *modet*, *caddt* ... be the corresponding static properties.

GEN(<u>stdcallinout</u> caddrout§ : $cadd_p$,
n§ : t,
mode1§ : mode1,
cadd1§ : cadd1,
...
moden§ : modet,
caddn§ : caddt) {59}

<u>Action</u> :
The action of the standard routine of access $cadd_p$ is performed on the *n§* parameters characterized by *modei§-caddi§*.

<u>Step</u> 4 : *BOST* management :
The *t BOST* top elements are deleted, this may involve the generation of ICI's for dynamic management of *dmr* and *gc*.
A new element is put at the top of *BOST* :
mode := <u>void</u>
cadd := (<u>nihil</u> 0).

17. OTHER ICIS

The ICI's which have not been mentioned explicitely in the description are now reviewed.

-*inprog* {40} and *outprog* {41} are generated at the beginning and at the end of each object program respectively. They are intended to perform appropriate initializations and finalizations.

-*newcard cardnb§* {103} is a command keeping track of the card number where the source program constructions giving rise to the ICI's appear. These commands allow to provide run-time error messages with more appropriate error diagnostic information.

-*prid iden§*{104} and *prnumb numb§*{105} keep track of pragmats which appear in the source program. They are used for three purposes (see [11])

(1) at compile-time, to require the printing of some tables as an aid to debugging.

(2) at run-time to interrupt program elaboration in order to be able to introduce new sets of data or to make some dump as an aid to debugging.

(3) at run-time to give the programmer the possibility of programming himself interruptions due to run-time errors.

- *stgcelem* {16}, *stwostincr* {19} , *minus* {21}, *jumpyes* {30}, *labformat* {32}, *stscope* {69}, *stinterstfl* {65}, *fillstateone* {68} and *rows* {84} used in the actual compiler for different purposes are not described in this book.

PART III : TRANSLATION INTO MACHINE CODE

0. GENERALITIES

PART III outlines the method used in the ALGOL-68-X8.1-compiler for generating machine code. This method has been designed in such a way that machine dependency is very well localized and parametrized, thus making even code generation quite portable. It is not at all intended to X8 specialists : references to X8 peculiarities are mentioned only occasionally in a few places and just as an illustration.
First, the methods used for solving general problems of machine code generation are described ; in particular, it is explained :

(1) how accesses provided by the intermediate code are transformed into actual addresses of machine instructions (III.1),

(2) how machine instructions are generated in a modular way using the above mentioned access transformation as a separate module (III.2),

(3) how local optimizations are applied to the generated code in order to improve its efficiency (III.3).

Some particular problems at the level of the loader are then analyzed (III.4).

Section III.5, gives information on how code is produced from the different intermediate code instructions and this using the general methods explained earlier and relying on a minimal set of registers.
In section III.6, some problems specific to the garbage collector are treated.

1. ACCESSES AND MACHINE ADDRESSES

In PART I and II, a number of accesses have been introduced and used at the level of intermediate code generation ; these accesses can be classified as follows :
(1) *Absolute accesses,* i.e. accesses allowing to define a value independently of any storage allocation, these accesses only correspond to *cadd = (constant v).*
(2) *Symbolic accesses,* i.e. accesses referring to some run-time device or constant provided with a symbolic representation which will be defined at load-time, such are :

(dirctab a),
(display bn),
(dirabs s),
(varabs s).

(3) *Dynamic accesses,* i.e. accesses depending on a run-time calculation ; these are the *RANST%* accesses using the *DISPLAY%* mechanism ; they are also called *RANST%* accesses. Such are for example *(diriden n.p), (indiden n.p),...* .

Remark 1.

In PART II.11.1, Remark 3, we have mentioned that it would be worthwhile to provide indirect accesses with an increment δ, for example *(indiden n.p;δ)* which would mean the following stored value address : *RANST%[DISPLAY%[n] +p] +δ*. In the sequel, we shall suppose that such an increment has been implemented.

Remark 2.

Actually, *RANST%* accesses do not contain *n.p* doublets but *bnc.α* doublets. In II.0.4.5.b.β, we have explained how *bnc.α* doublets allow to calculate *n.p* doublets through *BLOCKTAB§*, we do not describe this transformation any longer here ; it should be clear that after such a transformation, the number of distinctions amongst *RANST%* access classes can be reduced to 'direct', 'indirect' and 'variable' *RANST%* access classes :

(dirranst n.p),
(indranst n.p),
(varranst n.p).

However, for the sake of local optimizations (I.2.3.4) we must remember whether the value to be accessed or its indirect address is stored on *WOST%* or not ; such an information will be kept in an additional field *w*.

Remark 3.

Double indirect access (*i2iden n.p*) is locally used in PART II. The use of such an access could be easily avoided ; on the other hand, its implementation is similar to simple indirect accesses. For the sake of simplicity, double indirect access will not be mentioned any more.

1.1 ACCESS STRUCTURE

In order to ease the transformation of accesses into machine addresses, it seems worthwhile to structure them in a more appropriate way, while however keeping the same machine independency. This new structuration is characterized by the following mode :

```
mode access = (char class,
               struct (int hadd,
                           tadd) add,
               int symb,
               int level,
                   incr,
               bool w     )
```

The meaning of the different fields for a value *V* with *access A* is now explained : *class, add* and *symb* of *A* indicate how an integral value *I* can be obtained, integral value which later on, and according to *level* of *A* and *incr* of *A* will be considered *V* itself or a machine address through which *V* can be reached at run-time. There are two possible classes for *A* :

(1) *class of A = static* ; in this case *hadd = 0* and

$$I = tadd+S$$

where *S* is fixed at load-time ; *S* corresponds to the actual value of the field *symb* (*symbolic*).

(2) *class of A = display* ; in this case *add* is a doublet *n.p*, *symb* is irrelevant and

$$I = DISPLAY\%[n]+p$$

Level (of indirection) and *incr* indicate how *I* must be interpreted in order to reach the actual value *V*. We disitnguish three levels :

- *literal (level = -1) : V=I*
- *direct (level = 0)* : the static part of *V* is stored in a memory location starting at address *I* ; *incr* = 0 :

$$V = (MEM\%[I], MEM\%[I+1], \ldots).$$

- *indirect (level=1)* : the static part of is stored in a memory location, the address of which is the contents of MEM%[*I+incr*] :

$$V = (MEM\%[MEM\%[I+incr]], MEM\%[MEM\%[I+incr+1]] \ldots).$$

- *w* keeps track whether *V* is stored on *WOST%* or not.

cadd	access						psadd					
	class	add	symb	level	incr	w	class	add	symb	literal	w	GMI
(constant v)	static	v	0	-1	0	0	sdir	v	0	1	0	
(dircttab a)	static	a	constab	0	0	0	sdir	a	constab	0	0	
(varranst n.p)	display	n.p	0	-1	0	0	disp	n.p	0	1	0	
(dirranst n.p)	display	n.p	0	0	0	0/1	disp	n.p	0	0	0/1	
(indranst n.p;δ)	display	n.p	0	1	δ	0/1	indR	δ	0	0	0/1	LDR n.p
(display bn)	static	bn	display	0	0	0	sdir	bn	display	0	0	
(dirabs s)	static	0	s	0	0	0	sdir	0	s	0	0	
(varabs s)	static	0	s	-1	0	0	sdir	0	s	1	0	
	Machine independent						Machine dependent					

Table 1. Access transformations.

Table 1 situates the old *cadd*'s in the new frame ; obvious notational simplifications are used, in particular in columns *literal* and *w*, 0 means *false* and *1* means *true*.

1.2 PSEUDO-ADDRESSES

This section shows how accesses (as defined in PART I and as structured in III.1.1) are transformed in order to be directly utilizable in machine instructions (III.2). This transformation is necessarily hardware dependent, but it is performed by one single routine *CONVERTACCESS*, thus localizing machine dependency. This routine is intended to perform appropriate compile-time actions (including the generation of machine instructions) in order to simulate particular accesses when not available in the hardware :

-if *literal* addressing does not exist the corresponding value is caused to be stored in *CONSTAB§* and a direct access replaces the literal access.

-if *indirect* addressing is not available, it is simulated by means of an index register : machine instructions loading this index register are generated and the indirect access is replaced by an 'indexed access' using the index register loaded as explained above.

-if *display* addressing is not available, it is simulated by means of a particular register ; optimizations inhibiting the register to be loaded with a value it already contained can also be performed at this level, provided the static image of the old register contents is kept up-to-date during the whole code generation.

In order to be more concrete we shall assume that the available hardware has literal, direct and display addressing facilities, hence indirect addressing must be simulated by means of index registers. In this context, the routine *CONVERTACCESS* can be described with more precision. It has two parameters :

- a parameter of type *cadd* specifying a particular access,
- an index register R which can be used if necessary, to transform an indirect access into an indexed access.

CONVERTACCESS results in a so-called pseudo-address *(psadd)* which will be directly used by the code generator (III.2).

psadd can be formalized as follows :

```
mode psadd = struct (char class,
                     struct (int hadd,
                                 tadd)add,
                             int symb,
                             bool literal,
                                  w)
```

The meaning of the different fields for a value *V* with a *psadd P* is now explained :

Class, *add* and *symb* of *P* indicate how an integral value *I* can be obtained, integral value which later on, and according to *literal*, will be considered *V* itself or a machine address through which *V* can be reached at run-time. There are three possible classes for *P* :

(1) *class of P* = *sdir*, standing for simple direct address ;
in this case, *hadd = 0* :

$$I = tadd + S$$

where *S* is fixed at load-time ; *S* corresponds to the actual value of the field *symb*.

(2) *class of P* = *indR* standing for indexed addressing using the index register R ; actually there may be such a class for each hardware index register (in practice only two index registers are used).

$$I = tadd + S + contents(R)$$

(3) *class of P* = *disp* standing for *DISPLAY%* addressing ; in this case, *add* is a doublet *n.p*, *symb* is irrelevant and

$$I = DISPLAY\%[n] + p.$$

If *literal* is *true*, *I=V*, otherwise the static part of *V* is in a memory location at address *I* : *V = (MEM%[I], MEM%[I+1], ...)*

w keeps track whether *V* is stored on *WOST%* or not.

CONVERTACCESS performing all transformations from *cadd* to *access* (III.1.1) and from *access* to *psadd* is roughly described as follows :

proc CONVERTACCESS = (cadd cadd, register R) psadd :

co the result of the routine is the *psadd* corresponding to *cadd* ; the routine uses *BLOCKTAB§* for transforming doublets *bnc*.α into *n.p* ; table 1 shows the two steps of that transformation. The second step may involve the generation of some machine instructions. These are mentioned in column *GMI* of table 1 (see also III.2).
co

Two additional routines for pseudo-address transformation will be useful in the sequel, they are now described :

proc INREGPS = (psadd psaddx, register R) psadd :

co This routine is used to transform a *psaddx* in which *literal=false* into another *psadd* of the form

class := indR	
add := (0,0)	{in the sequel, this *psadd* is represented
symb := 0	by *(indR,0)*}
literal := false	
w := false	

Except if *psaddx* is already of the required form, the following generation takes place

GMI	*LDR = psaddx*

This means that *R* is loaded with the address represented by *psaddx* (see III.2). This routine is used when the address of a value has to be passed to a run-time routine through register *R*.

```
co.
proc DEREFPS (psadd psaddx, register R) psadd :
co psaddx is supposed to correspond to a name ; the routine delivers a psadd charac-
   terizing the value referred to by the name. co
   (literal of psaddx = true
          | (class of psaddx,
             add of psaddx,
             symb of psaddx,
             false,
             w of psaddx)
          | GMI [LDR psaddx] ;
             (indR, 0)
   ).
```

2. *METHOD OF CODE GENERATION*

In order to increase the modularity and the portability of the compiler, it is necessary to systematize the code generation. In the X8-compiler, code is generated by means of a single routine *GMI* interpreting the contents of a prebuilt table *GTAB*. Clearly, *GTAB* is machine dependent and is one of the few modules to be rewritten to adapt the compiler to a particular hardware. In this book for the sake of clarity, we do not refer to *GTAB* when we want to describe the generation of machine instructions ; instead a symbolic representation of the generated instructions is used. It is the conventions of this representation which are first explained. Thereafter, details of the actual process of code generation using *GTAB* are given.

2.1 *SYMBOLIC REPRESENTATION OF CODE GENERATION*

The generation of machine code is specified by *GMI* followed by a rectangle, prompting a call of the routine *GMI* ; in the rectangle, run-time actions for which code is generated are specified and this in two possible forms :

(1) by means of a block-diagram, when the action is sophisticated ; generally, what is actually generated in such a case is the call of a prestored run-time (library) routine (see also III.5.2).

(2) by means of a symbolic representation of the instructions to be generated, when the run-time action is more easily expressed in this form. The conventions which are used in the symbolic representation of an instruction are now explained :

<u>Case</u> A : if the address of the instruction is directly based on a *psadd*, the symbolic representation has four fields :

C	{*op-code*}	example	LDR
L	{*literal*}		=
P	{*psadd* }		*psadd*
I	{*incr* }		*+(reladd+3)*

C is a three-letter symbolic representation of the operation code of the instruction ; the meaning is generally obvious, e.g. LDR means "load register R", STR means "store the contents of register R" ... .

L is "=" when the operand defined by *P* and *I* has to be considered a literal operand ; clearly, in this case, *literal* <u>*of*</u> *P* must be <u>*true*</u>. Otherwise *L* is empty.

P specifies a particular *psadd*.

I is an increment ; it has the form '+ integral expression' and it means that the *tadd* <u>*of*</u> *psadd* has to be incremented by the value of the expression. Remark that both the expression and the *tadd* incrementation are performed at compile-time.

<u>Case</u> B : if the address of the instruction does not directly refer to a preexisting *psadd*, the instruction has a representation where a *psadd* is explicitely stated :

C {*op-code* }	example :	LDR
L {*literal* }		=
A {*address* }		*10*
I {*index* }		*,B*
S {*symbolic*}		*;constab*

C represents the instruction operation code as in case A.
L is "=" when the operand is a literal, it is empty otherwise.
A specifies the address properly so called ; it consists of an integral expression when the addressing is not <u>*display*</u> and a pair of integral expressions separated by a point if a <u>*display*</u> addressing is involved ; these expressions are calculated at compile-time.
I is ",X" when the index register X is involved, it is empty otherwise.
S is ";" followed by a symbolic run-time address or constant if such an item is involved, it is empty otherwise.

<u>Example</u>
Suppose we have to specify the machine code generation of the simplified ICI

```
standcall (caddrout§,
           cadd1§,
           cadd2§,
           caddres§)                        {54}
```

assuming that *caddrout§* specifies the standard operator <u>*op*</u>*(*<u>*int*</u>*,*<u>*int*</u>*)*<u>*int*</u> +,

```
        psadd1 := CONVERTACCESS (cadd1§,Y)
        psadd2 := CONVERTACCESS (cadd2§,X)
        psadd3 := CONVERTACCESS((caddres§,-)
            co caddres§ has always the form (dirwost ...)
               no index register is needed for the conversion  co.
        GMI      | LDY psadd1 |
                 | ADY psadd2 |
                 | STY psadd3 |
```

<u>*co*</u> Here we do not consider the fact that, for the sake of local optimizations, it is advisable to load an operand with a *WOST%* access *(w=*<u>*true*</u>*)* first (III.3) <u>*co*</u>
With the particular values

```
          cadd1§ : (indwost n.p)
          cadd2§ : (constant 3)
          caddres§ : (dirwost n'.p')
```

the above process corresponds to the following generation :

```
        GMI      | LDY  n.p   |
                 | LDY    0,Y |
                 | ADY =  3   |
                 | STY  n'.p' |
```

The process does apply to any sensible forms of *cadd's*.

2.2 ACTUAL IMPLEMENTATION OF CODE GENERATION

As stated above, code generation is implemented by means of the routine *GMI* interpreting the contents of a table *GTAB*. In *GTAB*, for each instruction to be specified, its operation code (op-code) and also other hardware dependent features (such as the variants pze, uyn in the case of the X8) are explicitely stated. However, the address is parametrized ; there are two mechanisms for address construction :

Case A : the address of the instruction is directly based on a preexisting *psadd* : then it is the address of the compile-time location where this *psadd* is found which is (symbolically) specified in the table ; moreover an increment to *tadd* is also specified under the form of the (symbolic) address of the compile-time location where this increment is found. Together with ***psadd***, an additional field *literal* is specified ; its meaning is analoguous to the one explained for *L* in case A of III.2.1.

Case B : the address of the instruction does not refer to a preexisting *psadd* : *GTAB* provides for the information to construct a *psadd* in an ad-hoc way, by means of a field of the mode *psadd1* :

```
mode psadd1 = struct (char class,
                      struct (ref int hadd,
                                      tadd)add,
                      int symb,
                      bool literal,
                            w)
```

the difference with *psadd* is that in the fields *hadd* and *tadd* it is the address of a compile-time location where the actual value can be found which is specified (symbolically). Hence, *hadd* and *tadd* may result from compile-time calculations and cannot be specified as such in *GTAB*. Moreover, as in case A, the address of a compile-time location where an increment to *tadd* is to be found is also specified.

The generation of a set of machine instructions is performed by the routine *GMI* which has as its parameter an entry point *gtabp* into *GTAB*.
The structure of *GTAB* is such that, at this entry point, the number *n* of instructions to be generated is found followed by the information for constructing these *n* instructions. For distinguishing the cases A and B above, in each instruction a special boolean field is provided. Formally we could write :

```
[1:...] [1:flex] ginst GTAB ;
mode ginst = struct (int opcode,
                     union (struct(ref psadd psadd, bool literal),
                            psadd1)psadd,
                     ref int incr,
                    {int pze, uyn})
```

Here, it is the union overhead which has to be interpreted in order to make the choice between the cases ; the fields *pze* and *uyn* are peculiar to the X8 and will easily be understood by the specialists.

Remark

It should be clear that *GTAB* is a preconstructed table and that it should be possible to "program" this table in a symbolic form, using compile-time variables and constants. In the X8-compiler, the macro-facilities of the assembler are used to build the table from its symbolic representation.

Example

Suppose we want to generate code by which a library routine *FILLSTRIDES%* is called. Suppose now this routine has two parameters : the address of a descriptor and its number of dimensions ; these parameters are for example provided in register R1 and R2 respectively. {The action of the routine *FILLSTRIDES%* is the calculation of the strides attached to each dimension according to the bounds supposed to be already filled in the descriptor}. For generating the call of the routine, we write

```
GMI     LDR1 =  psadd
        LDR2    nbdim
        LNK         0 ; FILLSTRIDES%
```

This is actually performed by means of the call

GMI (gtabp)

which assumes

(1) the following contents of *GTAB* :

GTAB

		opcode	psadd	incr	...
	...	...	...	...	...
gtabp:	1:3				
	{1}	LDR1	<u>*struct*</u>*:(psadd,* <u>*true*</u>*)*	0	
	{2}	LDR2	<u>*psadd1*</u> *: (*<u>*sdir*</u>*, (0, nbdim), 0,* <u>*false*</u>*,* <u>*false*</u>*)*	0	...
	{3}	LNK	<u>*psadd1*</u> *: (*<u>*sdir*</u>*, (0, 0), fillstrides,* <u>*false*</u>*,* <u>*false*</u>*)*	0	

(2) the following compile-time declarations :

<u>psadd</u> psadd := CONVERTACCESS (<u>cadd</u> <u>co</u> issued from the intermediate code *<u>co</u>)* ;

<u>int</u> nbdim ;

<u>int</u> fillstrides = *<u>co</u>* an integer representing the address of the run-time routine *FILLSTRIDES%* symbolically *<u>co</u>* ;

<u>int</u> LDR1= ..., LDR2= ..., LNK= ... ; <u>co</u> symbolic conventions for the op-codes *<u>co</u>*.

Eventually, *GMI* can be formalized as follows :

```
mode loadinst = co a mode representative of the structure of an instruction in a
                   form appropriate to the loader co
proc  GMI = (int gtabp) :
   for i to upb GTAB [gtabp]
         do co process instruction GTAB[gtabp] [i],
               i.e. put it in the appropriate loadinstr form and store it into the
               object program passing through the local optimizer co
         od.
```

3. *LOCAL OPTIMIZATIONS*

The principle of local optimizations is extremely simple [16] : when a new instruction is generated, it is compared with the last instruction in the object program to see whether one or both instructions cannot be cancelled. Precautions have been taken at the level of ICI generation :

(1) in order to ensure security ;

-*nooptimize* inhibits local optimizations when necessary (I.2.4.3 remark 1, II.0.4.5.e).

-*w* (III.1), deduced from the access class inhibits the cancelling of a "store instruction" when the corresponding access is not a *WOST%* access.

(2) in order to allow optimizations wherever possible :

-*loadreg* and *storereg* are generated in choice constructions and in case of routine calls and definition (I.2.3.4 , II.5.5 , II.14).

A number of practical considerations are now given in order to show how local optimizations have been actually implemented and to point out a number of peculiarities allowing to take a greater advantage of them.

A. It appeared that local optimizations may be implemented in a very simple way, by means of a buffer, without sensible loss of efficiency ; this method is now outlined. Each time an instruction has to be generated, it is compared with the contents of the buffer, which in turn containsthe lastly generated instruction ; several cases are possible :

- the buffer is empty : the new instruction is stored in the buffer.
- the buffer is not empty : an ad-hoc process is invoked by which the new instruction and possibly the contents of the buffer are cancelled or by which the contents of the buffer is pushed into the object program while the new instruction takes place into the buffer.
- the instruction contained in the buffer is pushed into the object program each time the ICI *nooptimize* is met.

The use of a buffer is also advantageous for compile-time efficiency ; in the buffer, the different fields of an instruction are in an unpacked form, which makes the accesses to its fields more efficient.

B. We refer to I.2.3.4, II.5.5 and II.11.1. Remark 1, for practical examples of local optimizations. In addition the following remarks are of interests :

a. Optimizing the use of Boolean values

A problem arises at the interface between modules resulting in a Boolean value and modules using it, considering that :

- A Boolean value is stored in a conventional way for example *0* for *false*, *1* for *true*.
- If the Boolean value results from operations on other Boolean values, calculations take generally place in conventional registers as for integral and real calculations.
- If the Boolean value results from relations, the result appears in a single bit comparison register *CREG%* which may be addressable or not.
- Finally a Boolean value may be used in conditional clauses for branching ; branching instructions are generally based on the contents of the *CREG%*.

The problem arises when we have to store a Boolean value contained in *CREG%* into a memory cell, and when we have to use a Boolean value stored in a memory cell for branching. With our principle of translating modules in an independent way, the use of the result of a module is unknown and it will always be stored in a *WOST%* cell. Conversely, branching based on a Boolean value will always have to deal with a Boolean value stored in a memory cell. The question is, how to proceed to recover efficiency by means of local optimizations? The solution lies in considering that we have an addressable *CREG%* at our disposal and to allow the generation of instructions LDC and STC through *GTAB*. Such instructions may take place in the buffer and be cancelled using the normal local optimization process of load- and store-instructions. However, if LDC and STC instructions are not available in the hardware (as it is the case for the X8), they are not pushed as such into the object program, but they are simulated by means of other actual hardware instructions.

The following examples illustrate the above mechanism and show how efficiency is retrieved :

Example 3.1

Source program

(a = b | ... | ...)

Intermediate code

=((int,int)bool, a, b, w)

jumpno(w,L)...

Machine code generated by *GMI*	Machine code actually stored
LDY *a*	LDY *w*
EQY *b*	EQY *b*
~~STC *w*~~	
~~LDC *w*~~	
IFJ *L*	IFJ *L*
...	...

Example 3.2

Source program

B := a=b

Intermediate code

=((int, int) bool, a, b, w)

:=(bool, w, B)

Machine code generated by *GMI*

```
LDY a
EQY b
STC w  ------->  LDY = 0
                 IFJ L
                 LDY = 1
                 L:STY w
LDY w
STY B
```

Machine code actually stored

```
    LDY a
    EQY b
    LDY = 0
    IFJ L
    LDY = 1
L:

    STY B
```

Example 3.3

Source program

(B | a | b)

Intermediate code

jumpno(B,L)

...

Machine code generated by *GMI*

```
LDC B  ------->  LDY B
                 EQY = 1

IFJ L
```

Machine code actually stored

```
LDY B
EQY = 1
IFJ L
```

Example 3.4

Source program

B or A

Intermediate code

or((bool,bool)bool,B,A,w)

Machine code

```
LDY B
ORY A
STY w
```

b. *Eliminating redundant goto's*

The local optimization mechanism can be used to eliminate redundant *goto's* which often appear in the code generated by a modular system like ours.

During machine code generation, a table (*LABTAB*) of correspondence between labels and relative machine addresses in the object program is generated. By means of this table the loader transforms labels into actual program addresses (an indication is given to it by a special value *labtabp* of the field *symb* in *GTAB*). Jumps (unconditional UNJ and others) and label definitions take place in the buffer defined above as other instructions. Indeed, they must inhibit local optimizations on load and store instructions surrounding them. Moreover, we take profit of their presence in the buffer to perform the following :

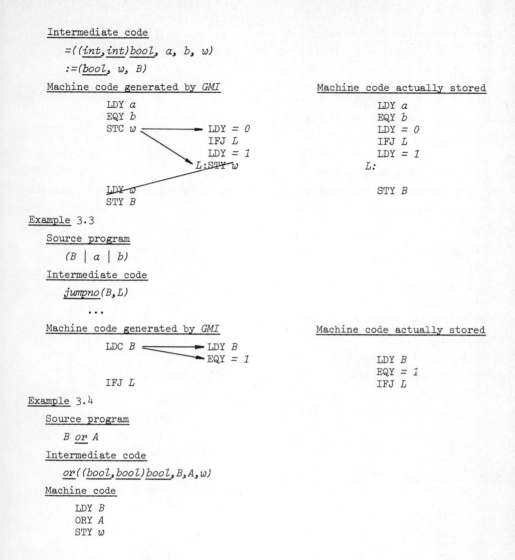

L' : UNJ L	causes the definition of L' to be equivalent to the one of L in *LABTAB* ; a chaining is implemented to take transitivity into account. In this way, L' is shortcut.
UNJ L L :	causes the cancelling of the jump
UNJ L UNJ L'	causes the cancelling of the second jump.

c. Ordering the operands of a formula

When translating a binary commutative operator, it is useful to load first, the operand which has a *WOST%* access *(w=true)*

Example 3.5

Source program

a+(b+c)

Intermediate code :

+((int, int) int, b, c, w)

+((int, int) int, a, w, w')

Machine code

1) Without the above precaution

Before local optimization	After local optimization
LDX *b* ADX *c* STX *w* LDX *a* ADX *w* STX *w'*	idem

2) With the above precaution

LDX *b* ADX *c* STX ~~*w*~~ ~~LDX~~ *w* ADX *a* STX *w'*	LDX *b* ADX *c* ADX *a* STX *w'*

4. *THE LOADER*(†)

The task of the loader is to put at appropriate places in the memory the different devices, routines and parts of program which must be available at run-time, and this in their definite hardware form, while trying to waste as few space as possible. The X8-compiler does not admit precompiled routines other than those defined by the compiler itself, such that no linkage editor task devolves upon the loader. The loader works in two steps :

(1) actual memory is allocated to the different run-time devices according to the information on their size furnished by the compiler for the particular program to be loaded.

(2) these devices are stored in the space allocated to them, while appropriate address transformations are performed.

The X8-loader is also given the task of checking the validity of generated instructions. Indeed, the X8 hardware though of modular conception has some peculiarities deviating from the general rules. It is prudent to have a kind of filter, before execution, giving an error message if an unacceptable instruction has been generated through *GTAB* interpretation. The filter relies on a kind of decision table *FILTAB* where the X8 hardware, general rules as well as peculiarities, has been described in an appropriate way. This feature has appeared to be very useful during the debugging phase of the compiler.

For designing the first task of the loader, we need to know which device must be available at each run-time moment. Two situations have to be distinguished, namely, outside and inside the garbage collection. Overlay is used in the implementation of these two situations (see fig.4.1).

(1) Outside the garbage collection we need :
  - *OBPROG%* : the object program in an executable form
  - *RTROUT%* : the library routines which are used in the particular *OBPROG%*
  - *CONSTAB%*
  - *DISPLAY%*
  - *VALSTACK%* : used in the elaboration of ICI's on data structures (see III.5.4)
  - *DECTAB%* : {could be avoided : II.0.4.2}.
  - *WORKSP%* : the working space allocated to *RANST%* and *HEAP%*

(2) Inside the garbage collector we need :
  - *GCPROG%* : the garbage collector program properly so called
  - *BITTAB%* : the bit table

(†) This section is rather technical, but its contents is not necessary for understanding the next sections.

- *HOLESTAB%* : the table of holes
- *DESCRTAB%* : keeping track of multiple values with interstices which have to be marked at the end of the process (see III.6.4)
- *TRACESTACK%* : a stack used when tracing values
- *VALSTACK%* : which must be updated during garbage collection (III.6.3)
- *DECTAB%* : {could be avoided : II.0.4.2}
- *WORKSP%* : to be traced (compacted, updated)

The size of these devices are represented by means of obvious notations ending with *sz*.

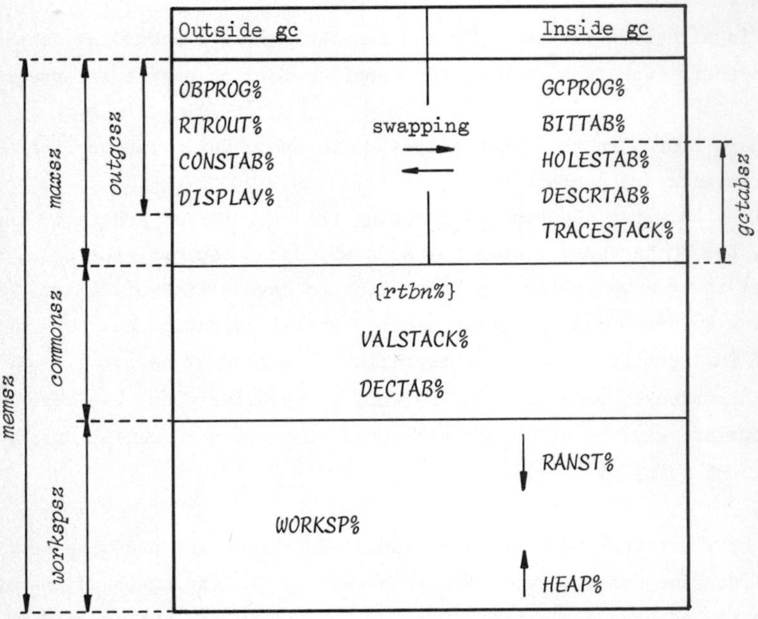

fig. 4.1

The following sizes are fixed a priori when the loader is entered :

- *obprogsz*
- *rtroutsz*(†)
- *constabsz*
- *displaysz*
- *valstacksz*
- *dectabsz*
- *gcprogsz*

(†) Not all library routines have to be present during the elaboration of each program ; which routines are needed is transmitted to the loader by the code generation phase by means of a table *ROUTTAB*.

Sizes which remain to be determined are :

- *workspsz*
- *bittabsz*
- *holestabsz*
- *descrtabsz*
- *tracestacksz*

The following considerations will guide the definition of these sizes.

(1) We shall suppose that in both situations (inside and outside the garbage collection) only the required information is present in direct access memory, and that consequently, swapping has to take place when switching from one situation to the other (fig. 4.1).

(2) Let us define

memsz = memory size

outgcsz = *obprogsz* + *rtroutsz* + *constabsz* + *displaysz*

outgcsz is fixed a priori

commonsz = *1* + *valstsz* + *dectabsz*

commonsz is fixed a priori

gctabsz = *holestabsz* + *descrtabsz* + *tracestacksz*.

maxsz = *max(outgcsz, gcprogsz* + *bittabsz* + *gctabsz)*

The following relations hold

bittabsz = *workspsz*   *bitswidth+1* {*bitswidth* = *27* in case of the X8}

workspsz = *memsz* − *commonsz* − *maxsz*.

These are not sufficient to settle all sizes, compromises must be chosen ; the most difficult point being to determine *holestabsz*, *descrtabsz* and *tracestacksz*, the size of which varies even for the same program from one gc call to the other. The best solution would be to eliminate *TRACESTACK%* by using a method similar to [10] and to store *HOLESTAB%* in the holes themselves ; *DESCRTAB%* could also be stored in the holes, however its size is reduced and the few space needed can be frozen for it. On the X8, a rough solution is used consisting in freezing a fixed space for *HOLESTAB%*, *DESCRTAB%* and *TRACESTACK%*. Up to now these limits have not been transgressed (see III.6.2).

Once the sizes of all devices have been fixed, the second task of the loader becomes straightforward : it loads devices of situation 1 and transmits appropriate parameters to the garbage collector calling routine to enable it to perform the swapping. Let us just point out a few details :

- while *OBPROG%* is loaded, addresses are given their final form using on the one hand *LABTAB§* filled during machine code generation and information on how symbolic addresses have to be transformed ; in particular, this transformation is influenced by the sizes calculated during the first phase of the loading.
- each instruction is checked for validity through *FILTAB§* before being stored in *OBPROG%*.

- in the source program, commands intended to *CONSTAB§* address updating are met ; they are executed using *LABTAB§* and the address allocated to *CONSTAB%*.
- only run-time routines needed by *OBPROG%* are loaded in *RTROUT%* ; information on which routine is needed is found in *ROUTTAB§* filled during code generation.

5. *TRANSLATION OF INTERMEDIATE CODE MODULES*

Intermediate code modules (instructions) are translated into machine code independently ; this improves the modularity of the code generation. Only a few precautions have to be taken is some modules in order to take the best profit of local optimizations :

(1) Registers are given a specialized task.

(2) When a module uses a *WOST%* value as one of its parameters, it is advisable, wherever possible, to start the module translation by an instruction loading this value in an appropriate register.

We distinguish three kinds of modules :

(1) Modules that can be translated by few machine code instructions directly generated as such in the object program. It is the case for most of the standard operators.

(2) Modules that are translated into a call of a library routine, routine possibly having some parameters. It is the case for routines constructing descriptors of multiple values for example.

(3) Modules that require a data structure scanning. It is the case of the modules *stwosti*, *assign*, ...

The problems inherent to these three classes will be treated in III.5.2, III.5.3 and III.5.4 respectively ; beforehand III.5.1 defines a-priori the minimal set of hardware registers required by the compiler, allowing a maximum of efficiency of the generated code.

5.1 *SET OF REGISTERS*

The general strategy for register allocation is based on the fact that efficiency of register use must be retrieved by means of local optimizations only ; this implies that registers are given a specialized task. In this line, the following set of registers is defined :

- Registers *XREG%* and *YREG%* are two paired registers for integral calculations.
- Register *FREG%* is a register for floating point calculations.
- Register *VREG%* is a register for boolean calculations.
- Register *WREG%* is a register for memory transfers.
- Registers *IREG%* and *JREG%* are two index registers.
- Register *DREG%* is a register used to simulate *DISPLAY%* addressing.

The above set of registers is not minimal, if general purpose registers are available, the same register can be used at different moments for performing different kinds of tasks. In the X8-compiler, the following subclasses of registers must be available at different run-time moments :

1. *XREG%*, *YREG%*, *IREG%* and *DREG%*
2. *FREG%*, *IREG%* and *DREG%*
3. *VREG%*, *IREG%* and *DREG%*
4. *IREG%*, *JREG%*, *WREG%* and *DREG%*

It is easy to decide in the light of the above subclasses whether the registers of a given hardware are sufficient to fit into the X8-code generator ; as an example, on the X8-compiler, registers are shared as follows :

XREG% : A

YREG% : S

FREG% : F(G)

VREG% : S

WREG% : F/G

IREG% : A/G

JREG% : S/G

DREG% : hardware *DISPLAY%* mechanism (D).

X8 B-register is used in library routines, taking profit of hardware stack-facilities.

5.2 SIMPLE MODULES

Simple modules are ICI's translated by the generation of a few machine instructions not invoking library routines. Most of these modules correspond to standard operators. For the translation of such modules, it is fundamental to have in mind the two precautions mentioned at the beginning of III.5. It is then very easy to verify that we take the best profit of local optimizations and that the minimal set of registers of III.5.1 is sufficient.

5.3 MODULES INVOLVING LIBRARY ROUTINES

When a module translation implies the generation of a long sequence of machine instructions, for the sake of space economy, these instructions are gathered into a library routine. Most of the time such routines must be provided with parameters known at compile-time, like accesses, information deduced from a mode (number of dimensions of a multiple value, static size of a value ...). Instead of generating the sequence of machine instructions itself, it is the instructions transmitting the parameters and calling the routine which are generated. The problem is now how to transmit the parameters of the routine.

(1) As far as enough registers are available, the most efficient solution for parameter transmission is to generate code by which registers are loaded with the actual parameters of the routine. For access transmission, the compile-time routine *INREGPS* (III.1.2) is used, for other parameters, instructions like

LDX = *nbdim*

where *nbdim* stands for the contents of a compile-time location, are generated.
(2) Suppose not enough registers are available, access transmission generally implies a dynamic effect ; *INREGPS* is still used, but moreover an instruction is generated to free the register by storing its contents in a run-time location local to the routine ;

STX 0 ; *access%*

For parameters which correspond to the contents of compile-time locations, a better solution exists : the compile-time value is stored in *CONSTAB§* and it is the *CONSTAB%* address which is passed on as a parameter of the routine ; this is particularly useful when several parameters of this second type have to be passed to the routine, they are stored in consecutive *CONSTAB§* locations and only one *CONSTAB%* address has to be furnished to the routine.

N.B. Some considerations on parameter transmission to library routines may influence storage allocation. An example will make this thing clear. The number of dimensions *nbdim* of a multiple value is part of the mode and is completely controlled at compile-time, it needs not to be stored in the descriptor. However, in a program manipulating multiple values, many calls to library routines are generated, having as parameters both the descriptor access and its number of dimensions. If follows that it is more efficient to store the number of dimensions in the descriptor than to generate instructions passing this number of dimensions to library routines a number of times. For similar reasons, it seems that the *bn* of a *BLOCK%* should be stored in its *H%*, that a run-time variable *rtbn%* should contain the *bn* of the current block and that a run-time variable *cardnb%* should contain the current card number. Note that in the last case, the run-time updating of *cardnb%* is only needed before the first module involving a run-time error message is encountered, and this before the first label definition and after each label definition on a line (card).

Example 5.1

Suppose we have to translate the module inacpar in case *caddrout§* is of the form (routct *constabp§*) as explained in II.5.2.

With proc *INCONSTAB* = (int *x*) :
(*CONSTAB§*[*constabpm*] := *x* ;
constabpm+:=1)

the compile-time actions are the following :

INCONSTAB (*bna§*)
INCONSTAB (*totsz§*)
INCONSTAB (*flex§*)
INCONSTAB (*tadd* of *caddres§*)
INCONSTAB (*gccres§*)
INCONSTAB (*dmrcres§*)

INCONSTAB (gcidb§)
INCONSTAB (h+sidsza§+dmrsza§)
INCONSTAB (gcsza§)
INCONSTAB (sidsza§)

GMI

LDJ = *constabpm-10*
LNK 0 ; *inacpar%*

At run-time the library routine *inacpar%* is executed ; its parameters are found in *CONSTAB§* at the address contained in register J. The action given in II.5.2, step 2.2 for the ICI *inacpar* is easily adapted to this situation.

Suppose now *caddrout§* is not of the form *(routct constabp)*, this means that the *CONSTAB* routine representation is only accessible at run-time ; the translation is then the following (II.5.3)

INREGPS(CONVERTACCESS (caddrout§,I),I)

co this causes the generation of (a) machine instruction(s) by which the address of the run-time routine representation is stored in register *I* co

INCONSTAB (bna§)
INCONSTAB (flex§)
INCONSTAB (tadd of caddres§)
INCONSTAB (gccres§)
INCONSTAB (dmrcres§)
INCONSTAB (h+sidsza§+dmrsza§)
INCONSTAB (gcsza§)
INCONSTAB (sidsza§)
INCONSTAB (swostcza§)

GMI

LDJ = *constabpm-9*
LNK 0 ; *inacpar1%*

At run-time, *inacpar1%* accesses its parameters through I and J.

N.B. It should be clear that *inacpar%* an *inacpar1%* are very similar and can be easily merged into one same routine.

5.4 MODULES IMPLYING DATA STRUCTURE SCANNING(†)

Modules (ICI) corresponding to copies of values on *RANST%* *(stwosti, stacpar, return, ...)*, to assignations *(assign {scope})*, modules related to name creation *(locvargen, locgen, ...)*, modules corresponding to formal bound checking *(checkformal)* and modules transputting values *(stdcallinout)* imply a data structure scanning.

These modules are provided with data accesses and a mode information as their parameters. Instead of interpreting the mode at run-time, the mode can be interpre-

(†) See also [20].

ted at compile-time and instructions are generated for handling the data structure at run-time. The code generated may consist of a few instructions for simple data structures or of many instructions for intricate ones. Here in particular, precautions must be taken in order to avoid that simple cases suffer from the existence of more complicated cases ; algorithms of translation of these modules must be particularly refined. On the other hand, when many instructions have to be generated for the translation of one of the above modules with a particular mode and when this module appears several times in the same program with the same parameter *mode*, it is advisable to generate one single routine and several calls. The parameters of such a routine will be accesses to data structures stored in index registers (*INREGPS* defined in III.1.2 is used to generate the instructions by which the registers are loaded). There are at most two such parameters in the modules such that two index registers are sufficient (for some modules and some hardwares a supplementary register is needed for moving memory zones).

The only problem for turning module translation into the generation of a routine and several calls is a compile-time bookkeeping telling for which module and which modes a routine has already been generated, and where such a routine appears in *OBPROG*. If we suppose that *DECTAB* has been compacted (i.e. a given mode appears only once), the bookkeeping reduces to associating to each *DECTAB* entry a chain consisting of information on the routines generated for the corresponding mode (i.e. for each routine, its address in *OBPROG* and the ICI operation code to which it corresponds). We now explain the principles used to generate code for data structure scanning.

5.4.1 DATA STRUCTURE SCANNING

A data structure actually consists of a tree in which 'plain values' (including names) are terminal nodes. Intermediate nodes consist of

- *structured values*, where fields have to be handled one after the other (recursively).
- *multiple values* generally having a dynamic number of branches (elements) ; hence a loop is generated, inside which elements are treated one by one.
- *union values* which in fact have only one branch at run-time but among several possible ones known at compile-time. The choice is dynamic and based on the union overheads. What has to be done is to generate code for all possible branches and a switch which, at run-time, will perform the choice amongst all alternatives. We recall that in the X8-compiler the switch is based on dynamic mode comparisons, which could be avoided (see II.0.4.2).

N.B. Although names are terminal nodes, it must be stressed that names referring to multiple values may be associated with a descriptor [14] which gives rise to some difficulties when such names have to be copied.

The major problem is met when dealing with multiple values ; solutions to this problem are outlined first. Another problem is to be able to generate very efficient code for transferring zones of memory, whichever they are ; this problem is solved by means of the routine *COPYCELLS* described thereafter.

Finally, we give a detailed description of the translation of the module *stwost* and we mention the peculiarities of the translation of the other modules on data structures.

Strategy used for scanning array elements

Suppose we have to scan the elements of a multiple value with an access characterized by a *psadd* ; in fact, this *psadd* is the access to the descriptor. Problems met when scanning the elements are the following :

A. Keeping track of the path in the data structure at run-time.
The address of the first element of an array is given by the *offset%* of its descriptor, this address will be put in an index register *IREG%* and the first element will be characterized by a *psadd* of the form *(indI,0)*. The problem is that the process is recursive and we cannot afford one new register each time a new descriptor is passed through. In practice, we shall use the same register and save its old value on a run-time stack we call *VALSTACK%* ; in this way, we are always able to retrieve the access of a descriptor after having scanned its elements. Two remarks have to be made on *VALSTACK%* :

a. The management of its pointer *valstackpm* is static and hence, its maximum size is known at compile-time.
b. *VALSTACK%* may contain *HEAP%* pointers which means that such pointers must be updated by the garbage collector when called and hence, appropriate information must be furnished to it, on where on *VALSTACK%* such pointers are found.

The management of the access when passing through and coming back to a descriptor is performed by means of the following compile-time routines :

proc THROUGHDESCR = (psadd psadd, int reladd, register R) psadd :
co *psadd* is saved on the multipurpose compile-time stack MSTACK. If *psadd* involves an index register *R1* (possibly R≡R1) its contents is saved on *VALSTACK%* together with appropriate garbage collection information ; the current *VALSTACK%* pointer *valstackpm* is incremented.
Instructions are generated to load register *R* with the *offset%* of the descriptor of access *psadd+reladd*. The routine results in a *psadd* of the form *(indR,0)*
co

proc psadd BACKDESCR = psadd :
co The routine results in the *psadd* restored from MSTACK ; if this *psadd* involves an index register, instructions are generated to restore its contents from *VALSTACK%* ; in this case *valstackpm* is decremented.
co

B. Incrementing the pointer of the current element.

For scanning the elements, a loop is generated, but the following must be remarked : the elements of the array may be not contiguous ; *iflag%* stored in the descriptor is characteristic of this situation, but this information is dynamic. As we shall see, scanning contiguous elements is much more efficient than scanning elements separated by 'holes'. If we want to optimize the execution in time, we generate instructions for the two strategies together with a switch based on *iflag%* ; this is what is done in the X8-compiler.

Notational conventions : the following notations with an obvious meaning are used to represent the fields of the current descriptor :

offset%

iflag%

$d\%_0$

$l\%_1, u\%_1, d\%_1$

...

$l\%_n, u\%_n, d\%_n$

moreover *add%* is supposed to be the address of the current elements ; in practice, index registers *IREG%* or *JREG%* are used for this purpose. The loop allowing to scan the elements of a multiple value is generated in two parts : an initialization and a finalization. We give now these two parts for arrays with and without interstices.

(1) No interstices

LOOP-INITIALIZATION0%

incr% := $d\%_n$;
max% := *offset%* + $d\%_0$;
add% := *offset%* ;
L :

LOOP-FINALIZATION0%

add% +:= *incr%* ;
(*add%*≠*max%* | goto *L*)

Remark

It should be clear that if the action of the loop limits itself to copying consecutive cells, what is generated is the call of a run-time routine *COPYCELLS%* with as its parameters $d\%_0$, the number of cells to be copied and the source and destination offsets (III.5.4.2).

(2) Interstices (first strategy)

The first strategy is based on a precalculation of the sizes of the holes which separate the elements of each dimension of the multiple value.

Notational conventions :

staticsize = the static size of one element.

$x\%_i$ $(l\%_i \leqslant x\%_i \leqslant u\%_i,\ i=1\ldots n)$ is a current counter in dimension i.

$h\%_i$ is the address increment associated with dimension i.

<u>Example</u> : suppose an array of 2 dimensions with bounds [*1:2,1:2*] (elements are hatched) :

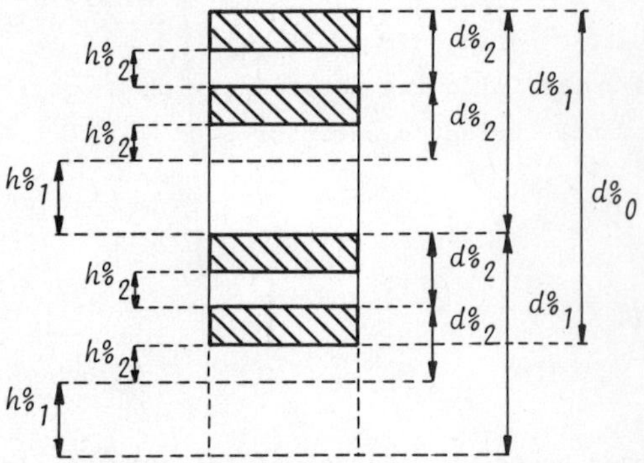

<u>*LOOP-INITIALIZATION1%*</u>

$x\%_n := l\%_n$;

$h\%_n := d\%_n - staticsize$;

<u>*for*</u> *i%* <u>*from*</u> *n-1* <u>*by*</u> *-1* <u>*to*</u> *1*

<u>*do*</u> $x\%_{i\%} := l\%_{i\%}$;

$h\%_{i\%} := d\%_{i\%} - (u\%_{i\%+1} - l\%_{i\%+1} + 1) * d\%_{i\%+1}$

<u>*od*</u> ;

add% := offset% ;

L :

<u>*LOOP- FINALIZATION1%*</u>

<u>*for*</u> *i%* <u>*from*</u> *n* <u>*by*</u> *-1* <u>*to*</u> *1*

<u>*do*</u> $(x\%_{i\%} = u\%_{i\%}$

$|\ x\%_{i\%} := l\%_{i\%}$

$|\ x\%_{i\%}$ +:= 1 ;

add% +:= $\sum_{g\%=i\%}^{n} h\%_{g\%}$ + *staticsize* ;

<u>*goto*</u> *L)*

<u>*od*</u>

<u>Remark</u>

This strategy requires too many calculations inside the loop, it is advantageously replaced by the second strategy.

(3) Interstices (second strategy)

This strategy is based on a precalculation of all possible sizes of the holes which separate the elements of the first dimension of the multiple value. There is one size $h\%_i$ per dimension i.

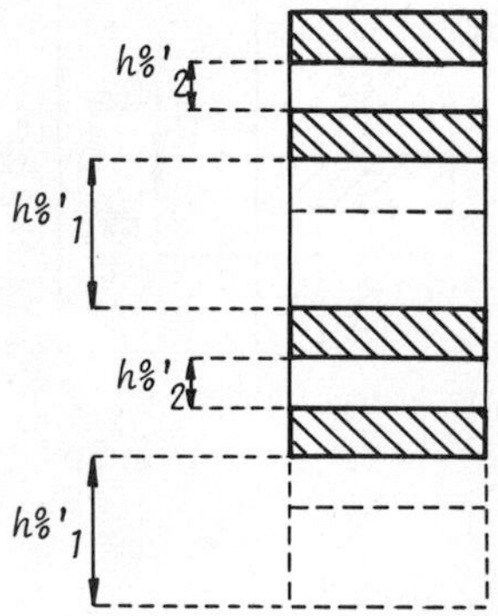

LOOP-INITIALIZATION2%

```
x%_n := l%_n ;
h%'_n := d%_n ;
for i% from n-1 by -1 to 1
do x%_i% := l%_i% ;
   h%'_i% := h%'_i%+1 + d%_i% - (u%_i%+1 - l%_i%+1 +1) * d%_i%+1
od ;
add% := offset% ;
L :
```

LOOP-FINALIZATION2%

```
for i% from n by -1 to 1
    do (x%_i% = u%_i%
        |x%_i% := l%_i%
        |x%_i% +:= 1 ;
         add% +:= h%'_i% ;
         goto L
    )
    od
```

(4) Interstices (third strategy)

This strategy uses one current pointer $a\%_i$ per dimension, the strides $d\%_i$ are used for their incrementation ; note that $add\% \equiv a\%_n$.

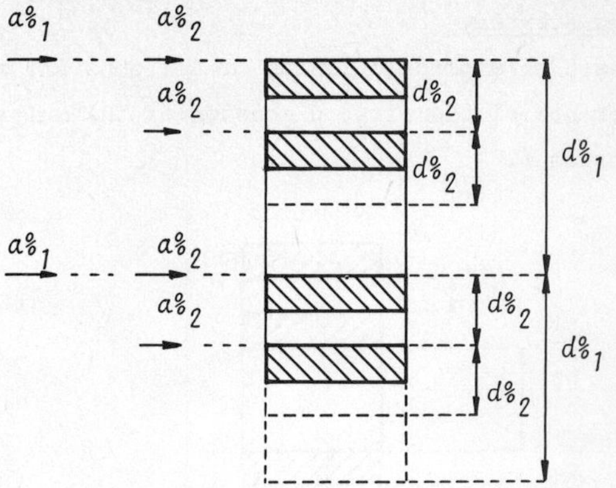


```
LOOP-INITIALIZATION3%
      x%n := l%n ;
      for i% to n-1
      do a%i% := offset% ;
         x%i% := l%i%
      od ;
      add% := offset% ;
      L :
LOOP-FINALIZATION3%
      if x%n ≠ u%n
         then add% +:= d%n ;
              x%n +:= 1 ;
              goto L
      fi ;
      for i% from n-1 by -1 to 1
      do if x%i% = u%i%
         then x%i% := l%i%
         else x%i% +:= 1 ;
              a%i% +:= d%i% ;
              for j% from n-1 by -1 to i%+1
              do a%j% := a%i% od ;
              add% := a%i% ;
              x%n := l%n ;
              goto L
         fi
      od
```

Remark

Though conceptually more simple, the third strategy is less efficient than the second one ; it is the second strategy which is used in the X8-compiler.

General remark

The actions taken inside the loop may involve a recursive use of *LOOP-INITIALIZATION%* and *LOOP-FINALIZATION%*. In this case the variables

(1) *incr%, max%, add%*

(2) $x\%_i$, $h\%_i$, *add%* $(i=1...n)$

(3) $x\%_i$, $h\%_i$, *add%* $(i=1...n)$

(4) $x\%_i$, $a\%_i$, *add%* $(i=1...n)$

must be saved on a run-time stack during the loop. *VALSTACK%* is used for this purpose ; again it is to be noted that the pointer *valstackpm* of this stack is controlled at compile-time and that the maximum size of *VALSTACK%* is static.

5.4.2 THE ROUTINE COPYCELLS

COPYCELLS is a compile-time routine used to generate code moving *n* consecutive cells, where *n* is known at compile-time ; it may involve the generation of a call of the run-time library routine *COPYCELLS%*. Such routines are used very often when manipulating data structures and they must be as efficient as possible. For this reason they are made hardware dependent.

proc *COPYCELLS* = (psadd *psadds, psaddo,* int *reladd, n)* :

co This routine generates instructions for copying *n* consecutive cells from *psadds+reladd* to *psaddo+reladd*. It uses hardware facilities, for example those which allow to transfer zones of memory. If such facilities do not exist, a register is used for copying the cells :

- for a small number of cells, load and store instructions are generated.
- for a large number of cells a loop is generated ; this loop may be generated explicitely or under the form of a call of the library routine *COPYCELLS%* (see below).

Remark that precautions have to be taken when the source access corresponds to varranst (routct or formatct). In this case what has to be copied is the dynamic representation of a name (routine or format). It consists of a *pointer%* and a *scope%* which is equal to *DISPLAY%*[*bnsc*].

co

proc *COPYCELLS%* = (int *n)* :

co this library (run-time) routine copies *n* consecutive memory cells from the address contained in *IREG%* to the address contained in *JREG%*. co

When a call of *COPYCELLS%* has to be generated for copying cells from *psadds+reladd* to *psaddo+reladd*, the following must take place :

psadds := INREGPS(psadds+reladd, IREG%)

psaddo := INREGPS(psaddo+reladd, JREG%)

This may involve the generation of run-time instructions

LDI *psadds+reladd*

LDJ *psaddo+reladd*

and simultaneously it makes

psadds := (indI, 0) ;

psaddo := (indJ, 0).

5.4.3 TRANSLATION OF THE MODULE *stwost*

The module *stwost* is used to copy data structures on *WOST%* ; this happens when results have to be transmitted at block or routine exit, when row and structure displays are constructed and finally when a copy of a value has to be forced on *WOST%*. This last case occurs in balancing process and when side-effects have to be avoided. The basic principle is simple : we copy the static part of the value using the source and the object accesses, thereafter the dynamic parts are copied on *RANST%* from *ranstpm%*. The essential difficulty is due to the fact that the source and object values may overlap, but the major problems are avoided if the rules of I.2.3.2, have been respected.

We now recall the strategy which can be used and which solves the problems of overlapping (with the above restrictions) as well as the problems of gc-protection. First of all, the protection of the source value, if any, is cancelled and the one of the object value is set up. The copy is performed by means of a recursive process at each step of which, static parts of source values are copied first as such, with their old pointers. These copied static parts are thus passed through a second time, if necessary, in order to update the descriptor pointers and to copy the corresponding elements always using the same strategy recursively. Note that the pointer is only updated after being sure there is space enough for copying the static parts of the elements, this allows the garbage collector to be called with full security. To copy the static parts, we use the routine *COPYCELLS* ; to pass through descriptors we use the general strategy explained at the beginning of III.5.3.1, applied to both source and object values. At this point four remarks must be made :

(1) The second pass through the static parts must rely on the object value only, given the source value may have been overwritten.

(2) The elements of source multiple values might be not contiguous, the copy will compact such elements thus gaining memory space and allowing a more efficient second scanning.

(3) Scanning the elements of a static part does not imply the generation of instructions for updating the current access even when this one involves an index register. What has to be done is to update a compile-time variable *reladd* (relative address) and to use an access of the form *psadd+reladd* in the instructions which are generated.

(4) The above process only requires two index registers I and J for the source and object value, and one register for memory transfer, unless special instructions are provided by hardware.

More precisely, the above process corresponds to the following sequence of actions:

Step 1 :

Space is reserved for the static part of the copy.

Step 2 :

The protection of the original value is cancelled if this value was stored on *WOST%* and the protection of the copy is set up.

Step 3 :

The static part of the value is copied as such.

Step 4 :

For the names which have been copied, which refer to a multiple value and for which the descriptor of the multiple value was stored in the space appended to the name, the pointer of this space, contained in the name, is updated. In this way all parts of the source value not yet copied are protected through the protection of the copy.

Step 5 :

If the value to be copied contains multiple values they are treated one by one, recursively and in sequential order by the following process :

Step 5.1 :

Space is reserved for the static part of the elements.

Step 5.2 :

The static parts of these elements are copied in the reserved space (with the old pointers as in step 3). Note that, it is the descriptor of the copy which must be used for accessing the elements, the original descriptor might have been overwritten. Note also that if the elements are not contiguous in the value, they may be compacted during the copy, thus gaining memory space and making further copies more efficient.

Step 5.3 :

Pointers of names referring to multiple values are updated as in step 4.

Step 5.4 :

If the elements contain in turn multiples values, these are treated one by one using step 5 recursively.

The algorithm corresponding to the translation of

```
stwost (mode§,
        cadds§,
        caddo§)
```

is now described as a typical example of data structure scanning ; it has the form of a recursive routine. The algorithm given here is not exactly the one of the X8-compiler, in the sense some compile-time optimizations have been eliminated for the sake of readability. Moreover, for the sake of simplicity, the problem relative to names referring to multiple values (step 4 and 5.3 above) are not treated ; this problem does not exist if descriptors resulting from *refslices* and *refrowings* are stored on *HEAP%*.

The following routines are used in the algorithm below :

```
proc RELEVANTW = (int modex) bool :
     co true if the value of mode modex contains multiple values co

proc SPACEREQUEST% = (int x) : co see III.6 co

proc COPYWOST(cadd cadds, caddo, int mode) :
begin
psadd psadds := CONVERTACCESS (cadds, IREG%) ,
      psaddo := CONVERTACCESS (caddo, JREG%) ;
COPYCELLS (psadd psadds, psaddo,0{reladd}, STATICSIZE(mode)) ;
(RELEVANTW(mode)  |valstackpm := 0 ;
                   COPYDYN(psaddo,loc int := 0, mode))
end

proc COPYDYN = (psadd psaddo,ref int reladd, int mode) :
begin
   (class of DECTAB[mode] = "struct" | goto STRUCT
   |:class of DECTAB[mode] = "union"  | goto UNION
  {|:class of DECTAB[mode] = "row"}   | goto ROW  ) ;
STRUCT : for each field of mode modef of the structured value of mode
         mode
         do
          (RELEVANTW(modef)
               |COPYDYN (psaddo,loc int := reladd,modef)) ;
          reladd +:= STATICSIZE (modef)
         od
UNION : GENSWITCHUN(psaddo,mode)
      co This call generates a jump to switch [ overhead of the value psaddo-mode] ;
         let modei be the current constituent mode of mode ; the switch can be cha-
         racterized as follows :
         (RELEVANTW(modei) | switch[i] := goto Li
                           | switch[i] := goto Lf)
      co
      for each constituent mode modei of the union mode mode
        do
         (RELEVANTW(modei)
           |GMI [Li :]   ;
            COPYDYN(psaddo,loc int := reladd + ovhszunion,modei) ;
            GMI [goto Lf] ) ;
        od ;
        GMI [Lf :]  ;
```

<u>co</u> Note that local optimizations automatically eliminate the last <u>goto</u> *Lf* preceding *Lf* definition <u>co</u>

ROW :

<u>co</u> We first give a rough diagram of the <u>run-time</u> algorithm which is generated

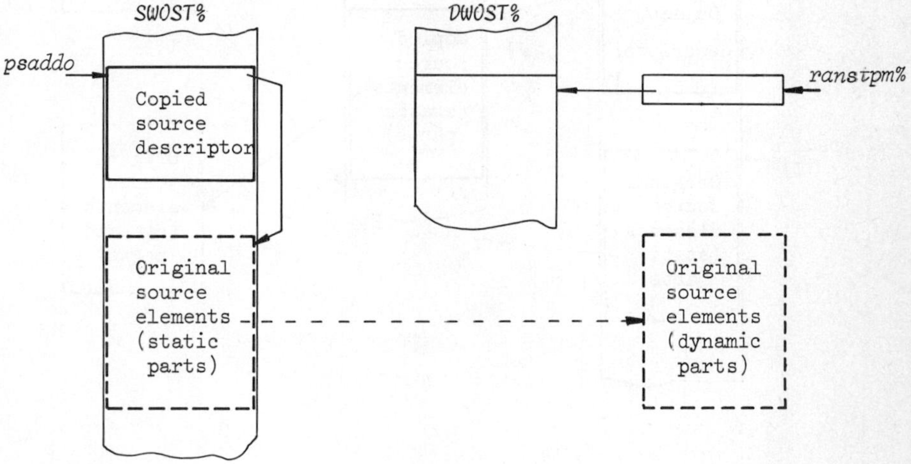

- *(d%$_0$=0 | offset% := ranstpm% ; <u>goto</u> Lf)* {see foot-note of page 293}
- Reserve space for the static part of the elements from *ranstpm%* {*ranstpm%* is not incremented yet}.
- *(iflag% = 0 | <u>goto</u> Lsq* {no interstices}*)* ;
- {There are interstices}
  - Initialize the loop for copying elements separated by interstices, i.e. calculate *h'i%*, initialize *xi%* and make *IREG%* and *JREG%* respectively equal to *offset%* {source} and *ranstpm%*{object}.

  Lo : Copy the static part of the current element as such from the location pointed to by *IREG%* to the location pointed to by *JREG%*
  - Loop finalization : increment *IREG%* according to precalculated hole sizes, and *JREG%* by *STATICSIZE*(mode element) given elements are copied into consecutive cells : (elements not exhausted | <u>goto</u> *Lo*)
  - Correct the *strides%* of the descriptor according to the fact copied elements are contiguous ;

    iflag% := 0 ;

    <u>goto</u> *Ld ;*

Lsq : COPYCELLS%(d%$_0$)

Ld : offset% := ranstpm% ;

ranstpm%+:= d%$_0$;

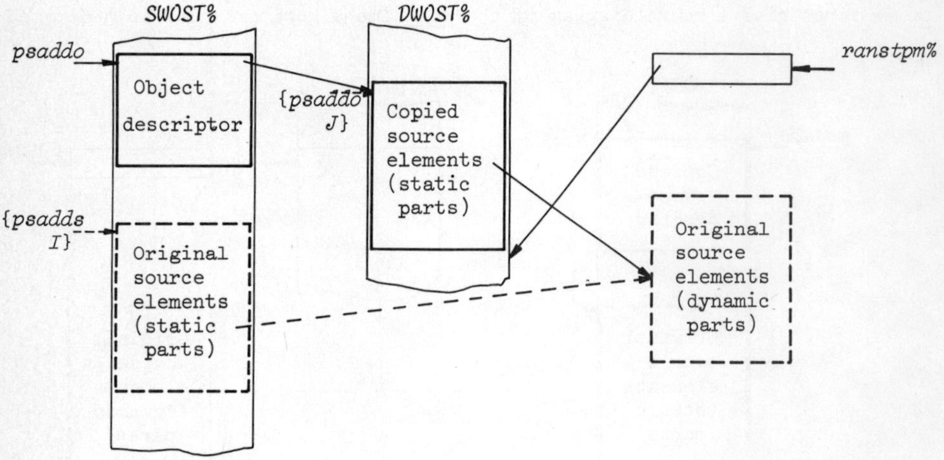

- {if elements themselves have dynamic parts, a second loop is performed in which dynamic parts of elements are treated recursively, note that here static parts of copied elements are contiguous}

Lf :

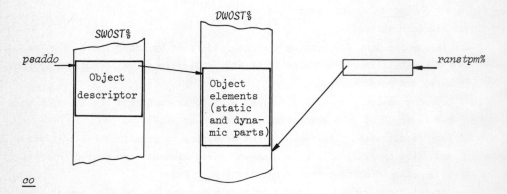

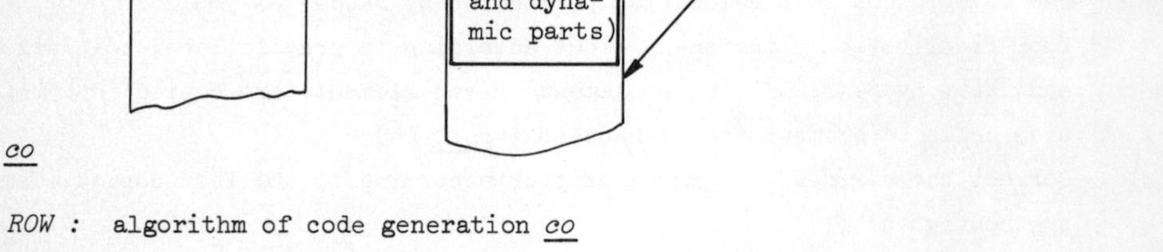

<u>co</u>

<u>co</u> *ROW* : algorithm of code generation <u>co</u>

(<u>int</u> *n* := {number of dimensions},

moder := {mode of one element},

staticsize := *STATICSIZE(moder)* ;

<u>co</u> Here we have to deal with a multiple value of access *psaddo+reladd* ; in order to simplify the notations, the fields of the descriptor are represented by their selector only : *offset%*, *iflag%*, $d\%_0$ ... $l\%_i$, $u\%_i$, $d\%_i$ <u>co</u>

GMI
```
co check if 0 element : co
(d%_0 = 0 | offset% := ranstpm%(†) ; goto Lf) ;
co Space is reserved for the static part of the elements : co
SPACEREQUEST%(d%_0) ;
co check whether elements are contiguous : co
(iflag% = 0  | goto Lsq)
```

co copy of non-contiguous elements into contiguous cells from *ranstpm%* co

GMI
```
co x%_i and h%_i are stored on VALSTACK% from valstackpm
   their value is calculated according to LOOP-INITIALIZATION2%
   for example co                                                ;
```

```
int savevalstpm  := valstackpm ;
valstackpm +:= 2*n co space for x%_i and h%_i co ;
psadds := THROUGHDESCR(psaddo,reladd,IREG%) ;
co by this, JREG% is saved on VALSTACK%, IREG% is overwritten by the offset% which
   gives access to the source elements (III.5.3.1) ;
   psadd_s := (indI, 0)  co
```

GMI
```
JREG% := ranstpm% ;
Lo :                     ;
```

```
psaddo := (indJ, 0) ;
          COPYCELLS(psadds, psaddo,0,staticsize) ;
```

GMI
```
co x%_i, h%_i are on VALSTACK% from  savevalstpm
   x%_i and IREG% incrementations are made according
   to  LOOP-FINALIZATION2% and JREG% +:= staticsize ;
   if the elements are not exhausted, goto Lo co        ;
```

```
psaddo := BACKDESCR :
valstackpm := savevalstpm :
```

GMI
```
co Descriptor strides are updated : co
   d%_n := staticsize ;
   for i% from n-1 by -1 to 1
   do d%_i% := (u%_i%+1 - l%_i%+1 +1) * d%_i%+1 od
   goto Ld ;
co Copy of contiguous elements : co
Lsq :                                                   ;
```

```
psadd_s := THROUGHDESCR(psaddo,reladd, IREG%) ;
```

(†) Forcing the *offset%* of *SWOST%* descriptors with 0 element to be equal to *ranstpm%* at the moment they are stored on *SWOST%* allows to deal with *DWOST%* memory recovery mechanism without further precautions.

```
GMI     | JREG% := ranstpm% ;     |
        | COPYCELLS% (d%0) ;      |  ;
psaddo := BACKDESCR ;
GMI     | Ld : offset% := ranstpm% ;  |
        |      ranstpm%+:=d%0 ;       |  ;
if RELEVANTW(moder)
   then psaddo := THROUGHDESCR(psaddo,reladd,JREG%) ;
     GMI   | max% := ranstpm% co to be saved on |
           | VALSTACK% co                       |
           | Lo' :                              |   ;
     COPYDYN(psaddo, loc int := 0, moder) ;
   GMI     | JREG% +:= staticsize ;                  |
           | while JREG% < max% co restored from     |
           | VALSTACK% co                            |
           | do goto Lo' od ;                        |   ;
     psaddo := BACKDESCR
fi ;
     GMI   | Lf : |
end
```

Remark

The above algorithm is a typical example of the application of the Bauer-Samelson principle. We see that in order to have the maximum of efficiency in all cases at run-time, we must distinguish these cases at compile-time. However sometimes the criterium allowing to choose a strategy is dynamic. In this case we must decide whether we want a good efficiency in space or time. If we choose efficiency in time, we generate algorithms for all cases and which one has to be applied is determined at run-time ; this clearly increases the length of the object programs and the design effort.

5.4.4 *TRANSLATION OF OTHER MODULES ON DATA STRUCTURES*

A. Generators

A generator is a construction by which a location is reserved for a data structure. Several strategies may be used for space reservation ; here, we describe a stepwise space reservation which among other things implies one single scanning of the data structure (see also II.2.2 Remark on dynamic space reservation).

Step 1 :

Space is reserved for the static part of the data structure.

<u>Step</u> 2 :

This reserved space is protected for the garbage collector.

<u>Step</u> 3 :

The reserved space is initialized :

-locations for references are set to *nil*.

-locations for procedures are filled with a flag making impossible a wrong interpretation of the uninitialized program pointer.

-locations for union overhead are filled with a flag making impossible a wrong interpretation of the uninitialized overhead.

-locations for descriptors are provided with information accounting that no elements are present yet ; this allows to proceed in full security in the step-wise reservation, the garbage collector relying on the unique protection of the whole location.

<u>Step</u> 4 :

Locations for multiple values whose descriptor is in the static part for which space has been reserved in step 1 are treated one by one as follows :

<u>Step</u> 4.1 :

The descriptor is filled according to the bounds provided by the generator, but track is kept that no elements are present yet.

<u>Step</u> 4.2 :

Space is reserved for the static parts of the elements.

<u>Step</u> 4.3 :

The static parts of the elements are initialized one by one as in step 3.

<u>Step</u> 4.4 :

If the elements contain in turn multiple values, they are treated one by one using step 4 recursively.

Space is reserved on *RANST%* for local generators and on *HEAP%* for heap generators. However locations for dynamic parts of flexible arrays (including arrays contained in union values) are also reserved on *HEAP%*.

It is to be noted that for reasons of uniformity in the accesses to subvalues, the static parts of a value and the static parts of the elements of an array are always stored towards increasing addresses.

<u>Example</u> 5.2 :

struct(ref real r, [1:n] int a, proc(int)int p, union(int,real)u)

<u>Step</u> 1

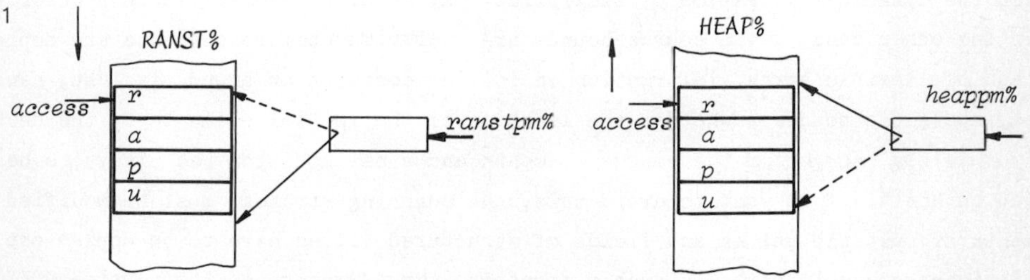

Step 2 and Step 3.

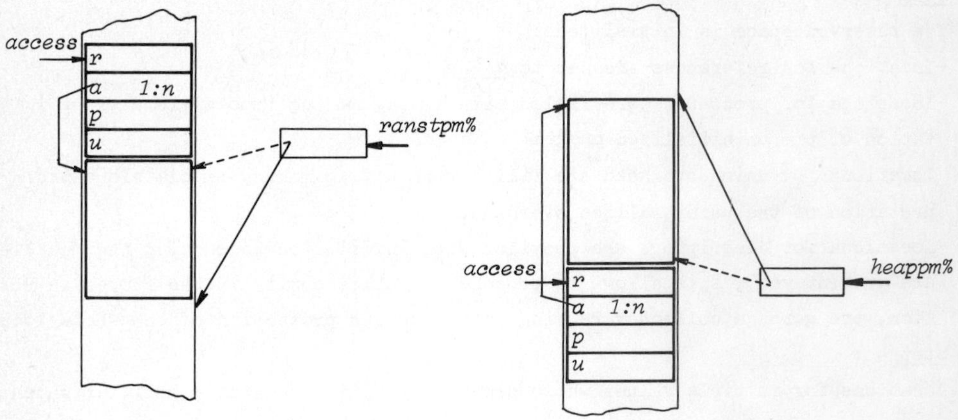

B. Assignations

The assignation differs from a *WOST%* copy under several aspects which are now reviewed :

(1) Assignation implies bound checking and hence, before copying the static part of the source in the object location, bound checking must be performed.

(2) Rule b4 (I.2.3.2.b) must be taken into consideration if elements of flexible arrays have to be copied on *HEAP%* during the assignation.

(3) For these elements, space must be reserved on *HEAP%* before the descriptor is updated, otherwise the garbage collector would fail. No other precaution must be taken for garbage collection, given source and destination are protected individually and that overlappings are not harmful as far as protection is concerned (II.12.1).

(4) However, overlappings may alter the copy, if no precautions are taken. A solution to this problem is to force a *WOST%* copy of the source when a dangerous overlapping arises : it is possible to decide at compile-time, for most of the current cases, whether an overlapping may take place : for the other cases a run-time check may decide whether an extra copy is needed or not.

Remark

Strictly speaking the above algorithm is not valid for ALGOL 68 not revised, given the dynamic information of flexibility may never be overwritten in a descriptor. On the other hand, given source bounds are overwritten before elements are copied, in case of flexible array, information on initial destination bounds is lost, hence, it is impossible to check whether the location of the initial elements of the destination is big enough for the source elements and a new location has always to be reserved on *HEAP%*. If we want to avoid this, the scanning strategy must be modified : elements of multiple values and fields of structured values have to be copied one by one static and dynamic part. In such a strategy, the advantage of the routine COPYCELLS is lost. However this can be avoided up to a certain point as explained now. In fact we can delay the copy of the static part of a data structure element up to the moment a descriptor is met, and accumulate copies by using *COPYCELLS* one time for several elements. More precisely, the static parts of a value consist of zones which can be copied as entities and separated by descriptors ; let ZI_i be such zones and D_j descriptors.

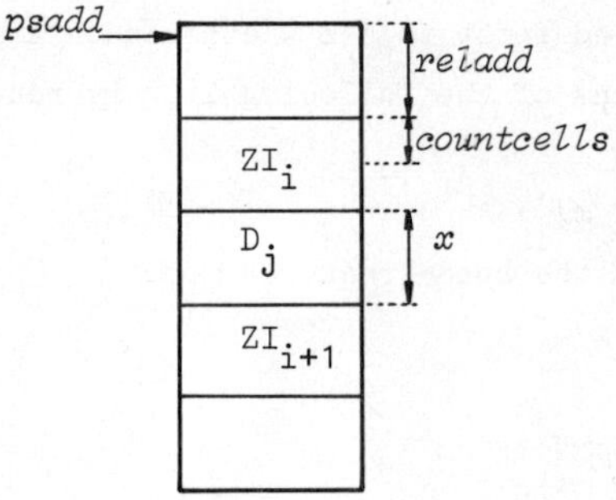

The process of copy is the following :

Suppose we start scanning zone ZI_i , with an access *psadd+reladd ;* instead of copying the zone elements as they are scanned, we just count the cells in *countcells ;* at the end of the ZI_i the following happens :

COPYCELLS(psadd+reladd, psaddo+reladd, countcells) ;
reladd +:= countcells ;
countcells := 0

D_j is then handled and thereafter :

reladd +:= x, with x = the size of D_j.

The process can go on with zone ZI_{i+1}

C. Transput of data structures

No particular problem arises, a strict left to right scanning allows to perform the straightening without difficulty.

6. FURTHER REMARKS ON GARBAGE COLLECTION

The compiler controls the calls of the garbage collector in the following sense : each time code has to be generated for increasing *ranstpm%* or decreasing *heappm%*, a run-time check is generated first to see whether such a space is available ; this check is performed by means of the following library routine :

```
proc SPACEREQUEST% = (int x) :
      co x is the size of the space required  co
   (heappm%-ranstpm%+1 < x
           |GARBCOLL% ;
            (heappm-ranstpm%+1 < x
                   |ALARM co not enough space co))
```

GARBCOLL% performs the garbage collection properly so called ; as explained in PART I it finds the necessary information in the *BLOCK%* headings *H%* linked by means of their dynamic chain *dch%* which starts at *rtbn%*. Our purpose here is not to come back to ge-geral principles explained elsewhere [9] , but to make a number of practical remarks on pecularities of the X8-implementation and on the experience gained with the use of the compiler.

6.1 THE INTERPRETATIVE METHOD

The X8 garbage collector is based on mode (*DECTAB%*) interpretation. A compiled garbage collector would not be significantly more complicated in principle, but it would ask for some additional desing effort. This effort is comparable with the one of translating a module like *stwost* in machine code. Principles lie on data structu-re scanning, but here names have to be passed through.
The experience shows that times involved by an interpretative garbage collector are not prohibitive. Clearly, times vary from one call to another but as an average, CPU time consumed for a *HEAP%* space of 10K memory cells is less than 1 second.

6.2 THE GARBAGE COLLECTOR WORKING SPACE

Garbage collector working space is allocated by the loader (III.4). This space consists of *HOLESTAB%*, *TRACESTACK%* and *DESCRTAB%*.
DESCRTAB%, except in very special programs, has a small size ; 0.1% of the whole working space (*RANST%* + *HEAP%*) seems to be sufficient.

HOLESTAB% is large for programs where the *HEAP%* is partitioned in small accessible zones separated by small zones of garbage.
TRACESTACK% is large when long lists have to be passed through.
It seems reasonable to admit that the number of holes is generally higher than the length of the longest list and to share the available space accordingly ; on the X8 the partitioning *holestabsz = 2 * tracestacksz* has been implemented.

6.3 GARBAGE COLLECTION DURING DATA STRUCTURE HANDLING

In III.5.4, it is shown how memory space is reserved in a step-wise way. As a consequence, the garbage collector may be called in the middle of the process of data structure handling.
(1) Precautions have to be taken in order to ensure a fool-proof protection of the data structures (see strategies of copy I.2.4.3.b, remark 3) and not to mislead the garbage collector (see initialization of location reserved by a generator, III. 5.4.4).
(2) The method allows to take a better profit of the memory during copies than methods based on global space reservation for data structures. Indeed, in case of a copy from *WOST%* to *WOST%*, the parts of the source data structure already copied become garbage one by one and can be directly freed for progressing in the copy.
(3) Pointers which are contained in index registers or on *VALSTACK%* at the moment of the garbage collection, must be updated properly. Hence the garbage collector must be provided with appropriate information allowing to retrieve such pointers.

6.4 MARKING ARRAYS WITH INTERSTICES

In a number of papers on ALGOL 68 garbage collection [9], it is stated that descriptors of subarrays must contain a pointer to the main descriptor. It appeared that this is not compulsory. Indeed, the descriptor of the subarray contains all the necessary information for marking the interstices which, for reasons of accessibility to the elements, must not be recovered by the garbage collector.
The problem is elsewhere : interstices must not be marked until the end of the marking process proper ; indeed if an interstice had been marked and would be accessible from somewhere else, the marking of the locations accessible through these interstices would be inhibited, which has to be avoided. If we want to avoid a special marking implying two bits/word in *BITTAB%* we must

- either collect the addresses of subarray descriptors in *DESCRTAB%* and use this table to mark the interstices at the end of the marking process proper.
- or at the level of the subarray, not only mark the interstices but also the locations accessible through them, which is not optimal as far as memory recovery is concerned.

6.5 FACILITIES FOR STATISTICAL INFORMATION

In the X8-compiler, each time the garbage collector is called the following information is printed :

- a counter,
- the card number of the construction causing the call,
- *ranstpm%* and *heappm%* before and after garbage collection,
- the duration of the garbage collection with and without swapping.

The data deduced from these printings are still too few to enable us to draw conclusion. However the following remark could be of some interests.

In [14] a solution is proposed which avoids the use of the *HEAP%* for storing descriptors of *refslices* and *refrowings*. This solution has been implemented but it can be disconnected ; thus allowing to make experiments. These have shown that simple programs such as the calculation of the determinant of a matrix (see [1] , 11.8) consume very much *HEAP%* space and lead very quickly to calls of the garbage collector.

CONCLUSION BIBLIOGRAPHY

APPENDICES

CONCLUSION

One of the main goals of the project was to gain a good experience in compiler methodology. This goal has been achieved ; we also developed principles and techniques in the run-time system design as well as in the static management and in their interface.

By implementing the language in its whole, we had to control a huge bulk of information and one may ask oneself if this is really worthwhile. To this question we answer that complexity is a problem in itself ; having succeeded to master it in a reliable way is quite an achievement ; this has been made possible by carefully choosing basic principles and applying them in a systematic and modular way.

Let us now try to evaluate the translation process on the basis of the following criteria ; *efficiency, security, portability* and *design effort.*

Beforehand, a number of general considerations must be made.

On the one hand, some of these criteria are many-sided, e.g. the efficiency must be split up into compile-time and run-time efficiency and both of these have two aspects : time and space. On the other hand, these criteria are conflicting :

- an increase in efficiency, security and portability must be paid by an increase in design effort.
- a higher level of security and portability generally decreases the efficiency.
- a higher level of run-time efficiency generally decreases the compile-time efficiency in space and/or time.
- a higher run-time efficiency in space generally causes a decrease in run-time efficiency in time and vice versa.

In the implementation described in this book the stress has been laid on run-time efficiency, security and portability while keeping a reasonable degree of compile-time efficiency. In a number of cases, some compromises have been made in order to keep the design effort inside reasonable limits. However the principle according to which "run-time efficiency of simple language features must not be affected by the presence of more intricate features" (Samelson-Bauer) has been constantly cared for.

Now, the evaluation proper can be formulated, it is based on the actual implementation on the X8.

(1) *Compile-time efficiency in time* fits into quite acceptable limits ; it amounts to

$$5 + 6x \text{ seconds}$$

where x is the length of the source program in pages (one page = 60 average lines) [4].

(2) *Compile-time efficiency in space :* the whole ALGOL 68 system including debugging facilities and initialized tables occupy 100K memory words of 27 bits, among which about 70K instructions. However the use of overlay techniques allows to run the compiler within a 32K words direct access memory.

(3) *Run-time efficiency in time :* comparisons with the ALGOL 60-X8 compiler show an average increase in efficiency of 30% in favour of the ALGOL 68-X8 compiler. This is not negligeable given the ALGOL 68 compiler has few restrictions, given its level of portability and the simplicity of the mechanism of local optimizations.

(4) *Run-time efficiency in space :* this efficiency is difficult to estimate, we have no comparative figures at our disposal. Comparing the length of the object program with the length of the source program is meaningless : one single assignation *(x:=y)* may give rise to a variable number of objects instructions depending on the mode of *x* and *y*, i.e. on the data structure being assigned.

(5) *Portability*

We distinguish two main aspects in portability :

- the language in which the compiler is written (a).
- the algorithm itself of compilation (b).

(a) The X8-compiler has been designed in an ALGOL 68-like language but hand-coded in assembly language. The language used for the design has been defined as our experience was growing ; as a consequence, the design needs some polishing before it can be accepted by a compiler.

(b) The second aspect, i.e. the portability of the algorithm itself of compilation (in particular the code generator) has been solved quite satisfactorily in the X8 compiler :

- the interface with the operating system is pretty well localized and can be easily modified.
- up to the production of intermediate code, only routines of lexical analysis dealing with internal representation of numbers (and possibly strings) have to be reconsidered to be transferred on a new hardware.
- the machine code generation itself, as it should be clear from this book, is surprisingly portable even on computers with a minimal hardware (III.5.1). For register allocation, only declarations making the correspondence between formal and actual registers must be specified according to each particular hardware.

  Moreover, only a few routines have been made machine dependent in order to take direct advantage of particular hardware facilities.

  These routines are :

CONVERTACCESS	(III.1.3)
INREGPS	(III.1.2)
DEREFPS	(III.1.2)
GMI	(III.2.2)
COPYCELLS	(III.5.4.2)

Also *GTAB*, (section III.2.2) containing instructions to be generated in an interpretative form, and its interpretation routine should be rewritten. Finally, the global optimizer and the loader should probably be modified.

(6) *Design effort*

Roughly speaking, the compiler has consumed 20 men-years, but what does it really mean?

- The reader will be aware of how far we have optimized, and how few restrictions we have introduced.
- The programming tools we had at our disposal were very poor : the X8 assembler.
- The hardware and in particular the memory at our disposal was underdimensioned. As an example we had no protected backing store to save the compiler ; this means that it had to be reintroduced from cards and paper tape at each set of corrections or additions!
- The majority of the members of the team were unexperienced when they entered the project.
- In the 20 men years, the time spent for learning the language is incorporated, and we started reading early versions of drafts. Also, time spent for programming the special purpose system supporting the compiler and all debugging facilities is incorporated in the 20 men years.
- Finally, we must add that much time has been spent in checking the compiler carefully, step by step ; only a very small number of easily locatable bugs have been discovered since the compiler has been operational. It must be stressed that during the debugging process, the existence of high-level (design) and low-level (programming) documentation, carefully kept up to date, has appeared to be of the utmost importance.

BIBLIOGRAPHY

[1] A. van Wijngaarden (ed), B. J. Mailloux, J. E. L. Peck, C. H. A. Koster, *Report on the algorithmic language ALGOL 68*, MR 101, Mathematisch Centrum, February 1969.

[2] K. Samelson, F. Bauer, *Sequential formula translation*, Comm. ACM, February 1960.

[3] B. Randell and L. J. Russell, *ALGOL 60 implementation*, Academic Press, 1964.

[4] Kruseman - Aretz, *Het object programma gegenereerd door de X8-ALGOL-60 vertaler van het MC*, MR 121, Mathematisch Centrum, Amsterdam, Feb. 71.

[5] D. Gries, *Compiler construction for digital computers*, Wiley, 1971.

[6] D. E. Knuth, *Semantics of context-free languages*, Mathematical systems theory, vol. 2, n° 1, 1968.

[7] E. Irons, *A Syntax Directed Compiler for ALGOL 60*, Comm. ACM, January 1961.

[8] A. van Wijngaarden et al., *Draft revised report on ALGOL 68*.

[9] J. E. L. Peck (Editor), *ALGOL 68 Implementation*, North Holland Publishing Company, 1971.

[10] G. Schorr, W. Waite, *An efficient machine-independent procedure for garbage collection in various data structures*, CACM, August 67.

[11] P. Branquart, J. P. Cardinael, J. P. Delescaille, J. Lewi, M. Vanbegin, *Output of the syntactic analyzer of the ALGOL 68-X8.1 compiler*, Technical Note N73, MBLE Res. Lab., Part I (June 1971), Part II (Dec. 1971), and P. Branquart, J. P. Cardinael, J. P. Delescaille, J. Lewi, M. Vanbegin, *User's manual of the ALGOL 68-X8.1 system*, June 1973.

[12] P. Branquart, J. Lewi, *A scheme of storage allocation and garbage collection for ALGOL 68*, Report R133, MBLE Res. Lab., April 1970 and *ALGOL 68 Implementation*, J. E. L. Peck (Editor), North Holland Publishing Company, 1971.

[13] P. Branquart, J. Lewi, J. P. Cardinael, *Local generators and the ALGOL 68 working stack*, Technical Note N62, MBLE Res. Lab., Sept. 1970.

[14] P. Branquart, J. Lewi, *On the implementation of local names in ALGOL 68*, Report R121, MBLE Res. Lab., Sept. 70 and *Proceedings of the International Computing Symposium*, Bonn 1970.

[15] P. Branquart, J. Lewi, *On the implementation of coercions in ALGOL 68*, Proceedings of the International Computing Symposium, Bonn 1970, and MBLE Res. Lab., Report R123 .

[16] W. M. Mc Keeman, *Peephole optimization*, Comm. ACM, July 1965.

[17] P. Branquart, J. Lewi, M. Sintzoff, P. Wodon, *The composition of semantics in ALGOL 68*, Report R125, MBLE Res. Lab., Feb. 1970 ; CACM, Nov. 1971.

[18] P. Branquart, J. Lewi and J. P. Cardinael, *Analysis of the parenthesis structure of ALGOL 68*, Report R130, MBLE Res. Lab., April 1970 and *ALGOL 68 Implementation*, J. E. L. Peck (Editor), North Holland Publishing Company, 1971.

[19] P. Branquart, J. P. Cardinael, J. Lewi, *An optimized translation process, application to ALGOL 68*, R224, MBLE Res. Lab., and ICS Davos 1973.

[20] P. Branquart, J. P. Cardinael, J. P. Delescaille, J. Lewi, M. Vanbegin, *Data structure handling in ALGOL 68 compilation*, Proceedings of ALGOL 68 III International Conference, Winnipeg, June 1974 and MBLE Res. Lab. Report R254.

[21] P. Branquart, J. P. Cardinael, J. Lewi, *An optimized translation process and its application to ALGOL 68*, Report R204, MBLE Res. Lab., Part I, September 1972 ; Part II, January 1974, Part III, February 1974, Part IV, May 1974.

[22] J. P. Delescaille and F. Heymans, *On keeping the EL-X8 alive ; emulation on the BS*. Technical Note N101, MBLE Res. Lab., October 1975.

APPENDIX 1 : ANOTHER SOLUTION FOR CONTROLLING THE *WOST%* GARBAGE COLLECTION INFORMATION.

The idea of the solution is not ours, but it seems to be originated from the ALGOL 68-R compiler implemented on the ICL series by I. Currie. The solution is very efficient as such, however, it will be shown how, combined with our system, it would give still better results. It is to be noted that in such a combination practically the whole *gc* management described in this book remains valid.

The solution consists in constructing at compile-time a table representative of all possible *SWOST%* contents ; let us call it *GCTAB*. Each table element consists of the garbage collection information for one *WOST%* value (mode and access for example). Moreover elements are linked by a chain field in such a way a pointer to a table element gives access (through the chain field) to all the elements representative of a *WOST%* contents at a given moment.

Suppose for example the *WOST%* contents varies as follows :

```
(1) A
(2) A  B
(3) A  B  C
(4) A  B
(5) A
(6) A  D
(7) A  D  E
```

The corresponding chain and entry points are scketched like this :

```
(1), (5)    A
(2), (4)    B
(3)         C
(6)         D
(7)         E
```

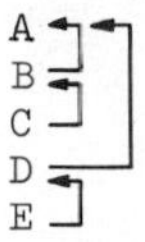

With this table, instead of having a dynamic *GCWOST%*, the garbage collection information for each *BLOCK%* reduces to a pointer *gcw%* stored in its *H%*, pointer to a *GCTAB* element. In principle, instructions are generated to update the *gcw%* of the current *BLOCK%* each time a value is stored or deleted from *WOST%* ; the corresponding static management requires a field on *BOST (gc1)* representative of the *GCTAB* entry point associated with the value.

Two optimizations are now possible :

(1) The first one corresponds to remark 2 at the end of I.2.4.3 : *gcw%* must not be updated at run-time if no garbage collection may take place during the time the corresponding value stays on *WOST%*. We can easily keep track of this fact by means of two new fields on *BLOCKTAB*, *gcp* and *gci* which are both pointers to *GCTAB*.

-*gcp* represents at each moment of the generation the actual *WOST%* state of the *BLOCK%*.

-*gci* is a static image of *gcw%* of that *BLOCK%*. Code updating *gcw%* will only be produced :

(a) when code risking to activate the garbage collector is produced, and

(b) when *gcp* and *gci* of the corresponding block are different.

(2) The second one corresponds to the minimization of the garbage collection information as explained in I.2.4.3.b, at the exception that what is minimized is the contents of *GCTAB* instead of *GCWOST%*. Clearly, the optimization is less advantageous here ; however some run-time actions may be saved given *gcp* will have to change less often and hence, instructions updating *gcw%* will have to be generated less frequently.

Practically, three compile-time routines allow to take care of the management of the *WOST%* garbage collection information :

(1) *PROTECT* will check whether a new value to be stored on *WOST%* has to be protected through *GCTAB* ; formulas given in II remain valid to make up that decision. When the value has to be protected through *GCTAB*, *gc1* in *BOST* and *gcp* in *BLOCKTAB* have to be updated.

(2) *DELETE* will cancel the protection of a given value deleted from *WOST%* by updating *gcp* in *BLOCKTAB*.

(3) *UPDATE* will generate *gcw%* updating code if it appears that on *BLOCKTAB* $gci \neq gcp$. This action is only to be taken when an ICI risking to call the garbage collector is to be generated. In *BLOCKTAB*, *gci* is updated accordingly.

APPENDIX 2 : SUMMARY OF THE SYNTAX

1. LBLOCK → lblock∇ BLOCKBODY

2.1 IDEDEC → idedec∇ FDECLARER iden = ACPAR
OPDEC → opdec∇ FDECLARER oper = ACPAR

2.2 LOCVARDEC → locvardec∇ ADECLARER variable |
locvardec∇ ADECLARER variable := SOURCE

2.3 HEAPVARDEC → heapvardec∇ ADECLARER variable
HEAPVARDEC → heapvardec∇ ADECLARER variable := SOURCE

3. LOCGEN → loc∇ ADECLARER
HEAPGEN → heap∇ ADECLARER

4. LABELDEC → labeldec∇ label :
GØTO → goto∇ label

5. CALL → call∇ PRIMCALL (ACPAR1, ACPAR2, ..., ACPARn)
FORMULA → dformula∇ operator OPERAND1 OPERAND2 |
mformula∇ operator OPERAND
ROUTDEN → routden∇ (FORPAR1, FORPAR2,... FORPARn) : ROUTBODY
FORPARi → FDECLARER fideni

6. DEPROC → deproc∇ DEPROCCOERCEND
PROC → proc∇ ROUTBODY

7. JPROC → jproc∇ label

8. CALLMODIND → callmodind∇ modind
MODEDEC → modedec∇ modind = ADECLARER

9. TRANSFORMAT → transformat∇ FORMATCOERCEND
FORMAT → format∇ DYNREP

11.1 SELECTION → selection∇ selector of SECONDARYSEL

11.2 DEREF → deref∇ DEREFCOERCEND

11.3 SLICE → slice∇ PRIMSLICE INDEXERS
INDEXERS → [INDEXER1 , ..., INDEXERn]
INDEXERi → TRIMMER |
INDEX

11.4 UNITED → uniting∇ UNCOERCEND

11.5 ROWING → rowing∇ ROWCOERCEND

```
12.1 ASSIGNATION → assignation∇ DESTINATION := SOURCE
```

12.2 IDREL → idrel∇ TERTL $\{:=: \mid :\neq:\}_1^1$ TERTR

12.3 CONFREL → confrel∇ TERTL $\{::= \mid ::\}_1^1$ TERTR

13. STDCALL → stdcall∇ (ACPAR1, ACPAR2, ..., ACAPRn)

14.2 SERIAL → LBLOCK | NONBLOCK

LBLOCK → lblock∇ BLOCKBODY

BLOCKBODY → NONBLOCK

NONBLOCK → SNONBLOCK | BALNONBLOCK

SNONBLOCK → PRELUDE last∇ LABUNIT

PRELUDE → $\{\{$DECLA ; | UNITV ; $\}_0^\infty$ DECLA ; $\}_0^1$ $\{$LABUNITVS$\}_0^1$

BALNONBLOCK → $\{$PRELUDE last∇ LABUNIT . LABELDEC$\}_0^1$

$\{$LABUNITVS last∇ LABUNIT . LABELDEC$\}_0^\infty$

LABUNITVS last∇ LABUNIT

LABUNITV → $\{$LABELDEC$\}_0^\infty$ UNITV

LABUNIT → $\{$LABELDEC$\}_0^\infty$ UNIT

LABUNITVS → $\{$LABUNITV ;$\}_0^\infty$

DECLA → IDEDEC | LOCVARDEC | HEAPVARDEC | OPDEC | MODEDEC

14.3 CONDCL → if∇ SERIALB CHOICECL fi

CHOICECL → then1∇ SERIAL |

thef∇ SERIALB CHOICECL |

then2∇ SERIAL1 else∇ SERIAL2 |

then3∇ SERIAL elsf∇ SERIALB CHOICECL

14.4 CASECL → case∇ CASECHOICE in∇ UNIT1, ... UNITn $\{$out∇ SERIAL$\}_0^1$ esac

CASECHOICE → UNITC | CASECONF

14.5 CASECONF → caseconf∇ mode1∇ TERTL1, ... moden∇ TERTLn $\{:: \mid ::=\}_1^1$ TERTR

15.1 COLLVOID → collvoid∇ (UNITV1, ..., UNITVn)

15.2 COLLROW → collrow∇ (UNITD1, ..., UNITDn)

15.3 COLLSTR → collstr∇ (UNITD1, ..., UNITDn)

16.3 FORCL → for∇ $\{$from∇ UNITF$\}_0^1$ $\{$by∇ UNITB$\}_0^1$

$\{$to∇ UNITT$\}_0^1$ $\{$foriden$\}_0^1$ $\{$while∇ SERIALW$\}_0^1$

do∇ UNITD

16.4 TRCALL → trcall∇ TRPRIM (UNIT1, ..., UNITn)

APPENDIX 3 : SUMMARY OF TOPST PROPERTIES

The table below shows how the fields *flextop* and *Δmem* of a *TOPST* element are initialized when a new *TOPST* element is set up by the activation of ρ(πα) or *NEWACTION (action)*. Other *TOPST* fields are initialized to 0. The letter T means that the corresponding field in the new element is copied from the old top one.

π(α)/action	*flextop*	*Δmem*
BLOCKBODY	T	0
FDECLARER	(*stat* 0)	0
ACPARi	(*stat* 1)	0
OPERANDi	"	0
ADECLARER	(*stat* 0)	0
SOURCE	(*stat* 1)	0
PRIMCALL	(*stat* 0)	0
FORPARi	"	0
ROUTBODY	(*dyn* bn)	0
DEPROCCOERCEND	(*stat* 0)	0
FORMATCOERCEND	"	0
DYNREP	"	0
SECONDARYSEL	T	T
DEREFCOERCEND	(*stat* 0)	0
PRIMSLICE	"	T
TRIMMER	"	0
INDEX	"	0
UNCOERCEND	(*stat* 1)	T+Δ*union*
ROWCOERCEND	(*stat* 1)	T+Δ*row*
DESTINATION	T	T
SOURCE	(*stat* 1)	T
TERTL	(*stat* 0)	0
TERTR	"	0
UNITV{i}	"	0
SERIALB	"	0
UNITC	"	0
TERTLi	"	0
collrow∇	T	T
UNITDi	(*stat* 1)	0
collstr∇	T	T
UNITF	(*stat* 0)	0
UNITB	"	0
UNITT	"	0
UNITD	"	0
SERIALW	"	0
TRPRIM	"	0
UNITi	"	0

APPENDIX 4 : SUMMARY OF THE NOTATIONS

1. MEM%

RANST% *(ranstpm%)*
HEAP% *(heappm%)*
DISPLAY%

BLOCK% | SBLOCK%
DBLOCK%

	Device	Static size	Current static pointers
SBLOCK%	H%	*h*	
	SIDST%	*sidsz*	*sidc*
	DMRWOST%	*dmrsz*	*dmrc*
	GCWOST%	*gcsz*	*gcc*
	SWOST%	*swostsz*	*swostc*
DBLOCK%	DIDST+LGST%		
	DWOST%		

2. H%

stch%
dch%
wp%
bn%
gcid% gcidp%
gcbodyflag%
gcw% gchp%
gcsz%

} lblocks and pblocks

result% swostp%
gcp%
dmrp%
flex%
prevflag%
retjump%

} pblocks only

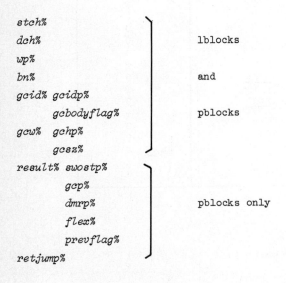

3. DYNAMIC VALUE REPRESENTATION

Name : *pointer%*
scope%

Rowname : *pointer%*
scope%
descr%

Descriptor : *offset%*
states%
iflag%
do%
{*li%*
ui%
di%}*

Union : *overhead%*
value%

Routine : *constabp%*
scope%

Format : *constabp%*
scope%

Tamrof : *offset%*
ndrep%
constabp%

4. BLOCKTAB (entry : *bnc*)

BLOCK%	Pseudo-$BLOCK\%_a$	Routine $BLOCK\%_b$
sidsz	$sidsz_a = sidsz_{b1}$	$sidsz_b = sidsz_{b1} + sidsz_{b2}$
dmrsz	$dmrsz_a$	$dmrsz_b$
gcsz	$gcsz_a$	$gcsz_b$
swostsz	$swostsz_a$	$swostsz_b$
gcid	$gcid_a$	$gcid_b$ {*gcbodyflag*}
bn	bn_a	bn_b

5. *ACCESS (cadd)*

Fundamental	Accessory
(*constant* v)	(*intct* v) (*boolct* v) (*bitsct* v) (*charct* v)
(*dircttab* a)	(*routct* a) (*formatct* a) (*tamrofct* a)
(*diriden* bnc.sidc) (*variden* bnc.sidc) (*indiden* bnc.sidc) (*dirwost* bnc.swostc) (*dirwost'* bnc.swostc) (*indwost* bnc.swostc) (*nihil* 0)	
	(*ddisplay* bn) (*dirabs* a) (*dirgcw* bnc.gcc) (*dirdmrw* bnc.dmrc) (*varabs* a) (*varwost* bnc.swostc) (*i2iden* bnc.sidc) (*i2wost* bnc.swostc) (*label* bnc.labnb)

6. SYMBTAB

Identifiers (*IDENTAB*)

Static property	Fields	Form
mode		
cadd	*class* *add* *hadd* *tadd*	(<u>*constant*</u> *v*) (<u>*dircttab*</u> *a*) (<u>*diriden*</u> *bnc.sidc*) (<u>*variden*</u> *bnc.sidc*) (<u>*label*</u> *bnc.labnb*)
scope	*insc* *outsc*	
flagdecl *flagused*		

Mode indications (*INDTAB*)

mode		
cadd		(<u>*label*</u> *bnc.lo*)

7. BOST

Static property	Fields	Form
mode		*dectabp*
cadd	*class* *add* *hadd* *tadd*	
smr	*hadd* *tadd*	*bnc.swostc*
dmr		(*stat* *bnc.swostc*) (*dyn* *bnc.dmrc*) *nil*
gc		*bnc.gcc* *nil*
or	*kindo*	*iden* *var* *gen* *nil*
	bno *derefo* *geno* {*flexo*} {*diago*}	
scope	*insc* *outsc*	
{*flexbot*}		
obprogp		

8. *TOPST*

Action	Fields	Form
flextop	*class* *spec*	(*stat* 0) (*stat* 1) (*dyn* bn)
Δmem *countbal* *countelem* *flagnextbal*		

9. *CONSTAB*

Routines

Non-standard	Standard	Jump
lo *bnsc* $sidsz_b$ $dmrsz_b$ $gcsz_b$ $swostsz_b$ $gcid_b$ *flagstand* {0} *flagjump* {0}	{specific} *flagstand* {1}	*lo* *bnsc* *flagjump* {1}

Formats

lo
ndrep
bnsc
formstringp

APPENDIX 5 : LIST OF INTERMEDIATE CODE INSTRUCTIONS

This appendix is a complete list of the ICI's. With each of them, a number is given between brackets ; this number is the page number where the definition of the ICI is found.

1	STWOST1	MODE CADDS CADDO	(105)
2	STWOST2	MODE CADDS CADDO	(105)
3	STWOST3	MODE CADDS CADDO	(105)
4	STWORD	CADDS CADDO	(97)
5	STADD	CADDS CADDO	(104)
6	STGCWOST	MODE CADD CADDGC	(94)
7	STDMRWOST	CADD CADDDMR	(106)
8	STACPAR	MODE CADDS CADDO	(109)
9	STDYNWOST1	MODE CADD	(197)
10	STDYNWOST2	MODE CADD	(197)
11	STDYNWOST3	MODE CADD	(197)
12	STSTATWOST	MODE CADDS CADDO	(105)
13	STGCNIL	CADDGC	(97)
14	PLUS	CADDS CADDO	(178)
15	STNDESCRWOST	MODE CADD	(184)

16	STGCELEM	BNCS	
		GCCS	
		BNCO	
		GCCO	(254)
17	STOVERHUNION	MODE	
		CADD	(195)
18	STPLUS	CADD1	
		CADD2	
		CADDO	(177)
19	STWOSTINCR	MODE	
		CADDS	
		INCR	
		CADDO	(254)
20	STNAMEINCR	CADDS	
		INCR	
		CADDO	(179)
21	MINUS	CADDS	
		CADDO	(254)
22	STWP	BNC	
		CADD	(241)
23	STOREREG	MODE	
		CADD	(224)
24	LOADREG	MODE	
		CADD	(224)
25	INCRRTWOSTPM	CADDINCR	(199)
26	HOLE		(222)
27	JUMP	LABNB	(139)
28	LABDEF	LABNB	(139)
29	JUMPNO	LABNB	
		CADD	(214)
30	JUMPYES	LABNB	
		CADD	(254)
31	GOTO	BNC	
		BNCID	
		LABNBID	
		SWOSTC	(122)
32	LABFORMAT	CONSTABP	(254)
33	UPDCONSTAB	MODE	
		CONSTABP	(142)
34	CHECKSTAND	LABNB	
		CADD	(136)

35	LABID	LABNB	(121)
36	CHECKLAB	LABNB	
		CADD	(148)
37	SWITCHCASE	LABNB	
		CADD1	
		CADD2	(230)
38	OBPROG	OBPROGP	(254)
39	BALTAB	BALTABP	(254)
40	INPROG		(254)
41	OUTPROG		(254)
42	INBLOCK	BNC	(102)
43	CALLMIND	LRETURN	
		BNCRES	
		SWOSTCRES	
		LBODY	(162)
44	OUTMIND	BNBODY	
		N	
		CADD1	
		.....	
		CADDN	(163)
45	INMIND	BNCBODY	(163)
46	CALLDYNREP	LRETURN	
		BNCRES	
		SWOSTCRES	
		CADDFORMAT	(167)
47	INDYNREP	BNCBODY	(170)
48	OUTDYNREP	BNBODY	
		N	
		CADD1	
		.....	
		CADDN	
		FORMATSTRINGP	(171)
49	INITDYNREP	CADDFORMAT	
		CADDREP	(169)
50	INACPAR	BNCA	
		FLEX	
		CADDROUT	
		CADDRES	
		GCCRES	
		DMRCRES	(130)
51	CHECKDYNREP	LABNB	
		CADDFORMAT	(169)

52	CALL	LRETURN CADDROUT BNCA	(132)
53	RETURN	MODERES CADDRES BNBODY	(140)
54	STANDCALL	NPAR DMRREC CADDROUT CADD1 ..... CADDN CADDRES DMRRES GCRES FLEX	(217)
55	STANDCALL1	LRETURN N BNCA CADDROUT CADD1 ..... CADDN	(137)
56	DEPROC	LRETURN CADDROUT CADDRES GCCRES DMRCRES FLEX	(146)
57	STANDDEPROC	LRETURN CADDROUT CADDRES GCCRES DMRCRES FLEX	(150)
58	CALLLAB	BNC CADDROUT	(157)
59	STDCALLINOUT	CADDROUT N MODE1 CADD1 ..... MODEN CADDN	(253)
60	CHECKFORMAL	MODE CADD N CADD1 ..... CADDN	(110)
61	CHECKFLEX	CADD	(186)

62	CHECKFLEXR	BNCROUT	
		CADD	(186)
63	TRIMMER	N%DIM	
		CADDS	
		CADDL	
		CADDU	
		CADDL'	
		CADDOFF	
		CADDT	(187)
64	INDEX	N%DIM	
		CADDS	
		CADDI	
		CADDOFF	(188)
65	STINTERSTFL	CADDFLAG	
		CADDESCR	(254)
66	STFILLSTRIDE	MODE	
		CADDESCR	(188)
67	STNAME	CADDPOINTER	
		CADDSCOPE	
		CADDO	(191)
68	FILLSTATEONE	CADDESCR	(254)
69	STSCOPE	CADDS	
		CADDO	(254)
70	ROWINGSCADES	MODEO	
		CADDS	
		CADDO	(202)
71	ROWINGVAR	MODEO	
		CADDS	
		CADDO	(203)
72	ROWINGSCAL1	MODEO	
		CADDS	
		CADDO	(204)
73	ROWINGSCAL2	MODEO	
		CADDS	
		CADDO	
		DMRCS	(203)
74	ROWINGROW	MODES	
		MODEO	
		CADDS	
		CADDO	(200)
75	ROWINGREFSCA	MODEO	
		CADDS	
		CADDO	(206)

76	ROWINGREFROW	MODES MODEO CADDS CADDO	(205)
77	ROWINGEMPTY	MODE CADD	(175)
78	CHECKBOUNDS	CADDL CADDU CADDT	(240)
79	STBOUNDS	CADDL CADDU CADDT	(239)
80	STOVERHDESCR	MODEO STATES CADDD CADDO	(239)
81	STFIRSTCOLLR	MODES MODEO CADDS CADDO	(240)
82	STNEXTCOLLR	MODES MODEO CADDS CADDO	(241)
83	STLITERALROW	MODE CADDS CADDO	(202)
84	ROWS	MODEPAR2 CADDROUT CADDPAR1 CADDPAR2 CADDRES	(254)
85	ASSIGN	MODE CADDS CADDD	(209)
86	ASSIGNSCOPE	MODE CADDS CADDD	(209)
87	LOCVARGEN	MODE CADD N CADD1 ..... CADDN	(112)

88	HEAPVARGEN	MODE	
		CADD	
		N	
		CADD1	
		.....	
		CADDN	(115)
89	FORTO	LABNB	
		CADDFORI	
		CADDBY	
		CADDTO	(250)
90	CHECKSCBLOCK	MODE	
		CADD	
		BN	(104)
91	IDREL=	MODESL	
		CADDSL	
		CADDSR	
		CADDO	(211)
92	IDREL|=	MODESL	
		CADDSL	
		CADDSR	
		CADDO	(211)
93	LOCGEN	MODE	
		CADD	
		CADDGC	
		N	
		CADD1	
		.....	
		CADDN	(118)
94	HEAPGEN	MODE	
		CADD	
		CADDGC	
		N	
		CADD1	
		.....	
		CADDN	(119)
95	CONFTO	MODEL	
		MODER	
		CADDR	
		CADDO	(213)
96	CONFTOBEC	MODEL	
		MODER	
		CADDO	
		CADDR	
		GCR	
		DMRR	
		CADD*R	
		GC*R	
		DMR*R	(213)

97	WIDEN	MODES	
		MODEO	
		CADDS	
		CADDO	(248)
98	STNIL	CADD	(174)
99	STSKIP	MODE	
		CADD	(173)
100	CONJWOST	CADD	(215)
101	CONJ	CADDS	
		CADDO	(215)
102	NOOPTIMIZE		(94)
103	NEWCARD	CARDNB	(254)
104	PRID	IDEN	(254)
105	PRNUMB	NUMB	(254)
106	CHECKNIL	CADD	(179)
107	CHECKOVERLAP	MODE	
		CADDS	
		CADDO	
		LABNB	(209)
108	STSTATACPAR	MODE	
		CADDS	
		CADDO	(109)
109	DEPROC1	LRETURN	
		CADDROUT	
		CADDRES	
		GCCRES	
		DMRCRES	
		FLEX	(152)
110	INBODY	BNCBODY	(154)

APPENDIX 6 : AN EXAMPLE OF COMPILATION

This example has been chosen very simple, it is only intended to give a flavour on how the successive stages of the compilation look like. (More examples can be found in [21]). The following comments on the output from the computer are useful :

(1) The source program text is first printed, its lines are numbered. The numbering, referred to as card number, is used in the next outputs as a reference to the source program.

(2) *DECTAB§* and

(3) *IDENTAB§* are self explaining. Note that the numbering in the first column is used for cross referencing.

(4) *BLOCKTAB§* must be explained :

<u>line 25100</u> : corresponds to the block 'program'.

<u>line 25103</u> : corresponds to 'particular program' with

-*bn=1* lexicographical depth number

-*sidsz=2* resulting from the way *Q(5)* is translated : the copy of the value of the primary *Q* is forced on *WOST%*, moreover, space is foreseen for the result of the call.

-*head* and *tail* are *IDENTAB§* pointers, keeping track of the declarations of the block, chained together ; they play the role of *gcid*.

<u>line 25106</u> : corresponds to the routine possessed by *P* with

-*bn=1*, i.e. the scope 0 of the routine +1.

-*sidsz=2* corresponding to parameter *X* and variable *A* (blocks are merged).

-*swostsz=1*, foreseen for the result of *10+X*.

<u>line 25109</u> : corresponds to the pseudo-block of the actual parameter of the call *Q(5)*, with

-*bn=2*, lexicographical depth number.

-*sidsz=1* for the integer parameter.

(5) Follows the linear prefixed form of the program i.e. *SOPROG* for the IC generation. This form is self-explaining. Note however that

- prefix markers start with '$',
- the lines **** CARD refer to the source program (1)
- the numbers 235, 236,... respectively refer to *IDENTAB§* entries 30584, 30588,...
- the number 232 refers to the operator <u>op</u>(<u>int</u>,<u>int</u>)<u>int</u> + in the initialized part of *INDTAB§* not printed here.
- coercions are kept in a separate table *COERCTAB* ; connections with *SOPROG*

are obtained through the specification field of the prefix markers of the coercends ; here : $ID and $DEN.

(6) The intermediate code (*OBPROG§*) should be easily understood in the light of PART II of this book. Only some details may differ from what has been described. Note moreover that *CONSTAB§* referred to in some ICI's is not printed here.

(7) The machine code in its relocatable form is then printed ; in this code, we find :

(a) instruction lines consisting of :

- the opcode using mnemonics. Note that A, S, G and F are registers and that SUBC means a subroutine call. The opcode may be preceded by one letter U, Y or N to mean a conditional execution of the instruction.
- an optional star the presence of which means (hardware) literal addressing.
- STAT, MPQ, MA and MS which are addressing types :
  -STAT means normal addressing.
  -MPQ means (hardware) display addressing.
  -MA (MS) means indexed addressing using A (S) register.
- the address field consisting of a pair of integers, the first one being only significant in case of display addressing. This field may be followed by P, Z or E, which causes the setting up of conditions, subsequently to the execution of the instruction.
- finally the field symbolic which is a symbolic representation of run-time routines or static working cells. In case it is 'LABTABPI' however, it has a special meaning, indicating to the loader that address conversion using *LABTAB§* is involved.

(b) loader commands :

-LABDEF for label definition.

-LABROUT and OFFSECT issued from the IC *updconstab* with mode parameters *proc* and *string* respectively.

(c) lines with '****' :

They correspond to references to the ICI's currently translated.

(8) The loader automatically prints the starting addresses of :

- the object program *OBPROG%*,
- *RANST%* and
- *HEAP%*

(9) The actual result of the program execution is finally printed.

1. SOURCE PROGRAM

```
(
 PROC P=(INT X)INT :(INT A:=10+X;
 ----  ---  ---  ---
                         A);
PR 51PR  PR 62PR   PR 63PR   PR 64PR
--  --   --  --    --  --    --  --
 PROC (INT  )INT Q:=P;
 ----  ---   ---
 PRINT(("RESULT=",Q(5)))
)
```

2. DECTAB

```
15500     PROC
                MODERES          INT
                NMBPAR            1
                PARAM1           INT
15503     PROC
                MODERES          INT
                NMBPAR            1
                PARAM1           INT
15506     REF                    15503
```

3. IDENTAB

	cadd			*used*	*mode*	*scope*		*chain*	*length*	*alpha*
30584	ROUTCT	0	1342	1	15500	0	0	0	1	P
30588	DIRIDEN	2	0	1	INT	0	0	30592	1	X
30592	VARIDEN	2	1	1	REF INT	1	1	0	1	A
30596	VARIDEN	1	0	1	15506	1	1	0	1	Q

4. BLOCKTAB

	swostsz	*sidsz*	*bn*	*head*	*gcsz*	*tail*	*dmrsz*
25100	0	0	0	0	0	0	0
25103	3	2	1	30596	0	30596	0
25106	1	2	1	30588	0	30592	0
25109	0	1	2	0	0	0	0

5. SOPROG

0	****CARD	1
1	****CARD	2
2	(CLO	2
3	<RAN	0
4	$CONSDE	0
5	DECLAR	15500
6	DEFID	235
7	(R	0
8	SCOPE	0
9	DECLAR	15500
10	(F	0
11	DECLAR	14570
12	DEFID	236
13	)F	0
14	DECLAR	14570
15	:	0
16	(CLO	1
17	<RAN	0
18	$LVARDE	0
19	DECLAR	14570
20	DEFID	237
21	:=*	0
22	$FORMUL	0
23	DYADOPE	232
24	$DEN	0
25	SINTCT	10
26	SEP	0
27	$ID	0
28	ID	236
29	;	0
30	$LASTUN	0
31	****CARD	3
32	$ID	1
33	ID	237
34	>NAR	0
35	)OLC	1
36	)R	0
37	;	0
38	$LVARDE	0
39	DECLAR	15503
40	****CARD	4
41	PRAGNUMB	62
42	PRAGNUMB	63
43	****CARD	5
44	PRAGNUMB	64
45	DEFID	238
46	:=*	0
47	$ID	0
48	ID	235
49	;	0
50	$LASTUN	0
51	$CALL	0
52	****CARD	6
53	$ID	0
54	ID	152
55	(AP	0
56	(COLL	1
57	COLLMOD	14555
58	$DEN	5
59	STRINCT	0
60	,	0
61	$CALL	7
62	$ID	3
63	ID	238
64	(AP	0
65	$DEN	0
66	SINTCT	5
67	)PA	0
68	)LLOC	1
69	)PA	0
70	****CARD	7
71	>NAR	0
72	)OLC	2

COERCTAB

0	END	0	0
1	DEREF	0	14587
2	END	0	0
3	DEREF	0	15506
4	END	0	0
5	[]OUTTYPE	8	14660
6	END	0	0
7	[]OUTTYPE	8	14570

6. *OBPROG§*

```
 0          INPROG

 1      ****CARD1

 2      ****CARD2

 3          INBLOCK     BNC                                     1

 4          JUMP        LABNB                                   3

 5      C2:
 6          LOCVARGEN   MODE                      INT
                        CADD         DIRIDEN           2        1
                        N                                       0

 9          STANDCALL   LRETURN                                 0
                        NLONG                                   0
                        N                                       2
                        BNC                                     2
                        DMRC         NIL*
                        CADDROUT     ROUTCT            0     1129
                        CADD 1       INTCT             0       10
                        CADD 2       DIRIDEN           2        0
                        CADDRES      DIRWOST           2        0
                        DMRCRES      NIL*
                        GCCRES                                  0
                        FLEX         STAT                       1

17          ASSIGN      MODES                     INT
                        CADDS        DIRWOST           2        0
                        CADDO        VARIDEN           2        1

20      ****CARD3

21          HOLE

22          UPDCONSTAB  MODE                                15500
                        CADD         ROUTCT            0     1342

24          RETURN      MODERES                   INT
                        CADDRES      DIRIDEN           2        1
                        BNBODY                                  1

27      C3:
28      ****CARD4

29          PRAGMAT          62

30          PRAGMAT          63

31      ****CARD5

32          PRAGMAT          64

33          LOCVARGEN   MODE                                15503
```

```
                           CADD        DIRIDEN     1        0
                           N                                0

36        ASSIGN           MODES                        15500
                           CADDS       ROUTCT      0     1342
                           CADDO       VARIDEN     1        0

39      ****CARD6

40        UPDCONSTAB       MODE                         14660
                           CADD        DIRCTTAB    0     1345

42        STWOST3          MODE                         15503
                           CADDS       DIRIDEN     1        0
                           CADDO       DIRWOST     1        0

45        INACPAR          BNCACPA                          3
                           FLEX        STAT                 0
                           CADDROUT    DIRIDEN     1        0
                           CADDRES     DIRWOST     1        2
                           GCCRSE                           0
                           DMRCRES                          0

49        STACPAR          MODE                INT
                           CADDS       INTCT       0        5
                           CADDO       DIRIDEN     3        0

52        CHECKSTAND       LABNB                            4
                           CADD        DIRWOST     1        0

54        CALL             LRETURN                          5
                           CADDROUT    DIRWOST     1        0
                           BNCACPA                          3

57      C4:
58        STANDCALL1       LRETURN                          5
                           N                                1
                           BNC                              3
                           CADDROUT    DIRWOST     1        0
                           CADD 1      DIRIDEN     3        0

62      C5:
63      ****CARD7

64        STDCALLINOUT     LRETURN                          0
                           N                                2
                           BNC                              1
                           DMRC        NIL*
                           CADDROUT    ROUTCT      0      565
                           MODE 1                       14660
                           CADD 1      DIRCTTAB    0     1345
                           MODE 2              INT
                           CADD 2      DIRWOST     1        2
                           CADDRES     NIHIL       0        0
                           DMRCRES     NIL*
                           GCCRES                       NILGC
                           FLEX        STAT                 0

75        HOLE

76        STADD            CADDS       DDISPLAY    0        1
```

```
                           CADDO     DIRABS      0     20

79         STWORD          CADDS     INTCT       0      0
                           CADDO     DIRABS      0     17

82         STWORD          CADDS     VARABS      0   4095
                           CADDO     DDISPLAY    0      1

85       ****CARD8

86       L1:
87         OUTPROG
```

7. MACHINE CODE

```
        opcode      lit  addtype   addr            symb
  0     LDA          *   STAT      0     11
  1     LDS          *   STAT      0      0
  2     LDG          *   STAT      0     11
  3     STG              STAT      0      0        INCRGC9
  4     LDG          *   STAT      0      0
  5     SUBC         *   STAT      0      0        INPROG9
        ****                                1
        ****                                2
        ****                                3
  6     LDG          *   STAT      0      2
  7     STG              STAT      0      0        CARDNB
  8     LDA          *   STAT      0      1
  9     LDS          *   STAT      0      0        GCINFOTAB
 10     LDG          *   STAT      0     16
 11     SUBC         *   STAT      0      0        INBLOCK19
 12     LDA          *   STAT      0     13
 13     LDS          *   STAT      0      0
 14     LDG          *   STAT      0      2
 15     SUBC         *   STAT      0      0        INBLOCK29
        ****                                4
        ****                                5
 16     GOTO         *   STAT      0     29        LABTABPI
        ****                                6
        ****                                9
        LABDEF                              2
 17     LDS          *   STAT      0     10
 18     ADS              MPQ       1     11
        ****                               17
        ****                               20
        ****                               21
        ****                               22
 19     STS              MPQ       1     12
        LABROUT                            17        LABTABPI
        ****                               24
 20     LDG              MPQ       1      4
 21     STG              STAT      0      0        RET.JUMP
 22     LDS              MPQ       1      5
 23     LDA          *   MPQ       1     12
 24     LDG          *   STAT      0      1
 25     SUBC         *   STAT      0      0        UPDATEDISP
 26     LDG              MA        0      0
 27     STG              MS        0      0
 28     GOTO             STAT      0      0        RET.JUMP
```

```
          ****                              27
          ****                              28
          ****                              29
          ****                              30
          ****                              31
          ****                              32
          ****                              33
          ****                              36
          LABDEF                             3
 29       LDG       *  STAT       0       1342    CONSTABPI
 30       STG          MPQ        1         11
 31       LDG          STAT       0          0    DISPLAYPI
          ****                              39
          ****                              40
 32       STG          MPQ        1         12
          OFFSECT                         1345
          ****                              42
 33       LDF          MPQ        1         11
          ****                              45
 34       STF          MPQ        1         13
 35       LDG       *  STAT       0          6
 36       STG          STAT       0          0    CARDNB
 37       LDG       *  STAT       0       1358    CONSTABPI
 38       LDS          MPQ        1         11
 39       SUBC      *  STAT       0          0    INACPARDYN
          ****                              49
 40       LDS       *  STAT       0          5
          ****                              52
 41       STS          MPQ        2         11
 42       LDA          MPQ        1         13  Z
 43   Y   LDS       *  STAT       0         14
 44   Y   GOTO      *  STAT       0          0    ALARM
 45   U   LDA          MA         0          0  P
          ****                              54
 46   N   GOTO      *  STAT       0         53    LABTABPI
 47       LDA       *  STAT       0         57    LABTABPI
 48       STA          STAT       0          0    RET.JUMP
 49       LDA       *  STAT       0          1
 50       LDS       *  MPQ        1         13
 51       LDG       *  STAT       0          2
 52       GOTO      *  STAT       0          0    CALLDYN
          ****                              57
          ****                              58
          LABDEF                             4
 53       LDG       *  STAT       0          6
 54       STG          STAT       0          0    CARDNB
 55       LDS       *  STAT       0         21
 56       GOTO      *  STAT       0          0    ALARM
          ****                              62
          ****                              63
          ****                              64
          LABDEF                             5
 57       SUBC      *  STAT       0          0    SAVETIME
 58       LDS       *  STAT       0       1345    CONSTABPI
 59       LDA          MS         0          2  Z
 60   Y   GOTO      *  STAT       0         70    LABTABPI
 61       LDA       *  STAT       0          0    VALSTPI
 62       LDG       *  STAT       0          1
 63       STG          STAT       0          2    VALSTPI
 64       LDG       *  STAT       0       1000
 65       SUBC      *  STAT       0          0    INITLOOPR9
          LABDEF                             6
 66       SUBC      *  STAT       0          0    PRINTCHARS
```

```
67     LDG        *  STAT    0     66    LABTABPI
68     LDA        *  STAT    0      0    VALSTPI
69     SUBC       *  STAT    0      0    FINALLOOPR9
       LABDEF                       7
70     LDS        *  MPQ     1     15
71     SUBC       *  STAT    0      0    PRINTINTS
72     SUBC       *  STAT    0      0    RESTTIME
       ****                        75
       ****                        76
73     LDA           STAT    0      1    DISPLAYPI
74     SBA        *  STAT    0    256
       ****                        79
75     STA           STAT    0      0    RTWOSTPM
76     LDS        *  STAT    0      0
       ****                        82
77     STS           STAT    0      0    RTBNA
78     LDS        *  STAT    0      0    NIL
       ****                        85
       ****                        86
79     STS           STAT    0      1    DISPLAYPI
       ****                        87
       LABDEF                       1
80     GOTO       *  STAT    0      0    FINAL9
```

8. *LOADER INDICATIONS*

```
OBPROGPI 11368
STACKPI  11449
HEAPPI   29700
```

9. *PROGRAM RESULT*

```
RESULT=        15
```